D0789437

Theories of Urban Politics

Theories of Urban Politics

Second Edition

Jonathan S. Davies and David L. Imbroscio

Los Angeles • London • New Delhi • Singapore • Washington DC

© Prelims, Introduction and editorial content – Jonathan S. Davies and David L. Imbroscio 2009

© Chapter 1 – Peter John 2009
© Chapter 2 – Alan Harding 2009
© Chapter 3 – Karen Mossberger 2009
© Chapter 4 – Mike Geddes 2009
© Chapter 5 – Serena Kataoka 2009
© Chapter 6 – Vivien Lowndes 2009
© Chapter 7 – Hank Savitch and Ronald Vogel 2009
© Chapter 8 – Stephen Greasley and Gerry Stoker 2009

© Chapter 9 – Anne Mette Kjaer 2009
© Chapter 10 – Richard Stren 2009
© Chapter 11 – Mara Sidney 2009
© Chapter 12 – J. Phillip Thompson 2009
© Chapter 13 – Judith A. Garber 2009
© Chapter 14 – Helen Sullivan 2009
© Chapter 15 – Gordana Rabrenovic 2009
© Chapter 16 – Clarence Stone 2009

First published 2009

Apart from any fair dealing for the purposes of research or private study, or criticism or review, as permitted under the Copyright, Designs and Patents Act, 1988, this publication may be reproduced, stored or transmitted in any form, or by any means, only with the prior permission in writing of the publishers, or in the case of reprographic reproduction, in accordance with the terms of licences issued by the Copyright Licensing Agency. Enquiries concerning reproduction outside those terms should be sent to the publishers.

SAGE Publications Ltd
1 Oliver's Yard
55 City Road
London EC1Y 1SP

SAGE Publications Inc.
2455 Teller Road
Thousand Oaks, California 91320

SAGE Publications India Pvt Ltd
B1/I 1 Mohan Cooperative Industrial Area
Mathura Road, New Delhi 110 044
India

SAGE Publications Asia-Pacific Pte Ltd
33 Pekin Street #02-01
Far East Square
Singapore 048763

Library of Congress Control Number available

British Library Cataloguing in Publication data

A catalogue record for this book is available from the British Library

ISBN 978-1-4129-2161-9
ISBN 978-1-4129-2162-6

Typeset by C&M Digitals (P) Ltd, Chennai, India

CONTENTS

Acknowledgements	vii
Notes on Contributors	viii
List of Tables and Figures	xi
Preface	xii

Introduction: Urban Politics in the Twenty-first Century   1
Jonathan S. Davies and David L. Imbroscio

PART I   PROLOGUE   15

1 Why Study *Urban* Politics?   17
   Peter John

PART II   POWER   25

2 The History of Community Power   27
   Alan Harding

3 Urban Regime Analysis   40
   Karen Mossberger

4 Marxism and Urban Politics   55
   Mike Geddes

5 'Posty' Urban Political Theory   73
   Serena Kataoka

PART III   GOVERNANCE   89

6 New Institutionalism and Urban Politics   91
   Vivien Lowndes

7 Regionalism and Urban Politics   106
   Hank Savitch and Ronald K. Vogel

8   Urban Political Leadership   125
    Stephen Greasley and Gerry Stoker

9   Governance and the Urban Bureaucracy   137
    Anne Mette Kjaer

10 Globalisation and Urban Issues in the Non-Western World   153
    Richard Stren

PART IV   CITIZENS   169

11 Poverty, Inequality and Social Exclusion   171
    Mara S. Sidney

12 Race and Urban Political Theory   188
    J. Phillip Thompson

13 Gender and Sexuality   204
    Judith A. Garber

14 Social Capital   221
    Helen Sullivan

15 Urban Social Movements   239
    Gordana Rabrenovic

PART V   CHALLENGES   255

16 Who is Governed? Local Citizens and the Political Order of Cities 257
    Clarence N. Stone

Index   274

ACKNOWLEDGEMENTS

The editors of this second edition wish to acknowledge and thank the editors of the first edition, professors David Judge, Gerry Stoker and Hal Wolman, without whose inspiration and hard work this volume would not have been possible. We also wish to thank our contributors for generously devoting much time and effort to their chapters and for their patience and openness to criticism and suggestion from the editors. The advice and counsel of our friends and colleagues Judy Garber, Clarence Stone and Ron Vogel were particularly helpful in shaping the overall structure of the book and chapter content in the initial phases of planning. Anne-Mette Kjaer, Vivien Lowndes, Peter John and Helen Sullivan, at the book panel at the Political Studies Association annual meeting in April 2006, provided very helpful insights into the general task of understanding what constitutes theories about politics at the urban scale. Also helpful were the reviews of the proposal proffered by Kevin Ward and Mark Evans. Thanks also go to Ali Modarres, Larry Bennett, Anne Caldwell and Andrea Blair who each provided useful feedback on elements of the project as it moved along. Our editor at Sage, David Mainwaring, has been a joy to work with on this project, in what we hope will be the first of several in a long and productive collaboration. We thank him specifically for providing just the right mix of patience and prodding in response to the inevitable delays experienced in the production of a complex project such as this. Finally, we dedicate this volume to our fathers, one of whom died just as we were completing it. From their teachings and guidance we draw continual inspiration.

NOTES ON CONTRIBUTORS

Jonathan S Davies is Reader in Public Policy in the Institute of Governance and Public Management at the University of Warwick. He graduated from the University of York (UK) with a DPhil in Politics in 2000. He is author of *Partnerships and Regimes: The Politics of Urban Regeneration in the UK* and co-editor, with Imbroscio, of the forthcoming Critical Urban Studies, New Directions and the Sage Library of Political Science collection on *Urban Politics*. He sits on the editorial board of *Policy Studies*. Davies has published numerous articles on critical issues in the study of governance, urban politics and public policy.

David L. Imbroscio is Professor of Political Science and Urban & Public Affairs at the University of Louisville, USA. He is author of *Reconstructing City Politics: Alternative Economic Development and Urban Regimes*, co-author of *Making a Place for Community: Local Democracy in a Global Era*, co-editor of the forthcoming Critical Urban Studies: New Directions, and he is currently finishing a book tentatively titled *Urban America Reconsidered*. His work also has appeared in several scholarly journals and edited collections. He serves on the Governing Board of the Urban Affairs Association and the Editorial Board of the *Journal of Urban Affairs*.

———————————————— Contributors ————————————————

Peter John is the Hallsworth Chair of Governance at the University of Manchester, where he is co-director of the Institute for Economic and Political Governance. He is author of *Analysing Public Policy* (1998) and *Local Governance in Western Europe* (2001).

Alan Harding is Professor of Urban and Regional Governance and Director of the Institute for Political and Economic Governance (ipeg) at the University of Manchester. He works in the broad field of urban and regional development, policy and governance, on which he has published widely.

Karen Mossberger is Associate Professor of Public Administration at the University of Illinois at Chicago. She teaches local government management and public policy. Her research interests include digital inequality and current projects on public–private partnerships for neighborhood regeneration in Chicago and regional collaboration to address poverty.

Mike Geddes is a Professorial Fellow in the Local Government Centre at the University of Warwick. His research has covered aspects of local governance ranging from local democracy and partnership to poverty and social exclusion. His current interest is in cross-national comparative analysis of local responses to neoliberalism in both the North and the South.

S.S. Kataoka is currently a doctoral candidate at the University of Victoria, in the Department of Political Science. Her background in interdisciplinary studies and community development enables her to do research that focuses on, and opens up, particular urban scenes.

Vivien Lowndes is Professor of Local Government Studies in the Local Governance Research Unit at De Montfort University. Her current research interests include citizen participation in local governance, faith and community cohesion, neighbourhood governance and local government reform.

Hank Savitch is the Brown and Williamson, Distinguished Research Professor at the University of Louisville (USA). An author of numerous books and articles, his co-authored work *Cities in the International Marketplace* was named the best book in the urban field by the American Political Science Association. He recently completed *Cities in a Time of Terror: Space, Territory and Local Resilience* (M.E. Sharpe).

Ronald K. Vogel is Chair of the Department of Political Science and Professor of Political Science and Urban & Public Affairs at the University of Louisville. His research focuses on comparative metropolitan and regional governance including the US, Canada, Japan, and Hong Kong.

Stephen Greasley is a research associate at the Institute for Political and Economic Governance at the University of Manchester. His research has focused on the impact of political leadership on democratic processes and policy outcomes at local level.

Gerry Stoker is Professor of Politics and Governance at the University of Southampton, UK. His current research deals with issues of governance in complex settings, political disenchantment in western democracies, citizen empowerment and strategies for encouraging civic behaviour among citizens. He is Director of the centre for Citizenship and Democracy (www.soton.ac.uk/ccd).

Anne-Mette Kjaer is Associate Professor at the University of Aarhus, Denmark. Her main areas of research are new forms of governance in comparative perspective, state capacity and public sector reforms in Africa, and the role of elites in implementing the new poverty agenda. Recent publications include *Governance*, and various articles in, among others, *Journal of Modern African Studies* and *Forum for Development Studies*.

Richard Stren is Professor Emeritus in the Department of Political Science of the University of Toronto, and the former director of the Centre for Urban and Community Studies. He has worked for many years in Africa and, more recently, Latin America on urban issues, and is author or editor of 18 books, including most recently *Decentralization and the Politics of Urban Development in West Africa* (with Dickson Eyoh).

Mara Sidney is Associate Professor of Political Science at Rutgers University-Newark. Her research focuses on housing discrimination, affordable housing, and urban education. She is the author of *Unfair Housing: How National Policy Shapes Local Action*, a co-author of *Multiethnic Moments: The Politics of Urban Education Reform*, and co-editor of *The Handbook of Public Policy Analysis*.

J. Phillip Thompson is Associate Professor of Urban Politics at the Massachusetts Institute of Technology. His book, *Double Trouble: Black Mayors, Black Communities and the Call for Deep Democracy* was recently published by Oxford University Press.

Judy Garber is Associate Professor of Political Science at the University of Alberta, in Edmonton. She has published on the constitutional powers of US cities to regulate land for redistributive purposes, feminist approaches to local community, the Christian Right's legal strategies, and critical theories of urban politics and public space.

Helen Sullivan is Research Director of the Centre for Public Service Partnerships at the University of Birmingham, where she also holds the Palmer Chair in Public Service Partnerships. She specializes in the study of collaboration in urban governance and has researched and published widely in this area.

Gordana Rabrenovic is Associate Professor of Sociology and Education and Director of the Brudnick Center on Violence and Conflict at Northeastern University. Her publications include the books *Community Builders: A Tale of Neighborhood Mobilization in Two Cities*, *Community Politics and Policy*, and *Why We Hate*, and edited volumes of the *American Behavioral Scientist*, *Hate Crimes and Ethnic Conflict* and *Responding to Hate Violence*.

Clarence N. Stone is Research Professor of Public Policy and Political Science at George Washington University and Professor Emeritus at the University of Maryland. His books include *Regime Politics* and *Economic Growth and Neighborhood Discontent*. His current research is about the politics of neighborhood revitalization.

LIST OF TABLES AND FIGURES

———————————————————— **Tables** ————————————————————

7.1 Theoretical frameworks on regionalism   108

9.1 Assumptions in the old public administration, the new public management
and governance theory   140

———————————————————— **Figures** ————————————————————

9.1 Authority migration   139

PREFACE

Published in 1995, the first edition of *Theories of Urban Politics*, edited by Professors David Judge, Gerry Stoker and Hal Wolman, was a huge success and a landmark for urban studies. It has inspired thousands of readers, no doubt encouraging many bright scholars to embark on careers in urban political research. That collection still resonates 13 years later and contemporary scholars would do well to return to it time and again. Yet, urban politics is a fast moving field and soon enough, the original editors realised that a second edition was required. Fortuitously for us, they did not have time to fulfil the task themselves and graciously entrusted us with this second edition. We owe them a debt of gratitude and hope that they, and all the readers who pick up the volume, are pleased with the outcome.

Urban politics is a pluralistic sub-field. It draws on many normative, methodological, and analytical traditions. It also draws inspiration from sibling social science and humanities disciplines spanning at least history, economics, geography, sociology, philosophy and law. Urban politics is thus inflected by myriad influences, an attribute that does not always find favour with critics. Such criticism was visibly and forcefully expressed in a recent polemic authored by Bryan D. Jones, a once prominent urbanist (and contributor to the first edition of *Theories*), and two of his graduate students, Joshua Sapotichne and Michelle Wolfe. Jones, who famously left the urban politics sub-field several years ago (Judd, 2005), and his co-authors took urban politics to task for failing to pay due attention to mainstream political science on the one hand and for failing to influence it on the other (Sapotichne et al., 2007). While several urbanists, including both co-editors of this volume and the author of its lead-off chapter, Peter John, took issue in various ways with their critique,[1] Sapotichne, Jones, and Wolfe performed a service by forcing us to think about the state of the urban politics field, both in relation to the discipline of political science and the broader social science arena. Crucially, they caused us to think about challenge and renewal. Do we subject our work to critical scrutiny sufficient to ensure that key perspectives evolve and respond to new intellectual and real-world challenges? Do urbanists have a proper perspective on the balance between theoretical continuity and change? In our view, the contributions to this volume offer a resounding 'yes' to these telling questions. It is our hope that readers will concur with this affirmative appraisal of the state of urban political theory.

Notes

1 See *Urban News: Newsletter of the Urban Politics Section (of the American Political Science Association)*, Spring 2008, 22(1). Available at: http://www.apsanet. org/~urban/

References

Judd, D.R. (2005) 'Everything is always going to Hell: urban scholars as end-times prophets,' *Urban Affairs Review*, 41 (2): 119–31.

Sapotichne, J., Jones, B.D. and Wolfe, M. (2007) 'Is urban politics a black hole? Analyzing the boundary between political science and urban politics,' *Urban Affairs Review*, 43 (1): 76–106.

Introduction

URBAN POLITICS IN THE TWENTY-FIRST CENTURY

Jonathan S. Davies and David L. Imbroscio

In bringing this volume together, we engaged in a vibrant dialogue with contributors and other colleagues. We held several conference panels on the book – notably at the 2006 and 2007 Urban Affairs Association annual meetings and the British Political Studies Association annual meeting in 2006. Colleagues at these events posed important questions to us as editors. What does it mean to study theories of urban politics? Specifically, is there anything distinctive about *urban* theory: is it merely general theory adapted to scale; or is there something distinctive about the urban such that urban theories are not generalisable to a broader canvas? Or since, as Richard Stren illustrates in this volume (Chapter 10), half of the world's population now inhabits urban spaces (see also Davis, 2006), is the study of the urban increasingly synonymous with the study of society at large? On a second dimension, it was suggested that we needed to think about the relationship between theory and practice in the field of urban politics. Does urban politics constitute the necessary fusion of theory and practice? If so, practice of what kind, and whose practice? That these searching questions were posed is itself an indication of the good health of the discipline. As editors, it was incumbent upon us to provide some direction to our contributors on how to address these issues. In very different ways, it is clear that all were able to meet the challenge. Here, we flesh out our thoughts as they evolved over the past couple of years.

Perhaps the most interesting question posed to us was 'what do we mean by theories of urban politics?' To begin with 'theory', the first key term in the volume title, we asked authors to engage empirical (or explanatory) theories in their respective subject areas rather than explicitly normative ones. Such guidance was, of course, given with the recognition of the impossibility of value-free social science, so we take as given the idea that empirical theory will be infused with normative influences and do not try to force a strict separation. Empirical theory seeks to explain observed phenomena, usually by establishing a number of conceptually linked and generalisable causal relationships about how some factors affect, or cause, phenomena to occur. Most of the urban political theories or theoretical propositions collected in this volume fit this general notion of empirical theory.

Such theories are, however, highly diverse, varying along several key dimensions. Some maintain a high degree of abstraction from direct observation, while others closely ground the abstract in the concrete and empirical. Some proceed largely inductively, building from empirical observation to hypotheses, while others are more deductive in nature, deriving hypotheses logically from an initial set of (non-observable) axioms. Theories in the volume also differ in their explanatory scope. Some seek to account for wide swaths of urban political outcomes, while others, focusing on more isolated urban phenomena, better fit the model of what Merton (1949) called theories of the 'middle range'. Perhaps the sharpest and clearest illustration of this theoretical diversity comes with the Marxism–regime theory comparison (see Chapters 3 and 4). Marxism employs considerable abstraction, deduces hypothesis from axioms about the nature of capitalism, and purports to explain much of the urban condition (and society at large). Urban regime theory, in contrast, focuses on the concrete existence of specific local governing coalitions, generates hypotheses rooted in empirical observation of such coalitions, and offers an explanation only for how local political arrangements mediate larger-order forces rather than for those forces themselves.

Concerning the second term in the title, 'urban', we suggested to the contributors that theory may be specialised where it makes distinctive conceptual generalisations about the character of *urban* politics; about, for example, the distinctive character of urban institutions like urban regimes. Or, it may draw on and adapt political theory at large to help us better understand urban political phenomena. And, there are grey areas. For example, urban regime theory, probably the most influential approach in the field since the late 1980s, owes many intellectual debts and is thoroughly cosmopolitan. In his extensive body of work (see Orr and Johnson, 2008), Clarence Stone credits many influences; from the political classics of the community power debate and neopluralism through to the sociologists Max Weber, Philip Abrams and Charles Tilly, who clarified his thinking respectively on social stratification, the nature of structure and agency and what he sees as the loose connections between the economic, political and ideational spheres. At the same time, it is arguable that there is a fundamentally 'urban' quality to regime theory. In Chapter 1, Peter John argues that a key feature of urban space is the 'propinquity' of political actors, a term which

> denotes the closeness of the urban space where actors interact frequently and tend to be small in number. The urban is politics in miniature and this creates a particular kind of political system rather than a mirror image of other levels. ...

The particularity to which regime theory points is the form of coalition arising from the need to mobilise governing resources at the urban scale. Krasner (1983: 2) defined international regime politics as 'sets of implicit or explicit principles, norms, rules and decision-making procedures around which actors' expectations converge ...'. This definition could be applied at the urban scale. The differences are partly methodological in that we can more easily study regime formation, maintenance and collapse close up; and partly analytical in that urban regime theory makes specific propositions about the development of urban governing regimes. It purports to explain why regimes are rare and difficult to mobilise, the conditions in which they are likely to emerge, how power is pre-empted and how governing agendas are constructed by actors with divergent but congruent interests. Thus, it purports to explain from the bottom-up why governing coalitions are likely, but not certain, to be biased against the lower classes. Each proposition is grounded in broader social science traditions, but at the same time hinges on conditions pertaining at the urban scale.

Peter John again helps us when we think about the distinction between the urban and the non-urban. Propinquity is a particular characteristic of the urban space, which does not usually apply at other scales of governing or when comparing the urban with the rural. In many parts of the US, Russia, Canada or China, the antonym 'remoteness' is more apposite than 'propinquity'. Yet, as John asks, '[i]s not rural life highly urbanised in many respects'? For example, since the 1970s China has pursued a policy of 'rural industrialization' (Liang et al., 2002). Alongside inexorable urbanisation, this policy is imperative for the sustenance of ever-growing mega-cities. Urbanisation, then, refers not only to the growth of cities, particularly in the developing world, but also the organisation of social life. It is an ongoing feature of contemporary capitalism affecting both cities and the countryside in equal measure. In this interpretation, the urbanisation of the rural has been occurring at least since the beginnings of the enclosure movement in England in the fifteenth century, which later gathered unstoppable momentum. It became a grotesque feature of so-called socialism in the USSR, where the forced collectivisation of agriculture effectively proletarianised the rural population. Seen this way, the urban is both form and process. And, as Kataoka argues in Chapter 5, following Lefebvre, it is also a matter of identity, disposition, psychology, culture and lifestyle.

Admittedly, we risk concept stretching in characterising the urban so expansively. Nevertheless, we believe that it is possible to assert convincingly that society is increasingly urbanised and at the same time delimit the concept. We do not claim that the urban encompasses every dimension of human experience. Nationalism, supra-national political institutions, parties, religious identities and the rise of social movements and environmentalism come to mind as features which, if they are at least part-constituted in the contemporary urban experience, are certainly not reducible to it. With that qualification, we suggest that to study the urban is, in many ways, to study the motor of contemporary human development.

'Politics' is the third key term in the title of the book. The question 'what is politics?' is itself sufficiently contentious to have spawned a substantial literature. A recent second edition of the book of the same title, edited by Leftwich (2004), provides an excellent overview of the key debates. One important question addressed by the book concerns the scope of politics, both as discipline and practice. Thus, is politics about the institutions of government, or more recently, governance? Can any debate in any context, public or private, about what a person or group ought to do, and how, be considered an instance of politics? Is politics a universal feature of all human societies, or is it bookended historically; for example, by the rise and eventual fall of class societies? Is politics essentially the same thing now as it has been throughout history? Perhaps of greatest interest for our purposes is what it means to talk about a discipline of urban politics as different from, say, sociology or economics? Such a question could easily lead to a lengthy discourse – indeed another book – on the historical conditions in which disciplinary silos evolved, their merits and limitations. For us, simply, politics is what our contributors have made of it. Thus, it is about the study of government, institutions and public engagement in dialogue and partnership with, or against, government. It is about the dynamic relationships between peoples, conflictual or otherwise. The volume shows that the field of urban politics cannot do other than address questions of livelihood and reproduction, space and migration and the web of relationships between state, market and citizen. Thus, inevitably, it transgresses other disciplines. Centrally, of course, urban politics is and always has been about power; its genesis, its acquisition, its forms and its uses.

Another question posed to us concerned the relationship between theory and practice in urban politics. On a broad canvas, this question is about the orientation of the discipline toward social questions and the role of urban scholars as practitioners and activists. Inspired by the urban movements and crises of the late 1960s, the Council of University Institutes for Urban Affairs was formed in Boston in 1969, succeeded by the Urban Affairs Association in 1981. The UAA is very clear that the urban field is both academic and professional, the Association welcoming faculty, students and professionals alike to its conferences and offering a platform to all. In a similar vein, the European Urban Research Association seeks to 'bridge the gap between academic, professional and policy interests, inform public debate and improve the quality of urban policy'.[1] In addition, while urban scholarship encompasses a plurality of political perspectives, it is also well known for its commitment to social justice. The mission of urban studies, then, is to engage in a critical dialogue with public policy and intervene widely in public discourse. There are, of course, very different ways of fulfilling this injunction; from researching and writing about practice, to engaging in practice as participant–observers; as policy makers, dissidents and activists.

All the contributors to this volume can credibly claim to have engaged with practice in one or more of the senses described above. As this is a book about theories, however, they were charged with demonstrating how theory characterises and explains empirical events. We asked them to explore the main theoretical claims and controversies in their designated area and ascertain how far these theories improved our understanding of urban political life – and thus, by implication, our capacity to engage effectively with it. They were asked to evaluate the strengths and limitations of the theories in question and explore how they might be developed to better explain and/or characterise the phenomena in question. *Theories of Urban Politics* addresses the relationship between theory and practice in this specific sense but we also hope that the book will find a wide readership beyond the faculty and influence debates, discussions and activities in the public arena.

---------------- **Design and structure** ----------------

Our objective was to produce a collection encapsulating the state of the discipline and pointing to contemporary and future research challenges. While this is a second edition, it is also a comprehensive rewrite. The current volume includes a mix of new contributors and contributors to the first edition. Previous contributors were invited to prepare new chapters on a different topic, thus ensuring that where chapters from the first edition have been retained, they have passed to a new author with a new perspective. Readers will notice that some chapters from the first edition have disappeared altogether, while others remain in a different form or are more or less completely new. The editors are responsible for the cut, which hangs on our judgement about the state of the discipline today and the challenges it faces. For example, regulation theory is now subsumed into the chapter on Marxism, because it has declined in influence since 1995. Pluralism and elite theory are integrated into the community power debate; not because they are less important, but because we had to recognise claims from newer approaches. On the other hand, chapters on urban social movements and leadership are retained intact because both themes have the same, or greater, prominence than in 1995. Themes rising up the agenda, in our judgement, include globalisation and urbanisation and postmodernism. In addition, we decided that overview chapters would be appropriate in opening and closing the volume. We asked Peter John to begin by explaining why it is important and rewarding to study urban politics, and Clarence Stone to conclude by outlining the key research questions confronting urban scholars. All contributors consider cross-national issues. Anglo–American issues feature strongly in most chapters, but many delve into broader literatures. Thus, we believe that the volume has global reach, pointing to challenges that will occupy scholars the world over in years to come. Inevitably, there is overlap between some of the contributions; for example, between community power and regime theory and Marxism and postmodernism. However, where overlap occurs, we do not see it as duplication; rather, we believe it casts an interesting light on different interpretations and styles.

Whereas the first edition of *Theories of Urban Politics* comprised 14 chapters, the second edition has 17. In a volume of around the same length, we have inevitably sacrificed depth for breadth. However, we believe the result bears us out, offering a wide ranging examination of theories, controversies and challenges but in sufficient depth for a robust evaluation of the relevant perspectives. In different ways, every chapter covers three specific issues: explication and critique of the dominant theoretical approaches, the application of theoretical approaches in conceptualising and researching the empirical world, and areas for future theoretical development and research. The exceptions are John's opening chapter and Stone's conclusion, where the authors were given more of a free hand.

The core of the book builds around three classic issues in the study of urban politics – who wields urban political power, the nature of urban governance, and how urban citizens both affect and are affected by these dynamics of power and governance. Apart from the first and the last, the chapters are organised under these three headings: power, governance and citizens.

Part I: Prologue

In Chapter 1, Peter John explores the reasons why new and established scholars should consider studying urban politics. He sets the scene for the rest of the volume by reflecting on the unique characteristics of urban politics; the rich literatures on power on the one hand, the reach of the urban concept on the other. John offers a particularly insightful explanation of the value of urban research. Urban spaces create propinquity and as such are more amenable to research than, say, national governments. They are also very numerous with hundreds of cities in any one country and thousands across the globe. Numerosity allows for large N comparisons which would be very difficult or impossible at the national scale. Moreover, large N international comparisons are easier at the urban scale, allowing urbanists to explore the patterns and diversity of political life across the globe (see also Sellers, 2005). John concludes that provided we are not downcast by neersayers, or tainted with an exaggerated sense of our importance, future scholars would do well to follow the path trodden by many of the great political scientists of the twentieth century who took urban politics as their starting point.

Part II: Power

A preponderance of urban political theory has been devoted to understanding the nature of urban power: its production, distribution, exercise and impact in its various faces. In Chapter 2, Alan Harding discusses some of the greats – Dahl, Hunter, Polsby and Lindblom – in the context of the community power debate. Harding takes us on a journey through the history of the debate, arguing that the work of community power scholars was formative of urban politics as an independent field of study. He demonstrates why the debate, much derided by commentators like Dowding (1996), remains relevant today. Harding argues that the influence of community power extends well beyond the literature commonly branded as such; notably (or notoriously) the elitism–pluralism debate. Certainly, the concern with power at the urban scale, which was central then remains central now. Harding charts the influence of community power on the later scholarship of the 1960s, 1970s and 1980s through the works of Lindblom, Peterson and Stone. The influence of community power upon the latter is discussed by Karen Mossberger in Chapter 3. Harding concludes that the challenge for the next generation of community power studies is cross-national; to develop common theoretical and methodological tools, which enable us to overcome the accusations of ethnocentrism levelled at approaches like regime theory.

Chapter 3 tackles the subject of urban regime analysis, which, as Mossberger points out, has been one of the most prevalent ways to study urban politics for over two decades.[2] Mossberger explains that one appeal of urban regime theory has been its ability to resolve the community power debates chronicled by Harding in Chapter 2. Regime theory portrays political power at the urban scale as characterised by neither pluralist fluidity and openness nor elite domination and control, while incorporating both political and economic influences on city politics. Mossberger focuses her discussion of regime analysis on the work of Clarence Stone, whose version, which he developed most thoroughly in his historical study of Atlanta, has been most frequently applied in urban research. Regime theory, she notes, incorporates the possibility of variation in regime agendas, and much of Stone's work and that of other regime theorists categorises various regime types. Another major strand of work attempts to apply, with varying results, the urban regime concept to non-US contexts. She points out, however, that scholars engaged in comparative efforts have increasingly eschewed urban regimes in favour of broader but related notions of 'governance' (see Part III). Mossberger concludes by asking whether these conceptual and theoretical developments sound the death knell for regime analysis. Her answer is a qualified no. Regime analysis will continue to be important to urban political research, she predicts, but it may be seen as only one manner in which governing arrangements can be conceptualised, especially in a comparative context.

In Chapter 2, Harding explains that by the 1970s, community power studies had fallen out of favour, with Marxist and neo-Weberian approaches increasingly dominant. Mike Geddes charts the development of Marxist urban scholarship from this period in Chapter 4. Geddes contends that despite the reverses experienced by the left over the past 20 years, Marxism remains highly relevant for understanding contemporary urban capitalism and the tasks facing those, notably in South America, who would resist it. He begins by exploring the period around the 1970s during which Marxist scholarship was at its most influential; particularly in the diverse works of Castells, Harvey and Lefebvre. He charts the subsequent development of Marxist approaches, including the 'postmodern Marxism' of Soja and influential criticisms; from scholars of postmodernist and socialist-feminist persuasions as well as those, like Storper, who suggest that Marxism is incapable of translating meta theory to the micro level of analysis. Yet, he argues, if Marxism faces daunting challenges, it still has much to contribute to understanding the trajectory and modes of resistance to contemporary neoliberalism. At the same time, it must prove itself equal to the challenges of the day; not least urbanisation and climate change.

Concluding Part 2, Serena Kataoka takes up some of the literatures explored by Geddes, notably the work of Lefebvre and Castells in exploring 'posty' urban politics (such as postmodernism, post-Marxism, post-structuralism). She sees the work of both prominent theorists as having strong post-structuralist affections, and therefore finds it surprising that post-structuralism has been largely forgotten in urban political theory, even within so-called 'posty' maps of the field. Post-structuralism, she notes, consists of an interpretative practice, termed critique, which seeks to delve deeper into the complexities of the familiar and reveal how structures act not merely as explanations but rather as the very means by which the familiar becomes so. Kataoka urges theorists to experiment with this post-structural critique, setting aside radical visions and ethics that, as Walter Benjamin's *flaneurie* and the idea of *governmentality* traced by Michel Foucault help us understand, only obscure the possibilities of urban politics and emergent political rationalities. Since the urban is not determined by any single structure, she finds the study of the urban to be inherently post-structural. Therefore, her aim is to (re)introduce post-structuralism into urban political theory, and toward that end she offers four ways urban theorists can begin experimenting with post-structural critique.

Part III: Governance

The notion of 'governance' is very broad, but centres loosely on the multiplicity and growing diversity of interests and actors in changing governing arenas. Part III examines the diverse theoretical challenges posed by developments in contemporary urban governance, enhancing our understanding of institutionalisation, regionalisation and re-scaling, leadership, the reform of the urban bureaucracy and development and urbanisation. Chapter 6, 'The New Institutionalism', is one of the new contributions in this edition. New institutionalism has become highly influential over the past decade, an example of theory from the wider field of political and social science prospering in studies of urban governance. In Chapter 6, Vivien Lowndes, a leading exponent, explains the emergence and subsequent development of neo-institutionalism in urban studies. Contrary to the inductive-descriptive approach of traditional institutional studies, the new institutionalism begins with theoretical propositions about the way institutions work, focusing in particular on the norms and rules governing political behaviour in given settings. Institutionalism itself is a broad church, encompassing structure-focused, cultural and rational choice explanations, which leads some to question whether it can reasonably be characterised as a single school of thought. But, Lowndes argues that the unifying proposition in institutional theory is the claim that institutions are the central component of political life and institutionalism (of whatever kind) and the most efficacious means of explaining it. She deploys three mini-case studies to demonstrate the versatility of institutional explanation in understanding political behaviour, the complexity of contemporary governance and the relationship between continuity and change at the urban scale. Challenges facing institutional theorists include the alleged incompatibility between its radically different understandings and the consequent methodological criticism that such a broad umbrella approach explains everything and nothing. How, then, can we know the influence of institutions when we see it? Nevertheless, Lowndes concludes that the approach offers significant insights into the nature of political constraint and the differentiation of localities, and thus can offer fruitful advice to urban policy makers about the opportunities and constraints on change at the local scale.

Since the first edition of *Theories of Urban Politics* was conceived over 15 years ago, interest in the possibilities and limits of urban governance at the regional scale has exploded. The urban politics literature from the mid-1990s on is replete with analyses of regional-level governance. As Hank Savitch and Ronald Vogel demonstrate in Chapter 7, however, regionalism has not been so much discovered as rediscovered, since such thinking (and its critique) dates back several decades. Scholars thus dubbed its reemergence in the 1990s 'new' regionalism, contrasting it with older forms. The chief contrast between old and new regionalism, Savitch and Vogel point out, is that the old regionalism sought to create formal *governments* on the metropolitan level to eliminate fragmentation, whereas the new regionalism stresses more informal modes of metropolitan *governance* to manage it. Persistent criticism of these regionalist visions has come from the public choice school. As Savitch and Vogel explain, this school embraces rather than condemns local governmental fragmentation, rejecting metropolitanism in favour of polycentrism. Most recently, a fourth theoretical approach to regionalism has emerged. This approach, which Savitch and Vogel following others label rescaling or reterritorialisation, develops a more comprehensive and sophisticated understanding of new regionalism, linking it with larger dynamics of state restructuring and global capitalism. Concluding, Savitch and Vogel find this last approach, exemplified by Neil Brenner's (2004) framing of 'new state spaces', especially exciting, seeing in it the potential to thrust urban politics back to the very heart of political science.

The starting point for Stephen Greasley and Gerry Stoker in their discussion of urban political leadership in Chapter 8 is the chapter on leadership by Clarence Stone in the first edition. Stone cautioned that adopting the Mayoral model would not necessarily result in strong local leadership. Despite this caution, there has been a trend towards the elected mayoral system or other models of executive leadership. Moreover, the challenge of political leadership remains high on the agenda of policy makers, politicians and public managers. Thus, the overview and critique offered by Greasley and Stoker is particularly timely, notably in the UK. They assess recent literatures on leadership, focusing on the relationship between three key factors: contextual influences on the performance of leaders, the characteristics of individual leaders and the distribution of decision-making powers between leaders and others in the local political system. The core theoretical concern for leadership studies is understanding the impact of individual actions in a complex social system. With respect to urban political leadership, this question manifests in the form of whether strong leader models make a positive difference in enhancing local democracy. Greasley and Stoker offer a qualified 'yes' to this question, suggesting that the immediate research challenge is to ascertain whether strong leader models of urban governance are better able to put forward a clear agenda and mobilise governing resources than others.

In Chapter 9, Anne Mette Kjaer explores the use of governance theory in studying changes to the urban bureaucracy. Governance theory, most closely associated with the work of Rod Rhodes (1997) in the UK, is concerned with the proliferation of governance by network, caused by the trend towards what Kjaer calls 'authority migration': the hollowing out of the state and diffusion of powers upwards to supranational institutions like the EU and downwards to the urban scale and outwards to the business, community and voluntary sectors. Thus, the task of the urban bureaucracy is coordinative. It is to mobilise and aggregate governing resources fragmented by these centrifugal trends. Hence, governance theory shares common cause with the concerns of leadership, institutional and regime theorists as well as a concern with the mobilisation of community and social capital. Kjaer draws attention to the many criticisms of governance theory, particularly the claim that network governance is in fact tightly controlled by national governments and the dispersal of state power upwards, downwards and outwards radically overstated. Hence, one of the weaknesses in governance theory is that it does not adequately theorise the relationship between hierarchy market and network modes of social coordination. Kjaer concludes by challenging governance theorists to think further about the conditions in which networks might function without hierarchical interventions, the implications of conflict for the management of networks and the relative prevalence of success and failure in particular modes of governance.

Nearly all extant urban political theory has been developed and applied in the context of the Western, or developed, world. The rapid urbanisation of the developing world, driven in part by powerful forces of globalisation, demanded attention be paid in this edition to urban issues in the non-Western context. We have hence dedicated Chapter 10, authored by Richard Stren, to this subject; to recognise the importance of this phenomenon and attempt to better understand it. Stren's survey of the literature reveals that few theoretical treatments of developing world urbanisation incorporate the analysis of the political in any sustained way. One key reason for this lacuna, he points out, is that international organisations concerned with urban problems in the developing world, such as the World Bank and UN-HABITAT, have failed to support work with politics – especially local politics – as its object of study. Stren predicts, however, that the growing recognition of the importance of developing world cities will spur a parallel growth in scholarly research focused on political questions. In particular, the intensity of the social and environmental problems plaguing such cities will demand a better understanding of, in his words, 'the complex politics of urban development of 80 percent of the world's population'.

Part IV: Citizens

Part IV is concerned more directly with the role of the urban citizen in politics. The dynamics of urban power covered in Part II and the institutions and processes of urban governance covered in Part III both deeply affect this citizenry. Urban citizens experience lives shaped by the forces of power and governance; yet they also engage in struggles to reshape these forces. To better understand the role played by citizens in urban politics, the first three chapters in this section focus on their differential experiences by class, race and gender. The remaining two chapters examine social capital and urban social movements as key elements in the struggle of the urban citizenry to create and recreate its political milieu.

Leading off this section, Mara Sidney in Chapter 11 addresses the vexing problem of poor people's marginalisation in urban politics. She identifies and explicates three broad theoretical approaches used to understand this marginalisation and how it might be ameliorated, usefully labeled 'politics first', 'economics first', and a 'problem-centred' approach associated with the European concept of social exclusion. In this explication, Sidney uncovers numerous cross-cutting themes and points of difference among the three. Nonprofit and community-based organisations are central to each approach's vision of poverty amelioration, but the approaches vary as to whether they emphasise policy or process changes. The three approaches also engage the role of ideas and political discourse and the possibilities and limits of the local scale. Sidney closes by identifying four directions for further theory development. Better theory is needed concerning variation across policy sectors and the role of conflict in securing benefits for the disadvantaged. She similarly suggests more theoretic attention be paid to differences among various sub-groups of the poor, while making a compelling case for scholars analysing poverty in cities to develop and apply constructivist and interpretive theories and methods.

J. Phillip Thompson next engages the related issue of race in Chapter 12. Urban political theory, Thompson argues, has failed, at its peril, to put the theorisation of race at its center. As a result, many of the field's most significant and enduring research problems remain unsolved. Three fundamental questions regarding race remain especially neglected. The first concerns the radical basis of society; in particular, whether white racism produces a fundamental racial divide, rivaling that of class, in social life and politics. The second asks why poor blacks are so economically marginalised decades after the civil rights movement in America. The third asks whether, in light of the black experience, state power should be conceptualised as genuinely democratic or fundamentally repressive. Thompson suggests that critical appraisals of the role of race in cities not only sharpen empirical inquiry; such appraisals also introduce a host of analytic and strategic questions wholly different from conventional urban political studies. The powerful backdrop to these efforts to better theorise race in US urban politics is the high level of immigration that is rapidly altering its racial landscape. Thompson next explains the political significance of this changing landscape and contrasts the American experience with that in Britain. Finally, Thompson compellingly calls for re-imagining current notions of political community and citizenship, so that minority advancement is not pitted against that of whites and immigrant advancement is not pitted against that of the struggling native-born. The former, he points out, is the unfinished civil rights revolution; the latter, the unfinished human rights revolution.

In Chapter 13, Judith Garber highlights the major contributions of gender theories to urban studies in four areas. These are, first, the development of an interdisciplinary vocabulary and conceptual framework for talking about the influences of gender on urban politics; secondly, contesting and correcting the dominant Marxist and postmodern theories about urban political economy; thirdly, understanding 'gender' expansively, so as to include sexuality and, indeed, various identities and sources of power/oppression; and fourthly, an examination of the ways in which urban space – in its physical and metaphorical guises – simultaneously construct each other. The theories she discusses provide empirically grounded as well as abstract models of cities that can both guide our thinking about the functioning (and dysfunctioning) of familiar gender relations and help us envision new configurations of citizenship, family, work and other gender-based dimensions of urbanity.

The concept of social capital is another mainstream political science concept that has become very influential at the urban scale, when it was barely known in the field in 1995. In Chapter 14, Helen Sullivan undertakes a critical examination of the concept and its application in urban politics. Social capital refers to the generation of shared values and norms, 'lubricated through trust, in generating and maintaining social order'. Sullivan contrasts different approaches to the study of social capital; from Bourdieu, who saw it as something we possess which explains how the class order is maintained, to Putnam who saw it as something desirable, but often lacking and therefore to be acquired. Putnam has become very influential in urban politics, where the acquisition of social capital is seen by many as aiding the revitalisation of cities, communities and the institutions of governance; particularly in the network era. Social capital theory has become influential in studies of community organising and development, where the relative merits of acquiring 'bonding' and 'bridging' capital are much debated. Sullivan suggests that the concept, while problematic, has merits and has generated important insights into urban politics. However, important challenges remain. How do we conceptualise the development of 'good' and 'bad' social capital and situate social capital analysis in a broader analysis of urban power? In what circumstances can social capital of what kind aid in democratic renewal and empowerment? And what empirical evidence can we bring to bear on the question of how social capital enhances well-being? Such questions are likely to be salient in the urban field for years to come.

Chapter 15 on urban social movements by Gordana Rabrenovic anchors the Citizens section of the book. Given the subject's significance to many areas of urban politics, it is one of the few carried over intact from the first edition. Rabrenovic begins by nodding, as several in this volume have, to our more globalised and urbanised world. These trajectories continue to augment the importance of urban social movements, as urban issues will continue to dominate the agenda of social movement organisations around the world. She begins, as many students of urban social movements do, with the groundbreaking work of Castells in the 1970s. Rabrenovic notes, however, that over time the concept of an urban social movement broadened to include other, less radical examples of grassroots organising and political mobilisation. She next explains three prominent theoretical approaches drawn upon to understand social-movement dynamics – resource mobilisation theory, political opportunity structure theory and framing theory. These approaches are illustrated with examples of social movements combating homelessness, highway construction and hate against immigrants. Rabrenovic concludes by pointing to numerous lacunae within the urban social movement literature. She also underscores the importance of globalisation to our understanding of contemporary urban social movements, both as a source of the urban ills against which movements mobilise and as a force linking localised mobilisations with broader transnational ones.

Part V: Challenges

Finally, in Chapter 16, Clarence Stone addresses some of the challenges lying ahead for urban political theory and practice. Stone urges scholars to resist the pervasive political pessimism and fatalism to which much urban scholarship has too often capitulated. What is needed, he contends, is 'fresh thinking' about urban politics and its possibilities. In particular, Stone offers a nine-step research programme to refashion a new urban scholarship explicitly built around the goal of redesigning local institutions to better realise democratic ideals. Just as Harold Lasswell famously sought to formulate 'a policy science of democracy', Stone (1951) seeks to formulate what might be understood as an 'urban political theory of democracy'. He exhorts scholars to take up the great international challenge of how to build just cities, in which citizens wish and are able to engage in political discourse.

We hope and believe that this exciting collection will provide ample inspiration for those embarking upon, or continuing their careers in, the study and practice of urban politics. Evidently, there will be gaps that some readers will regret. Frantic change seems to be a pervasive feature in the urban political landscape and perhaps the concept of urban political change itself merits further theorisation and comparative analysis. Continuous change also means that by 2020, a third edition of *Theories of Urban Politics* may well be required. It is foolhardy to predict what such a volume might contain. But, at the methodological level, urban political power is likely to remain at the centre of controversy, as it is in politics at large. Intra and cross-national comparative urban studies are likely to proliferate and should be encouraged (Sellers, 2005). Urban politics will continue to transgress and engage in productive dialogue with other disciplines; particularly economics, sociology and geography. Urbanisation will almost certainly be an even more urgent concern by 2020. The political agency of the vast, and growing, urban poor needs to be centre-stage in political analysis, as does the concomitant problem of what social justice might mean for them, and others, in a world rapidly polarising along the lines of space, wealth, health and power. On a truly global scale, questions of climate change and environmental justice are likely to be of even greater import than they are now. Urban politics 'as if nature mattered' (Carter, 2004) is almost certain to demand greater attention than it has received here. At the institutional level, Kjaer shows how over the last 20 years, network theories have become pervasive, alongside network modes of governance. In 2020 we will almost certainly need to reflect on the evolution of network theories and network governance. Will regime theory still lead the field? Will the spread of collaborative, cross-sectoral governance continue? Or, will the fashion for network forms of political organisation and analysis pass as quickly as it emerged centre-stage in the late 1980s? However, in order to navigate change, it is certain that future studies of urban politics will have to maintain continuity in one important respect: the critical, reflective and reflexive disposition that characterises so much scholarship in the field, amply demonstrated in this volume. In this respect, we hope that *Theories of Urban Politics* offers readers a stimulating tour of both the great theoretical challenges of today and the means by which they may be fruitfully studied far into the future.

Notes

1 See http://www.udel.edu/uaa/about_uaa/index.html and http://www.eura.org/pdfcharter 2006.pdf. Both accessed 25 January 2008.
2 A prevalence is unmistakably apparent in this volume. Urban regime theory makes an appearance in the coverage of multiple subjects, including community power, poverty, social movements, leadership, race, bureaucracy and new institutionalism.

───────────────── **References** ─────────────────

Brenner, N. (2004) *New State Spaces: Urban Goverance and the Rescaling of Statehood.* Oxford: Oxford University Press.

Carter, N. (2004) 'Politics as if nature mattered', in A. Leftwich (ed.), *What is Politics?* Cambridge: Polity Press. pp. 182–95.

Davis, M. (2005) *Planet of Slums.* New York: Verso.

Dowding, K. (2006) *Power.* Buckingham: Open University Press.

Judge, D., Stoker, G. and Wolman, H. (eds) (1995) *Theories of Urban Politics.* London: Sage.

Krasner, S.D. (ed.) (1983) *International Regimes,* 1st edn. Ithaca: Cornell University Press.

Lasswell, H. (1951) 'The policy orientation', in D. Lerner and H. Lasswell (eds), *The Policy Sciences.* Stanford: Stanford University Press. pp. 3–15.

Leftwich, A. (ed.) (2004) *What is Politics?* Cambridge: Polity Press.

Liang, Z., Chen, Y.P. and Gu, Y. (2002) 'Rural industrialization and internal migration in China', *Urban Studies,* 39 (2): 2175–87.

Merton, R. (1949) *Social Theory and Social Structure.* New York: The Free Press.

Orr, M. and V.C. Johnson (eds) (2008) *Power in the City: Clarence Stone and the Politics of Inequality.* Lawrence, KS: University Press of Kansas.

Rhodes, R.A.W. (1997) *Understanding Governance: Policy Networks, Governance, Reflexivity and Accountability.* Buckingham: Open University Press.

Sellers, J. (2004) 'Replacing the nation: an agenda for comparative urban politics', *Urban Affairs Review,* 40 (4): 419–45.

Part I

PROLOGUE

1

WHY STUDY *URBAN* POLITICS?

Peter John

At its most straightforward, urban politics is about authoritative decision-making at a smaller scale than national units – the politics of the sub-national level. Examples of urban politics are a mayor's decision about what policy to follow in a city, the consequences of a neighbourhood participation exercise, or the decision of a locally important business to relocate away from an area, with a loss of jobs and income. In other words, urban is local. Of course, it is not possible to separate out neatly the local from national or even international politics as each one affects the other, particularly in an era of ever-deepening global influences (Sellers, 2005); and national decision-makers affect what happens in places like cities just as local decisions have a knock-on effect higher up. But the focus of the interest is at the sub-national level with particular reference to the political actors and institutions operating there. As with all definitions in the social sciences, the context is multidimensional and the boundaries are fuzzy, but it is usually clear when a topic is primarily about urban politics and when it is not.

Urban in the dictionary means relating to a city, which denotes dense built-up areas and centres of population as opposed to rural and less populated places. Indeed, most of the study of urban politics is about cities, which means that some writers think that urban politics is about 'the politics in urbanised communities' (Stoker, 1998: 120). But such a limitation marginalises vast tracts of non-urban areas – and the people who live and work there – and also counts out units that transcend urban areas, such as regions. In any case, it is also impossible to define where the boundary is between urban and non-urban. And what about suburban areas? Is not rural life highly urbanised in many respects? There is also a geographic bias in the use of language, with most researchers in Europe happy with the local politics tag, whereas the US has the urban politics definition. Probably the urban epithet is winning over, with its extensive use in the less developed world and in Asia. In Europe since the 1970s, there has been a move to replace the use of the term 'local' with 'urban' (Young, 1975; Dunleavy, 1980), partly to emulate US intellectual endeavours, but also to signal that local politics is not as a previous generation of scholars assumed it was; that is mainly about describing local political institutions and expressing the ideal of local self-government. Urban is associated with the importance of city processes, such as population movements, employment changes, and the political conflicts that arise from the intensity of economic competition and ethnic diversity of many cities, something that is heightened by the increasing urbanisation of modern life across the world.

So urban politics is, on the one hand, a description and analysis of a spatial scale of operation, but, on the other, it is about the wider socio-political-economic processes associated with cities and urban areas – and is concerned with the links between the two. In part, this focus can be on the various policy problems, such as inner city deprivation or environmental damage, and possible solutions to them. But the interest is also theoretical, about how economic power and class politics play out in the city and take a particular form because of the spatial location and particular structural constraints in operation. The question of economic power and city politics goes to the heart of the classic pluralist–elitist debate in the 1950s and 1960s, which consolidated urban politics as a sub-discipline, with Dahl and his associates arguing for a description of a more open and accessible political system than their elitist counterparts, who studied the closed and high status elites who appeared to govern cities (see Chapter 2 for a detailed discussion). As Geddes demonstrates in Chapter 4, power is also central to the long-running Marxist contribution to the analysis of the power of the city, appearing in the 1970s (Pickvance, 1995; Geddes, Chapter 4 in this volume), such as in the work of Castells (1974, 1978) in Europe and Saunders (1980) in the UK, coming to prominence with the work of Harvey (1973) and Davis (1990), and continuing in more recent debates led by Cox (2001). With such a focus on the concepts, it is no surprise that philosophical takes on urban theory themselves constitute an academic industry. In fact, almost any theoretical topic can be aligned with urban politics – rational choice, post-Fordism, postmodernism are a few that have been tried. The succession of theoretical edifices has been described by Dunleavy as a series of tanks lying wrecked on the academic road, each one tried, exploded and then abandoned.[1] Thus the urban political field is highly flexible and diverse, something that urbanists tend to like about their subject. It also makes the definitional issue rather irrelevant. As Stoker (1998) comments, what matters for definition is the practice of studying urban politics, making the topic what academics do at a particular point in time. Urban politics becomes a 'flag of convenience', allowing researchers to pursue their topic of interest.

Even if we do not wish to conflate urban with the study of cities, most urbanists tend to be fans of these places, and believe them to be interesting even if they recognise the negative side in the forms of conflict, pollution and crime. It is also no surprise that urbanists like cities as places to study and live, with their diversity of lifestyles and groups; their celebration of ethnicity; and large choice of consumption, whether it is food, the arts, clothes or housing. In that sense, most urbanists use their leisure for some enjoyable participant observation.

In spite of the attractions of cities, the 'why' question for urbanists often elicits some panic as well as self-confident justification. Urbanists are inclined to look over their shoulders at others in supposedly more exciting fields, such as international relations and global terror. Academics get a buzz from what they study from its relevance and importance, such as an exciting and newsworthy topic, or that one embodies salient political values. But urban political scientists sometimes feel too modest about theirs. Urban or local governments are usually subordinate to other levels of government, with less powers and responsibilities, and where key decisions about powers and finances get taken at other levels. This diminutive status in politics can make people think that the topic is less important than the prominent dealings of nation states or international organisations (Wolman and Goldsmith, 1992: 1). In the English case, the lack of importance is underlined by the poor way in which local government has been treated by the sovereign parliament and executive in the years since the mid-1970s, with the loss of its powers and controls over finance along with intense legal regulation by the centre (John, 1994), which successive governments have done nothing to correct, and if anything have heightened. Indeed, a recent study highlights just how few functions and resources locally elected governments control in their area (Wilks-Heeg and Clayton, 2006). Partly, this subordination is the result of the unusual centralisation of English life in its constitutional arrangements; it also reflects the contempt for local government by the London political elite, which a study of senior politicians and civil servants revealed through a series of off-the-record interviews (Jones and Travers, 1996). Partly, because local government is perceived to administer things that others consider to be dull, such as bin emptying, street cleaning, drainage, and building quality, it is assumed the administration and decision-making of these activities are similarly tedious. And one prominent public figure, Lord Redcliffe-Maud, even described local government as 'sewage without tears'.[2] Then there is the British equation of local government with bureaucratic routine, petty-fogging red tape, corruption, small mindedness, mediocrity, embodying the limited nature of social culture outside the great metropolis, where it is hard to see grand opera, for example. Such is what the London elite would have others believe, but such public perception may rub off on students of urban politics who may think the subject boring and have to defend its choice to their families who may share the popular misconceptions. However, the British case is extreme – a cause for academic interest rather than the opposite – as local government has a greater importance in national life in France and the USA where local politicians are national figures.

In fact, it is possible to find the very features that make local government unattractive to some appealing to others. Sewage may be about the machinations of minor bureaucrats, but it can illustrate issues of power and collective action problems. There is a fashionable set of research in historical studies about rubbish, dirt, waste, which illustrate the nature of the urban space.[3] In fact, the very grittiness, action-centredness and practicality of the problems that typical urban governments face create research opportunities for the budding urbanist, a topic this chapter returns to.

Enthusiasm for the interesting aspects of urban politics should not be confused with belief in the topic. A lot of writers assume that the very characteristics that others despise in urban politics can actually be a reason for studying it. Thus the subordination of urban political institutions and the practical policy-orientated aspects of urban policy become fetishised. Because local government is supposed to embody certain values, following them through may be an attractive route for the researcher or at least a background set of concerns that inform a study. Such normative preoccupations are very common in research, and often influence that important early decision to opt for a topic of study. Someone who is interested in the state of the environment studies green politics, a feminist studies women and so on. The belief in the values of political decentralisation thus may influence the topic choice. These values are implicit in the arguments of local representative organisations, local bureaucrats and politicians and some academics that seek to defend their autonomy and believe that local democracy is by definition a good thing. They are usually about the relevance and appropriateness of locally informed choices, based on the group of people affected by a set of decisions, a set of arguments going back to J.S. Mill in *Representative Government*. Related to this is the value of pluralism in the grand polity (Sharpe, 1970), allowing a thousand flowers to bloom. Not only is such diversity a good thing in itself, but it allows for innovation. From this core, local government has been seen to embody a host of desirable political values, such as equality and diversity. This is not the place to have a detailed review of the theory of local government, except to say that such attempts usually fail because the empirics fail to support the argument – there is nothing special in local government terms of representation, pluralism and innovation, and much of the opposite can be found. It is impossible to create a range of public goods for local government which do not involve other levels of government making a universal justification of self-government activities something of a chimera. In any case, the so-called values are so vague that it is hard to come up with a specific justification of local government actions or institutions (Stoker, 2005). Moreover, value-driven research rarely makes for good social science as it encourages the researcher to confirm an initial set of values.

In any case, most social scientists find that, in the business of doing research, value concerns often take the back seat because the main project becomes that of explanation and engagement with the theoretical problems of the discipline. In many ways, the topic of study may not be relevant. It is possible to imagine many topics that appear to be dull on the outside but become fascinating as the research develops. In that sense, it does not matter what to study, but how to do it. Here we have what may be called the 'Swiss cowbell theory of dissertation topic choice'. The thought experiment works like this: imagine a research student who has to start a dissertation on Swiss cowbells (say because of a funding opportunity), who is initially disheartened by the topic, but then comes to examine the variation in cowbell sizes and sounds, invents a theory of political cooperation and conflict based on their ownership and display, which is tested by a model of the appearance of different styles and so on. Then a successful career beckons. If the cowbell theory were true, then all that would matter is that the student chooses something and sticks with it – the payoff comes in time. Choosing on the basis of initial interest and fashion does not matter because all researchers end up doing the same sort of thing, and a good researcher will create an interesting piece of work no matter how different the subject. What the initial interest does is to get people started. And in fact, accident often plays a role in starting people off on a course of study, such as a tip from a teacher or an early project that turns into a longer dissertation. Once the early choices have been made, it is easy to move to the next linked research project. Path dependence means that there are economies from staying in the same kind of work because knowledge and expertise pay off, and high transactions costs rule out a topic change. Reputation means that others ask for chapters and contributions, and research grant proposals have the right curriculum vitae to back them up.

If it is the case that topics only vary to the extent to which the researcher has engaged with them rather than some intrinsic level of interest, then what should govern the choice of topic? Issues of practicality and tractability now come to the fore. And here urban politics has some unique advantages, especially for the beginning student; and if they were more widely known about, would make international relations researchers green with envy, particularly when they have sunk their precious investment of time and resources into studying something so inaccessible as an international political movement, for example.

Urban politics has two main characteristics that derive from its location in multiple and often small units below the level of the state – the first is propinquity; the second is numerosity (see John, 2006 for an outline of the argument). Propinquity denotes the closeness of the urban space where actors interact frequently and tend to be small in number. The urban is politics in miniature and this creates a particular kind of political system rather than a mirror image of other levels, largely to do with smaller numbers of the elite and the ease at which its members can interact. And it is no surprise that one of the enduring themes of the study of urban politics is political power, not because power only operates at the local level, but that an urban space is a convenient and tractable unit for studying such a difficult phenomenon and power takes a particular form in a localised space, which partly explains the profusion of community power studies of the 1960s, the Marxist accounts of the 1970s and 1980s, and the regime case studies of the 1990s. It is possible for one person to make the rounds of the whole local political elite, such as the author and Alistair Cole did for their study of four cities in Britain and France (Cole and John, 2001), so much so that the researchers became a rather over-familiar sight in the waiting rooms of their case study municipalities. Trying that in Whitehall or Washington would require an army of researchers who would still be overwhelmed by the exercise.

Propinquity also means the actors are close to what they administer – there is a coal face aspect to urban politics where policy and implementation are near to the political process (see Yates, 1977), and where politics extends way beyond the formal institutions into the realms of governance and civil society. For the political scientist who wants to study real-world phenomena, but still look at the role of political actors, the urban space is appropriate, and more interesting than the field offices of a large central government department, for example. Thus the student of terror can get much more of a handle of the origins and impact of terrorism by studying the local factors leading to recruitment and the policies adopted to counteract it. As Tip O'Neal (O'Neill and Hymel, 1995) said, 'all politics is local'. When dug down, the local aspects of political phenomena are usually at work because actors usually relate to particular places for electoral support where they make contact with their followers; on the policy side, decision-makers need to address the practicalities and politics of implementation in particular places, which end up being the places that local government administers and the wide array of governmental and non-governmental organisations interact to try to solve collective action problems. Typically, urban problems intersect with a wide variety of fields, and propinquity means that questions of society, race and poverty closely intersect with politics. Thus urban political scientists have a rich vein of interdisciplinary work to draw upon without becoming economists, sociologists, lawyers and social policy experts. Propinquity has some even more obvious advantages as it is possible to study out of one's back door as universities are usually located in or near to cities or towns accessible to the urban researcher. Apart from the cost and convenience of the bus rather than the airplane, it is usually the case that urban political actors are willing to see a local researcher (though the backyard can create problems too). Even if the urban area is overseas, it is usually easier to get access than to the offices of a national government, for example.

Numerosity is the multiple occurrences of local governments, often amounting to many hundreds. For statistical projects hungry for large numbers, urban politics is a feast because the large N means that it is acceptable to deploy a test based on a 95 percent confidence interval with the idea that some of the natural variation in observations comes from chance, which means it is possible to make inferences when things do not happen by chance. This is a massive advantage because the nation state has only one observation or a limited number. Even comparative politics projects can only have a handful of cases, which can be multiplied by having observations over time, but not by that much. By contrast, it is possible to perform routine statistical tests in urban politics, such as to find out where there is a relationship between political parties and public expenditure for example, which has stimulated a plethora of output studies (e.g. Boyne, 1985).

Numerosity is not just of advantage to the statistically literate, it is a boon to the qualitative researcher as the abundance of local government units means that there are many cases from which to choose. This convenient factor means that the researcher can select cases on variations of the independent variable as well as ensure that the dependent variable varies too. By being rigorous on selection, it is possible to re-create scientific conditions in the data with just a few cases. In this sense, research in urban politics is much closer to meeting the ideals of *Designing Social Inquiry* (King et al., 1994) than most projects in the comparative country field.

Rather than be downhearted at the lowly status of urban politics or over-inflated by an exaggerated sense of its virtues, the urban researcher should be glad that the topic offers many natural advantages as well as offering interesting places like cities to study. Research is easier and is more tractable than at other levels of government. It offers more possibilities for good social science because numerosity ensures variation in the units and propinquity enhances quality of and access to the data. It is no surprise that urban politics was the starting point for several major political scientists such as Dahl, Polsby and Lowi in the US, and Dunleavy and Newton in the UK. Given the natural advantages, it would not be surprising if more scholars found the urban route in the twenty-first century.

Notes

1 Comment made at an urban politics panel at the UK Political Studies Association annual conference, Leicester, 1993.
2 As reported in Peter Hamant (ed.), 1978, *The Empire Club of Canada Speeches 1977–1978*. Toronto, Canada: The Empire Club Foundation. pp. 41–54.
3 See the London Consortium course, 'Shit and civilization: our ambivalent relationship to ordure in the city, culture, and the psyche'.

References

Boyne, G. (1985) 'Theory, methodology and results in political science: the case of output studies', *British Journal of Political Science*, 15: 473–515.
Castells, M. (1974) *Monopolville: L'entreprise, l'Etat, l'urbain*. Paris: Mouton.
Castells, M. (1978) *City, Class and Power*. London: Macmillan.
Cole, A. and John, P. (2001) *Local Governance in England and France*. London: Routledge.
Cox, K. (2001) 'Territory, politics and the urban', *Political Geography*, 20: 745–62.
Davis, M. (1990) *City of Quartz: Excavating the Future in Los Angeles*. London: Verso.
Dunleavy, P. (1980) *Urban Political Analysis*. London: Macmillan.
Harvey, D. (1973) *Social Justice and the City*. London: Arnold.
John, P. (1994) 'Central-local relations in the 1980s and 1990s: towards a policy learning approach', *Local Government Studies*, 20 (3): 412–36.
John, P. (2006) 'Methodologies and research methods in urban political science' in H. Baldersheim and H. Wollmann (eds), *The Comparative Study of Local Government and Politics. Overview and Synthesis*. Opladen: Barbara Budrich Publishers (World of Political Science series).
Jones, G. and Travers, G. (1996) *Attitudes to Local Government in Westminster and Whitehall*. Commission for Local Democracy Report No. 14 (May 1995).
King, G., Keohane, R. and Verba, S. (1994) *Designing Social Inquiry*. Princeton, NJ: Princeton University Press.
O'Neill, T. and Hymel, G. (1995) *All Politics is Local: And Other Rules of the Game*. Adams Media Corporation.
Pickvance, C. (1995) 'Marxist theories of urban politics', in D. Judge, G. Stokes and H. Wolman (eds), *Theories of Urban Politics*. London: Sage.
Saunders, P. (1980) *Urban Politics*. Harmondsworth: Penguin.
Sellers, J. (2005) 'Re-placing the nation. An agenda for comparative urban politics', *Urban Affairs Review*, 40: 419–45.
Sharpe, L.J. (1970) 'Theories and values of local government', *Political Studies*, 18 (2): 153–74.
Stoker, G. (1998) 'Theory and urban politics', *International Political Science Review*, 19 (2): 119–29.
Stoker, G. (2005) *What is Local Government For?* London: New Local Government Network.
Wilks-Heeg, S. and Clayton, S. (2006) *Whose Town is it Anyway?* York: Joseph Rowntree Charitable Trust.
Wolman, H. and Goldsmith, M. (1992) *Urban Politics and Policy*. Oxford: Blackwell.
Yates, D. (1977) *The Ungovernable City*. Cambridge, MA: MIT Press.
Young, K. (ed.) (1975) *Essays on the Study of Urban Politics*. London: Macmillan.

Part II

POWER

2

THE HISTORY OF COMMUNITY POWER

Alan Harding

Why bother with community power?

In some respects, beginning the substantive section of a contemporary book on theories of urban politics with a discussion of the history of community power research may seem faintly eccentric. After all, as subsequent chapters demonstrate, academic commentary on urban politics, and within urban studies more generally, is increasingly concerned with the impact of processes of globalisation on urban development patterns and the challenges that are seen to arise for urban governance, broadly defined. The concerns of the original community power theorists of the 1950s and 1960s were, by comparison, highly localised, even parochial. Furthermore, in a book intended for a trans-Atlantic readership, it must be acknowledged that the direct impact of the US-dominated community power debate in the UK was sufficiently muted that Crewe could write, long after the controversies it engendered had begun to subside, that 'with the exception of some unpublished doctoral theses, there exist no studies of community power in Britain' (Crewe, 1974: 35). In this context, and in light of the fact that the community power debate, by common consent, did not produce the final words on the politics of power or the concept of community, it might be tempting, at least from a UK perspective, to concur with Dowding et al. (1993: 1) that 'rarely has a focus for study and a set of competing methods been so thoroughly discredited, vanishing behind us with so little residual trace'.

That summary judgement, however, severely underestimates the historical importance and legacy of community power theory. Whilst the original community power debate was inevitably a product of its place and time – parts of the urban US in the 1950s and 1960s – its contribution to the development of urban studies is substantial in at least three senses. First, it established urban politics as a focus for study in its own right rather than effectively assuming that politics was something that 'urban' academics might choose to engage in outside of their scholarly, 'non-political' day jobs. Secondly, whilst it failed, ultimately, to provide any resolution to the complex questions about the nature and measurement of power that it raised, by comparison with other paradigmatic approaches within urban studies before and since, it was a model of clarity in terms of conceptual foundations and methodologies. Thirdly, notwithstanding the fact that it is now virtually invisible to all but a small group of urban scholars interested in the history of their subject, it wielded significant, if indirect, influence over subsequent academic approaches to understanding the politics of urban development, including some that had more significant trans-Atlantic impact.

The remainder of this chapter elaborates upon the merits and legacy of the community power debate whilst not denying its limitations. It makes two overall assumptions. First, what was originally understood by the term 'community power debate', whilst it was critical in establishing an academic focus on the politics of urban development, by no means exhausts all the most important work in the field it opened up. Thus a 'history of community power' cannot limit itself entirely to a commentary upon the debate itself. Secondly, given the way in which the influence of different schools and approaches within urban theory ebb and flow, sometimes appearing to be overturned abruptly but more often metamorphosing over time into something substantially different, we should not expect the 'debt' that later approaches owe to community power theorists will necessarily be transparent, far less openly acknowledged.

The chapter proceeds in four stages. The next section locates the community power debate within the context of the evolution of urban theory and demonstrates how it put 'politics', broadly defined, centre-stage for the first time. It then provides a brief overview of the nature and parameters of the community power debate with reference to the work of its key protagonists. The third section assesses the controversies to which the debate gave rise but was unable to resolve. It also notes certain key limitations of community power studies that were less remarked upon at the time but were implicitly acknowledged by later approaches to the politics of (US) urban development that drew some inspiration from them. The fourth section links the concerns of the community power debate to that later generation of urban political economy and provides an account of changes in the intellectual climate that encouraged a return to the concerns of community power researchers but in rather different form. The final section briefly summarises the legacy of the community power debate and the challenges that the developments in urban theory it helped to inspire continue to face.

Community power: bringing in politics

The study of community power surfaced in the 1950s at a time when the influence of the once-dominant Chicago School of urban sociology had begun to wane and most new developments in urban theory were increasingly being associated with urban geography and spatial analysis. It was a significant departure from both. The ecological approach for which the Chicago School had become famous drew heavily upon Darwinian notions of competition and natural selection. It adapted these biological concepts to the study of social groups, rather than species, and used them in attempts to account for the dynamic process through which different groups of city-dwellers became 'sorted' into the areas and neighbourhoods to which their capabilities and circumstances were best suited and, from there, for the development of the physical form of cities. Work within urban geography and spatial analysis, by contrast, drew more upon neo-classical economics than evolutionary biology. It employed the notion of distance minimisation – a spatial version of the utility-maximisation principle favoured by economists – as a basic assumption about how people satisfy their wants and needs and built various explanations of the development of cities and urban systems around it.

Both of these broad schools of urban social science were classically positivist in their orientation and methods. They based explanations of the observable *outcomes* of human behaviour – as represented by patterns of migration, social segregation and land-use, the locational behaviour of firms, the size and location of urban areas and so on – on assumptions about the imperatives driving the individual agents that collectively produced them but with scant reference to the intentions, motivations or interaction of those agents. For all their differences, both approaches effectively assumed that the production of cities and urban life was dependent upon blind imperatives – be it quasi-biological programming or the 'hidden hand of the market' – rather than intentionality. In short, they saw cities as more accidental than planned.

This is not to argue that either school was entirely disinterested in collective decision-making for or within cities. Prominent figures within the Chicago School, for example, whilst they were sometimes derided as 'social Darwinists', were prominent social reformers keen to use the findings of their research to inform policies on urban development. Many urban geographers and spatial analysts, similarly, considered their work to be essential to the 'technical' resolution of urban problems at a time when belief in the potential of well-intended social engineering was at its height. Neither school, however, saw collective urban decision-making processes as particularly relevant objects of study in their own right.

Community power theorists, by contrast, put decision-making processes for and/or within cities at the centre of their work. For them, the way in which urban environments and urban life were consciously shaped by those with the responsibility or power to do so was just as important as the impact of myriad decisions, by households or businesses, that 'inadvertently' drove urban change. In short, they were interested in urban politics, broadly defined, and specifically concerned with the way collective decisions were shaped by various agents. For all the differences between them, the main protagonists in the community power debate – pluralists and elite theorists of one form or another – agreed upon two things. First, there was an important sub-set of 'urban' decisions, associated mainly with the institutions of urban government, that was concerned with 'place-shaping' as an end in itself, not simply as a bi-product of instrumental choices. Secondly, power – within this sub-set of decisions as elsewhere – was ultimately a property of people, not of abstractions. Community power theorists were 'methodologically individualist'; they saw individuals as the basic explanatory unit for all social phenomena in the last instance.

The core question arising from these concerns for the first wave of community power studies was 'who runs cities?' It was posed, most famously, by Hunter (1953) who, in attempting to assess 'who runs Regional City' – actually Atlanta, Georgia – adopted what became known as 'reputational analysis'. Methodologically, this proceeded in two main stages. First, Hunter tested the extent to which 'four groups that may be assumed to have power connections ... [in] ... business, government, civic associations, and "society" activities' (Hunter, 1953: 11) were reputed to be powerful by their peers. Having ranked the responses and identified a long list of perceived 'community influentials', he then interviewed the top-ranked individuals to ascertain who amongst them was seen as most powerful, how they interacted, how they grouped themselves in relation to key 'community projects' and how their influence over these projects was channelled. Using this method, Hunter claimed to identify a small clique of 'policy-makers' that collectively determined all the major place-shaping choices taken within the city. The clique was overwhelmingly dominated by senior executives of the city's key businesses. Only one member – Atlanta's mayor – held public office. Hunter was therefore able to offer 'scientific' evidence that local representative democracy – at least in this case – provided a smokescreen for dominant economic interests and that nothing in the governance of Atlanta moved if it did not originate within, or gain the approval of, a business-dominated elite. This conclusion established Hunter as the father of US urban elite theory.

Genuine debate amongst community power researchers was triggered by the publication of Dahl's classic study of New Haven in 1961. Dahl, a political scientist, eschewed the more sociological approach to the measurement of power employed by Hunter and instead looked for evidence of the way power was actually used in particular decision-making situations. He applied 'decisional analysis' in attempting to answer a slightly different question – 'who (if anyone) governs New Haven?' – and came to the conclusion that no one did in an absolute sense. Having examined decision-making controversies in a number of discrete policy areas and assessed whose preferences prevailed, Dahl argued that whilst some individuals were particularly influential within one area, none exerted influence across the board. In other words, power, although by no means equally shared across all social groups, was sufficiently diffused for rule by an elite – particularly an unelected one – to be impossible. This conclusion, and the work it built upon, established Dahl as the leading US pluralist thinker, not just within urban studies but more generally. Other community power studies (e.g. Banfield, 1966) supported his argument that local representative democracy 'worked' in so far as many different groups could influence decisions and there were enough checks and balances within the system to prevent the centralisation or abuse of power.

The 'debate' reconsidered

Because elite theorists and pluralists came to what appeared to be radically different conclusions about the merits of representative democracy within the urban US, it is understandable that the community power debate was dominated by attempts to assess which, if either, was 'right'. Given that both approaches had been remarkably clear about their conceptual assumptions and methods, the natural focus of the debate was on methodology. Following Dahl's intervention, pluralist approaches were criticised in turn by neo-elite theorists who did not favour Hunter's reputational method but insisted that decisional analysis was also inadequate for the purposes of measuring power. Neo-elitists argued that the decision points studied by pluralists were purely arbitrary and that decisional analysis was blind to the way policy agendas were set. Pluralists, they argued, could not prove that the decisions they studied represented the most important points at which power was exercised, nor that the issues those decisions dealt with were critical to a city's most powerful people. For neo-elitists, the power used to make concrete, controversial decisions represented only one face of power. A second face, involving 'non-decision making', sees the powerful act to ensure that only those issues that are comparatively innocuous to them ever reach the point of decision. Thus the weak mini-elites identified by pluralists in different policy areas may have been decisive in disputes over issues that were on agendas laid before them, but those agendas could already have been manipulated and neutralised so as to be unthreatening to the 'real' elite (Bachrach and Baratz, 1962). The key question posed by neo-elite theorists – effectively, 'who sets urban agenda and why aren't they challenged?' – was less amenable to research methodologies that focused upon local decision-making processes.

By the early 1970s, much of the energy unleashed within urban studies by the community power debate had dissipated as the methodological controversies it provoked began to outgrow their urban origins. Although some subsequent attempts to 'resolve' the community power debate retained a nominal urban focus (Polsby, 1980), for the most part, theoretical work on power was taken forward by political and social theorists who had no particular academic interest in cities and preferred in-principle conceptual argument to the empirical testing of propositions (Lukes, 1974; Foucault, 1980). In retrospect, the decline and/or 'de-urbanisation' of the concerns raised within community power research and the way researchers had gone about addressing them are unsurprising. On one hand, concerns about 'urban' power relations began to be dominated by 'radical' neo-Marxist and neo-Weberian scholars who favoured broader and/or more structural approaches – based upon the relationship between classes, status groups and tiers of government within the 'capitalist state' – over the methodological individualism of community power theorists (see Geddes in Chapter 4). On the other, critics were right to suggest that methodologically individualist approaches to power found it hard to cope with the idea that the exercise of power may not be associated with conflict and that people may be quiescent for reasons other than their satisfaction with decisions. In trying to allow for such possibilities, subsequent theories of power had to delve deeper into abstractions, such as the role of ideology and the difference between 'real' and perceived needs, which are less readily observable and amenable to empirical testing (see Dowding, 1996 for a review).

Just as important, however, is the fact that community power theorists were generally more concerned with power than they were with 'communities' or their relationship to 'places'. For Hunter and Dahl, the 'communities' of Atlanta and New Haven were interesting not so much in themselves but in so far as they could be treated as microcosms of the larger (US) society of which they formed a part. Indeed, there was neither consensus nor very much discussion about what comprised the 'communities' in question. For Dahl, whose focus was on local political decision-making, the New Haven 'community' was effectively taken to be those people who lived or worked in the area defined by the boundaries of the local authority that had jurisdiction over the core of the conurbation; in other words, the 'city', administratively defined. Hunter had a looser spatial conception of community in which the 'non-elite' was effectively assumed to comprise city residents whose interests were poorly served by the powerful but the 'elite' was not necessarily so spatially constrained. Whilst it would have been surprising if Hunter's methods had identified members of the Atlanta elite operating to a radically different spatial geography, this was certainly possible, given that the criteria that determined 'membership' of the elite focused upon evidence of perceived or actual influence over key decisions impacting upon the city, irrespective of where those involved lived.

The 'urban' focus of community power studies, then, was rather vague and based largely on convenience for the researcher and the assumption that empirical research findings derived at the level of the city could be generalised. In the methodological debate triggered by community power studies, this assumption was rarely challenged. In retrospect, however, the notion that cities could be treated as self-contained and independent entities was an important shortcoming that later work in the field of urban political economy had to address. The platform provided by pluralists and elite theorists ensured that such efforts did not take place in a vacuum but could build, in particular, upon three propositions that effectively flowed from community power studies. First, whilst the nature of cities and processes of urban development are, in many respects, the unintended and largely incidental aggregate outcomes of countless individual decisions, the context within which such decisions are made is substantially shaped by an urban politics that revolves around collective, place-shaping choices. Secondly, the way place-shaping decisions are made does not conform to standard textbook descriptions of the policy-making process within liberal democracies, whereby elected politicians ostensibly translate the desires of the majority of citizens into policies and programmes that are then implemented by apolitical executives. Thirdly, and even though community power theorists occupy different positions along a continuum on the issue, the textbooks are wrong because they underestimate the capacity of business groups and business 'needs' to shape policy agenda and decisions.

Where the notion of 'cities as microcosms' was deficient was in not sufficiently recognising or assessing the extent to which key local actors involved in place-making decisions – be they in the public or private sectors – were able to act autonomously. From today's vantage point, this oversight seems surprising. After all, it is now widely accepted that the institutions of urban government are embedded within complex, hierarchical systems of 'multi-level governance' and have to find ways of operating within the legislative, regulatory and financial constraints that apply in their particular 'space-times'. Similarly, in a world of footloose global capital and huge multinational enterprises, it is axiomatic that many of the businesses located within any given city, and especially the largest and most 'powerful' ones, are neither dependent upon a local market nor limited to a single urban location. It is possible to be lenient towards the original community power theorists in so far as (a) capital was more 'localised' in the urban US in the 1950s and 1960s than it is today, and (b) there was, and remains, a high degree of 'home rule' amongst local authorities within the US governmental system which, certainly in comparison to much of Europe, limits the extent of direct interventions into local politics by higher levels of government. However, these lacunae, whilst they may have been smaller at the point at which the community power debate was at its peak, were never negligible, grew in importance over time, and had to be addressed by any subsequent approach to the politics of urban development which took public–private sector interaction seriously.

US urban political economy: community power revisited?

Most accounts of the history of community power research end with the neo-elitist critique of Dahl. Again with hindsight, though, it is clear that attempts to develop methodologically individualist accounts of the politics of urban development, that is to say ones that take human agency seriously, suffered no more than a temporary lull. The late 1970s and 1980s, in fact, witnessed a resurgence of variations of community power research in the form of a 'new', again US-dominated, urban political economy. One key strand within this somewhat amorphous 'school', the growth coalition/machine thesis (Molotch, 1976; Logan and Molotch, 1987), can be interpreted as a modernised elite theory approach whilst the other discussed by Karen Mossberger in the next chapter, urban regime theory (Elkin, 1987; Stone, 1989), has pluralist antecedents. That these links back to the community power debate are not highlighted more emphatically reflects two things: the transformation of pluralist thinking in the intervening years and the fact that these two strands of US urban political economy saw themselves not so much as refining a tradition as responding to a very specific, contemporary intellectual 'enemy'.

The transformation of pluralism is best reflected in the work of Charles Lindblom, the father of neo-pluralism, who took upon himself the task of modifying traditional pluralist analysis in response to critics from neo-Marxist and elite theory schools. His analysis started from the observation that the separate but interlinked decisions made through the organs of representative government and by the business community represent the two core systems of authority in market-based, liberal democratic societies, in that they jointly have the most telling effect on the levels and distribution of economic and social welfare. From there, he argued that business interests are privileged, far more than any other group in civil society, when it comes to influencing public policy choices because of what he calls the 'structural' and 'instrumental' power of business.

Structural power is a reflection of the critical importance of business decisions – over jobs, remuneration, standards of living and so on – in providing public welfare. Public officials, be they elected or appointed, cannot, consequently, be indifferent to business performance because social well-being, along with a government's popularity and the availability of public revenues, depend upon it. Business interests are automatically regarded by government officials 'not ... simply as the representatives of special interests ... [but] ... as ... performing functions that [they] regard as indispensable' (Lindblom, 1977: 175). In recognising and responding to the inescapable reliance of governments on business performance, a public official, he argued, 'does not have to be bribed, duped or pressured to do so. Nor does he [*sic*] have to be an uncritical admirer of businessmen' (*ibid.*). Furthermore, this recognition that business preferences have disproportionate influence over public policy agenda invites 'no conspiracy theory of politics ... [and] ... no crude allegation of a power elite' (*ibid.*).

The 'structural' power of business interests is supplemented by the 'instrumental' power afforded via partisan interest group activity. Business groups, Lindblom argued, are able to mobilise their case particularly effectively and be reassured that it will be given an attentive hearing for two reasons. First, they have material advantages in terms of financial and organisational resources. No other group can, for example, so readily funnel enterprise profits into 'friendly' political parties and causes or deploy a ready-made bureaucracy in the lobbying of public officials or quasi-political campaigning. Secondly, and irrespective of the self-organising power of the business community, public officials will tend to be more concerned to elicit the views of business organisations in the process of policy-making than those of other groups. Business leaders are 'admitted to circles of explicit negotiation, bargaining, and reciprocal persuasion, from which ordinary citizens are excluded' (*ibid.*: 179) and given a privileged status over other interest groups because they 'are there ... in their capacity as "public" officials' (*ibid.*); that is, as decision-makers with a critical influence over public welfare. Lindblom did not argue that business interests necessarily dictate policy choices. There is no necessary consensus among business interests, and business demands may exceed what public officials are prepared to concede. Nevertheless, 'conflict between government and business ... is not evidence of a lack of privilege' since 'it will always lie ... within a range of dispute constrained by their understanding that ... they do not wish to destroy or seriously undermine the function of the other' (*ibid.*).

If neo-pluralism indirectly inspired the new urban political economy, a more obvious catalyst was the public choice-influenced approach to urban politics set out in Paul Peterson's 1981 book, *City Limits* (Peterson, 1981; Logan and Swanstrom, 1990). Peterson's argument, essentially, was that cities effectively 'die' if they are deserted by people and firms in big enough numbers. 'They' therefore have no choice but to try to capture and retain potentially mobile businesses and residents, and the income they can provide, if they are to survive. That means city administrations are compelled by the logic of their circumstances to compete against each other by engaging in what Peterson calls 'developmental politics'; that is, by devising strategies to improve local circumstances with respect to economic development and employment growth. As a result, they are left with little scope for what he calls 'redistributive politics'. City administrations cannot behave like latter-day Robin Hoods, taking from the rich to give to the poor. There are strict limits to their capacity to use resources gathered largely from the more affluent sections of the urban population to provide goods and services which primarily benefit their poorer counterparts.

'New' US urban political economists did not take issue with the idea that city administrations engage in competition for firms and households. Neither did they deny the importance of local developmental politics nor the existence of significant intra- and inter-urban inequalities. Rather, they objected to two features of Peterson's analysis. The first was his assertion that local politics hardly matters and that the environment in which city administrations operate determines all their significant choices. The second was his implication that cities have a single set of 'interests' which can be understood without reference to preferences that are actually expressed, by city residents and users, through the political system or other channels. Not all of the new generation of urban political economists disagreed violently with Peterson's conclusions but they did take issue with the way he reached them (Sanders and Stone, 1987a, 1987b; Peterson, 1987). For them, cities and urban life are produced and reproduced, not by the playing out of some externally imposed logic, but by struggles and bargains between different groups and interests within cities. The outcomes of these struggles and bargains, they argued, far from serving 'the good of the city' in any general sense, inevitably reward some groups and disadvantage others.

The concerns of the original community power debate, and particularly its insistence upon methodologically individualist approaches to 'urban' decision-making, once filtered through the lens of neo-pluralism and, given coherence by a common, public choice-based 'enemy', helped galvanise the new urban political economy. The growth coalition thesis, in particular, returned to Hunter's main theme: the extent to which business activists dominate place-shaping decisions. It did so in a classically methodologically individualist way, arguing that 'the activism of entrepreneurs is, and always has been, a critical force in shaping the urban system' (Logan and Molotch, 1987: 52). Logan and Molotch's analysis proceeds from a distinction, borrowed from Marxism, between the use-values and exchange-values of property. It then suggests that growth machines – coalitions of local interests acting out of partisan motivations but espousing a pervasive ideology of 'value-free development' – are the dominant force in urban development.

The core coalition 'players' are said to be the most place-bound elements of capital; rentiers (property owners), who wish to enhance the exchange (and hence rental or sale) values of their holdings by intensifying the uses to which they are put. Rentiers are joined by other private sector interests – some of them 'place-bound', others not – such as developers, financiers, construction interests, regional banks and development-dependent professional practices which profit directly from the intensification process and by those who benefit in tangential fashion from the increased demand for products and services induced by economic growth. Paramount among the latter are the local media and local utility companies, both general 'growth statesmen' whose sales are boosted by most forms of growth. Auxiliary growth coalition activists are argued to include universities, cultural institutions, professional sports clubs, labour unions, the self-employed and small retailers.

This cast list of key players in 'parochial capital' roughly describes a business elite that wields power over the pattern of urban development by virtue of its control over material and knowledge assets and, critically, its ability to smooth access to and attract 'metropolitan capital' (i.e. inward investment). Logan and Molotch's (implicit) methodology thus relies on judgements about the 'positional', rather than reputational and personal, characteristics of a rather wider and better specified group of key interests than was employed by earlier elite theorists. In their view, coalitions need not always embrace all these interests, far less those of the wider community whose concern with property revolves more around use than exchange values. In most circumstances, though, selective combinations of these forces support urban growth strategies, the nature of which will be determined by the interests involved and their 'reading' of prevailing economic circumstances and future prospects.

Challenges by groups, such as neighbourhood organisations, espousing the politics of use-values are not considered impossible. Anti-growth movements, or others prepared to countenance only selective growth, can be powerful, particularly in affluent areas where residents consider the benefits of growth to be outweighed by the costs, for example in environmental degradation or loss of community exclusivity. When growth machines lose momentum though, corporate capital, normally aloof from local issues, can play a critical role in remobilising them and restoring their dominance. The case of Cleveland, where a populist Mayor was unseated after intense corporate lobbying and campaigning, is a case in point (Swanstrom, 1985).

In stressing the indirect and occasionally direct influence of the actual or perceived needs of corporate or metropolitan capital on the nature of urban politics, the growth coalition thesis went further than had earlier elite and pluralist approaches in demonstrating that supra-local business decisions and activities play an important part in shaping the urban development strategies advocated by coalitions of local business interests. It therefore addressed, at least in part, one of the lacunae identified above. Where it was less successful was in demonstrating why it was that local governments are 'primarily concerned with increasing growth' (Logan and Molotch, 1987: 53) and hence broadly supportive of local growth coalitions.

Mossberger's chapter (this volume) describes how urban regime theory, the second key strand of the new urban political economy, was rather more successful in describing why, and in what circumstances, local governments pursue developmental as opposed to redistributive goals. The key point to note in relation to this chapter is that it did so through taking on board neo-pluralist arguments. This is readily observable in the way Stone helped 'urbanise' neo-pluralism in a key essay on 'community decision-making'. In an analysis that mirrored Lindblom, Stone (1980: 979) argued that 'public officials form their alliances, make their decisions and plan their futures in a context in which strategically important resources are hierarchically arranged' (Stone, 1980: 979). This hierarchical arrangement of resources means a less-than-equal distribution of power between individuals and groups which cannot be overcome, as classical pluralists suggest, by the sheer force of an interest group's preferences or the extent of its mobilisation.

For Stone, those who derive most advantage from skewed patterns of control over resources – leading figures in key public and private institutions – have 'systemic power' which affords them the *potential* to have more influence over place-shaping decisions than others, and 'command power', which helps them achieve compliance within their organisations and from other individuals or groups in the wider community over whom the organisation has effective authority. Systemic and command power provide the basis for domination; that is, a form of control which does not rely upon the consent of the controlled. Because power is diffused across a wide range of institutions, though, domination over a limited number of 'subjects' is not always enough. It is augmented by coalition power, through which independent organisations join forces to achieve mutually desired goals, and pre-emptive power, through which coalitions, once they have linked a sufficiently broad group of asset holders together, effectively prevent alternative coalitions forming. Thus the process that saw Dahl's 'urban' observations 'scaled up' into a more general conception of pluralist politics happened in reverse with neo-pluralism as it was 'scaled down' to the urban level.

Two cheers for community power analysis

The foregoing discussion has hopefully demonstrated that the original community power debate, for all its limitations, made an important breakthrough in establishing urban politics as a key and enduring focus within urban theory and has continued, if only indirectly, to inform later generations of theorists interested in the politics of urban development. It is unlikely that this legacy will ever entirely disappear, not just because, as John argues, cities continue to provide more manageable sites of study for researchers than entities of a larger scale, but also because of the inherent attractiveness of methodologically individualist approaches which hold out the promise of explaining social phenomena, in the last instance, through the observation of human agents. For both these reasons, urban research that can broadly be described as being within the community power tradition will likely continue to provide an intellectual 'home' for those who are suspicious of structural explanations within social science.

Whether any one approach to community power will ever be capable of supporting genuinely comparative research, be it transatlantic or broader still in its scope, however, is a moot point. On one hand, the more recent generation of US urban political economy clearly triggered greater interest outside the US than the community power debate did. The reason for that, however, appears to have more to do with the recent onset of forms of state restructuring, particularly in Western Europe, that have encouraged a greater focus on urban developmental politics than with the inherent cross-national transferability of approaches developed in the US. As a result, attempts to translate the broad frameworks employed within US urban political economy into other national contexts have tended to produce unsatisfactory results and/or to conclude that those frameworks, ultimately, were too US-centric to be applied successfully (see, e.g., Harding, 1999 on UK applications).

At one level, it is perhaps asking too much that particular sets of concepts and methods that were devised primarily to analyse experiences within one national context should provide an adequate basis for cross-national research. Logan and Molotch (1987: 149), for example, concluded as much about their own work when they noted, with reference to the UK, that:

> A strong land-use authority vested in the national government combined with the central funding of local services and the heavy taxing of speculative transactions undermines some

of the energy of a growth machine system. Central government, working closely with elites in the production sphere, has relatively greater direct impact on the distribution of development than in the US, where parochial rentiers have a more central role.

Paradoxically, though, what they were conceding in making that observation is that some modification of the argument put forward by the much-criticised Peterson – that the inter-governmental legislative, financial and organisational–cultural constraints within which urban governments work is as important in defining the nature of urban politics as the activities of agents at the urban scale – may have more analytical purchase than many of the new generation of US urban political economists were willing to concede.

If the next generation of community power research is to facilitate genuine cross-national comparison, it will need to connect analytical work on inter-governmentalism and state restructuring in a globalising age with the more detailed, agent-centred urban research with which it has traditionally been more associated. That is not a trivial task, but it is one to which this volume, as a whole, can hopefully contribute.

References

Bachrach, P. and Baratz, M.S. (1962) 'Two faces of power', *American Political Science Review*, 56: 947–52.

Crewe, I. (1974) *British Political Sociology Yearbook, Vol.1: Elites in Western Democracy.* London: Croom Helm.

Dahl, R.A. (1961) *Who Governs?* New Haven, CT: Yale University Press.

Dowding, K. (1996) *Power.* Buckingham: Open University Press.

Dowding, K., Dunleavy, P., King, D. and Margetts, H. (1993) 'Rational choice and community power structures: a new research agenda'. Paper presented to the American Political Science Association conference, Panel 12, Washington, DC.

Elkin, S.L. (1987) *City and Regime in the American Republic.* Chicago, IL.: University of Chicago Press.

Foucault, M. (1980) *Power/Knowledge.* New York: Pantheon.

Harding, A. (1999) 'American urban political economy, urban theory, and UK research', *British Journal of Political Science*, 29 (3): 447–72.

Hunter, F. (1953) *Community Power Structure: A Study of Decision Makers.* Chapel Hill, NC: University of North Carolina Press.

Lindblom, C.E. (1977) *Politics and Markets: The World's Political-economic Systems.* New York: Basic Books.

Logan, J.R. and Molotch, H. (1987) *Urban Fortunes: The Political Economy of Place.* London: University of California Press.

Logan, J. and Swanstrom, T. (eds) (1990) *Beyond the City Limits: Urban Policy and Economic Restructuring in Comparative Perspective.* Philadelphia, PA: Temple University Press.

Lukes, S. (1974) *Power: A Radical View.* London: Macmillan.

Molotch, H. (1976) 'The city as growth machine', *American Journal of Sociology*, 82 (2): 309–55.

Peterson, P. (1981) *City Limits.* Chicago, IL: University of Chicago Press.

Peterson, P. (1987) 'Analyzing development politics: a response to Sanders and Stone', *Urban Affairs Quarterly*, 22: 540–7.

Polsby, N.W. (1980) *Community Power and Political Theory*, 2nd edn. New Haven, CT: Yale University Press.

Sanders, H.T. and Stone, C.L. (1987a) 'Developmental politics reconsidered', *Urban Affairs Quarterly*, 22: 521–39.

Sanders, H.T. and Stone, C.L. (1987b) 'Competing paradigms: a rejoinder to Peterson', *Urban Affairs Quarterly*, 22: 548–51.

Stone, C.L. (1980) 'Systemic power in community decision making: a restatement of stratification theory', *American Political Science Review*, 74 (4): 978–90.

Stone, C.L. (1989) *Regime Politics: Governing Atlanta 1946–1988*. Lawrence: University Press of Kansas.

Swanstrom, T. (1985) *The Crisis of Growth Politics: Cleveland, Kucinich, and the Challenge of Urban Populism*. Philadelphia, PA: Temple University Press.

3

URBAN REGIME ANALYSIS

Karen Mossberger

For over two decades now, urban regime analysis has been one of the most prevalent approaches to the study of urban politics. Several variations of urban regime analysis have developed, with somewhat different purposes. In all of its forms, the urban regime concept has described formal and informal modes of collaboration between public and private sectors, arguing that the fragmentation of power between a market economy and popularly elected political institutions makes such cooperation necessary in order to realise important local policy goals. Regime analysis therefore touches fundamental questions of politics, such as the nature of power and the potential for democratic governance.

The appeal of urban regime analysis has been its ability to explain urban politics by incorporating both political and economic influences, resolving prior debates over elitism, pluralism and economic determinism in urban politics, as Chapter 2 shows. Regime analysis depicts local actors as constrained by their environment (for example, by fiscal and economic necessity), but also as capable of reshaping that environment through cross-sectoral governing arrangements. Regime typologies suggest that these arrangements vary not only because of differences in historical trends and local conditions, but because of the particular agendas and decisions of local political actors.

In practice, however, urban regime research has traditionally stressed the role of business and economic development in urban policy. This has resulted in two dilemmas for urban regime analysis, both of which have led toward more general concepts of urban governance and collaboration, gradually moving away from the political economy origins of regime analysis in order to explain more of urban politics. First, because urban regime research was originally rooted in the highly decentralised and fragmented policy environment of American local government, the lure of applying it cross-nationally required some modification and raised issues about the comparability of studies. Secondly, some researchers have debated how urban regimes in the US can address poverty, alternative economic agendas, or social issues beyond economic development. While urban regime analysis has argued that politics is important as well as structural economic constraints, one dilemma for regime analysts is understanding how governing arrangements that prioritise social justice can evolve and be maintained in the American context. Recently, regime scholars have looked more closely at collaboration around specific policy issues in urban areas, such as education, public safety, and AIDS education, and have employed the insights of earlier regime studies to explore the mobilisation of a broader range of interests through 'civic capacity' (Stone, 1998; Stone et al., 2001).

What is an urban regime?

A 'regime' connotes a set of governing arrangements, and in its usage over the past few decades, it indicates collaboration across institutional boundaries – beyond the formal apparatus of government in the case of urban regimes.[1] The traditional focus in urban regime analysis has been on formal and informal modes of collaboration between business and government. This recognises the fragmentation of authority and interdependence between the policy-making capacity of democratic institutions and the wealth-generating resources of the market economy.

As Harding demonstrates in his discussion of community power studies during the 1950s and 1960s, business domination of local politics had long been a normative concern and a topic of empirical debate, from Floyd Hunter's (1953) study of Atlanta's local power structure, to Dahl's (1961) pluralist portrait of New Haven. During the late 1970s and 1980s, American cities experienced economic restructuring and dramatic cuts in intergovernmental aid. As firms moved to the suburbs, the sunbelt and offshore locations, cities battled against each other to maintain and attract investment. Against this backdrop, Paul Peterson's 1981 book, *City Limits*, helped to shift the terms of the debate from elite domination of cities to the incentives and constraints created by economic and fiscal structures. Peterson argued that city policy was driven by competitive needs for economic growth, and that development was in the interest of the 'city as a whole' (1981: 148). The policy consequence of this competition for development was that cities could not afford to engage in redistributive policy. Generous social policies would attract poor people and strain local resources, and repel businesses and affluent residents fleeing high taxes. Elections, social movements, political organising, and other aspects of democratic politics were by implication of little significance at the local level, for local agendas favoured the development of business and the upscaling of neighbourhoods by necessity. According to Peterson, 'economic limits shape not only urban public policy but also the pattern of local politics. Local issues are less pressing, local conflicts are less intense …' (1981: 210).

Proponents of urban regime analysis depicted a more complex relationship, with greater potential for politics and autonomy at the local level. According to early work on urban regimes by Susan and Norman Fainstein, 'urban redevelopment cannot … be explained through either a purely economic analysis or a study of local politics divorced from the economic relations that confine it' (Fainstein and Fainstein, 1983a: 1). They define the local regime as the 'circle of powerful administrators and elected officials who move in and out of office', in order to distinguish it from the more stable and overarching entity of the local 'state' (1983b: 256). Regimes, or city governments, negotiate between the demands of social movements and electoral politics on the one hand, and the forces of capital on the other. As the prior quote from the Fainsteins suggests, politics is bounded by the economic relations of the capitalist system, but political concessions may be made to social movements and popular causes.

For Stephen Elkin, regimes do not signify class control or elected governments, but are 'constitutive' or formative institutions (Elkin, 1987: 108, 115–19). The regime in the United States is a 'commercial republic' bridging the divide between a democratic state and a privately controlled market, where property rights should foster citizenship and economic development should further the republican aims of community. Elkin's concern is how to revitalise local democratic political institutions so that economic development policy serves the public interest rather than narrow business interests (1987: 18, 144–5). Mechanisms such as neighbourhood assemblies and referenda are needed for more deliberative democracy that would draw in a wider range of participants. Elkin mentions some possible alternative policies for economic development that more vigorously democratic cities might adopt, such as repayment of initial public investment in private enterprises, and the encouragement of production for local use rather than export (1987: 171, 178–9).

For Clarence Stone, urban regimes are governing arrangements also, but more concretely, they are embodied within the actions of a governing coalition, 'an informal yet relatively stable group with *access to institutional resources* that enable it to have a sustained role in making governing decisions' (original emphasis, Stone, 1989: 4). Business is typically an important partner in the governing coalition because of the resources it commands. Like Elkin, Stone (1993) describes urban regime analysis as a political economy perspective. These various definitions recognise the significance of both economic constraints and political action.

Stone's version of urban regime analysis has been used most frequently in subsequent research,[2] and it is his narrative of Atlanta from 1946–1988 that has served as the prototype for an urban regime. Stone's Atlanta demonstrates how participants overcome the problem of fragmented authority and resources through what he calls the social production model of power.

Negotiating power in Atlanta's urban regime

Stone's (1989) history of Atlanta provided evidence of a stable governing coalition that cut across more than four decades. The coalition included white downtown business groups, Black middle class organisations, and elected officials from a succession of city administrations. The process of coalition-building occurred gradually, however, through many years of interaction and bargaining. White mayors and downtown business owners confronted the rising political power of an increasingly African-American electorate, and civil rights organisations recognised the economic and political resources that an enlightened business leadership could contribute toward greater racial progress. While their primary interests were not the same, elected officials, business leaders, and the Black middle class cooperated over a number of years to shape the governing arrangements of Atlanta. Coalition formation reflected the interplay of structural forces and change in American society, but Atlanta made choices that were different from those of many other cities in the south. The biracial governing coalition presided over an agenda that contained the congruent goals of downtown development and desegregation, encapsulated in the slogan, 'The city too busy to hate'.

Urban regimes embody the social production model of power, or 'power to' accomplish goals rather than 'power over' others (Stone, 1989: 229). Stone sees power in this model as coalitional rather than unilateral, and preferences as open to change through cooperation with others (Stone, 1989: 851–2). Change requires the incorporation of actors with strategic resources into relationships that provide the capacity to act around congruent concerns.

Atlanta's regime resolved the problem of collective action – forging and maintaining active collaboration over time – through control of selective incentives and small opportunities. Large purposes such as civil rights and downtown revitalisation provided direction for Atlanta's regime, according to Stone, but were insufficient to secure participation over the long term. Selective material incentives used to reward regime participants played a key role in eliciting cooperation. The contracts generated by projects like downtown development offered an abundance of selective incentives or side payments for regime participants, including minority business owners. Incentives were not always based on material self-interest, however. Small opportunities such as job training programmes, community theatre programmes, or parks represent lesser collective goals that could be achieved through cooperation with the regime. Selective incentives and small opportunities make some regime agendas easier to sustain than others.

Variation and policy choice

The possibility of variation in regime agendas, however, distinguishes regime analysis from other political economy approaches that developed around the same time, such as the 'growth machine' concept (Molotch, 1976; Logan and Molotch, 1987). Local growth coalitions have a singular agenda, but a number of regime typologies suggest that diverse agendas may be carried out by concessionary (Fainstein and Fainstein, 1983b) or even progressive regimes (Stone and Sanders, 1987; Stone, 1993). For the Fainsteins, regime types are largely the result of different historical eras in federal policy and the capitalist economy (1983b: 276). Their concern is to explain change over time in response to developments at both the federal and local levels. Concessionary regimes in the United States represented the presence of intergovernmental aid for social policies and the demands of organised social movements in cities during the 1960s and early 1970s. Entrepreneurial regimes in the Fainstein typology emerged because of cuts in federal grants and local attempts to cope with such cuts. Even within these historical periods, however, cities made distinct choices and pursued different policies. Elkin's regime types encompass geographical variation as well as historical differences, with pluralist political economies resembling Dahl's New Haven in the Northeast and Midwest during the 1950s and 1960s, followed by federalist political economies in the mid-1960s. Entrepreneurial political economies like Dallas have strong business involvement in civic and political affairs, and have traditionally arisen in the Southwest (Elkin, 1987: Chapters 3 and 4).

Regime typologies for Stone are not based on historical periods or geographic patterns, but on variation in participants and their agendas (Stone and Sanders, 1987; Stone, 1993). In this sense, local agency plays the greatest role in Stone's formulation. But, the mobilisation of resources and cooperation around an agenda is contingent, and sustained attention to issues requires that they be embedded within collaborative governing arrangements. For the Fainsteins, social movements can employ outside pressure to influence regime agendas, but for Stone, the question is how to sustain change through inclusion in the governing coalition.

Stone (1993) categorises regimes in the US as maintenance, development, middle-class progressive, or lower-class opportunity expansion regimes. On the face of it, this suggests regime diversity. Yet, these types can also be thought of as arrayed along a continuum in terms of the difficulty of regime building and the expected strength of regime collaboration. Maintenance (or caretaker) regimes have little need for resource mobilisation, and are therefore easiest to achieve, though they generate few benefits and are more likely to appear in small towns rather than large cities facing competitive pressures. Development regimes (like Atlanta) entail a greater degree of difficulty because of their activist agenda. Still, they are able to garner resources from politically and economically powerful partners such as business. Development regimes also generate selective incentives as side payments for cooperation. Environmental or social agendas are more difficult to mobilise resources around and sustain, in part because they lack the structural advantages and material resources that support economic development agendas, and in part because they generate fewer selective incentives for regime participants. Middle-class progressive regimes (that espouse environmental or historic preservation or neighbourhood concerns) may clash with development-oriented business elites and they generate fewer selective incentives. Lower-class opportunity expansion regimes (Stone, 1993), or human capital agendas that emphasise education and economic opportunity for the poor, are most problematic.

The typology implies that mobilising support around an agenda of social justice entails extraordinary effort, and perhaps unusual circumstances, at the least. Stone and Pierannunzi (2000) illustrate this point in their later account of Atlanta in the 1990s, arguing that poor Atlantans lacked the organisational capacity of the Black middle class, and their interests were neglected on the regime agenda. In the early years of the regime, middle-class African-American participants advocated for low-income housing, but later, as they emerged in a leadership position in Atlanta, issues benefiting the poor receded from the agenda. Atlanta's regime was able to espouse desegregation as a goal, but it fell short of addressing issues of poverty and social inequality.

The capacity to act, then, is embodied for Stone in the strategic use of congruent goals and resources to build coalitions and 'power to'. This is the paradox for creating more inclusive regime agendas. Resources are not equally distributed and not all potential partnerships are equally attractive (Stone, 1989: 175–6). Some interests must expend greater resources than others to influence policy, because they lack systemic advantages (Stone, 1980). Selective incentives are also not equally available for all prospective agendas. In general, the path of least resistance for a regime agenda is slighting social equity (Stone, 1989: xii, 1994).

This creates what Jonathan Davies (2002) has elsewhere referred to as a normative as well as a theoretical dilemma for regime analysis. There is a long tradition of regime scholarship that discusses the potential for progressive regimes (Stone and Sanders, 1987; DeLeon, 1992; Stone, 1993; Orr and Stoker, 1994; Ferman, 1996; Imbroscio, 1997, 1998), but the evidence for the viability of such regimes is sparse. Progressive agendas appear to be short-lived or limited in scope, particularly in the American political context where cities are largely dependent upon own-source revenues, and are therefore more sensitive to capital mobility. In cases where neighbourhood groups have achieved some measure of membership in governing coalitions, their participation may diminish over time (Ferman, 1996; Rast, 2005).

Exporting regime analysis to other national contexts is one way of understanding possibilities for regime change, and for what is essential in governing arrangements across a wider variety of cities. There has indeed been strong interest in this broader application, as well as questions about how to adapt the framework for more general use.

Regimes in cross-national perspective

At the same time that urban regime analysis developed in the United States, economic restructuring and changes in the welfare state in many countries seemed to be increasing pressures for economic development policy at the local level. Governments in many countries advocated privatisation, market mechanisms, and public–private partnerships much like those long existing in the US. Many urban researchers argue that globalisation produced greater local and regional competition as well (Sellers, 2002: 2). This raised the possibility that developed countries were experiencing similar trends, and that urban regime analysis could explain new forms of governance appearing in many places. Because power is to some extent fragmented between state and market in all capitalist democracies, the basic premise of the urban regime framework promised at least some general applicability.

Comparison can also strengthen theory, using a larger canvas to portray, isolate and explain the causes and consequences of similarities and differences between cities (Pierre, 2005; Denters and Mossberger, 2006). The comparative use of urban regime analysis can offer a more general explanation for the conditions under which we see the development of urban regimes, and variations in regimes. Does the social production model describe the exercise of power in other political systems? What difference does a regime make for policy outcomes or local agendas across different cities – and countries?

There are a number of cross-national studies completed in Western Europe that demonstrate both potential and cross-national problems in applying the urban regime framework outside the US. In a study of 11 cities in the US, Germany and France, Sellers (2002: 369–70) finds stable urban regimes in all three countries, particularly where there were locally dependent businesses. He also discovers cities with less stable regimes, as well as instances in all three countries where there was no stable regime. The ability to incorporate social and environmental issues on the agenda was stronger in Germany and France, and agendas tended to be more comprehensive in cities with stable regimes.

Other researchers have found evidence of public–private partnerships that resembled regimes, but in many cases the assessment that they were comparable to American regimes was qualified. The regional capitals of Leeds and Lille feature business involvement in local coalitions, including networks of informal ties in Leeds, although these were not fully developed regimes according to the authors of the study (John and Cole, 1998). Other coalitions built around the politics of local development emerge as an important issue even in highly centralised France, although development is stimulated by concerns for creating local jobs, and local tax revenues are less of a concern than in the US because of equalisation grants for French cities (Levine, 1994). Harding (1994) argues that the potential of regime analysis in the UK is to highlight the role of informal relationships and networks that were often neglected in earlier studies of local government. This more general shift in attention may be a contribution of regime research even where governing arrangements don't fit previous notions of regimes.

Some studies stress cross-national differences between urban partnerships. Bristol's progrowth coalition has been compared to American urban regimes in some respects (DiGaetano and Klemanski, 1993). Bassett (1996), however, argues that economic development policy in Bristol resembles a discrete policy network with vertical links to central government, rather than a governing coalition that influences city-wide priorities. Stewart (1996) concludes that much of the Bristol experience is comparable to regimes such as Atlanta, but that local authorities have less autonomy and more central government intervention. Local cross-sectoral cooperation was often shallow and largely symbolic in the English public–private partnerships that Davies studied, but he did find evidence of more genuine collaboration in one of the cities he examined. Davies identifies the top-down, centralised character of English partnerships as problematic for the regime concept (Davies, 2003). Comparing Amsterdam, Copenhagen, Edinburgh, Hamburg and Manchester over a 15-year period, Harding (1997) perceives growing concern over local economic development in all cities, shared by businesses as well as national and local governments. Redevelopment, however, is generally top-down rather than generated by informal coalitions at the local level, and development coalitions competed with many other priorities on city agendas.

European institutional contexts offer markedly different patterns of resources, authority and incentives for cross-sectoral collaboration at the local level. The United States is unusual for its decentralised form of federalism, which grants local governments a relatively high degree of intergovernmental autonomy, but creates dependence on the local tax base. Both of these factors encourage the pattern of business involvement in local affairs. In Europe, higher levels of fiscal support from central governments, more comprehensive planning controls, more public ownership of municipal land and other factors lessen the need for business involvement as a critical factor for the 'power to' achieve development and support local services. In some countries, business is more centralised (as in the UK), or corporatist arrangements are largely worked out through the national parties. Stronger parties more generally lend a national character to political relationships at the local level, in contrast with the US. There have been debates over the applicability of regime analysis in Canada as well (Leo, 2003).

Comparison doesn't require that all cases are the same, for we can compare along certain dimensions, or examine the impact of differences. What is necessary is a thorough understanding of these differences and conceptual frameworks that take these into account. Many cross-national studies have therefore modified the urban regime concept (DiGaetano and Klemanski, 1993; Stoker and Mossberger, 1994; Kantor et al., 1997; DiGaetano and Lawless, 1999; Dowding et al., 1999). Problems can occur, however, when those modifications ignore core dimensions of the concept. This is especially true for case studies, which are the most common method employed in regime research. Without a common framework, it is difficult to draw parallels between cases and to aggregate results. If comparison is to contribute to theory-building, there should be some basis for generalisation beyond the specific detail of cases.

One way of coping with this problem is to define a set of minimal, defining criteria that provides for some flexibility in application (Sartori, 1984, 1991). Mossberger and Stoker (2001) proposes a set of four defining criteria for urban regimes, based on Stone's earlier work (Stone and Sanders, 1987; Stone, 1989, 1993). They define urban regimes as 'coalitions based on informal networks as well as formal relationships' (2001: 829), which have (1) partners drawn from government and non-governmental sources, requiring, but not limited to, business participation; (2) collaboration based on social production; (3) identifiable policy agendas that can be related to the participants in the coalition; and a long-standing pattern of cooperation rather than a temporary coalition. On the topic of selective incentives, Stoker and Mossberger (1994) regard them as only one possible motivation for cooperation within regimes. They see motivations for participation as more diverse, particularly within other countries, and even in the US, where the sense of community or tradition (in organic regimes) and ideology or image revitalisation (in symbolic regimes) may also play a role.

Another strategy for comparison, however, is to consider urban regimes as one type of a more general phenomenon – urban governance. Rising higher on the 'ladder of abstraction' allows researchers to encompass more varied cases (Sartori, 1984). Sellers (2002) employs the urban regime framework, but fits both regimes and non-regimes within the larger category of urban governance. DiGaetano and Klemanski (1999) examine both 'power to' and 'power over' in instances of urban governance in cities in the US and UK. Other urban governance frameworks add culture to the political and economic factors more usually discussed in urban regime analysis. DiGaetano and Strom (2003) blend cultural, institutional and rational actor approaches to the study of urban governance. Savitch and Kantor (2002) explore city choices in ten Western European and North American cities, within differing contexts of markets, intergovernmental relations, local politics and local political culture.

Pierre (2005) advocates comparative research in urban governance as an alternative to urban regime analysis.

> A governance perspective on urban politics directs the observer to look beyond the institutions of the local state and to search for processes and mechanisms through which significant and resource-full actors coordinate their actions and resources in the pursuit of collectively defined objectives. (Pierre, 2005: 452)

Governance, as a more general concept, clearly shares many of the defining characteristics of urban regime analysis such as governing arrangements that include actors beyond the formal institutions of government, and the need to mobilise resources to achieve the capacity to act. As with regime analysis, power is fragmented and policy-making does not rest solely with the state. However, there are few assumptions about who participates in governance beyond those in formal positions in the local state, whether cooperation is mandated by higher levels of government or is generated by local interdependence and priorities, is project-oriented and short-term, or is ongoing and engaged in setting city-wide priorities, etc. This greater flexibility makes governance attractive as a comparative concept that travels across national boundaries. Yet, if urban regime analysis is undertheorised because of its dependence on specific cases and the American context, as Pierre (2005) suggests, presently the idea of governance is even more so, because it can be so many things.

Perspective on revising the regime concept

There have been a number of criticisms of the regime framework among American scholars as well, and different suggestions for revising regime analysis. Many of the critiques seek to address the priority of distributional or social issues on regime agendas.

David Imbroscio (2004) urges urban regime analysts to acknowledge the developmental imperatives of cities, but provide an alternative to corporate-centred development strategies. For Imbroscio, Elkin's concept of the public interest in a commercial republic calls for challenging conventional economic development as ineffective and showing that superior alternatives exist. These might include local economic self-reliance, the development of locally rooted networks of small businesses, local public or non-profit ownership of some enterprises, and employee ownership (Imbroscio, 1998, 2004). Analytic tools such as public balance sheets, which show the costs and benefits of current strategies and alternatives, can be used to open public discourse around existing policies (Imbroscio, 2004). Debates over Imbroscio's recommendations focus on whether this position sufficiently recognises the need for mobilising participants with the political resources to sustain such an agenda (Rast, 2005; Stone, 2005).

Some critics maintain that the political economy focus of urban regime analysis neglects other issues in urban politics. These include the politics of identity and the urban character of the lesbian and gay movement (Bailey, 1999), or the role of civic cultures that vary across cities (Reese and Rosenfeld, 2001). Other studies moving away from the political economy perspective have used Elkin's thinking on the constitutive character of regimes and citizenship to explore participation and governance in a more limited policy context – AIDS policy in Christchurch, New Zealand (Brown, 1999). Using philosophical approaches such as communitarianism, modernism and feminism, Brown uncovers different motivations for collaboration, such as community and identity. These motivations supplement the exchange relationships that characterise regimes that bridge the state and market divide.

While Brown cites Elkin, his focus on the internal dynamics of coalition-building is also compatible with Stone's version of regime analysis, particularly Stone's most recent work. In what he terms a restatement of urban regime analysis, Stone (2005) draws upon the social movement literature to reconsider the role of purpose in regimes. He notes that the Atlanta study did not give due credit to the role of purpose in civic collaboration, despite the recognition of small opportunities for collective gain as well as selective incentives and individual material interests. Some participants in Atlanta's regime, such as the Black middle class, were also partly motivated to cooperate in order to achieve progress toward larger goals such as civil rights. For others, commitment to the shared purpose of the 'city too busy to hate' developed more gradually through collaboration. This reconsideration of purpose effectively loosens the requirement for selective incentives as the predominant motivation in regimes, most abundantly generated by development projects. Based on his co-authored research on urban education, Stone writes that purpose also played a role in sustaining alliances in cases where educational reform has had a consistent presence on city agendas. Stone's chapter in this volume elaborates on the role of purpose in collaboration and governance.

Stone has also recently offered a stripped-down and more general definition of regimes. This is perhaps less of a restatement than his reconsideration of selective incentives. But, it distils some of the features of the Atlanta regime, while omitting others. Stone (2005: 329; see also 2001) defines four interrelated factors as 'the core elements of a model of local governance,' involving:

- an agenda to address a distinct set of problems
- a governing coalition formed around the agenda, typically including both governmental and non-governmental members
- resources for the pursuit of the agenda, brought to bear by members of the governing coalition and
- given the absence of a system of command, a scheme of cooperation through which the members of the governing coalition align their contribution to the task of governing.

The intent is to leave open a number of issues as a matter of empirical investigation, while asserting that collaboration is focused on a distinct agenda, and based on the particular set of participants, resources and mode of cooperation. In comparison,

Stone's earlier work stressed the role of business as one key set of participants, and depicted regimes as long-standing examples of cooperation rather than temporary coalitions (Mossberger and Stoker, 2001). According to Stone's more recent work (2005), the key participants vary with the agenda. In part, this reflects the critique that business is less important for governing arrangements in European cities, but also Stone's current research on educational policy and human capital as well. Stone (2005) suggests that with varied schemes of cooperation, regime partners may see issues such as low-income housing or equal educational opportunity in poor schools as part of a larger community interest, and that large purposes may drive regime participation as well as selective incentives or small opportunities.

Turning toward issues such as education policy and public safety has allowed Stone and others to examine the potential for wider participation and social inclusion in the governing arrangements within these policy areas. The concept of 'civic capacity' (Stone, 1998; Stone et al., 2001) applies the insights of urban regime analysis to the subsystems that govern specific issue areas. The relationship to regime analysis is evident, for civic capacity is needed 'to devise and employ formal and informal mechanisms to collectively solve problems' (2001: 27). Civic capacity is more participatory than the elite-based interaction in urban regimes, however, for the involvement of parents and community-based organisations is necessary to alter the status quo in educational subsystems. Similarly, Stone (2005) has considered the governing arrangements in public safety needed to link communities with police. For Stone and his co-authors (2001; Stone, 2005), influencing policy requires changing governing arrangements within policy sub-systems rather than winning sporadic victories through interest group pressure. But in contrast to the largely closed systems of urban regimes, civic capacity seems to require greater inclusion for more appropriate and responsive policy. Both civic capacity and a broader concept of regimes hold out the theoretical possibility of greater variation and wider participation in city policy-making, but further research will reveal the extent to which this can be realised, and under what conditions.

The future of urban regime analysis

Urban regime analysis began as a way to explain the informal relationships that overcome the fragmentation of authority between states and markets in capitalist democracies, and the fundamental tensions these create for democratic governance and the well-being of cities. Over the years, urban regime analysis has tended to become more general, to explain governing arrangements beyond economic development, and beyond the American context. Both civic capacity and Stone's recent arguments about the core concepts of regime analysis represent a broadening of the regime framework. At the same time, scholars using regime analysis in the comparative context have also increasingly turned toward the broader, but related idea of governance. Urban regime analysis has never been simply an economic approach, for in its different versions, it has also included social movements (Fainstein and Fainstein,

1983a), political theory (Elkin, 1987), and organisation theory and sociology (Stone, 1989). Yet political economy was a common thread that has become less central to many regime studies over the past few decades, with some exceptions.[3] In many ways, Stone's more recent framework is quite close to the general concept of urban governance described by Pierre.

Does this mean that urban regimes have faded away, transformed into urban governance? One distinct contribution of regime analysis is the social production model of power. For Stone, this explained the systemic power of business in the US, but it also depicts power more generally as contingent and based on achieving the capacity to act rather than on formal institutional authority. In comparison to the less defined assumptions of 'interdependence' in governance (or network analysis in public policy and public administration), the scheme of cooperation in urban regimes and civic capacity offers some more concrete and testable assumptions. Further research might compare the role of large purposes, selective incentives and small opportunities in fostering cooperation and achieving the capacity to act. This may well vary in city-wide governing coalitions, broader mobilisations of issue-specific civic capacity and cross-nationally.

Urban regime analysis is also consistent with attention to the changing role of the state across a number of fields of research. The public administration literature, for example, now commonly refers to governance rather than government (Rhodes, 1997), and implementation networks (Kickert et al., 1997; O'Toole, 1997; Milward and Provan, 2000). Some network research in public administration directly cites the influence of urban regimes (Agranoff and McGuire, 2001). This indicates the relevance of the regime framework for understanding the larger social environment in which cities exist. Regime analysis will continue to be an important aspect of urban political research, but it may be only one way of conceptualising governing arrangements and the efforts to create and sustain them, particularly in a comparative perspective. Far from superseding the prior work on urban regimes, the more general idea of urban governance gains meaning in relation to the concept of urban regimes, and how different instances of governance compare with urban regimes. Civic capacity provides a way to extend the insights of regime analysis within specific policy areas or even at the neighbourhood level. Looking toward the future, the question is whether these variations on regime analysis can explain local governing arrangements more broadly in Western democracies, and can show points of leverage for democratic participation and effective policy in cities.

Notes

1 See, for example, Krasner, 1983 on international regimes where there are formal and informal arrangements governing international collaboration in a policy area.
2 For exceptions, however, see Michael Brown, 1999 and Imbroscio, 1998, which rely on Stephen Elkin.
3 See, for example, Imbroscio (1997, 1998, 2004). For a quite different approach, but one also rooted in political economy, see Lauria (1997).

References

Agranoff, Robert and McGuire, Michael (2001) 'Big questions in public network management research', *Journal of Public Administration Research and Theory*, 11 (3): 295–326.

Bailey, Robert (1999) *Gay Politics, Urban Politics*. New York: Columbia University Press.

Bassett, Keith (1996) 'Partnerships, business elites and urban politics: new forms of governance in an English city?', *Urban Studies*, 33: 539–55.

Brown, Michael (1999) 'Reconceptualizing public and private in urban regime theory: governance in AIDS politics', *International Journal of Urban and Regional Research*, 23 (1): 45–69.

Dahl, Robert A. (1961) *Who Governs? Power and Democracy in an American City*. New Haven, CT: Yale University Press.

Davies, Jonathan S. (2002) 'Urban regime theory: a normative-empirical critique', *Journal of Urban Affairs*, 24 (1): 1–17.

Davies, Jonathan S. (2003) 'Partnerships vs. regimes: why regime theory cannot explain urban coalitions in the UK', *Journal of Urban Affairs*, 25 (3): 253–76.

DeLeon, Richard E. (1992) *Left Coast Politics: Progressive Politics in San Francisco, 1975–1991*. Lawrence, KS: University Press of Kansas.

Denters, Bas and Mossberger, Karen (2006) 'Building blocks for a methodology for comparative urban political research', *Urban Affairs Review*, 41 (4): 550–71.

DiGaetano, Alan S. and Klemanski, John S. (1993) 'Urban regimes in comparative perspective: the politics of urban development in Britain', *Urban Affairs Quarterly*, 29: 54–83.

DiGaetano, Alan S. and Klemanski, John S. (1999) *Power and City Governance: Comparative Perspectives on Urban Development*. Minneapolis, MN: University of Minnesota Press.

DiGaetano, Alan and Lawless, Paul (1999) 'Urban governance and industrial decline: governing structures and policy agendas in Birmingham and Sheffield, England and Detroit, Michigan, 1980–1997', *Urban Affairs Review*, 34: 546–77.

DiGaetano, Alan and Strom, Elizabeth (2003) 'Comparative urban governance: an integrated approach', *Urban Affairs Review*, 38 (3): 356–95.

Dowding, Keith, Dunleavy, Patrick, King, Desmond, Margetts, Helen and Rydin, Yvonne (1999) 'Regime politics in London local government', *Urban Affairs Review*, 34: 515–45.

Elkin, Stephen L. (1987) *City and Regime in the American Republic*. Chicago, IL: University of Chicago Press.

Fainstein, Susan S. and Fainstein, Norman I. (1983a) 'Economic change, national policy, and the system of cities', in Susan S. Fainstein, Norman I. Fainstein, Richard Child Hill, Dennis Judd and Peter Smith, *Restructuring the City: The Political Economy of Urban Redevelopment*. New York: Longman. pp. 1–26.

Fainstein, Susan S. and Fainstein, Norman I. (1983b) 'Regime strategies, communal resistance, and economic forces', in Susan S. Fainstein, Norman I. Fainstein, Richard Child Hill, Dennis Judd and Peter Smith, *Restructuring the City: The Political Economy of Urban Redevelopment*. New York: Longman. pp. 245–82.

Ferman, Barbara (1996) *Challenging the Growth Machine*. Lawrence, KS: University Press of Kansas.

Harding, Alan (1994) 'Urban regimes and growth machines: toward a cross-national research agenda', *Urban Affairs Quarterly*, 29 (3): 356–82.

Harding, Alan (1997) 'Urban regimes in a Europe of the cities?', *European Urban and Regional Studies*, 4: 291–314.

Hunter, Floyd (1953) *Community Power Structure: A Study of Decision Makers*. Chapel Hill, NC: University of North Carolina Press.

Imbroscio, David (1997) *Reconstructing City Politics*. Thousand Oaks, CA: Sage.

Imbroscio, David (1998) 'Reformulating urban regime theory: the division of labor between state and market reconsidered,' *Journal of Urban Affairs*, 20 (3): 233–48.

Imbroscio, David L. (2004) 'The imperative of economics in urban political analysis: a reply to Clarence N. Stone', *Journal of Urban Affairs*, 26 (1): 21–6.

John, Peter and Cole, Alastair (1998) 'Urban regimes and local governance in Britain and France: policy adoption and coordination in Leeds and Lille', *Urban Affairs Review*, 33: 382–404.

Kantor, Paul, Savitch, Hank V. and Haddock, Serena Vicari (1997) 'The political economy of urban regimes: a comparative perspective', *Urban Affairs Review*, 32: 348–77.

Kickert, Walter J.M., Klijn, Erik-Hans and Koppenjan, Joop F.M. (eds) (1997) *Managing Complex Networks: Strategies in the Public Sector*. London: Sage.

Krasner, Stephen D. (1983) 'Structural causes and regime consequences: regimes as intervening variables', in Stephen D. Krasner (ed.), *International Regimes*. Ithaca, NY: Cornell University Press. pp. 1–21.

Lauria, Mickey (1997) *Reconstructing Urban Regime Theory*. Thousand Oaks, CA: Sage.

Leo, Christopher (2003) 'Are there urban regimes in Canada? Comment on: Timothy Cobban's "The political economy of urban redevelopment: Downtown revitalization in London, Ontario, 1993–2002"', *Canadian Journal of Urban Research*, 12.

Levine, Myron A. (1994) 'The transformation of urban politics in France: the roots of growth politics and urban regimes', *Urban Affairs Quarterly*, 29: 383–410.

Logan, John R. and Molotch, Harvey L. (1987) *Urban Fortunes: The Political Economy of Place*. Berkeley, CA: University of California Press.

Milward, H. Brinton and Provan, Keith G. (2000) 'Governing the hollow state', *Journal of Public Administration Research and Theory*, 10 (2): 359–80.

Molotch, Harvey L. (1976) 'The city as a growth machine', *American Journal of Sociology*, 82 (2): 309–30.

Mossberger, Karen and Stoker, Gerry (2001) 'The evolution of urban regime theory: the challenge of conceptualization', *Urban Affairs Review*, 36 (6): 810–35.

Orr, Marion E. and Stoker, Gerry (1994) 'Urban regimes and leadership in Detroit', *Urban Affairs Quarterly*, 30 (1): 40–73.

O'Toole, Laurence J. (1997) 'Treating networks seriously: practical and research-based agendas in public administration', *Public Administration Review*, 57: 45–52.

Peterson, Paul (1981) *City Limits*. Chicago, IL: University of Chicago Press.

Pierre, Jon (2005) 'Comparative urban governance: uncovering complex causalities', *Urban Affairs Review*, 40 (4): 446–62.

Rast, Joel (2005) 'The politics of alternative economic development: revisiting the Stone–Imbroscio debate', *Journal of Urban Affairs*, 27 (1): 53–69.

Reese, Laura and Rosenfeld, Raymond A. (2001) 'Yes, but …: questioning the conventional wisdom about economic development', *Economic Development Quarterly*, 15: 299–312.

Rhodes, R.A.W. (1997) *Understanding Governance: Policy Networks, Governance, Reflexivity and Accountability*. Buckingham: Open University Press.

Sartori, Giovanni (1984) 'Guidelines for concept analysis', in Giovanni Sartori (ed.), *Social Science Concepts: A Systematic Analysis*. Beverly Hills, CA: Sage.

Sartori, Giovanni (1991) 'Comparing and miscomparing', *Journal of Theoretical Politics*, 3: 243–57.

Savitch, Hank V. and Kantor, Paul (2002) *Cities in the International Marketplace*. Princeton, NJ: Princeton University Press.

Sellers, Jefferey M. (2002) *Governing from Below: Urban Regions and the Global Economy*. Cambridge: Cambridge University Press.

Stewart, Murray (1996) 'Too little, too late: the politics of local complacency', *Journal of Urban Affairs*, 18: 199–237.

Stoker, Gerry and Mossberger, Karen (1994) 'Urban regime theory in comparative perspective', *Environment and Planning C: Government and Policy*, 12: 195–212.

Stone, Clarence N. (1980) 'Systemic power in community decision making: a restatement of stratification theory', *American Political Science Review*, 74: 978–91.

Stone, Clarence N. (1989) *Regime Politics: Governing Atlanta 1946–1988*. Lawrence, KS: University Press of Kansas.

Stone, Clarence N. (1993) 'Urban regimes and the capacity to govern: a political economy approach', *Journal of Urban Affairs*, 15: 1–28.

Stone, Clarence N. (ed.) (1998) *Changing Urban Education*. Lawrence, KS: University Press of Kansas.

Stone, Clarence N. (2001) 'The Atlanta experience re-examined: the link between agenda and regime change', *International Journal of Urban and Regional Research*, 25 (1): 20–34.

Stone, Clarence N. (2005) 'Looking back to look forward: reflections on urban regime analysis', *Urban Affairs Review*, 40 (3): 309–41.

Stone, Clarence N. and Pierannunzi, Carol (2000) 'Atlanta's biracial coalition in transition.' Paper presented at the annual meeting of the American Political Science Association, 31 August–3 September, Washington, DC.

Stone, Clarence N. and Sanders, Heywood T. (1987) *The Politics of Urban Development*. Lawrence, KS: University Press of Kansas.

Stone, Clarence N., Henig, Jeffrey R., Jones, Bryan D. and Pierannunzi, Carol (2001) *Building Civic Capacity: The Politics of Reforming Urban Schools*. Lawrence, KS: University Press of Kansas.

4

MARXISM AND URBAN POLITICS

Mike Geddes

This chapter offers a critical review of Marxist theories of urban politics.[1] Given the scope of the endeavour, it is necessarily selective.

Marxist theories of urban politics are defined here as those which situate 'the urban' and 'politics' within a Marxist theorisation of capitalism. This implies:

- that the urban is conceived as a locus of the contradictory and crisis-ridden process of capital accumulation
- that capitalist class relations provide a fundamental perspective on urban politics
- a recognition of the ideological content of categories such as 'the urban' and of the bourgeois separation of the 'political', the 'social' and the 'economic'.

The chapter starts with a brief review of key authors from the 'golden age' of Marxist theorisation of urban politics in the 1960s and 1970s (Harvey, Castells, Lefebvre) and considers criticisms of this work. This is however well-trodden ground, and therefore recognition is then given to more recent contributions including those from other parts of the globe, and especially to the question of the contribution of Marxist perspectives in the era of globalisation and neoliberalism. A specific focus is on the relationship of urban politics to the state. For Marxists, the state is a capitalist state – a form into which the contradictions of capital may move. The chapter will discuss Marxist analysis of the (local) state, and various forms of opposition to it based on Marxist principles. Given that the objective of Marxism is not just to understand but to change the world, the chapter will be concerned with the variety of ways in which Marxist theorisation has informed, or attempted to inform, attempts to contest, overthrow or reform (urban) capitalism. The chapter addresses the four main issues which concern all the chapters of this book (presentation of theory, illustrations and applications, critiques, and evaluation and future challenges) but does so by interweaving concerns with theory and practice, and the development and critique of theory, throughout rather than by treating them separately.

The founding fathers: humanist, structuralist
and classical Marxist urbanism

Most discussions of Marxism and urban politics inevitably refer back – as well as of course to Marx – to the 1960s and 1970s, and the series of major works by Henri Lefebvre, Manuel Castells and David Harvey. This body of work, as Merrifield (2002: 8) puts it, insisted that Marxists must 'focus as much on urbanism as industrialism, on streets as much as factories'.[2]

The initial reference point for a Marxist urbanism is the work of Lefebvre, whose combination of a theoretical insistence on the capitalist 'production of space' as a crucial concern for Marxism, with a politics of urban revolutionism, was built on the early, humanist Marx. Lefebvre's spatial Marxist humanism, as Merrifield summarises it, argued that the capital/labour contradiction was now first and 'foremost a contradiction of urban society, not industrial society ... the battle for and over urban space becomes the stage and stake in the modern class struggle'. Lefebvre (1991) contrasted the new commodified urban 'space of the spectacle' and the bureaucratic and political authoritarianism which produced it, both in the remaking of old cities and in new towns, with the lived space of everyday experience, in a new attempt to 'decode space and empower socialists in their analyses of, and struggles against, modern urbanising capitalism'. Lefebvre's own politics reflected an uneasy blend of on–off adherence to the Communist Party and an instinctive appreciation of spontaneity as expressed in the street, the authentic arena of everyday life not occupied by institutions, reflected in his collaboration with the Situationist International and his conception of a 'right to the city' (Merrifield, 2002: 80–90; Shields, 2004).

The tensions in Lefebvre's politics were apparent in his ambiguous response to the events of 1968 in France, and in the aftermath of 1968 his influence was eclipsed by that of Castells' structuralist Marxist urbanism. Castells criticised Lefebvre for straying too far from Marxism in subordinating industrialism to urbanism and exploitation to the alienation of everyday life (Merrifield, 2002: 116–7), arguing that in abandoning the fundaments of Marxism, Lefebvre was aligning himself with the ideological perspectives of bourgeois urban studies.

Castells therefore attempted (what was for him) a scientific Marxist analysis of the urban, rooted in Althusser's structuralism, which means 'to analyse space as an expression of the social structure ... studying its shaping by elements of the economic system, the political system, the ideological system' (Castells, 1997: 126, quoted by Merrifield, 2002: 117). His study of Dunkirk, *Monopolville* (Castells, 1974), laid the basis for his later work, offering an empirically detailed and theoretically structured analysis of:

> the movements of capital, the large multinational enterprises and the interventions of the state; the production of a new urban system as a structure of contradictions; class relations and their articulation to urban contradictions; local politics and the transformation of the institutional system ...

While monopoly capital was very much present in his work, Castells, like Lefebvre to this extent, focused (following Althusser), on the urban as the sphere of reproduction rather than production, and – less like Lefebvre – on the urban as the site of collective consumption. While cities for Castells are indeed places where capital accumulation and production take place, the urban can be defined 'in terms of collective reproduction of labour power and the city in terms of a unit of this process of reproduction' (Merrifield, 2002: 119). The capitalist state is central to this conception of the city as the chief provider of collective consumption and as the manager and regulator of the urban system. But, while the state may thus offset crises of overproduction and profitability, its role in collective consumption politicises important aspects of everyday life, prompting urban struggles around consumption and reproduction, and the formation of new 'urban social movements', involving not only the working class but groups traditionally distant from the working class movement, such as white collar workers and non-working women. In *City, Class and Power*, Castells (1978) likens these activist groupings to an 'urban trade unionism', opening the possibility that 'the articulation of new social struggles with alternative democratic politics can lead to a left wing electoral victory based on a programme opening the way for socialism' (quoted by Merrifield, 2002: 125). In taking the view that urban social movements can progressively work within as well as against the state, Castells reflected the terrain opened up by Poulantzas' theorisation of the relative autonomy of the state. Examples of this 'new urban left' politics are discussed further below.

Castells' engagement with urban social movements drew him however progressively away from Marxism. In contrast, David Harvey has remained consistent in his Marxism since his first Marxist book, *Social Justice and the City* (1973). Where Castells focused on collective consumption as the core of the 'urban', Harvey's work foregrounds the accumulation process, and specifically the urban space of land and property analysed through classical Marxist conceptions of rent and secondary circuits of capital such as construction, property, finance, landlordism, etc. For Harvey, 'the urban system is conditioned by relative and monopoly rental and property values, as is the circulation and direction of surplus value flowing through the built environment' (Merrifield, 2002: 138). Part of his analysis has been to chart the shift in the local state from the social democratic managerialism of the 1960s to the urban entrepreneurialism of the 1980s and 1990s (Harvey, 2001b).

Consistent with the classical Marxism of his analysis, Harvey has espoused a class politics. While becoming increasingly aware of the heterogeneity of the 'new social movements', Harvey has been 'wary of what fragmentation would mean for a united Left' (Merrifield, 2002: 151). Thus, in response to the postmodern challenge (discussed below), he has recognised the importance of race, gender and difference as something 'omnipresent from the very beginning in any attempt to grasp the dialectics of social change' but – in contrast to Castells – has insisted on the need to work them in to the fundamental Marxist categories of capital and class. As will be discussed below, this position has not satisfied many of his Marxist or non-Marxist critics. In one of his most concrete engagements with urban politics, the struggle against the closure of the Cowley car plant in Oxford in the 1980s, Harvey equally distanced himself from a 'workerist' position in which the struggle within the factory is paramount, arguing that:

some consideration had to be given to the future of socialism in Oxford under conditions in which the working class solidarities that had been built around the plant were plainly weakening and even threatened with elimination. This meant the search for some broader coalition of forces, both to support the workers in the plant and to perpetuate the socialist cause.

This led Harvey to question traditional left defence of jobs in the motor industry in anything but the short run, partly because of the nature of these 'shit jobs' themselves but also because of ecological concerns about the motor car. These questions led on to a concern about the tension between conservatism and revolutionary objectives in struggles such as that in Cowley/Oxford, and with the parallel tension between local and wider perspectives in such struggles. In an engagement with Raymond Williams' writings (Williams, 1989), Harvey works with Williams' phrase 'militant particularism' in defining a position which attempts to bridge the local and the global and the need for short-term defence with long-term social transformation – 'ideas forged out of the affirmative experience of solidarities in one place get generalised and universalised as a working model for a new form of society that will benefit all of humanity' (Harvey, 2001a: 172). Here Harvey's analytical work on the urban accumulation process is brought to bear on urban politics in a way which suggests that classical Marxism can be the reverse of one dimensional.

Criticism and evolution

In the first edition of *Theories of Urban Politics,* Pickvance took issue with Marxist theories of urban politics (Pickvance, 1995). Pickvance argued that Marxist theories of urban politics offer both alternative explanations of topics addressed by 'more conventional' theories, and also identify new objects for study. In particular, he considered that the centrality of capital accumulation and class conflict in Marxist approaches leads to a perspective which links the economic and political spheres, which is important in an age of academic specialisation. Thus Marxist work in urban politics, he allows, has drawn attention to the role of economic interests and class conflict in urban policy. Questions about how class is reproduced through urban policy, and the role of the local state in the reproduction of labour power, are distinctively Marxist contributions. However, for Pickvance, the problems of Marxist approaches seemed to outweigh these positives. First, he is particularly critical of those Marxists whom he regards as functionalist, in the sense that they regard the (local) state as an 'instrument' of the dominant class with little autonomy from the interests of that class, and of the class reductionism of some Marxists. Pickvance also argued that Marxist writing as a whole 'has diverted attention from the study of political parties, elections and voting behaviour, and from the study of the internal functioning of the local state'.

More fundamentally, Pickvance questioned what he saw as the abstraction of Marxist analyses, and their 'application' to concrete situations with little attention to mediating processes. The 'apparently sponge-like character of Marxist theory' and a critical and selective attitude towards evidence means that class interests can be imputed to actors and events in arguments which make causal inferences without a seeming need for 'proof'. Thus 'the genuine problems for Marxist theory are: the abstraction of its concepts; the assertion that contradictory processes co-exist; and the critical and selective stance towards evidence' (Pickvance, 1995: 272).

By the time Pickvance was making these criticisms, Castells had already turned away from Marxism towards Weberian sociology, but a much wider body of Marxist literature had either already made its appearance or was about to do so. Three examples will have to suffice to illustrate the evolution of Marxist approaches in the 1980s and 1990s. Perhaps most clearly in the Marxist tradition, the work of Neil Smith takes up the concern of Lefebvre, the early Castells and Harvey to show how and why space matters to capitalism and capitalism to space (Castree, 2004). In *Uneven Development*, Smith argued that uneven development is a systematic and necessary aspect of modern capitalism, and one that can only be adequately understood through the concept of scale (Smith, 1991). Thus, for Smith, the urban is one point on a 'scale of scales', that runs from the body, the home and the community to the region, the nation and the global. Contra Castells, Smith defines the urban primarily as the scale of the labour market and the urban land market (Smith, 1992). This leads him to the conception of a 'spatialised politics' 'that recognises the importance of space in everyday life and shows struggles over the control of space to be flashpoints for power and resistance' (Castree, 2004: 265). In particular, he suggests, the concentration of labour power in the city facilitates political organisation, and urban fiscal crises bring cutbacks in services and employment around which city-wide organisation can develop.

Ed Soja's work represents an ongoing attempt to map out a postmodern Marxism, or a Marxist postmodernism. In opposition to the dominant current of postmodernism which rejects meta-narratives, Soja (1989) attempts to 'tie postmodernism tightly to the certainties of historical materialism', arguing that the postmodern epoch should be 'read as the latest manifestation of a series of waves of capitalist development, and that the aim of postmodern social theory is to make sense of the capitalist restructuring that has brought this epoch into being' (Latham, 2004). Soja has sought to take from postmodernism important perspectives such as an openness to different perspectives (and thus potentially a broader-based left politics), though in the event his attempt to build a bridge between Marxism and postmodernism has often satisfied neither. This is in some contrast to Mike Davis who, while rooted in Marxism as well as a wider body of radical theory, often displays the openness to multiple perspectives which the postmodernists demand. Davis' detailed, lively and careful analyses of 'gangs, land-grabbing elites, extremist policing and highly politicised conservative homeowners' in Los Angeles in *City of Quartz* (Davis, 1990) and subsequent books wear their Marxist theory lightly and eschew abstract statements about left politics but nonetheless display a 'fierce class consciousness, a stress on how long-term historical processes impact on everyday life and a strongly humanised, even individualised, account of the impact of capitalism on the lives of Angelenos' (McNeill, 2004).

The attempted accommodations of some Marxists with postmodernism does not mean, of course, that the critics have been stilled – quite the reverse. Storper (2001) represents an example of a contemporary 'sympathetic' critique. Storper seeks to 'stress the substantial achievements of Marxist-inspired radical political economy, while criticising its utopian impulses and suggesting the need for an updated radical political economy' (2001: 156). The 'substantial achievements' of accounts rooted in Western Marxism are, he suggests:

- the recognition that capitalism is not a self-guiding system as markets have failures and contradictions
- the importance of power to both the development of capitalism and distributional outcomes
- the tension between the market and democracy.

However, for Storper, 'the overall Marxist view of the economics of capitalist development no longer carries very much weight'. While

> the strong point of Marxism is that it considers capitalism as a system: its fundamental nature is based on property relations and their corresponding social relations ... this has also become its great limitation: it has never been able to go beyond large scale descriptions to cause-and-effect analyses of the internal dynamics and processes of capitalism. For this, it would require microanalytic foundations and passageways between them and the macro-description it does so well. Because of the failure to build a true multi-level theory, when Marxists use their basic descriptive categories to try and say things about short- or long-term evolutionary processes of the system, they generally do not do so very well. (Storper, 2001: 158)

Moreover 'even the notion of revolution, so dear to Marx ... has been seriously questioned as the principal source of democratisation and development ... and ... there is no Marxist "metanarrative of social transformation" left' (2001: 158–9). Storper thus rejects not only Marxism as a practical analytical methodology but the Marxist political project.

Storper's criticisms are echoed and extended by critics from the postmodern urbanist school which has emerged very strongly since the 1990s. To take perhaps the best known instance, Dear criticises both Harvey and Soja, but especially Harvey, for his continuing commitment to historical materialism and to the attempt at a 'profoundly modernist' reconstruction of urban theory. According to Dear, this attempt is marked by three cardinal errors: the absence of any sustained engagement with 'difference'; a lack of critical reflection about his own epistemological stance; and misunderstandings or misrepresentations concerning the politics of postmodernity (Dear, 2000: 76). First, Dear argues not only that Harvey marginalises issues such as gender (see further below) but that his 'totalising (Marxist) discourse ignores different voices of all kinds – from the insights of non-Marxist social theorists to voices on nature and the environment'. Secondly, he is immune to critical analysis of his own historical materialism, continuing to hold that 'all aspects of social processes can be unproblematically encompassed within fundamental historical materialist categories'; that if 'the real world' can be fitted into Marxist categories, then no further proof is needed (2000: 78–9). Thirdly, Dear argues that Harvey's alignment with Marxism on the grounds of its ability to link social thought to progressive political action ignores not only the way in which modernist politics have been 'absorbed for evil purposes or improper applications' (2000: 79), but also what Dear sees as the emancipatory potential of postmodern politics which celebrate difference:

> by insisting on totalising and reductionist visions, Soja and Harvey squander the insights from different voices and alternative subjectivities. Difference is relegated to the status of an obstacle hindering a coherent theoretical and political praxis. (2000: 81)

More than a little aggressively himself, Dear characterises the Marxist urbanism of Harvey and Soja as 'hegemonic belligerence'.

The modernism/postmodernism debate has also stimulated feminist critiques of Marxist urbanism. In a well known essay, Massey accuses Harvey (*The Condition of Postmodernity*) and Soja (*Postmodern Geographies*) of 'flexible sexism', on the grounds of the 'denial, by both these books, of feminism and the contribution it has recently made', including the contention that 'political action and intellectual activity have been more closely linked together in fields such as feminist studies ... than they have been in more mainstream white male work, including much Marxism' (Massey, 1991: 31–4). Massey's main contention is that in Soja and Harvey, structures such as patriarchy are reduced to 'noises off'. Characterising the public urban spaces such as those celebrated by Lefebvre as gendered ('The public city which is celebrated in the enthusiastic descriptions of the dawn of modernism was a city for men'), she asserts that 'modernism is about more than a particular articulation of the power relations of time, space and money' and contends that Harvey completely misses the other power relations by which space is also structured. While noting Harvey's acknowledgement of the need to recognise the importance of race, gender and difference, she points out that this is only within an analysis in which 'everything must be subordinated to – just as theoretically it is reduced to – a question of class', and feminism is reduced to a 'local' struggle while class struggle is presumed to be general. Massey rejects this 'continued subordination for all those "people in parentheses"' and concludes that 'I am absolutely in favour of thinking through issues of gender "within the overall frame of historical materialist enquiry"' but 'materialism is far wider than an emphasis upon the power of money and capital circulation' and, while 'we need to think through ways of constructing "the unity of the emancipatory struggle"... this emphatically cannot be achieved by forcing all struggles under "the overall frame of ... class politics"' (all quotes from Massey, 1991: 47–55).

Similar issues arise in relation to race: while some analyses of race and urban politics have sought to link race to class, for example in characterising the local state in the American South as a 'southern racial state' (James, 1988), others are more squarely in a black radical tradition, as in Vargas' depiction of politics in the Los Angeles inner city and the Brazilian favelas (Vargas, 2003).

One further important strand of Marxist or neo-Marxist analysis is regulation theory. As summarised by Painter (1995) in the first edition of *Theories of Urban Politics*, regulation theory developed in the 1980s as an attempt by, initially, a group of French Marxist economists (Aglietta, Boyer, Lipietz) to try to explain how and why the crisis-ridden nature of capitalism did not result in constant 'actual' crisis: how is crisis managed or postponed for long periods, such as that of the postwar boom in the advanced capitalist countries? In addressing this question, regulation theory developed a number of core concepts, especially those of a 'regime of accumulation (which specifies the nature of the economic relationship between investment, production and consumption) and mode of regulation (which specifies the political and sociocultural institutions and practices which secure that relationship)' (Painter, 1995: 277). As attempts were made to understand the breakdown of the postwar boom and subsequent patterns of capitalist development, regulation theory became closely associated with conceptions of Fordism (characterising the regime of accumulation of the postwar boom) and post-Fordism.

Regulation theory became influential, especially among geographers (Goodwin et al., 1993), in the analysis of urban politics and policy, often following Jessop's (1990) account, rooted in a version of Marxist state theory, of the transition from a Keynesian Welfare state to a Schumpeterian Workfare State, of the varieties of 'post-Fordisms' and of the enhanced importance of sub-local space and urban governance. Painter and Goodwin (2000) identified four key elements of local state restructuring accompanying changes in the post-Fordist mode of regulation: a shift from welfare to workfare; from government-centred political management to a mode of governance which stresses entrepreneurial local leadership and public–private cooperation; fiscal austerity; and economic promotion through a range of local supply-side policies. For non-Marxist critics, though, regulation theory does not escape from the problems of Marxism more generally, such as functionalism and economic determinism (Painter, 1995: 290). For some Marxists, regulation theory, and even more the concepts of Fordism and post-Fordism, veered away from crucial aspects of Marxist analysis, especially insofar as they tended to reproduce the Althusserian separation between the economic and the political, and, in foregrounding the stability of regimes of accumulation and modes of regulation such as Fordism, de-emphasised the contradictory nature of capital as a class relation. Attempts to build bridges between regulationist approaches and non-Marxist approaches to urban politics, such as regime theory (Lauria, 1997) gives more weight to such criticisms. Moreover, the concept of post-Fordism proved extremely difficult to specify adequately, and increasingly (as is discussed below) has been supplanted by the concept of neoliberalism.

Throughout these various developments, the main criticisms of Marxist urbanism have remained consistent, even while some if not all critics wish to recognise some important Marxist contributions. In summary:

• Marxist exclusivism limits its ability to draw strength from other traditions.
• Marxists have failed to translate meta-theory into convincing micro-analysis.
• Marxist revolutionary class politics is no longer (if it ever was) an adequate strategy for progressive social change.

We will return later to these criticisms. First however we explore two contrasting instances where Marxism has had an important influence on urban politics – the new urban left of the 1980s in the UK and Western Europe, and aspects of urban politics in the contemporary context of neoliberalism in both the North and the South.

The new urban left

The 'new left' emerged in Western Europe at the time when tensions within social democracy and the social democratic state were mounting, and there was a revival of interest in so-called 'Western Marxism' (Anderson, 1976) following the long period of Fordist boom, and disillusionment with actually existing communism. In Italy, the revival of the 'eurocommunist' Italian Communist Party (PCI) both nationally and locally in the 1970s brought to prominence the policies pursued by the PCI in control of a number of cities, most famously 'Red Bologna' (Jaggi et al., 1977). Reflecting the PCI conceptions of revolution as a process rather than a single revolutionary moment, and of the mass party not as a vanguard leading the working class from outside the state but as a mediating force between the working class and the state which should operate inside the state, the PCI administration in Bologna developed an urban politics and programme emphasising a radical extension of democratic participation and the transformation of bureaucratic structures, as the platform for a series of policies – from transport and urban planning to health and education – which, while aware of the dangers of the idea of 'socialism in one city' were intended to offer 'elements of a passage towards socialism'.

In the UK in the 1970s, Marxist analysis had begun to have an influence on urban issues, most notably through the work of some of the Community Development Projects set up in deprived urban areas by the Home Office. Biting the hand that fed them, the CDPs produced radical analyses of urban problems and of the failure of the state to do more than manage problems of urban policy, locating urban problems in a class analysis of the impact of capitalist crisis and the contradictions of the capitalist state (CDP, 1977a and b). A critique of reformism and the state, *In and Against the State* (London–Edinburgh Weekend Return Group, 1979) was similarly influential in outlining the contours of a local politics which was both 'in and against' the state, aiming to construct a 'new kind of settlement between the cultural politics of communities and the political culture of the state' (Shaw, 2003).

In the early 1980s, political control of a number of major urban areas in England, including Greater London, the West Midlands conurbation and Sheffield, were captured by left-wing Labour Party groups influenced – though again far from exclusively – by Marxist thinking. These administrations – characterised as the new urban left – attempted to implement radical urban politics and policies, of which those of the Greater London Council are an exemplar, in sharp distinction from 'municipal Labourism'.

The GLC's urban politics sought a 'rainbow alliance' between communities and community activists, left trade unionists, feminists and the unemployed. At the core of the policy programme were a set of highly ambitious strategies, especially the London Industrial Strategy (GLC, 1985). The LIS was influenced by regulationist and related theories, which were interpreted in the GLC as offering the possibility of a progressive transition to a post-Fordist economy, drawing on the potential for 'flexible specialisation'. The LIS advocated an urban policy of 'restructuring for labour' which aimed to defend communities against the worst effects of capitalist crisis while at the same time advancing the material position of labour by means of a range of interventions in industrial sectors and firms. At the same time, a property strategy was intended to make common cause between the local state and community activists opposing property-led regeneration; a women's committee was established with substantial funds to invest in womens' group projects; and high-profile transport policies reduced public transport fares. These 'local socialist' policies and politics thus acknowledged the critique of 'traditional' Marxist politics and analysis for its failure to acknowledge 'difference' and the new social movements, and tried to steer a path between a revolutionary and a reformist politics – influential figures in the GLC described their politics as one of 'prefiguring' socialism (Mackintosh and Wainwright, 1987). In contrast to the focus of Castells and others on the urban as the sphere of collective consumption, new urban left politics, while not altogether neglecting consumption issues, were primarily oriented to the spheres of finance and production foregrounded by Harvey and others.

For the traditional Marxist left, such new urban left politics was subject to hostile critique as an unrealistic strategy of 'socialism in one city', and in particular as a politics located primarily in the local state rather than in the organised working class, with the ever-present danger of the new left (Labour) leadership selling out (Howard, 1995). It is important to note that this new urban left politics was contemporary with struggles such as that of the National Union of Miners against the Thatcher Conservative government, and while both were defeated by Thatcher, it is notable that the new urban left was unable to marshall the mass support which the miners did (Geddes, 1988). For others, the new urban left overemphasised the space for restructuring for labour which the transition from Fordism to post-Fordism offered (Nolan and O'Donnell, 1987), and showed a naivety about the possibility of working 'in and against the market' with sections of capital in order to 'restructure for labour' (Cochrane, 1988; Eisenschitz and Gough, 1993). For a brief while, however, the new urban left seemed to offer the possibility of a 'new terrain of class struggle' (Cockburn, 1977), both in and against the local state and in and against the market, a Marxist-influenced path away from the dead end of municipal Labourism. In the event, with the abolition by the Thatcher government of the big city local governments which had been the new left's power base, Labourist local managerialism gave way to an entrepreneurialist local politics (Harvey, 2001b) as neoliberalism (rather than a progressive post-Fordism) took hold.

Urban politics under neoliberalism

The term neoliberalism has two linked senses: the wider sense of a 'new capitalism', the historical outcome of the restoration of the power of the capitalist class in the context of advanced managerialist capitalism; and a narrower sense, as a set of policies to restore capitalist power and lead to a new phase of development (Dumenil and Levy, 2002). In his most recent work, David Harvey has emphasised that neoliberalism must be understood as a political project 'to re-establish the conditions for capital accumulation and to restore the power of economic elites', arguing that when theoretical neo-liberal principles clash with the need to restore or sustain capitalist class power, 'then the principles are either abandoned or become so twisted as to be unrecognisable' (Harvey, 2005: 19).

Marxist analysis argues that neoliberalism has transformed urban politics. Harvey himself (2005: Ch 4) suggests that a specific incident in urban politics – the fiscal crisis of the New York City government – was one of the key moments in the shift to neoliberalism. In a context in which capitalist restructuring and deindustrialisation had been eroding the economic base of the city, and suburban flight by the middle class had left the central city impoverished, public investment and employment had been seen as the solution to the 1960s 'urban crisis'. But in the mid-1970s, the Nixon administration and the financial institutions refused further support, pushing the city into bankruptcy in 'a coup by the financial institutions against the democratically elected government of New York City', resulting in the imposition of 'fiscal discipline' accompanied by cuts in public expenditure, employment and social programmes, prefiguring the national debt crises of countries from Mexico to Korea in the 1980s (Harvey, 2005: 45–8).

More generally, the reshaping of cities as 'spaces of neoliberalism' has stimulated a new Marxist or neo-Marxist literature, which seeks at the same time to reflect the diversity of ' neoliberalisms' across the globe while identifying more universal features of neo-liberal urban space. Harvey himself emphasises the uneven geographical development of neoliberalism. Jessop notes how key global neo-liberal strategies envisage a growing

role for cities in managing the interface between the local economy and global flows, between the potentially conflicting demands of local sustainability and local well-being and those of international competitiveness, and between the challenges of social exclusion and global polarisation and the continuing demands for liberalisation, deregulation, privatisation and so on. (Jessop, 2002: 466)

Keil argues that globalisation remakes local state institutions 'to accomplish two kinds of integration and articulation in the formation processes of the world city' – their external integration in the global economy and the internal integration of fragmented societies (1998: 640). Brenner and Theodore (2002) associate the deregulation of capital and of financial and labour markets in North America and Western Europe, at all levels from the global to the local, with local policies

of competitiveness, fiscal austerity and privatisation, and the thoroughgoing reconfiguration of the local state apparatus. They term this restructuring the 'neoliberali-
sation of urban space' presenting the process of 'neo-liberal localisation' as one of
destructive creation in which the old local state apparatus is replaced by new forms:
an attack on the old bureaucratic 'silos' and the local politicians associated with
them, and the creation of managerialist and networked institutions; the elimination
of public monopoly local services and their replacement by competitive contracting
and privatised provision; and the dismantling of traditional compensatory regional
policies and their replacement by localised, competitive entrepreneurial strategies.

Harvey argues that neoliberalism can only be properly understood by reference to
what he terms 'accumulation by dispossession'. Arguing that neoliberalism has been
notably unsuccessful in stimulating capital accumulation, he suggests that 'the main
substantive achievement of neo-liberalisation, however, has been to redistribute, rather
than to generate, wealth and income' by means of 'the continuation and proliferation
of accumulation processes which Marx had treated as "primitive" or "original" during
the rise of capitalism' (2005: 159). A fundamental feature of accumulation by dispossession is the increase in inequality which it entails, not as an unintended consequence
but as a structural feature of the restoration of the power of capital. Harvey suggests
that accumulation by dispossession comprises four main features:

- Privatisation and commodification of public utilities, social welfare provision, institutions, intellectual property rights and other domains has opened up new fields for
  accumulation while rolling back the gains of decades of class struggle.
- Financial deregulation has allowed redistribution of value on a massive scale through
  asset stripping, debt promotion and speculation.
- The management and manipulation of crises at all levels from the individual to the
  global has become a major means of redistribution of wealth from poor countries and
  individuals to the rich.
- The neo-liberal state becomes a prime agent of redistributive policies, reversing
  any flow from the upper to the lower classes that may have happened under social
  democracy. (2005: 160–4)

These features of neoliberalism are extremely apparent in the advanced world, but
even more so in the South, where neo-liberal structural adjustment regimes imposed
by transnational institutions such as the IMF and World Bank have hegemonised
political options in many countries. While urban inequalities have intensified in
Europe and North America, they pale by comparison with those in the South. In his
most recent work, Mike Davis explores the growth of mega-cities, and especially of
slums in the South, where 'urbanisation ... has been radically decoupled from industrialisation, even from development per se' as a result of neoliberalism – specifically
the debt crisis of the 1970s and the subsequent IMF-led restructuring of Third World
economies in the 1980s and the retreat of the state, including the local state as a
provider of services (Davis, 2004: 9, 19–20). Residents of slums now constitute 78 percent of the urban population of the least developed countries and at least a third of
the global urban population. Slums overlap with, though are not identical to, the

global informal working class, 'almost one billion strong, making it the fastest growing and most unprecedented social class on earth' (2004: 24). Asking whether such a potentially potent social force can actually possess historical agency, Davis suggests that struggles of informal workers have tended to be episodic, focused on immediate consumption issues and attracted to populist and indeed religious saviours in the form of fundamentalist Christianity and Islam rather than to Marxist politics.

A particularly interesting example of the hegemony of neoliberalism is that of South Africa, which in the space of a decade from the mid-1990s has made a double transition – not only from apartheid to bourgeois democracy, but from the Marxist-influenced mass movement radicalism of the ANC at the time of the transition to the policies of the ANC in government.

Bond argues that urban politics and policies in South Africa are propelled by twin imperatives: the domination of urban policy by the prioritisation of urban entrepreneurial competition, in line with the World Bank's urban policy prescriptions, implying the lowering of social costs; and the reprivatisation of essential elements of social reproduction, especially but not only urban services such as transport, sewage, water, electricity and aspects of healthcare, services which are of particular importance to women and children (Bond, 2000, 2005). These neo-liberal policies, Bond argues, are associated with a resegregation of South African cities, no longer (essentially) on racial but on class lines, as the well off entrench themselves (as in Davis' Los Angeles) in protected enclaves while other urban areas 'embody even more severe inequality and uneven development than occurred under apartheid', impacting particularly on women, young people and disabled people (Bond, 2005: 341). He argues that the accession to power of the ANC meant that many of the leading activists in the mass popular movements which brought it to power have moved into government in an 'elite transition' and a 'highly circumscribed political democratisation', echoing Harvey's emphasis on the ambiguity of the neo-liberal state regarding democracy. There has been widespread urban resistance to state and municipal policies on housing, urban infrastructure and access to affordable water, electricity and other urban services by reformed community groups and urban movements, but concessions from government have been strictly limited: privatisation has been slowed rather than halted or reversed, and social spending has been increased only fractionally.

If the struggle in South Africa was the focus of world attention in the closing years of the twentieth century, the spotlight seems to have now turned to Latin America. While the revolutionary democracy established by the Sandinistas in Nicaragua in the 1980s was eroded by the unremitting hostility of the US (Disney, 2003), the struggle for 'democratisation from below' of the long-running Zapatista movement in Mexico, an explicitly class-based movement in opposition to capitalism and neo-liberal state policies (Stahler-Sholk, 2001), had a major impact throughout the continent. Left governments have more recently been elected on platforms of opposition to neoliberalism in Venezuela, Brazil and Bolivia. While the programme of the Lula government in Brazil has become bogged down in problems of corruption and increasingly subordinated to global capital, the victory of Evo Morales and the Movimiento al Socialismo coalition in Bolivia has given new impetus to the opposition to neoliberalism. The MAS coalition loosely and precariously combines urban miners and rural coca growers, trade unions, workers and peasants, indigenous, European and *mestizo* elements, and its largely unexpected victory in the 2005 presidential election built on a series of struggles over a number of years: against the US-backed coca eradication pro-gramme; against IMF-imposed tax increases; to retain control over the processing of Bolivian gas and for hydrocarbon nationalisation; and the successful defeat of pri-vatisation in the Cochabamba 'Water War' (Hylton and Thompson, 2005; Hylton, 2006; see also Webber, 2005). The MAS success is evidence that it is in the South that opposition to neo-liberal 'accumulation by appropriation' is currently most active and effective. Other recent writing about opposition to neoliberalism (Leitner et al., 2007) and left urban politics in Latin America (Chavez and Goldfrank, 2005) lends further weight to this view.

Concluding comments: assessment and challenges

From its initial primary concern with the urban in Europe and North America, Marxist urban analysis is now increasingly concerned with the South, especially as the global hegemony of neoliberalism has exposed both similarities and differences between North and South (Peck, 2004). The Marxist critique of neoliberalism has brought powerful new concepts to bear (accumulation by dispossession) while engagement with the South has questioned some Northern perspectives (southern slum cities decoupled from formal production, southern political movements in which 'the urban' is not necessarily in advance of 'the rural' but in which urban and rural strug-gles interpenetrate). Recognition of 'southern' and 'rural' issues and perspectives is a challenge for urban political theory in general, not just Marxist approaches.

The charge that Marxism is unable to translate meta-theory into robust micro-analysis remains a relevant warning for Marxists today, as a tendency to argue by assertion undoubtedly still exists (though it is not at all clear that this is a specifically Marxist sin). However, Marxist urban analysis has produced robust empirical work – from Castells' *Monopolville* to some of Harvey's work such as *Limits to Capital* and numerous others. At its best, therefore, Marxism can indeed produce substantial, multi-level urban analysis, while the meta-theory which is the essence of the Marxist tradition ensures that it does not – like some non-Marxist work – descend into naive empiricism.

The postmodern criticism of Marxist exclusivism and its unwillingness to draw from other paradigms – especially those also seeking to analyse exploitation and oppression – can still be levelled at some Marxist writing. But then, so can a criticism of non-Marxist analysis for its unwillingness to recognise and incorporate the important contributions of Marxism. More importantly however, there is now a serious desire by many Marxists to recognise race, gender and other dimensions of 'difference' as key elements in patterns of exploitation and oppression. There remain, however, major challenges here. The many attempts to build bridges between analyses based on class, gender and race have pointed some ways forward, even if proposals for a unified theory of class, race and gender (Sacks, 1989) have not fully convinced. In particular, the arguments that class analysis needs to afford more recognition to the mutually constituting processes of class and gender (Pollert, 1996; Gottfried, 1998) as well as race to unwaged as well as waged work, to a wider 'social proletariat' (Byrne, 1997) and to the collective relation of communities to both employers and the state rather than just that of individuals to employers, are challenges which need to be taken up in the analysis of urban politics. For some, these lead to the notion of a broader historical materialism, encompassing but not limited to Marxism or to 'Western rationalism' (Gordon, 2005). Such perspectives pose opportunities but also threats to Marxist analysis, in that what often now seems to be occurring is some blurring of the boundaries between Marxism and some other radical analytical perspectives, for example in the work of Mike Davis. Such a blurring may well gloss over important theoretical differences (which in turn can have political implications) but may at the same time produce more 'plurally radical' analyses. Similarly, in the new urban left of the 1980s and many contemporary radical social and political movements in Latin America and elsewhere in the South, Marxism is one of a number of influences alongside, and intertwined with others in radical left urban politics (Chavez and Goldfrank, 2005), in a relationship which is sometimes dynamic, sometimes problematic. The challenge for Marxist urban analysis is to ensure that specifically Marxist contributions continue to be a major formative influence within the radical urban left.

Marxism brings to such contexts its characteristic meta-perspectives – such as the identification of neoliberalism not just as a set of ideas but as a ruling class strategy, and its insistence on class relations as fundamental to political strategy and practice. Clearly however, the collapse of 'actually existing socialism', among other factors, has removed many of the historical certainties of the Marxist political project. While much of the recent Marxist and neo-Marxist analysis of urban politics under neoliberalism argues for resistance (expressed as opposition to privatisation for example), and sometimes for socialism, the contours of the Marxist alternative are often unclear. For example, does the reshaping of the local state into a 'market-state' by neoliberalism mean, as has been argued (CARF, 2003) that strategies which view the local state as a potentially positive terrain of struggle are no longer viable?

Finally, environmental sustainability, especially under the impact of climate change induced by the accumulation imperative of global capitalism, is very probably the most serious issue for 'urban politics' today, with many of the world's most populated urban areas under threat of destruction. While ecological issues are not foregrounded in much Marxist writing, there are notable exceptions, such as Lipietz' melding of regulation theory and ecology (Lipietz, 1989) and Foster's contemporary critique of the impact of neoliberalism on the environment and his case for a Marxist ecological politics (Foster, 2002). For Harvey (1996) and O'Connor (1998), the possibility of a sustainable capitalism is at best intensely problematic and probably impossible. As Hudson (2005) suggests, though, blueprints for a more sustainable world frequently involve a combination of a radical socialisation and relocalisation of the global neo-liberal economy. If this is the case, the ecological crisis represents both the greatest challenge, but also the greatest opportunity, for a Marxist urban politics.

There are therefore formidable challenges to Marxist urban analysis. However, the rethinking of Marxist praxis, evident from the European new left of the 1980s to the oppositional movements in the South today, provides evidence not of the political bankruptcy of Marxism but of its continuing relevance to radical urban politics.

Notes

1 I am grateful to Jonathan Davies and David Imbroscio for entrusting this chapter to me, and to Madeleine Wahlberg for bibliographic searches for the chapter.
2 This section of the chapter is heavily indebted to Merrifield's lively discussion of the work and politics of Lefebvre, Castells and Harvey.

References

Anderson, P. (1976) *Considerations on Western Marxism*. London: New Left Books.
Bond, P. (2000) *Cities of Gold, Townships of Coal: Essays on South Africa's New Urban Crisis*. Trenton, NJ and Asmara, Eritrea: Africa World Press.
Bond, P. (2005) 'Globalisation/commodification or deglobalisation/decommodification in urban South Africa', *Policy Studies*, 26 (3/4): 337–58.
Brenner, N. and Theodore, N. (2002) *Spaces of Neoliberalism: Urban Restructuring in North America and Western Europe*. Oxford: Blackwell.
Byrne, D. (1997) 'Social exclusion and capitalism: the reserve army across time and space', *Critial Social Policy*, 17: 27–51.
CARF (2003) 'Racism and the market state: an interview with A. Sivanandan', *Race and Class*, 44 (4): 71–6.
Castells, M. (1974) *Monopolville: L'entreprise, l'Etat, l'urbain*. Paris: Mouton.
Castells, M. (1978) *City, Class and Power*. London: Macmillan.
Castells, M. (1997) *The Urban Question: A Marxist Approach*. London: Edward Arnold.
Castree, N. (2004) 'Neil Smith', in P. Hubbard, R. Kitchin and G. Valentine, *Key Thinkers on Space and Place*. London: Sage.
CDP (1977a) *Gilding the Ghetto: The State and the Poverty Experiments*. London: CDP Inter-project Editorial Team.
CDP (1977b) *The Costs of Industrial Change*. London: National CDP Information and Intelligence Unit.
Chavez, D. and Goldfrank, B. (2005) *The Left in the City: Participatory Local Governments in Latin America*. London: Latin America Bureau.
Cochrane, A. (1988) 'In and against the market? The development of socialist economic strategies in Britain, 1981–1986', *Policy and Politics*, 16 (3): 159–68.
Cockburn, C. (1977) *The Local State: Management of Cities and People*. London: Pluto Press.
Davis, M. (1990) *City of Quartz: Excavating the Future in Los Angeles*. London: Verso.
Davis, M. (2004) 'Planet of slums: urban involution and the informal proletariat', *New Left Review*, 26: 5–34.
Dear, M. (2000) *The Postmodern Urban Condition*. Oxford: Blackwell.
Disney, J.L. (2003) 'Democratization, civil society and women's organising in post-revolutionary Mozambique and Nicaragua', *New Political Science*, 25 (4): 533–60.
Dumenil, G. and Levy, D. (2002) 'The nature and contradictions of neoliberalism', in L. Panitch and C. Leys (eds), *Socialist Register 2002*. London: Merlin.
Eisenschitz, A. and Gough, J. (1993) *The Politics of Local Economic Development*. Basingstoke: Macmillan.

Foster, J.B. (2002) *Ecology against Capitalism*. New York: Monthly Review Press.

Geddes, M. (1988) 'The capitalist state and the local economy: restructuring for labour and beyond', *Capital and Class*, 35: 85–120.

Goodwin, M., Duncan, S. and Halford, S. (1993) 'Regulation theory, the local state and the transition to urban politics', *Environment and Planning D: Society and Space*, 11 (1): 67–88.

Gordon, A. (2005) 'Cedric Robinson's anthropology of Marxism', *Race and Class*, 47 (2): 23–38.

Gottfried, H. (1998) 'Beyond patriarchy: theorising class and gender', *Sociology*, 32 (3): 451–68.

Greater London Council (GLC) (1985) *The London Industrial Strategy*. London: GLC.

Harvey, D. (1973) *Social Justice and the City*. London: Arnold.

Harvey, D. (1989) *The Condition of Postmodernity*. Oxford: Blackwell.

Harvey, D. (1996) *Justice, Nature and the Geography of Difference*. Oxford: Blackwell.

Harvey, D. (2001a) 'Militant particularism and global ambition: the conceptual politics of place, space and environment in the work of Raymond Williams', in D. Harvey, *Spaces of Capital: Towards a Critical Geography*. Edinburgh: Edinburgh University Press.

Harvey, D. (2001b) 'From managerialism to entrepreneurialism: the transformation of urban governance in late capitalism', in D. Harvey, *Spaces of Capital : Towards a Critical Geography*. Edinburgh: Edinburgh University Press.

Harvey, D. (2005) *A Brief History of Neoliberalism*. Oxford: OUP.

Howard, N. (1995) 'The rise and fall of socialism in one city', *International Socialism*, 69.

Hudson, R. (2005) 'Towards sustainable economic practices, flows and spaces: or is the necessary impossible and the impossible necessary?', *Sustainable Development*, 13: 239–52.

Hylton, F. (2006) 'The landslide in Bolivia', *New Left Review*, 37: 69–72.

Hylton, F. and Thomson, S. (2005) 'The chequered rainbow', *New Left Review*, 35: 41–64.

Jaggi, M., Muller, R. and Schmidt, S. (1977) *Red Bologna*. London: Writers and Readers.

James, D.R. (1988) 'The transformation of the southern racial state: class and race determinants of local-state structures', *American Sociological Review*, 53: 191–208.

Jessop, B. (1990) *State Theory: Putting Capitalist States in their Place*. Cambridge: Polity Press.

Jessop, B. (2002) 'Liberalism, neoliberalism and urban governance: a state-theoretical perspective', in N. Brenner and N. Theodore, *Spaces of Neoliberalism: Urban Restructuring in North America and Western Europe*. Oxford: Blackwell.

Keil, R. (1998) 'Globalisation makes states: perspectives on local governance in the age of the world city', *Review of International Political Economy*, 5 (4): 616–46.

Latham, A. (2004) 'Edward Soja', in P. Hubbard, R. Kitchin and G. Valentine, *Key Thinkers on Space and Place*. London: Sage.

Lauria, M. (ed.) (1997) *Reconstructing Urban Regime Theory: Regulating Urban Politics in the Global Economy*. London: Sage.

Lefebvre, H. (1991) *The Production of Space*. Oxford: Blackwell.

Leitner, H., Peck, J. and Sheppard, E.S. (2007) *Contesting Neoliberalism: Urban Frontiers*. New York: Guilford.

Lipietz, A. (1989) *Towards a New Economic Order: Postfordism, Ecology and Democracy*. Cambridge: Polity.

London–Edinburgh Weekend Return Group (1979) *In and Against the State*. London: Pluto Press.

Mackintosh, M. and Wainwright, H. (1987) *A Taste of Power: The Politics of Local Economics*. London: Verso.

Massey, D. (1991) 'Flexible sexism', *Environment and Planning D: Society and Space*, 9: 31–57.

McNeill, D. (2004) 'Mike Davis', in P. Hubbard, R. Kitchin and G. Valentine, *Key Thinkers on Space and Place*. London: Sage.

Merrifield, A. (2002) *Metromarxism: A Marxist Tale of the City*. London and New York: Routledge.

Nolan, P. and O'Donnell, K. (1987) 'Taming the market economy: a critical assessment of the GLC's experiment in restructuring for labour', *Cambridge Journal of Economics*, 11: 251–63.

O'Connor, J. (1998) *Natural Causes: Essays on Ecological Marxism*. New York: Guilford.

Painter, J. (1995) 'Regulation theory, post-fordism and urban politics', pp. 276–96. In D. Judge, G. Stoker and H. Wolman (eds), *Theories of Urban Politics*. London: Sage.

Painter, J. and Goodwin, M. (2000) 'Local governance after fordism: a regulationist perspective', in G. Stoker (ed.), *The New Politics of British Local Governance*. Basingstoke: Macmillan.

Peck, J. (2004) 'Geography and public policy: constructions of neoliberalism', *Progress in Human Geography*, 28: 392–405.

Pickvance, C. (1995) 'Marxist theories of urban politics', pp. 253–75. In D. Judge, G. Stoker and H. Wolman (eds), *Theories of Urban Politics*. London: Sage.

Pollert, A. (1996) 'Gender and class revisited: the poverty of "patriarchy"', *Sociology*, 30: 639–59.

Sacks, K.B. (1989) 'Towards a unified theory of class, race and gender', *American Ethnologist*, 16 (3): 534–50.

Shaw, M. (2003) 'Classic texts', *Community Development Journal*, 38 (4): 361–6.

Shields, R. (2004) 'Henri Lefebvre', in P. Hubbard, R. Kitchin and G. Valentine, *Key Thinkers on Space and Place*. London: Sage.

Smith, N. (1991) *Uneven Development: Nature, Capital and the Production of Space*. Oxford: Blackwell.

Smith, N. (1992) 'Contours of a spatialised politics: homeless vehicles and the production of geographical scale', *Social Text*, 33: 54–81.

Soja, E. (1989) *Postmodern Geographies: The Reassertion of Space in Critical Social Theory*. London: Verso.

Stahler-Sholk, R. (2001) 'Globalisation and social movement resistance: the Zapatista rebellion in Chiapas, Mexico', *New Political Science*, 23 (4): 493–516.

Storper, M. (2001) 'The poverty of radical theory today: from the false promise of Marxism to the mirage of the cultural turn', *International Journal of Urban and Regional Research*, 25 (1): 155–79.

Vargas, J.C. (2003) 'The inner city and the favela', *Race and Class*, 44 (4): 19–40.

Webber, J.R. (2005) 'Left-indigenous struggles in Bolivia: searching for revolutionary democracy', *Monthly Review*, 57 (4): 34–48.

Williams, R. (1989) *Resources of Hope*. London: Verso.

5

'POSTY' URBAN POLITICAL THEORY

Serena Kataoka

In face of the proliferating use of the prefix 'post-' to describe forms of politics and to indicate new approaches to understanding those forms, it seems both responsible and timely to include a chapter on 'posty' urban political theory in this collection. The three chapters in Part I have traced challenges to the assumption that political structures are the containers of power. Each has invoked the importance of economic and social structures, whether in terms of the power of the business elite in local coalitions, social stratification (i.e. class) in the distribution of power in urban regimes, or global capitalism in empowering neo-liberal localisation. What is significant is not so much that the structures are multiplied, but that they are intertwined, which releases power from the political structure into the *interplay* across and between various structures. Such rejection of the separation of the economic, social and political is a distinctly Marxist approach, whether explicit or implicit. There are two broad 'posty' trajectories following upon this approach: one progressive and the other critical.

Previous chapters have alluded to *progressive* trajectories, such as 'postmodernism' and 'post-Marxism'. Such terms use the prefix 'post-' to assert a difference between the present and the past (Matthewman and Hoey, 2006: 533). In a chapter of this sort, however, the use of such terminology would reproduce an evolutionary impression of the way that urban political theory advances, by implying that pre-'posty' theories such as Marxism are doomed to become extinct as 'posty' theories exercise their superior ability to grapple with the contemporary challenges of urban politics (on post-Marxism, see Laclau and Mouffe, 2001). Given the particularly 'global' character of the latter challenges, the purported extinction would probably be linked in most people's minds to 'globalism' or 'globalisation'. Such a progressivist account might seem timely, but it would neglect the responsibility of political theorists to ask into the politics of our attachment to progress (and to the globalism, modernism, nationalism, colonialism, urbanism and so on that are linked to our ideas of progress) and thus to explore the political implications of our own, often unconscious commitments. The approaches that we need to consider in this chapter put ideas of progress, be it political or intellectual, into question.

This chapter will examine a largely forgotten *critical* trajectory of 'posty' urban political theory, generally referred to as 'post-structuralism'. Post-structuralism consists of *an interpretative practice*, termed 'critique,' exemplified in Gilles Deleuze's reading of

Nietzsche (Hoy, 2004: 19–56). To engage in critique is not necessarily to reject struc-turalist accounts of things (such as Marxism), which suggest that the apparent world can be explained by abstract structures that are in tension with one another, such as the economy and society. Instead, practising critique is to linger 'in consideration of' structuralism (Deleuze, 2004: 170–92). Lingering enables post-structuralist works to delve deeper into the complexities of familiar things, exposing how structures are not simply explanations, but are the very means of producing things so they seem famil-iar; for instance, we come to think of ourselves as economic agents with economic problems once we understand ourselves as living in a world that is structured by the economy. Interpretation takes worlds as consisting of compositions of sorts that we can read (i.e. interpret) in order to get at structuralist ways of producing those worlds, their conditions of possibility and unrealised possibilities (Kurasawa, 1998: 83–96).

Currently, post-structuralism is not even a feature of 'posty' maps of the field (e.g. Dear and Dishman, 2002; Short, 2004; for an exception, see Parker, 2004). However, there were two formal introductions of post-structuralism in what Geddes refers to as the 'golden age' of Marxist urban political theory. As the second section will highlight, Manuel Castells and Henri Lefebvre were both trying to shake commonsense ideas about the urban and capitalism, in an attempt to get at the social relations by which these apparent structures are produced. Considering that two prominent urban polit-ical theorists came onto the scene with post-structural affections, it seems surprising that post-structuralism has been largely forgotten in the field. Even though Lefebvre is remembered as a post-structuralist of sorts, those taking up his work have been more interested in his radicalism, than in delving into the complexities of the urban. To be fair, so too was Lefebvre. This chapter will show how radicals following upon him miss important insights of other post-structuralist works that were becoming popularised during the 'golden age' of (post-structural) Marxist theory. Radical planners' cos-mopolitan visions obscure the possibilities of urban politics, which this chapter will suggest are perceptible if we adopt a disposition more open to the everyday, such as Walter Benjamin's *flâneurie*. Similarly, activists' radically 'free' ethics obscure emergent political rationalities such as the *governmentality* traced by Michel Foucault. This chapter will suggest setting aside radical visions and ethics (in order to stop playing into progress), and to experiment with post-structural critique.

As will be briefly noted in the third section of this chapter, a criticism implicit in the radical impulse is that post-structuralism does not offer us hope or values for the future. Such criticism would be important to entertain if it spoke to the primary pur-pose of urban political theory, but it does not. Urban political theory involves think-ing through urban politics. Our studies can enable radical planners and/or activists to strategise more effectively. If urban political theorists opt out of such thinking in order to respond to the seemingly urgent demands for planning and/or activism, we do so at the risk of unwittingly reproducing the very crises that generated the demands in the first place.

In so far as the urban is not determined by any one structure, the study of *the urban is inherently post-structural*. By way of conclusion, this chapter will offer up four ways to experiment with post-structuralism: disciplinary, evolutionary, practising critique and scenic. It is not clear whether readers will take up any of these approaches in experiments with post-structuralism. Such future telling is best left to the experts, with their crystal balls, bags of bones and calculators.

(Re)introducing post-structuralism

'Astonished' by the 'urban question', Castells determined to write a book attenuating it (Castells, 1979 [1972]: 1). He was shocked by the way that what he called 'urban ideology' skewed scholars' perceptions of the urban, so he set out to demonstrate the uselessness of negatively defining the urban (as something other than the natural). Castells asserted that the urban consists of the reproduction of labour, a function determined by the 'base' of state capitalism; at the same time, the reproductive social relations make the functioning of state capitalism possible. In short, the urban is a 'superstructure' (Althusser, 2001 [1971]). It was this mobilisation of Althusser's structural Marxism that led to Castells' reputation as a structuralist (Bradley, 1981; Zukin, 1987). *The Urban Question* was swept up in a materialist movement within urban planning (Fainstein, 1983; Harvey, 1988 [1973]). It is worth noting that urban planning was conceived 'as an alternative to politics' (Friedmann, 1987: 105), and that even in this radical variant, the capture of power is sought after in order to transform its use, to overcome inequities that are thought to generate politics.

It seems to have been forgotten that in *The Urban Question*, Castells chastised the founding father of structuralism, Levi-Strauss, for treating societies as though they were mere repositories of symbols posited by an unconscious signifying structure (Castells, 1979 [1972]: 216). He asserted that societies are made up of social relations that are informed by and enable an economic base that consists of *practices*. In an afterword included in the second run of the book, Castells railed against his disciplinary casting as a structuralist (Castells, 1979 [1972]: 452). Nonetheless, he was unable to shake the trade name until the 1990s, when his work became oriented around the impact of emergent technologies on the configurations of the economy, society and the state (Castells, 1996). Whether or not one considers Castells to be a post-structural urban theorist, his struggles against structuralism are certainly characteristic of a movement that asserts the significance of practices while resisting the imposition of a single signifying structure. In the case of Castells' early work, the particular role of the urban superstructure is cast in relation to the regional economic system (Castells, 1979 [1972]: 444–5), which raises the question of how the regional economy might constitute the determining structure of the urban. The latter is a question that illustrates his struggle with the apparent structuralism of his own account.

If there is any influential urban theorist whose works are read as post-structuralist, it is Henri Lefebvre. His declaration of the 'right to the city' was zealously taken up by his students during the May 1968 uprisings in France (Lefebvre, 1968). Such lively and widespread engagement with his recasting of the city as a political problem of access to 'social centrality' is likely to be what so astonished Castells, who in criticising the 'urban ideology', specifically targeted Lefebvre (Castells, 1979 [1972]: 86–95). Strikingly,

Lefebvre's ideas were vindicated not only by the revolutionary moment, but also by the students' failure to sustain that moment. Lefebvre had cautioned against proceeding without a strategy (Shields, 1999: 225). We can read his counsel in *The Urban Revolution*, which was published a couple of years after the uprisings (Lefebvre, 2003).

Lefebvre's post-structural approach is not so much a denigration of structuralism, as it is an opening up to the complexity of the urban itself. He posits the urban as a phenomenon that 'astonishes us' (Lefebvre, 2003: 45). In order to apprehend this shockingly complex and massive phenomenon, he develops a method of 'radical critique.' This method's 'critical reflection provides an orientation, which opens pathways and reveals a horizon' (Lefebvre, 2003: 66). Orientation is provided by way of a radical disposition, situated within an unfolding urban revolution. Urbanism as a way of life has only been partially realised because the urban has not been adequately articulated as a way of ordering culture, power and values in a 'socio-logic' (Lefebvre, 2003: 78). Hence the pathway opened up by radical critique is an 'urban strategy' that consists of focusing all social scientific study on the urban. Such study disentangles the urban (from the rural and the industrial for instance), thereby exposing the urban as a *political practice* whereby we make our social reality (cf. de Certeau, 1988; Bourdieu, 1989), and whereby 'modalities of daily life' are actualised in people's particular dispositions (Lefebvre, 2003: 51). Finally, radical critique provides the global city as a utopic horizon in which urbanism as a way of life has been completely realised.

Lefebvre gestures towards the horizon of the global city with his introductory hypothesis: 'Society has been completely urbanised'. Beginning with this 'impossible possibility'. Lefebvre theorises the completely urbanised society as the global city. It is an 'elsewhere', a u-topia that enables us to get a sense for another way of life without living it, as opposed to currently fashionable theorisations of actual cities serving as nodes in a global socio-economic system (Sassen, 1991). Thinking through the global city, Lefebvre theorises the urban as an 'immanent dialectic' (Lefebvre, 2003: 36–41). This dialectic moves between the differentiating properties of an urban strategy that is presently thought through disparate disciplines, and the centralising values of a u-topic urban society (Lefebvre, 2003: 117–120). As a materialist, Lefebvre is not satisfied with this abstract conception of the urban. So, rather than raising the urban up out of the everyday (even through Marx's revolutionary metaphysics), he treats the urban as a 'concrete contradiction'. Just as the line of sight has a body that it looks through (i.e. the eye), the immanent dialectic has a body (i.e. the everyday life of the city) that can see itself as moving contradiction (i.e. the urban) only through the reflection of the values of urban society. He terms this process of reflection 'urban thought', and credits it with the rediscovery of the global city (Lefebvre, 2003: 37). Hence, the global city is at once an inspirational source of values for social movements, and an 'elsewhere' beyond our everyday apprehension. It is the horizon revealed by urban thought, for radical critique of the urban.

In sum, the contradiction of the actual urban strategy and the virtual urban society are surpassed by a synthesis in Lefebvre himself, through the practice of urban thought. He conceives of the urban as the *movements* gathering together and differentiating ways of knowing and ways of living. But rather than delving into the complexities of these movements, Lefebvre gives them the structure of an incomplete urban revolution. His radical critique is meant to direct urban movements towards sustainable revolution by: (1) strategically focusing scientific study on 'the everyday'; and (2) envisioning the global urban society as the context in which we can claim 'rights to the city'. Each of these revolutionary imperatives has been taken up by radical planners and activists respectively, as will be examined in the following two sub-sections.

The everyday

Perhaps Lefebvre's most significant contribution to urban theory is his assertion that we can encounter the political in 'the everyday' (Lefebvre, 1991). Scholars in various fields have engaged in studies of everyday urban life, but they do not seem to be concerned with politics *per se*. Exceptional in this regard are radical urban planning theorists, who are explicitly politicising a field that is largely governed by technical rationality, by looking to everyday planning processes (e.g. Flyvberg, 2002; Hillier, 2002; Healey, 2006). Most notably, Leonie Sandercock engages in analyses of community-based initiatives that actively and creatively meet communities' needs (e.g. Sandercock, 2003: 143–5). Characterising these initiatives as examples of 'insurgent planning', she draws from them an 'insurgent sensibility' that is attentive to the city's emotions, senses and spirit, as well as its materiality (Sandercock, 2003: 10). Here is where Sandercock's approach differs from Lefebvre's. In the materiality of everyday life, Lefebvre discovers the mundane modes of industrial oppression, as distinct from urban sociality; distinguishing between the industrial and the urban is the first step of his scientific study of the urban. In contrast, Sandercock tries to make herself vulnerable to the urban itself (cf. Ellin, 2003), and thus is able to sense qualities that exceed scientific categories, such as fear of the other. Her insurgent sensibility is certainly more open than Lefebvre's urban strategy, but Walter Benjamin's *flâneurie* provides a disposition that is even more open to the minutiae and nuances of the everyday life of cities (Benjamin, 1983).

Despite having died before the 'golden era', Benjamin was only nine years Lefebvre's senior, and he gained more widespread recognition with the 1968 publication of a collection of his essays under the title *Illuminations* (Benjamin, 1986 [1968]: 1–3). The first essay in that collection can be read as a discursion on the *flâneur's* disposition as a collector of sorts (Benjamin, 1978: 59–67). The *flâneur* strolls through the city, simultaneously observing city life and participating in it, as imaged in the dandy walking a turtle along Paris streets (Benjamin, 1997). Unpacking his book collection, Benjamin characterises collecting as a 'mental climate' whose desire moves both by the open *curiosity* of a child, and the 'tactical instinct' of a wise elder. The collector frees books from booksellers' catalogues, and puts them into relation with one another in his collection. Similarly, while strolling through the city, the *flâneur* curiously transforms everything encountered into signs, mystically reads those signs, and thereby frees qualities of these encounters from scientific ordering. So *flâneurie* involves collecting everything and nothing in particular as a way of making oneself available to sensing the style of the city (i.e. being struck by city-ness). Urban reveries collected in this way only convey a sense of chance encounters in a city, and so they speak neither to the *flâneur's* style, nor to the city as a whole. This chance order is exemplified in the incomplete collection of Benjamin's snippets of his wanders through Paris (Benjamin, 1999 [1935]). Readers of Benjamin's *Arcades* necessarily become *flâneurs* of a sort, wandering through 'convoluted' indexes of notes, quotes and such. The work does not offer any one meaning proper to Benjamin or Paris, only myriad possibilities for interpretation.

While Sandercock provides a disposition that is similar to *flâneurie* in that it is sensitive to seemingly ephemeral qualities of cities, she draws away from Benjamin's openness by framing these qualities within a radical vision. She envisions 'cosmopolis' as a radically democratic utopia from which we can draw cosmopolitan values, such as being open to difference and working through conflict. Her cosmopolis rises up from the cacophony of difference below, and therefore is distinct from her colleagues' versions of cosmopolitanism, which tend to be theorised in the abstract terms of citizenship, on the level of the 'kosmos', of the universe (Douglass and Friedmann, 1998; Flyvbjerg, 1998; Amin, 2005; Markell, 2006). But like Lefebvre's meta-theoretical global city, cosmopolis is a whole that settles the contradiction between everyday and a u-topic society by providing a horizon of transformation. For example, with cosmopolitan ethics, we ought to be able to transform qualities of multicultural cities, such as fear of the other, into a sense of belonging. While hopeful, such stories of transformation narrate over the everyday. Ironically, therefore, radical visionaries assert the importance of the everyday as a site of study, while simultaneously obscuring it with u-topic visions.

For those of us who are interested in thinking through urban politics, the challenge posed by this analysis is to resist the comfort of hope, in order to make ourselves available to the unrealised possibilities of the everyday. But how might we do this? For an example, we might look to Sandercock's analysis of the Collingwood Neighbourhood House (CNH) in Vancouver BC – a community centre of sorts that responds to the needs of residents by providing services ranging from immigrant settlement to cultural parades. Her curiosity about how people create a sense of belonging leads her to map the *conditions of possibility* for CNH's effectiveness as an 'intercultural organization'. For example, she notes the intersection of a shift in national multiculturalism thinking, a leftist party taking leadership of the municipal council and anticipation of the city hosting an Expo (Sandercock, 2003: 145). If we were to more thoroughly seek after the conditions of possibility for CNH, we might note an interviewee's passing comment that 'the racists' moved to Surrey, a largely unplanned suburb (Sandercock and Attili, 2006). Hence, the displacement of racism was another condition of possibility of CNH. Collingwood was founded as an intercultural neighbourhood through the transformation of residents' values, such that racism ceased to make sense, and so racism must necessarily lie beyond it (whether in the suburbs or in private). A post-structural critique would resist the radical impulse of progress towards cosmopolis (or any u-topia whatever), and linger a bit longer in the encounter with racism (on encounter, see Whitehall, 2003). Listening evermore carefully, such a critique would highlight not only how racism is made the object of intercultural criticism, or how racism is embodied in displaced subjects, but more importantly, how racism as a *possibility* can be encountered otherwise. While there might be strategic reasons to explain away or displace nonsense, such as racism or reveries, the task of thinking through urban politics requires that we make ourselves available to the generally unrealised possibilities of the urban, however frightening or romantic they might seem at first glance.

'Rights to the city'

Beneath the cacophony of everyday life, Lefebvre highlights the pervasive contradiction between capitalism and urbanism. His revolutionary call for 'rights to the city' invokes the political freedom of the urban, as a way of countering the seemingly total reign of capitalism. In May 1968, his students took up this call, exercising their political freedom in Paris streets, thereby freeing these spaces from the stranglehold of capitalism. In short, the city they claimed and produced consisted of 'free' space. Similarly inspired riots took place in the People's Park at UC Berkeley in 1969, but Don Mitchell's analysis of the process by which the park came to be cemented over with volleyball courts for the leisure classes suggests that 'free' space may no longer be viable (Mitchell, 1995). Nonetheless, he concludes that struggles 'over and within' public spaces are key because our society produces homelessness, and the homeless occupy public space whether they choose to or not (Mitchell, 1995: 128). Their lack of choice is contrary to the democratic ethic that we are all free to choose to be part of the public, to participate in city politics. The contradiction that concerns Mitchell is between the democratic ethic, and that which seems to be beyond its capacity for explanation. Hence, he finds the action of city politics in the struggle between those creating *safe* democratic spaces (e.g. securitising public space and technologically mediating civic activities) and activists attempting to create *free* democratic spaces. Lost in the ongoing focus on public space as the site of democratic urban politics (e.g. Mitchell, 2003) is the reign of capitalism that so concerned Lefebvre.

In his analysis of the revitalisation of downtown Seattle, Timothy Gibson highlights the fundamental discursive struggle by which the 'vitality' of downtown is defined as singularly economic, beneath the apparent struggle over the location of a public hygiene centre (Gibson, 2004). While inviting readers to consider 'how particular spaces are *used* and *signified* in the process of daily life' (emphasis added, Gibson, 2004: 275), his discourse analysis focuses largely upon language. Downtown developers effectively mobilised commonsense understandings of vitality as singularly economic, and so the hygiene centre was not secured as a public space downtown. Nonetheless, activists are engaged in an ongoing struggle to rearticulate the discourse of 'vitality' in terms of the local histories of people mixing across socioeconomic and racial categories. Gibson invests activists and academics with the capacity to change the governing discourse to a more situated discourse whose inclusiveness evidences a *democratic ethic* (Gibson, 2004: 272–80). However, Foucault's 'genealogies' suggest that the shift from one discourse to another is not so intentional, since it involves not only language, but also a myriad of seemingly unrelated techniques, methods and so forth.

Foucault was inspired by the uprisings of 1968 (as quoted in Rabinow, 1984: 53) to draw back from 'archaeological' analyses exposing the governing discourse – the language and practices that constitute our topics of conversation (e.g. Foucault, 1989 [1966]) – in order to highlight discursive shifts. Taking up Nietzsche's 'genealogy', Foucault was able to get at the complex and mundane mechanisms that by *chance* interact in such a way as to enable a discourse to function as a governing rationality. Most famously, his genealogy of the prison traces the shift from sovereign to disciplinary society (Foucault, 1995 [1977]). Following upon Foucault, Nikolas Rose's analysis of 'third space' community suggests that with the loss of political guarantees made by the state, and moral guarantees made by society, a 'new diagram of power' is emerging (Rose, 1999: 167–96). What he calls 'government through community' works through a rationality of 'ethico-politics', in which *we make ourselves subjects by taking on the responsibility for self-governing and thinking ethically*, both as individuals and as members of communities. While demonstrating how ethico-politics works in neo-liberal friendly initiatives such as Thatcher's back to work programme, Rose holds out the possibility for a 'radical ethico-politics'. As opposed to the morality that informs neo-liberal community, he proposes an 'ethic of creativity' through which we can agonistically construct ways of living in 'becoming communities' (Rose, 1999: 195–6). Differently put, the ethic of creativity informs collectivising such that ways of life are always being created, and so communities cannot settle into norms that would fix 'free' individuals. Thus, Rose proposes to avert the offences of ethico-politics, by shifting the function of ethical freedom from controlling the individual to collectivising.

To be clear, Rose's proposal takes seriously Foucault's insight that we cannot simply plan an escape from a governing discourse, and so it is best understood as an attempt to change the configuration of ethico-political community. Whether we consider such change to be 'radical' must depend on our understanding of its *depth*. The depth to which Foucault's analysis directs us can be read in the vignette of the 'carceral city' (cf. Davis, 1990), which concludes his genealogy of the prison. It is a city (i.e. without a sovereign or a social contract), centred upon 'a multiple network of diverse elements – walls, space, institution, rules, discourse' (Foucault, 1995 [1977]: 307). Power relations, forces and bodies are formed and reformed as 'disciplinary individuals' through a myriad of 'carceral' mechanisms that are invoked over transgressions of 'the apparatus of production – "commerce" and "industry"' (Foucault, 1995 [1977]: 308). Thus, the carceral city is situated in a capitalist domain, with its warlike ways (Foucault, 1995 [1977]: 168). No attempt to clarify a strategy for reconfiguring the city is proposed. What is radical about Foucault's vignette is the way that it makes the carceral city sensible (its elements and force-full domain), as distinct from the common sense that city space is produced through social relations guided by ethical imperatives – of moral reform, economic development and even Rose's creativity. Radical politics of the depth that interests Foucault involves 'a re-partitioning of the sensible world' (Shapiro, 2006: 10). By depicting the carceral city for us, Foucault illustrates that we can get a sense for other cities, if we are simultaneously attentive to the workings of discourse and its domains (such as capitalism). Rather than assuming a contradiction between capitalism and urbanism, and re-visioning the city accordingly, genealogy enables us to convey something of the complexity of urban politics. While Foucault's analysis well traces power-full forces, we might trace forces of desire, and how they are at play in constituting neighbourhoods, for instance.

This section has (re)introduced post-structuralism in the field of urban political theory, from the 'golden age' of Marxist urban theory through to contemporary planners and activists. It has highlighted how the radical impulse of post-structuralism has been limited throughout by a 'progressive' orientation exemplified by Lefebvre's incomplete urban revolution. Radical planners envision u-topias towards which we can progress, and radical activists imagine ethics that can progress freedom. In spite of all this progress, they neglect the urban movements noted by Lefebvre's post-structural analysis – gathering together and differentiating ways of knowing and ways of living. By (re)introducing other post-structuralist works, this section has illustrated a couple of ways that we might get a sense for urban movements. Following Benjamin, we can become curious about the minutiae of everyday life, and linger in moments when we are struck by city-ness. Extending this approach, we can try to get a sense for how city-ness is commonly made sensible (i.e. its politics), and to refuse common sense in order to affirm its unrealised possibilities. Following Foucault, we can become attentive to discourses and their domains. Suddenly apparent are the complex relations of forces, techniques, bodies, and so forth. Since discourse is not simply constituted in contradiction to another discourse, there can be no revolution of one over another. A post-structural radical politics thus consists of experimenting with other ways of ordering the sensible. Urban studies that focus on power are radical in so far as they enable us to get a sense for forces and techniques that are obscured in studies focused on governmental institutions. And we need not assume that studies of power have made complete sense of *urban* politics – how we encounter the urban is posed as a political question that we can hold open.

Criticism of critique

In 'progressive' desires to transform the urban – whether through politicising planning or creating 'free' spaces – we can read an implicit criticism of post-structural critique: it does not provide hope or ethics for another way of life. But while securing hopeful cities and ethical communities seems to be the purview of radical planners and activists, it is not necessarily (and certainly not primarily) the purpose of urban political theory. The practice of theorising urban politics is: much broader, in that it is attentive to various dimensions of politics, not just planning processes or unjust constraints upon freedom; and much more specific, in that it is grounded in the everyday, rather than becoming abstracted by radical visions and radical ethics. If we are to take thinking through urban politics seriously, we must take the time to do so. As noted by eminent cultural and political theorists, contemporary forms of power produce crises, whose seeming urgency makes it difficult for us to justify pausing to think things through (Baudrillard, 2002; Zizek, 2002). But to respond to apparent crises with cosmopolitan visions or creative ethics, before pausing to get a better sense for the politics of an urban scene, is reckless. So prior to strategising, there is a role for urban political theory to play in producing careful analyses of urban scenes that highlight their conditions of possibility, unrealised possibilities and implications (cf. Shaw, 2002). It is important to acknowledge, however, that radicals of all political stripes could use such analyses to the advantage of their particular interests.

Inviting critique

Having (re)introduced post-structuralism as the modality of distinguished Marxist strategies, this chapter will conclude by sketching four ways that we students of urban politics can use critique to think through the urban as an open question, so as to get at some of the complexities of its politics.

First, if we were to take up a disciplinary approach, we would see post-structural theory as largely absent inside the field of urban political theory, the golden age of Marxist urban theory notwithstanding. Hence, its role in the field would have to be secured from outside – as for example through an intervention by cultural studies (e.g. Bell and Leong, 1998; Seigworth and Wise, 2000), sociology (e.g. Agger, 1992; Westwood and Williams, 1997), or geography (e.g. Aitchison et al., 2000; Anderson, 2003). Post-structural analyses from other fields could be accepted, but they would not easily settle into a field founded on the assumption that its disciplinary territory is known, as in the assumption that politics is a function of power. It is precisely such assumptions that post-structural analyses challenge in favour of encountering things in their complexity. One might jump to the conclusion that post-structuralism poses a threat to the security of the discipline, or inversely, that it provides security by creating opportunities for enriching the knowledge of the discipline. A more reasonable interpretation would be that post-structuralism is not concerned with the security of disciplines, and it has techniques that could be useful in studies of urban politics. So post-structural critique would be useful for those who are primarily concerned with the discipline's purported object of study. The challenge would be to pose urban politics as an open question, rather than leading with probes about particular forms of political power, for instance.

Secondly, if we were to adopt an evolutionary approach, we might trace Lefebvre's post-structuralism back to Louis Wirth's urbanism as a way of life. In 1925 (prior to the terminology of post-structuralism), Wirth effectively mobilised 'urban reveries' – Simmel's cultural studies – in developing the concept of a 'city mentality' (Wirth, 1967 [1925]). It is a *culture*, which differentiates the urban from the rural in its naturalness. Lefebvre further differentiated urbanism, by arguing that it is a political culture, as opposed to industrialisation's pacification. Tracing a post-structural lineage following upon Lefebvre could take us towards Warren Magnusson's examination of the global city: 'the city that has become the world, the world that has become the city' (Magnusson, 2000b: 291). To emphasise, this *actual* global city is distinct from Lefebvre's *hypothetical* global city. In order to make sense of the global city, Magnusson conceptualises a 'hyperspace' that consists of urbanism, whose fundamental political practice is the creation and maintenance of our environments through the jockeying of social movements' claims, such as those of sovereignty, property, gender and so on (Magnusson, 2000a). Importantly, there is no apparent order to this jockeying, which means to say that there is neither a sovereign authority (see Magnusson and Walker, 1988), nor rules of communication (cf. Habermas, 1984) informing the distribution of urbanism. Magnusson's urbanism locates politics in the less predictable interactions of social movements. This chapter might pose as a continuation of this evolutionary line, taking hyperspace as an indifferent 'plane of immanence' (Deleuze, 1986 [1983]: 59), and urbanism as presentations of that plane. Rather than making hyperspace a groundless ground of urbanism upon which *claims* to other ways of life can be made, an indifferent plane only provides for *propositions* of that plane. Inviting theorisations of urbanism as a way of presenting the plane would seem a fitting way to leave off this evolutionary story.

However, the very project of theory-building is counter to post-structuralism, which implies that we can think otherwise at any moment. Reading a particular set of works together may be of use, but we need not pretend that their relation is a function of evolution. For example, the set of Wirth, Lefebvre and Magnusson is useful for opening up disciplinary understandings of the urban to culture, for politicising that culture, and for decentring those politics. Shaking the common sense that the urban is coextensive with city space, and that politics is power centred in that space, may make it easier for our disciplined minds to pose urban politics as an open question. Openness to sensing the complexity of urban politics is characteristic of post-structuralism, as this chapter has tried to convey. If the purpose of this chapter were to plan a city or mobilise an activist community, a different reading of the 'urbanism as a way of life' set would be called for.

Thirdly, if we were to offer a critique of the urban, we would linger in the golden age of Marxist urban theory just a moment longer, with Deleuze's *Difference and Repetition* (Deleuze, 1994). To be clear, mobilising Deleuze's thinking through difference is distinct from the fashionable trend of mining his work for playful metaphors – such as rhizomes – that lend flair to largely conventional proscriptions for playing contemporary politics (e.g. Amin and Thrift, 2002; Hardt and Negri, 2000). Similarly, it does not commit us to his metaphorical treatment of the urban, as an indifferent cityscape that is in line with postmodern accounts; he was not an urban theorist (Deleuze, 1986 [1983]: 208). Following upon Deleuze's reading of Nietzsche, the urban would itself be taken as a composition (of interpretations and forces), composed by a play of difference that is neither negative nor based on contradiction. Deleuze identifies three movements of difference. One is the difference between compositions, such as Wirth's *differentiation* between the urban and the rural, which produces a 'multiplicity' of social forms. Another is the difference of a composition in relation to itself, as in the modulation of social movements' claims traced by Magnusson, which *distributes* urban ways of life; the urban is ever 'becoming' urban. Lefebvre was onto the structuralism of the urban in so far as he identified its functions of gathering together and distributing. But he did not admit the deeper difference that Deleuze notes, the difference of the system as a whole (i.e. chance). Rather than the order lent to the urban by Lefebvre's incomplete revolution, critique allows for the chance interplay of differentiation and distribution. Hence, upon a shocking encounter with the urban, we would linger in the gap that prefigures such shock. Lingering thus, we might get a sense for the schema of urban movements, and in turn, affirm unrealised possibilities of the urban. Thus, like Marx, critique refuses the comfort of assuming that we can escape from capitalism by way of a strategy, instead seeking the overcoming of capitalism within its relations; the same can be said for urbanism, globalism and so forth.

Fourthly, if we were to experiment with a scenic approach, we would propose a literal definition of the urban as a moment in which we are struck by city-ness. While this would seem to posit an elusive object of study, most every study of the urban begins with or touches off on a vignette of an urban scene that conveys some sense of the city-ness that scholars are struck by (e.g. Weber, 1966 [1958]: 10; Jacobs, 1993: 10). So theorists of urban politics are already in the habit of encountering the urban through scenes, but there is a tendency to narrate over these encounters (Holston, 1999). Italo Calvino's *Invisible Cities* (Calvino, 1974 [1972]) would be provided as an example of a work of urban political theory that problematises narration by its very form. It is written as a play (i.e. a series of scenes), whose 'dialogue' consists of Marco Polo describing various cities to Kublai Khan (cf. Trinh, 1992). Out of Polo's stories, Khan narrates his discovery of the elemental order of his otherwise over-extended and disintegrating empire (Calvino, 1974 [1972]: 43). It is an ironic narrative, however, because the order that Khan perceives undoes the narrative order. The 'elements' he senses structure the play. All of the scenes are given one of eleven titles, each of which correspond to an element of cities, and the scenes expressing each element are numbered in order of appearance. So rather than following Khan's narrative discovery of the elements by reading the play from start to finish, one could read all the scenes entitled 'Cities and desire' from '1' (the third scene) through to '5' (the sixteenth scene), for example. Since all of the elements have five scenes, none is weightier than another. If Calvino wanted us to take Khan's journey of discovery (through Polo's storytelling) seriously, he would have entitled the work *His Invisible Empire*, or something of the sort. Instead, Calvino uses scene titles to draw attention to the deeper structure of the 'elements' of cities, and he maintains an open politics by presenting these elements as singularities, in particular cities/scenes. Thus, we would end by recommending that readers experiment with other ways of presenting the urban that holds its politics open.

In a sense, these are four attempts to seduce students of urban politics into experimenting with post-structural critique. Such sachés move with a perceptible confidence that those who mobilise post-structural critique become enamoured with the sense of getting at the complexities of urban politics – as illustrated in the profile of politics in post-structural urban studies in other fields. However, these moves are inflected with a subtle fear that if theorists of urban politics continue to forget post-structuralism, radical urban planners and activists will become fully responsible for thinking through contemporary urban politics. Given the preoccupation of the former with collaboration and the latter with globalisation, there would surely be many sensibilities and possibilities missed, while we students of urban politics stood around telling stories of ourselves as 'progressive'. Readers will likely find one of the four entrées into practising post-structural critique more attractive than the others, regardless of its implications, which is fine. No oaths are being requested.

References

Agger, Ben (1992) *Cultural Studies as Critical Theory*. London; Washington, DC: Falmer Press.
Aitchison, Cara, MacLeod, Nicola E. and Shaw, Stephen J. (2000) *Leisure and Tourism Landscapes: Social and Cultural Geographies*. London; New York: Routledge.
Althusser, Louis (2001 [1971]) *Lenin and Philosophy and Other Essays*, Ben Brewster (trans.). New York: Monthly Review Press.
Amin, Ash (2005) 'Local community on trial,' *Economy and Society*, 34 (4): 612–33.
Amin, Ash and Thrift, Nigel (2002) *Cities: Reimagining the Urban*. Cambridge; Malden, MA: Polity.
Anderson, Kay (2003) *Handbook of Cultural Geography*. London; Thousand Oaks, CA: Sage.
Baudrillard, Jean (2002) *Spirit of Terrorism and Requiem for the Two Towers*. New York: Verso.
Bell, Michael and Leong, Sze Tsung (1998) *Slow Space*. New York: Monacelli Press.
Benjamin, Walter (1978) *Illuminations* Hannah Arendt, (ed.) New York: Schocken Books.
Benjamin, Walter (1983) *Charles Baudelaire: A Lyrical Poet in the Era of High Capitalism*, Harry Zohn (trans.). London: Verso.
Benjamin, Walter (1986 [1968]) *Illuminations*, Hannah Arendt, (ed.). Harry Zohn (trans.). New York: Schocken Books.
Benjamin, Walter (1997) *Charles Baudelaire: A Lyrical Poet in the Era of High Capitalism*, Harry Zohn (trans.). New York: Verso.
Benjamin, Walter (1999 [1935]) *The Arcades Project*, Rolf Tiedemann (ed.), Howard Eiland and Kevin McLaughlin (trans.). Cambridge, MA: Belknapp Press of Harvard University Press.
Bourdieu, Pierre (1989) *The Logic of Practice*, Richard Nice (trans.). Cambridge: Polity.
Bradley, Raymond (1981) 'Review: [the urban question]', *Social Forces*, 59 (3): 845–7.
Calvino, Italo (1974 [1972]) *Invisible Cities*, William Weaver (trans.). San Diego: Harcourt.
Castells, Manuel (1979 [1972]) *The urban question: A Marxist Approach*, Alan Sheridan (trans.). Cambridge, MA: MIT Press.
Castells, Manuel (1996) *The Rise of the Network Society*. Cambridge, MA: Blackwell Publishers.
Davis, Mike (1990) *City of Quartz: Excavating the Future in Los Angeles*. London: Verso.
de Certeau, Michel (1988) *The Practice of Everyday Life*, Steven Rendall (trans.). Berkeley: University of California Press.
Dear, Michael J. and Dishman, J. Dallas (2002) *From Chicago to L.A.: Making Sense of Urban Theory*. Thousand Oaks, CA: Sage Publications.
Deleuze, Gilles (1986 [1983]) *Cinema 1: The Movement-Image*, Hugh Tomlinson Barbara Habberjam (trans.). Minneapolis: University of Minnesota.
Deleuze, Gilles (1994) *Difference and Repetition*. New York: Columbia University Press.
Deleuze, Gilles (2004) 'How do we recognize structuralism?', in David Lapoujade (ed.), *Desert Islands and Other Texts, 1953–1974*. Los Angeles, CA: Semiotexte; distributed by MIT Press.
Douglass, Mike and Friedmann, John (1998) *Cities for Citizens: Planning and the Rise of Civil Society in a Global Age*. New York: John Wiley & Sons.
Ellin, Nan (2003) 'A vulnerable urbanism', in *Re-envisioning Landscape/Architecture*. Barcelona: ACTAR, pp. 222–35.
Fainstein, Susan S. (1983) *Restructuring the City: The Political Economy of Urban Redevelopment*. New York: Longman.
Flyvbjerg, Bent (1998) *Rationality and Power: Democracy in Practice*, Steven Sampson (trans.). Chicago: University of Chicago Press.

Flyvberg, B. (2002) 'Bringing power to planning research: one researcher's praxis story', *Journal of Planning Education & Research*, 21 (4): 355–68.

Foucault, Michel (1989 [1966]) *The Order of Things: An Archaeology of the Human Sciences*. London; New York: Routledge.

Foucault, Michel (1995 [1977]) *Discipline and Punish: The Birth of the Prison*, Alan Sheridan (trans.). 2nd edn. New York: Vintage Books.

Friedmann, John (1987) *Planning in the Public Domain: From Knowledge to Action*. Princeton, NJ: Princeton University Press.

Gibson, Timothy A. (2004) *Securing the Spectacular City: The Politics of Revitalization and Homelessness in Downtown Seattle*. Lanham, MD: Lexington Books.

Habermas, Jürgen (1984) *The Theory of Communicative Action*, Thomas McCarthy (trans.). Boston: Beacon Press.

Hardt, Michael and Negri, Antonio (2000) *Empire*. Cambridge, MA: Harvard University Press.

Harvey, David (1988 [1973]) *Social Justice and the City*. Oxford: Basil Blackwell.

Healey, P. (2006) *Collaborative Planning: Shaping Places in Fragmented Societies*, 2nd edn. Basingstoke, NY: Palgrave Macmillan.

Hillier, J. (2002) *Shadows of Power: An Allegory of Prudence in Land-use Planning*. London; New York: Routledge.

Holston, James (1999) 'Spaces of insurgent citizenship', in James Holston (ed.), *Cities and Citizenship*. Durham: Duke University Press. pp. 155–73.

Hoy, David Couzens (2004) *Critical Resistance: From Poststructuralism to Post-Critique*. Cambridge, MA: MIT Press.

Jacobs, Jane (1993) *The Death and Life of Great American Cities*, Modern Library edn. New York: Modern Library.

Kurasawa, Fuyuki (1998) 'The adventures of the structure', *Thesis Eleven*, 55: 83–96.

Laclau, Ernesto and Mouffe, Chantal (2001) *Hegemony and Socialist Strategy: Towards a Radical Democratic Politics,* 2nd edn. London; New York: Verso.

Lefebvre, Henri (1968) *Le Droit à La Ville*. Paris: Anthropos.

Lefebvre, Henri (1991) *Critique of Everyday Life*. London; New York: Verso.

Lefebvre, Henri (2003) *The Urban Revolution*. Minneapolis: University of Minnesota Press.

Magnusson, Warren (2000a) 'Hyperspace: a political ontology of the global city', in Richard V. Ericson and Nico Stehr (eds), *Governing Modern Societies*. Toronto: University of Toronto Press. pp. 80–104.

Magnusson, Warren (2000b) 'Politicizing the global city', in Engin Isin (ed.), *Democracy, Citizenship, and the Global City*. London: Routledge. pp. 289–306.

Magnusson, Warren and Walker, R.B.J. (1988) 'De-centring the state: political theory and Canadian political economy', *Studies in Political Economy: A Socialist Review*, 26: 37–71.

Markell, Patchen (2006) 'The rule of the people: Arendt, Arche, and democracy', *American Political Science Review*, 100 (1): 1–14.

Matthewman, Steve and Hoey, Douglas (2006) 'What happened to postmodernism?', *Sociology*, 40 (3): 529–47.

Mitchell, Don (1995) 'The end of public space? People's park, definitions of the public, and democracy', *Annals of the Association of American Geographers*, 85 (1): 108–33.

Mitchell, Don (2003) *The Right to the City: Social Justice and the Fight for Public Space*. New York: Guilford Press.

Parker, Simon (2004) *Urban Theory and the Urban Experience: Encountering the City*. London; New York: Routledge.

Rabinow, Paul (1984) *Foucault Reader*. New York: Random House.

Rose, Nikolas S. (1999) *Powers of Freedom: Reframing Political Thought*. Cambridge; New York, NY: Cambridge University Press.

Sandercock, Leonie (2003) *Cosmopolis II: Mongrel Cities in the 21st Century*. London; New York: Continuum.

Sandercock, Leonie and Attili, Giovanni (2006) *Where Strangers Become Neighbours: The Story of the Collingwood Neighbourhood House* [DVD]. Vancouver: School of Community and Regional Planning, UBC.

Sassen, Saskia (1991) *The Global City: New York, London, Tokyo.* Princeton, NJ: Princeton University Press.

Seigworth, G.J. and Wise, J. Macgregor (2000) 'Deleuze and Guattari in *Cultural Studies*', *Cultural Studies*, 14 (2): Special Issue.

Shapiro, Michael J. (2006) 'After Kant: re-thinking hermeneutics and aesthetics', *The Good Society*, 15 (1): 7–10.

Shaw, Karena (2002) 'Indigeneity and the international', *Millennium: Journal of International Studies*, 31 (16): 55–81.

Shields, Rob (1999) *Lefebvre, Love and Struggle: Spatial Dialectics.* New York: Routledge.

Short, John Rennie (2004) *Urban Theory: A Critical Assessment.* Hampshire, NY: Palgrave Macmillan.

Trinh, T. Minh-Ha (1992) *Framer Framed.* New York: Routledge.

Weber, Max (1966 [1958]) *The City*, Don Martindale and Gertrud Neuwirth (trans.). 3rd edn. New York: Free Press.

Westwood, Sallie and Williams, John (1997) *Imagining Cities: Scripts, Signs, Memory.* London; New York: Routledge.

Whitehall, Geoffrey (2003) 'The problem of the "world and beyond"', in Jutta Weldes (ed.), *To Seek Out New Worlds: Science Fiction and World Politics.* New York: Palgrave Macmillan.

Wirth, Louis (1967 [1925]) 'A bibliography of the urban community', in Robert E. Park, Ernest W. Burgess and Roderick D. McKenzie (eds), *The City*. Chicago: University of Chicago Press. pp. 161–228.

Zizek, Slavoj (2002) *Welcome to the Desert of the Real!: Five Essays on September 11 and Related Dates.* London; New York: Verso.

Zukin, Sharon (1987) 'Urban social movements', *American Journal of Sociology*, 93: 459.

Part III

GOVERNANCE

6

NEW INSTITUTIONALISM AND
URBAN POLITICS

Vivien Lowndes

Up until the 1950s, institutionalism was political science. Outside of political theory, the core activity within political science was the description of constitutions, legal systems and government structures, and their comparison over time and across countries. Urban politics was no exception. But the scope of US urban politics began to expand with the birth of the 'community power' debate which sought to discover 'who (really) governs' (see Harding, this volume). Both pluralists and elitists declined to take at face value the official pronouncements of government bodies and their constitutional accounts of decision-making. Later, public choice theorists and neo-Marxists, from very different perspectives, also came to question the centrality of formal institutions to urban political outcomes.

In Britain, where the structure and role of local government was more extensive, the critique took longer to bite. In 1979, Peter Saunders bemoaned the continuing assumption that 'the contours of political power at the local level correspond to the formal institutions of local government; that power resides in the town hall … and nowhere else' (1979: 328). But, by the 1980s, changes within the apparatus of local government itself provided further stimulus to critical analysis. The organisation of local government was becoming increasingly fragmented: functions were passed to non-elected agencies; private and voluntary bodies gained new roles as contractors and 'partners'; and the internal management of local authorities was transformed through decentralisation, 'down-sizing' and the creation of internal markets. Recognising the multiplicity of actors now involved in urban politics (and influenced by theoretical advances in both Europe and the US), British scholars increasingly turned their attention to problems of coordination or 'governance', whether through studies of policy networks, urban regimes or new public management (Stoker, 1995; Rhodes, 1997; Lowndes, 1999).

Do the theoretical and empirical developments of the last 15 years signify a final triumph over institutionalism in the study of urban politics? The narrow institutional approach criticised by Saunders is clearly no longer relevant. But, at the same time, there is a strong case for the rehabilitation of institutional theory in order to analyse the emergence of novel and diverse arrangements for urban governance. Institutions have not become any less important in urban politics, but they have changed. The new-style institutions on the urban political scene call for new-style institutional analysis. Rather than returning to the descriptive and atheoretical style of the 1950s, we can draw inspiration from the 'new institutionalism' that has emerged not just in political science but also in economics, sociology and organisation studies (Lowndes, 1996).

New institutionalism differs from its older sister in at least three important respects. First, it is concerned not only with formal rules and structures but also with the informal conventions and coalitions that shape political behaviour. Secondly, it does not take political institutions at face value; instead, it takes a critical look at the way in which they embody values and power relationships. Thirdly, new institutionalism rejects the determinism of earlier approaches. While institutions constrain individual behaviour, they are also (paradoxically) human creations, which change and evolve through the agency of actors.

The chapter starts by providing a brief account of the core premises of new institutionalism. The next section shows why new institutionalism is particularly well suited to the analysis of changing processes of urban governance. Three case studies, based on the author's own research, are then provided in order to exemplify and develop the theoretical case. The chapter finishes with a consideration of the outstanding dilemmas that confront the new urban institutionalists.

New institutionalism: core premises

The new institutionalism emerged in the 1980s as a reaction to the dominance of 'undersocialised' accounts of social, economic and political behaviour. Behaviourism and first-generation rational choice theory (themselves reactions to the 'old institutionalism') regarded institutions as epiphenomenal – the simple aggregation of individual actions. In their seminal article, March and Olsen (1984: 747) argued quite simply that 'the organisation of political life makes a difference', and asserted a more autonomous role for institutions in shaping political behaviour.

Traditional institutionalism employed a descriptive–inductive method (drawing conclusions from empirical investigation), but the new institutionalism takes a deductive approach that starts from theoretical propositions about the way institutions work. Consequently, there is not one 'new institutionalism' but many: in 1996, Hall and Taylor identified three variants; by 1999, Guy Peters had discovered seven! The basic theoretical cleavage has been between normative and (second-generation) rational choice perspectives. The normative version argues that political institutions influence behaviour by shaping individuals' 'values, norms, interests, identities and beliefs' (March and Olsen, 1989: 17). The rational choice version argues that, while institutional factors do not 'produce behaviour', they do affect 'the structure of a situation' in which actions are selected, primarily through influencing incentives and information flows (Ostrom, 1986: 5–7). 'Historical institutionalism', which represents the most extensive body of empirical work to date, draws upon *both* normative and rational choice perspectives (Hall and Taylor, 1996: 940). More recently, a 'discursive institutionalism' has emerged which sees institutions as shaping behaviour through frames of meaning – the ideas and narratives that are used to explain, deliberate or legitimise political action (Schmidt, 2006: 99).

Do we need to choose between normative, rational choice and discursive accounts? Some commentators have insisted that these positions express fundamentally different ontological positions (Hay and Wincott, 1998: 953), while others have argued that the distance between competing variants is actually small and decreasing, with new institutionalism holding out the promise of a 'rapprochement' between traditionally warring factions of political science (Goodin and Klingemann, 1996: 11). Indeed, the special character of institutions may lie precisely in the fact that they are 'over-determined': in robust institutional arrangements, regulative, normative and cognitive mechanisms work together to shape behaviour (Scott, 2001: 51). While theoreticians inevitably emphasise the distinctive features of each variant, Vivien Schmidt (2006: 116) reminds us that 'problem-oriented scholars tend to mix approaches all the time, using whichever approaches seem the most appropriate to explaining their object of study'.

Where does a pragmatic approach of this sort leave us? Can we specify a theoretical core for the new institutionalism that is able to distinguish it from other frameworks discussed in this book? Peters (2005: 164) provides the best summary:

> The fundamental issue holding all these various approaches … together is simply that they consider institutions the central component of political life. In these theories institutions are the variable that explain political life in the most direct and parsimonious manner, and they are also the factors that themselves require explanation. The basic argument is that institutions *do* matter, and that they matter more than anything else that could be used to explain political decisions.

So, new institutionalists contend that the greatest theoretical leverage is to be gained by studying the institutional frameworks within which political actors operate. By studying the rules, values and ideas embodied in and expressed through these institutional frameworks, it is possible to understand better (and even predict) the behaviour and decisions of actors. This is not to say that individuals are unimportant: indeed, it is political actors themselves who are the creators and shapers of institutions. What interests new institutionalists is the complex relationship 'between institutional architects, institutionalised subjects and institutional environments' (Hay and Wincott, 1998: 957). We now consider what new institutionalism has to offer urban politics and, in so doing, explore key concepts in further detail.

What does new institutionalism have to offer urban politics?

For our purposes, a new institutionalist framework is particularly appropriate because it provides tools with which to analyse:

- the overarching rules of urban politics and governance
- the complex nature of urban governance environments
- the contested and uncertain nature of change within urban politics and governance.

The overarching rules of urban politics and governance

For new institutionalists, institutions are not the same as organisations. As Huntington noted, as early as 1968, institutions are 'stable, valued and recurring patterns of behaviour'. Institutions can best be understood as the 'rules of the game'. Organisations – like individuals – are players within that game. In urban politics, relevant 'rules' may be consciously designed and clearly specified – like constitutions and structure plans, community strategies, or performance plans and agreements. Alternatively, rules may take the form of unwritten customs and codes. Informal rules may support 'positive' patterns of behaviour, like 'community leadership', the 'public service ethos' or 'continuous improvement'; equally they may underpin 'negative' frameworks like departmentalism, paternalism or social exclusion.

The players within the 'game' of urban governance are diverse, and include organisations (the elected local authority, other service agencies, political parties, voluntary organisations) and individuals (politicians, bureaucrats, service professionals, community activists, electors). Interestingly, Prime Minister Tony Blair (1998: 10) used the new institutionalist imagery of players in a game to describe the state of British urban governance: 'There are all sorts of players on the local pitch jostling for position where previously the council was the main game in town'.

The institutions of urban politics cannot, therefore, be reduced to the specific organisation of the elected local authority. Urban policy-making and service delivery now involve private and voluntary as well as public sector actors; partnerships and networks are as important as hierarchical intra-organisational relationships. To paraphrase Fox and Miller (1995: 92), the institutions of local governance exist within, between and around particular organisations. A new institutionalist perspective allows us to 'grasp systems of interaction across formal barriers' (Bogason, 2000: 61). The fragmentation of elected local government and the growing importance of multi-actor networks serves to clarify what has, in fact, always been the case: that 'institutions' are not the same as 'organisations', and that informal conventions can be as important as formal constitutions. As Alan Harding (1995: 49) has pointed out, informal coalitions have become more visible now that 'partnership' is on every policy-maker's lips.

Institutional innovations in urban politics increasingly involve rules and conventions that shape the behaviour of many different organisations, acting both individually and in partnership. This emerging amalgam of rules and organisations makes up the 'institutional matrix' of local governance (to borrow a phrase from the economist

Douglass North, 1990). The practical separation of *local governance* from *local government* calls for clearer analytical distinctions: new institutionalism can provide these.

A new institutionalist perspective allows us to identify and track changes in different sets of rules within the overall institutional matrix of local governance, and to study the interaction of formal and informal rules, and old and new elements. There is no necessary assumption that different rule sets (political, managerial, professional, constitutional) will move in the same direction or with the same speed, or that they will be in some way compatible or reinforcing. There will, however, be knock-on effects between rules in different domains. As Ostrom (1999: 39) notes: 'the impact on incentives and behavior of one type of rule is not independent of the configuration of other rules'.

Another merit of a new institutionalist analysis is its value-critical stance. A new institutionalist perspective ensures that the normative dimension to urban politics is not lost, as governance becomes increasingly de-coupled from the 'capital P' politics of elected local government. Governance is not reduced to a technical problem of 'system coordination'. The overarching rules of governance are far from neutral. Rules create 'positions' within governance (e.g. council leader, committee chair, partnership member); they determine how participants enter or leave these positions; what actions they are permitted to take, and what outcomes they are allowed to affect (see Ostrom, 1986: 5). More informally, they determine what behaviour is deemed 'appropriate' in different situations (March and Olsen, 1989: 38).

It follows that institutional rules embody power relations by privileging certain positions and certain courses of action over others – they express 'patterns of distributional advantage' (Knight, 1992: 9). As Pierre (1999: 390) argues, 'the structure of governance – the inclusion or exclusion of different actors and the selection of instruments – is not value neutral but embedded in and sustains political values'. Institutions are 'carriers' of interests and values 'above and beyond immediate political control' (Pierre, 1998: 193). This is why, as we shall see, institutional change is never a purely technical matter. Any challenge to existing institutional settlements is likely to be met by resistance; indeed, shifting power relations may be one of the *goals* of institutional reform (for example, empowering political leaders vis-à-vis other elected councillors, or politicians vis-à-vis professionals, or citizens vis-à-vis bureaucrats).

The complex nature of urban governance environments

New institutionalists are interested in the interaction between political institutions and wider institutional frameworks (in contrast to the 'inward looking' character of traditional institutional analysis). New institutionalists' concerns are particularly relevant to the study of urban politics, given the constraints afforded by institutional frameworks at higher levels of government *and* at the local level. According to Goodin and Klingemann (1996: 18), institutional rules are 'nested within an ever-ascending hierarchy of yet-more-fundamental, yet-more-authoritative rules and regimes and practices and procedures'. There is no necessary association between the emergence of 'local governance' and any increase in local autonomy. In Britain, high degrees of institutional differentiation have been accompanied by a large degree of central control over the resources and operation of local governance. Even among the decentralising countries of the European Union, local actors continue to act within institutional constraints established and maintained by central government. As Mike Goldsmith (2002: 91) argues:

> ... central government control – by which is meant the rules of the intergovernmental game – is a crucial piece in the establishment of local government systems, in that the position of local government in state systems is decided by the nature of the constitution (written or unwritten) and by the interpretation of and formal changes to it through legislation and judicial decisions.

Indeed, in an environment of 'multi-level governance', the picture becomes yet more complex with growing roles for supranational bodies like the European Union and, in many countries, for regional government. Urban governance is also subject to international conventions (for instance on climate change), whilst also having to work with private sector partners whose structures and strategies are truly global (in fields like waste management or informatics, for example).

New institutionalists have also turned their attention to the 'bottom-up' influence of *locally specific* institutional constraints. The social capital debate is concerned with the relationship between institutions of civil society and the performance of political institutions (Putnam, 2000; Lowndes and Wilson, 2001). From an organisation theory perspective, Clegg (1990: 163) shows how locally specific institutional environments serve to reinforce or undermine society-wide institutional frameworks. The legitimacy (and effectiveness) of local governance is, at least in part, related to its affinity with the conventions and organisational traditions of a particular locality. Local governance is embedded in locally specific institutional frameworks of both a political nature (e.g. patterns of party organisation or municipal traditions) and a non-political nature (e.g. the structures and conventions of local business life and of community activity). Although the degree of embeddedness may vary from place to place (and over time), local institutional environments create opportunities in local governance 'to do not only different things but also the same things differently' (Clegg, 1990: 151). Looking across Western Europe, Peter John (2001: 133) argues that 'local particularities' are becoming more evident with the growing importance of networks and less formalised patterns of governance.

'Top-down' and 'bottom-up' institutional influences interact in important ways. The extent of local distinctiveness in urban politics is related to the degree of autonomy and diversity that higher levels of government will tolerate. At the same time, the impact of higher-level regulation or influence is mediated by the strength of local institutional commitments. New institutionalist perspectives are particularly pertinent to analysing the multi-level character of contemporary urban politics.

The contested and uncertain nature of change in urban politics and governance

Stability is a defining feature of institutions, and traditional institutional approaches can be criticised as 'a-temporal and lacking in a sense of dynamic and change'

(Harding, 1998: 71). New institutionalists, however, argue that institutions are processes, not 'things'. They are concerned with the dynamic processes of institutionalisation that sustain rules over time. March and Olsen (1989: 16) refer to institutions as 'islands of imperfect and temporary organisation in potential inchoate political worlds'. What drives institutionalisation – and what interrupts it – is a matter of debate. Rational choice scholars hold that institutional arrangements persist as long as they serve the utility of dominant political actors (Shepsle, 1989: 134). Normative institutionalists argue that institutions change when 'their value premises have changed or because they are considered incompatible with other values' (Offe, 1996: 685). For discursive institutionalists, change arises out of the interaction of 'epistemic communities' or 'advocacy coalitions' seeking to promote new ideas and narratives (Schmidt, 2006: 113). In a pragmatic vein, Robert Goodin (1996: 24) argues that institutional change typically proceeds through a combination of accident, evolution and intention.

New institutionalists underline the difficulties involved in attempts at the intentional redesign of political institutions. In urban politics, as elsewhere, new institutions are likely to be resisted (or 'hijacked') by those who benefit from existing arrangements or see new rules as hostile to their interests (Lowndes, 1999). New institutional arrangements are frequently adapted in ways that suit locally specific institutional environments. Organisations and groups have an immense capacity 'to co-opt, absorb or deflect new initiatives' (Newman, 2001: 28). 'Old' and 'new' institutions frequently coexist within urban politics, reflecting the balance of power between different groups of actors, as well as signalling the (inevitably) unfinished business of reform. Historical institutionalists go further in arguing that all political institutions are 'path dependent' (see Pierson, 2004). Once a particular institutional design has become embedded, the effects of positive feedback make it very costly to change direction. Path dependency creates a powerful cycle of self-reinforcing activity and there is no reason to assume that the institutional option which becomes 'locked in' is superior to the alternatives that were foregone. In fact, this becomes increasingly less likely as external environments change.

In a period of frenetic activity directed at 'modernising' or 'reinventing' urban governance, new institutionalists are able to distinguish between *organisational* and *institutional change*. While the former involves no more than structural reorganisation, the latter requires that the actual 'rules of behaviour' are altered through specifying and embedding new norms, incentives and sanctions – and developing an associated 'institutional software' of persuasive arguments and convincing discourses (Dryzek, 1996: 204). Elinor Ostrom (1999: 38) draws our attention to the difference between rules-in-form and rules-in-use, which she defines as the distinctive ensemble of 'dos and don'ts that one learns on the ground'. Rather than being a technical exercise, institutional change is inevitably a value-laden, contested and context-dependent process, which typically throws up unanticipated outcomes.

Although new institutionalists argue that attempts at institutional reform rarely satisfy their initiators' intentions, they also contend that such programmes are of enormous importance. Attempts at reform provide an opportunity for 'the discovery, clarification and elaboration' of the values that undergird existing and alternative institutional arrangements, and the way in which they can contribute to the 'good society' (March and Olsen, 1989: 90). Despite the difficulties involved, recent decades have seen no shortage of attempts to shape the institutions of urban politics and governance. Because institutions embody values and power relationships, the prospect of their redesign is likely to continue to seduce politicians – and rightly so!

Putting new institutionalism to work: three case studies

We now exemplify these arguments through three case studies, each of which addresses an important issue in urban politics and governance. We explain briefly the question at hand and then show how new institutionalist insights can cast light upon the phenomenon. Based on the author's original UK-based research, the case studies inevitably reflect a particular cut on new institutionalism (which is a diverse body of theory), and a particular set of empirical realities. The value of the exercise, however, is to show how concepts from new institutionalism can be operationalised in research on urban politics. The iteration between theoretical premises and empirical observation also yields a more nuanced understanding of urban political institutions and processes of change in urban governance.

Case study 1 – Rules matter: explaining local differences in urban political participation

Why do levels of political participation vary between localities? This question, which is significant in the light of traditional theoretical justifications for local self-government, has acquired a new urgency in the context of current (international) policy concern about declining electoral turnouts and methods for stimulating higher levels of participation. The conventional explanation is that areas with higher socioeconomic status (SES) have higher levels of participation (Verba et al., 1995). In Britain, SES does indeed account for most of the variation between localities. However, there are localities that are out of synch with their predicted level of participation. What are the factors that determine why some wealthy areas have unusually low levels of participation, and some disadvantaged areas have vibrant local polities? Can an understanding of these 'deviant' cases contribute to the development of urban political participation?

To investigate this phenomenon, we looked at four pairs of local authorities (see Lowndes et al., 2006). Each pair had a similar SES but different levels of participation, taking into account both electoral and non-electoral activities aimed at influencing local decision-making. The research considered the proposition from social capital theory that norms of trust and high levels of associational activity were associated with political participation (Putnam, 2000). We found that, within our sample, there were localities with high social capital and low participation, and low social capital and high participation. Insights from new institutionalism drew our attention to differences in the institutional frameworks within which citizen participation took place (or didn't). Although formal structures were similar in most localities, the way in which these were elaborated and embedded in rules-in-use made a big difference to citizens' willingness to participate. Indeed, skills and capacities for participation associated with both SES and social capital remained 'latent' where rules-in-use were not conducive, but were activated in those localities where rules enabled and made attractive practices of citizen participation.

Three different rule sets were found to be particularly important. In the party political domain, rules-in-use that favoured strong party competition and regular leadership changes were linked to more active citizen participation. In public management, the formal rules and informal conventions governing interactions between citizens and front-line staff engaged in service delivery were as important as the availability of specialist bodies and forums for participation. Rules-in-use relating to public service delivery affected citizens' perception of the accessibility and responsiveness of the local authority at a general level. Finally, in the civic domain, we found variation in the formal and informal mechanisms that existed to link different local organisations and their activities (networks, umbrella bodies), and the extent to which they provided channels for communication with local policy-makers (forums, scrutiny).

We concluded that rules-in-use in the political, managerial and civic domains combined to produce locally distinctive institutional configurations that enabled, or constrained, public participation. Differences between 'rules-in-use' in each domain were important, but so too were the varied ways in which rules interacted with one another.

As well as throwing light upon the reasons behind differences in citizen participation, the research had a positive message for policy-makers and practitioners. By framing and sustaining rules-in-use, public bodies can provide additional and malleable incentives for participation (beyond SES and social capital, which are notoriously difficult for policy-makers to influence). They can also seek to establish a normative context in which participation is seen as 'appropriate' behaviour (by citizens and decision-makers alike).

Case study 2 – Institutional environments matter: exploring urban political leadership

The Local Government Act 2000 sought to bring a new form of strong, individualised leadership to urban politics in England, aiming at greater accountability, a more outward-oriented focus, and a reduced role for adversarial party politics. The traditional committee system of decision-making was replaced (in all but the smallest local authorities) by new executive arrangements. Local authorities could opt for a directly elected mayor with cabinet or council manager, or a leader and cabinet selected from within the ruling political group(s). Survey evidence shows that the latter, more conservative, option was chosen by over 80 percent of English local authorities; it also reveals that, in writing their individual constitutions, local authorities have tended to minimise the delegation of decision-making powers to individual leaders (Stoker et al., 2003).

But what has happened inside local councils? Is the new institutional framework imposed by the government shaping political behaviour in the ways that were intended? Or has its impact been minimised as suggested by the survey evidence? We undertook case study research in a range of local authorities that had adopted different formal structures (see Lowndes and Leach, 2004; Leach and Lowndes, 2007). We found that the legislation had not generated any move to a more uniform pattern of political leadership. Neither did we find any simple distinction between strong and weak leaders. Looking at rules-in-use rather than rules-in-form, we encountered a picture of considerable diversity within both mayoral and non-mayoral authorities. We concluded that the government's ideal-type of urban political leadership had, to date, been realised only sporadically and partially.

Why is this? Our research highlighted the way in which complex, overlapping institutional environments had shaped the emergence of new rules for urban political leadership. Using Ostrom's distinction, we looked at the way in which collective (or legislative) rules had been translated into operational rules. Local authorities had detected and exploited considerable freedom in the writing of their own constitutions. Constitutions were crafted to reflect existing locally specific conventions about how politics was practised in specific localities (e.g. to maximise the role of the full council in relation to policy-making, or to involve more councillors in decision-making by appointing advisers to cabinet portfolio holders). The embeddedness of formal rules in local institutional environments was further exemplified in the interpretation of the new constitutions, once in place. Depending upon pre-existing local conventions, strong and weak leadership was observed within *both* mayoral and non-mayoral set-ups; similarly, the degree of outward-orientation related as much to established expectations about consultation, as to the formal detail of the new arrangements. Locally specific institutional elements either reinforced or undermined the formal rules for political leadership promulgated by central government.

In addition to these bottom-up pressures, the process of developing new rules for urban political leadership was also, paradoxically, circumscribed by top-down pressures emanating from central government. Leadership practices were being shaped by the incentives and constraints embodied in other elements of the government's modernisation agenda (including, for instance, regional governance and 'comprehensive performance assessment'). Different institutional innovations were not necessarily compatible, and local political actors were left to negotiate a way through tangled webs of regulations, incentives and normative exhortations.

The research revealed the importance of what Hay and Wincott referred to as the interaction 'between institutional architects, institutionalised subjects and institutional environments'. Leaders themselves did not react passively to the external imposition of new rules and structures; rather they interpreted and adapted these in the context of local institutional environments and the competing demands of different top-down innovations. The way in which leadership institutions developed on the ground depended on individual leaders' skill and imagination in navigating between institutional environments, acknowledging competing demands and exercising selectivity and prioritisation in terms of their own roles, and the sharing of leadership responsibilities with a wider group. The research confirmed that challenges to existing institutional settlements are generally met by resistance from some quarters. It takes a skilled institutional architect to navigate between overlapping institutional environments, and to secure change not just in formal rules and structures but also in the conventions and expectations that subtly, but effectively, shape political behaviour.

Case study 3 – How urban politics changes (and stays the same)

This research was stimulated by the seeming incompatibility of two arguments about the pace of change in British urban politics since the 1980s (see Lowndes, 2005). On the one hand, we hear a lot about the 'transformation' of urban politics and governance in the context of 'new public management' and new executive arrangements inside elected local councils, alongside new roles for non-elected bodies, commercial and voluntary sector contractors and multi-agency partnerships. But on the other hand, it is often also argued that – despite several hundred pieces of legislation – local authorities still look very much like they did in 1979: a collection of professionally driven service departments and a form of politics dominated by committee conventions, the party group and the whip.

Are these accounts of British urban governance compatible? If not, which one is (more) correct? Insights from new institutionalism helped to address this conundrum: first, in developing a clearer understanding of the object of analysis, avoiding any unified conception of local government (or, indeed, local governance); second, in focusing upon the coexistence, and interaction, of forces for continuity and change.

The research conceptualised local governance as an 'institutional matrix', made up of distinct (but interacting) rule sets. It found that different rule sets had changed at different rates and in different directions, reflecting power relationships and the 'embeddedness' of local governance in specific historical and spatial contexts. Detailed investigation identified a sharp contrast between the inertia and innovation that had characterised, respectively, the political and managerial domains of local governance. Further research revealed that there also exist creative spaces in between these extremes of institutional stability and volatility. We used the term 'institutional entrepreneur' to refer to the way in which everyday actors seek to adapt 'the rules of the game' in order to meet the demands of uncertain and changing environments, and to protect (or further) their own interests. The research investigates the strategies of such entrepreneurs, showing – for instance – how actors 'borrowed' practices from other arenas, 'remembered' past practices and put them to new uses, and 'shared' the outcomes of institutional experimentation within their wider networks.

The research illuminated the dynamics of institutional change in urban politics. Dominant theoretical models have focused on stop/go models of change – path dependency punctuated by critical junctures – with a focus on exogenous triggers to change (Streeck and Thelen, 2005). This research suggested that change in urban politics is better understood as an emergent process, in which endogenous and exogenous factors combine in the fashioning of new hybrid forms of 'recombinant governance' (Crouch, 2005). Rules-in-use emerge as actors (inhabiting specific local institutional environments) react to, and engage with, external interventions in the formal institutional architecture of urban politics. Lanzara (1998) has coined the term 'institutional *bricolage*' to refer to the patching together of diverse institutional elements – old and new, formal and informal – in elaborating new rules and roles of urban politics. In policy terms, institutional reformers might be well advised to come up with strategies better able to harness this creative energy.

Conclusions and dilemmas

In the 1960s and 1970s, urban political scientists turned their backs on the crude institutionalism of the time, arguing that political decision-making and outcomes could not be explained with reference only to the formal structures and constitutions of elected local government. Institutionalism has, however, been rediscovered as scholars seek to understand change in the urban political landscape. Theoretically, the conviction that 'institutions matter' has once again become respectable. Empirically, the constraints through which urban politics operates have become evermore diverse and entangled.

The new institutionalism is not a single theory. It is better considered as a 'broad, if variegated, approach to politics', held together by Peters' assertion that 'institutions are the variable that explain most of political life, and they are also the factors that require explanation' (Peters, 1999: 150). Unlike its older sister, new institutionalism employs an expansive definition of its subject matter (including informal conventions alongside formal rules and structures) and starts from explicit theoretical premises about the ways in which institutions shape behaviour. Most importantly, perhaps, new institutionalists concern themselves with the ongoing interaction between individual actors and the institutions that constrain them. Individuals and institutions are seen as mutually constitutive. Although there are many 'new institutionalisms', the distance between them seems to be narrowing (Goodin and Klingemann, 1996: 10–11). The special significance of the new institutionalism lies precisely in its capacity to defuse the unconstructive stand-off between structuralists and behaviouralists that has bedevilled not just urban politics but political science more generally.

New institutionalism has much to offer the study of urban politics. At the same time, urban politics presents a particularly fertile field in which to test and refine new institutionalist concepts. Avenues for further research are many. As urban governance fragments, new institutionalists are well placed to map emerging 'rules of the game' and the ways in which they shape the behaviour of local political actors – be they politicians, professionals, activists or ordinary citizens. How do contracts and networks coexist with bureaucratic hierarchies in urban service provision? How do public opinion polls and citizen panels influence politicians vis-à-vis local elections and public meetings? Do incentives and information flows emanating from supranational bodies reinforce or undermine existing regulatory regimes? Identifying overlapping trajectories of change and continuity is a vital research task. Changes in the formal architecture of urban governance are interacting with established rules-in-use, which are themselves embedded in local institutional environments and express particular values and power relationships. Further research is needed on the processes of rule-making, rule-breaking and rule-shaping that are under way in different domains of urban politics.

Questions remain, of course, for the new generation of urban institutionalists. At a theoretical level, sceptics ask whether the cohabitation of rational choice and normative theory is sustainable and, moreover, intellectually defensible (see Hay and Wincott, 1998). In attempting to have our new institutionalist cake and eat it, do we lose theoretical leverage? Do we trade a capacity to explain and predict for nothing more than thick description? New institutionalists are responding through the development of a major body of empirical work designed to test and elaborate concepts (Peters, 2005). And, in some quarters, they are defending thick description for its ability to illuminate the essentially contested and context-dependent character of political institutions (see Bevir and Rhodes, 2006).

At a methodological level, new institutionalism has been criticised for conceptual stretching and the associated dangers of non-falsifiability (see Peters, 1996: 215–6). If we expand the definition of institution to include informal understandings, how can we know when institutions constrain and when they don't? (Actors who ignore formal rules could be seen as following another, invisible, set of informal rules.) The difficulty of identifying and measuring rules-in-use is considerable. New institutionalists are responding by experimenting with a broad repertoire of techniques, which range from ethnography to laboratory studies, historical case studies to game theory (see Ostrom et al., 1996).

At a policy level, new institutionalists have been criticised for stating the obvious – that institutional change is hard to control – and retreating into an 'anything is possible' position that over-emphasises contingency and fails to provide helpful advice to practitioners (Jordan, 1990). But, as we have seen, new institutionalists are able to identify the specific nature of the constraints upon institutional design: that is, the power relationships and the value premises inherent in existing institutional arrangements, and the embedded nature of political institutions. As the juggernaut of local government reform rolls on, new institutionalists can offer advice to urban policy-makers. As this chapter has shown, the most effective reform strategies are likely to be those that seek to debate values and build persuasive arguments and 'institutional software'; and exploit (rather than frustrate) the efforts of those intelligent 'entrepreneurs' on the ground who are able to combine and recombine institutional resources in responding to the new challenges of urban politics.

References

Bevir, M. and Rhodes, R. (2006) *Governance Stories*. London: Routledge.
Blair, T. (1998) *Leading the Way: A New Vision for Local Government*. London: IPPR.
Bogason, P. (2000) *Public Policy and Local Governance: Institutions in Post-Modern Society*. Cheltenham: Elgar.
Clegg, S. (1990) *Modern Organisations*. London: Sage.

Crouch, C. (2005) *Capitalist Diversity and Change: Recombinant Governance and Institutional Entrepreneurs*. Oxford: Oxford University Press.

Dryzek, J. (1996) 'The informal logic of institutional design', in R. Goodin (ed.), *The Theory of Institutional Design*. Cambridge: CUP.

Fox, C. and Miller, H. (1995) *Postmodern Public Administration*. Thousand Oaks, CA: Sage.

Goldsmith, M. (2002) 'Central control over local government – a Western European comparison', *Local Government Studies*, 28 (3): 91–112.

Goodin, R. (1996) 'Institutions and their design', in R. Goodin (ed.), *The Theory of Institutional Design*. Cambridge: CUP.

Goodin, R. and Klingemann, H. (1996) 'Political science: the discipline', in R. Goodin and H. Klingemann (eds), *A New Handbook of Political Science*. Oxford: OUP.

Hall, P. and Taylor, R. (1996) 'Political science and the three new institutionalisms', *Political Studies*, 44 (4): 936–57.

Harding, A. (1995) 'Elite theory and growth machines', in D. Judge, G. Stoker and H. Wolman (eds), *Theories of Urban Politics*. London: Sage.

Harding, A. (1998) 'Public–private partnerships in the UK', in J. Pierre (ed.), *Partnerships in Urban Governance*. London: Macmillan.

Hay, C. and Wincott, D. (1998) 'Structure, agency and historical institutionalism', *Political Studies*, 46: 951–7.

Huntington, S. (1968) *Political Order in Changing Societies*. New Haven: Yale University Press.

John, P. (2001) *Local Governance in Western Europe*. London: Sage.

Jordan, G. (1990) 'Policy community realism *versus* 'new' institutionalist ambiguity', *Political Studies*, 38: 470–84.

Knight, J. (1992) *Institutions and Social Conflict*. Cambridge: CUP.

Lanzara, G. (1998) 'Self-destructive processes in institution building and some modest countervailing mechanisms', *European Journal of Political Research*, 33: 1–39.

Leach, S and Lowndes, V. (2007) 'Of roles and rules: analysing the changing relationship between political leaders and chief executives in local government', *Public Policy and Administration*, 22 (2): 183–200.

Lowndes, V. (1996) 'Varieties of new institutionalism: a critical appraisal', *Public Administration*, 74 (2): 181–97.

Lowndes, V. (1999) 'Management change in local governance', in G. Stoker (ed.), *The New Management of British Local Governance*. London: Macmillan.

Lowndes, V. (2005) 'Something old, something new, something borrowed … how institutions change (and stay the same) in local governance', *Policy Studies*, 26 (3): 291–309.

Lowndes, V. and Leach, S. (2004) 'Understanding local political leadership: constitutions, contexts and capabilities', *Local Government Studies*, 30 (4): 557–75.

Lowndes, V. and Wilson, D. (2001) 'Social capital and local governance: exploring the institutional design variable', *Political Studies*, 49: 629–47.

Lowndes, V., Pratchett, L. and Stoker, G. (2006) 'Local political participation: the impact of rules-in-use', *Public Administration*, 84 (3): 539–61.

March, J. and Olsen, J. (1984) 'The new institutionalism: organisational factors in political life', *American Political Science Review*, 78: 734–49.

March, J. and Olsen J. (1989) *Rediscovering Institutions*. New York: Free Press.

Newman, J. (2001) *Modernising Governance: New Labour, Policy and Society*. London: Sage.

North, D. (1990) *Institutions, Institutional Change and Economic Performance*. Cambridge: Cambridge University Press.

Offe, C. (1996) 'Political economy: sociological perspectives', in R. Goodin and H. Klingemann (eds), *A New Handbook of Political Science*. Oxford: OUP.

Ostrom, E. (1986) 'An agenda for the study of institutions', *Public Choice*, 48: 3–25.

Ostrom, E. (1999) 'Institutional rational choice: an assessment of the institutional analysis and development framework', in P. Sabatier (ed.), *Theories of the Policy Process*. Boulder, CO: Westview. pp. 35–72.

Ostrom, E., Gardner, R. and Walker, J. (1996) *Rules, Games, and Common-Pool Resources*. Ann Arbor, MI: University of Michigan Press.

Peters, G. (1996) ' Political institutions, old and new', in R. Goodin and H. Klingemann (eds), *A New Handbook of Political Science*. Oxford: OUP.

Peters, G. (1999) *Institutional Theory in Political Science: The 'New Institutionalism'*. London: Pinter.

Peters, G. (2005) *Institutional Theory in Political Science: The 'New Institutionalism'*, 2nd edn. London: Continuum.

Pierre, J. (1998) 'Public–private partnerships and urban governance: introduction', in J. Pierre (ed.), *Partnerships in Urban Governance*. London: Macmillan.

Pierre, J. (1999) 'Models of urban governance: the institutional dimension of urban politics', *Urban Affairs Review*, 34 (3): 372–96.

Pierson, P. (2004) *Politics in Time*. Princeton, NJ: Princeton University Press.

Putnam, R. (2000) *Bowling Alone*. New York: Simon and Schuster.

Rhodes, R. (1997) *Understanding Governance*. Buckingham: Open University Press.

Saunders, P. (1979) *Urban Politics: A Sociological Interpretation*. London: Hutchinson.

Schmidt, V. (2006) 'Institutionalism', in C. Hay, M. Lister and D. Marsh (eds), *The State: Theories and Issues*. Basingstoke: Palgrave.

Scott, W. (2001) *Institutions and Organisations*, 2nd edn. Thousand Oaks, CA: Sage.

Shepsle, K. (1989) 'Studying institutions: some lessons from the rational choice approach', *Journal of Theoretical Politics*, 1 (2): 131–47.

Stoker, G. (1995) 'Regime theory and urban politics', in D. Judge, G. Stoker and H. Wolman (eds), *Theories of Urban Politics*. London: Sage.

Stoker, G., Gains, F., Greasley, S., Jolus, P., Rao, N. and Harding, A. (2003) Evaluating Local Governance (ELG) report. London: Office of the Deputy Prime Minister.

Streeck, W. and Thelen, K. (eds) (2005) *Beyond Continuity: Institutional Change in Modern Political Economies*. Oxford: OUP.

Verba, S., Schlozman, K. and Brady, H. (1995) *Voice and Equality: Civic Voluntarism in American Politics*. Cambridge, MA: Harvard University Press.

7

REGIONALISM AND URBAN POLITICS

Hank Savitch and Ronald K. Vogel

Urban scholars have studied questions of metropolitan and regional governance for more than a century utilising four main theoretical framings. First, the *metropolitan government school* sought to have the core city capture growth on the urban fringe so that cities would be metropolitan cities and by definition city government would be metropolitan government. The values underlying the theory were concern for *efficiency* and *equity*. This approach dominated political science from the early 1900s to the 1950s. Indeed, many of the leading works were published in prominent political science journals and there was little differentiating scholars and practitioners. This wave of regionalism is often referred to now as *old regionalism*.

Secondly, the *public choice school* arose in the 1950s and 1960s to account, in part, for the extensive public service delivery system in the metropolis that was not under a core central city government. If there was metropolitan governance, it was not due to an overarching metropolitan government, but rather a series of interlocal agreements and cooperation. The theory is based upon the market model. Cities compete to provide citizens and businesses with the good public services at a low cost or face losing population and companies to growing suburbs. The underlying values are reliance on markets rather than hierarchical organisation to ensure efficiency and effectiveness in public service delivery. Public choice was more empirically based and tended to neglect concern for equity. The local public economies approach of the 1960s and 1970s modified the public choice school by recognising that metropolitan governance arrangements were structured and not just shaped by market processes. The public choice school generally was at odds with most metropolitan policy-makers and practitioners who continued to advocate metropolitan government.

The *new regionalism* is the third major theory of metropolitan and regional governance. This approach evolved in the 1990s. Given the practical difficulties of establishing metropolitan government, less emphasis is placed on structural reform. New regionalists highlighted the continuing problem of city–suburban disparities, particularly in the US context. The public choice school's failure to acknowledge the inability of the market process to address the equity problem was also apparent. Combining the advance offered by the new 'local public economies' school highlighting a more complex metropolitan governance arrangement and the more pragmatic approach to metropolitan reform, a more nuanced and problem-oriented strategy of 'metropolitan governance without government' evolved.

The fourth and most recent theoretical approach to metropolitan and regional governance is *rescaling or reterritorialisation,* which provides a broader theoretical context to account for the new regionalism. Critiques of new regionalism highlighted the lack of empirical evidence to support the so-called successes of metropolitan governance without government. More importantly, Neil Brenner (2004) proposed a more comprehensive and sophisticated understanding of the new regionalism. He proposed that 'new state spaces', that is city-regions, were best understood as part of a larger restructuring of the state in this latest stage of global capitalism.

Each of the theoretical frameworks on metropolitan government is summarised in Table 7.1. In the remainder of the chapter, we review more carefully the theories regarding metropolitan government, the historical evolution of scholarship, and contemporary framings of the issues. We then consider future directions for research in the field.

The metropolitan government school

G. Ross Stephens and Nelson Wikstrom (2000) provide a comprehensive review of the evolution of theories of metropolitan government. Classic studies include Chester Maxey (1922) 'The political integration of metropolitan communities'; Paul Studenski (1930) *The Government of Metropolitan Areas in the United States* and Victor Jones (1942) *Metropolitan Government* (see Stephens and Wikstrom, 2000). The central concern of these scholars was that fragmentation of local government leads to inefficient and ineffective public services. Fragmentation divides the metropolis which is a single social and economic community. As a consequence, there is great inequality in the distribution and finance of public services, problems coordinating services, and an inability to address regional problems. Robert Wood (1958, 1961) provided the strongest indictment of the chaotic and fragmented system of metropolitan government. He charged the system was antidemocratic since citizens could not determine who was responsible for what policies and services. Wood was highly sceptical of the claim that small town government represented the Jeffersonian ideal given the low level of voter turnout in suburban elections. Scott Greer (1962) suggested that suburban governments dealt with narrow and parochial issues that trivialise politics.

The proposed solution is structural change to produce political integration in the metropolis. More incremental approaches such as annexation were viewed as insufficient since there is so much citizen opposition to central city expansion. Initial metropolitan reform focused on city–county consolidation to create a metropolitan city. Indeed, a number of central cities in the US consolidated with their county governments in the 1800s, including New Orleans (1805), Philadelphia (1854), San Francisco (1856) and New York (1898).

Table 7.1   Theoretical frameworks on regionalism

	Metropolitan government (Old regionalism)	Public choice (Polycentrism)	New regionalism	Rescaling and reterritorialisation
Time-frame	1900–1960s	1950s–1990s	1990 to present	2006 to present
Core focus	Efficiency	Effectiveness	Equity	City competitiveness
Pattern of urban development	Monocentric	Multi-centred metropolis but core still dominant	Multi-centred metropolis but core less dominant	Megalopolis
Problem	Fragmentation	Centralisation	Equity and competitiveness	Competitiveness
Solution	Hierarchy Establish metropolitan government (e.g., annexation, consolidation, or new tier)	Market Rely on market competition, which leads cities to keep taxes low, provide good public services, and a good business climate to attract businesses and residents	Hierarchy/cooperation Government plus governance in city-region; focus on strategic metropolitan decisions either through consolidation or governance arrangements	Rescaling/Restructuring Economic globalisation leading to sub-national (local) state restructuring involving realignment of boundaries, roles, functions, and resources and relations with private and non-governmental actors
Major critique	Evidence that consolidation may lead to higher costs and lack of responsiveness (Bish and Ostrom, 1979) Two-tier metropolitan	Lack of equity as poor can't move easily (Warren et al., 1992) Citizens do not behave as Tiebout model predicts and they lack information	Selective and weak regionalism (Frisken and Norris, 2001; Lefèvre, 1998) Unlikely to reduce disparities (Altshuler et al., 1999)	Tendency towards economic determinism, high level of abstraction, and 'absence of politics' (Le Galès, 2006; also see Beauregard, 2006)

Table 7.1 (Continued)

	Metropolitan government (Old regionalism)	Public choice (Polycentrism)	New regionalism	Rescaling and reterritorialisation
	government leads to better infrastructure development and planning but not equity (Self, 1982) Problem of minority dilution (Powell, 2000) Political infeasibility (Downs, 1994)	about tax and services provided by localities to make informed choices about location (Lyons et al., 1992)	Misnomer and reflects 'post-fordist urban restructuring and neoliberal ... state retrenchment' (Brenner, 2002)	Provides higher level theory of what is driving state restructuring but little normative guidance on whether the local region should embrace or resist
Selected works	• Charles Beard (1923) • William Robson (1939) • Robert Wood (1961) • US ACIR (1976)	• Charles Tiebout (1956) • Vincent Ostrom et al. (1961) • Roger Parks and Ronald Oakerson (1989)	• David Rusk (1993) • H.V. Savitch and Ronald K. Vogel (1996) • Altshuler et al. (1999)	• Neil Brenner (2004) • Michael Keating et al. (2003)
Empirical reference points	New York City (1898) Toronto (1954) Miami (1958) London (1965)	Los Angeles (Lakewood Plan) St. Louis Pittsburgh	Louisville (1986–2000) Bologna Rotterdam Portland	World cities

In the early and mid-twentieth century, city–county consolidation and the more incremental annexation approach proved increasingly difficult to pass. The metropolitan reform agenda turned to establishing an overarching metropolitan government with responsibility for providing area-wide or regional services on top of the existing municipal system responsible for more local or neighbourhood services. These recommendations were embraced by groups such as the US Advisory Commission on Intergovernmental Relations (1976), the Committee for Economic Development (CED) (1970) and the League of Women Voters (1974). In the US, the main obstacle to implementing these reforms is that they require the authorising of state legislation or constitutional change and by convention must be submitted to the voters in a referendum.

Metropolitan government is associated with a number of benefits. First, metropolitan government reduces fiscal imbalances between central cities and suburbs through metropolitan-wide tax and finance schemes. Secondly, metropolitan governments provide a capacity to engage in strategic planning for the region. Thirdly, metropolitan governments facilitate large-scale transportation planning and adoption of more balanced transportation policy including the development of mass transit (Self, 1982; Barlow, 1991; Keating, 1995).

There are a number of criticisms of metropolitan government. First, there is little evidence that greater efficiencies or economies of scale actually occur with the establishment of metropolitan government or city–county consolidation (Horan and Taylor, 1977; Benton and Gamble, 1983; Condrey, 1994). A piercing critique of the metropolitan government approach is provided by Robert Bish and Vincent Ostrom (1979) in the book, *Understanding Urban Government: Metropolitan Reform Reconsidered*. They point out that the metropolitan government school lacks empirical evidence that services provided by a number of local governments are more costly, inefficient or unresponsive to citizens. Rather, they find the metropolitan reform agenda rests on a series of untested assumptions. Elinor Ostrom's withering critique of moncentrist government's faulty assumption and its lack of evidence added to the credibility of public choice (2000). So effective was the public choice critique that there is now widespread scholarly consensus that metropolitan government does not lead to greater efficiency or effectiveness (Altshuler et al., 1999).

Secondly, creating metropolitan governments threatens political gains of the minorities, especially blacks in the US. In Jacksonville, Nashville, Louisville and Indianapolis, blacks suffered significant decline in political power (Vogel and Harrigan, 2007: 285–7). The power base of minorities is weakened in the new city and the metropolitan government ends up being dominated by the suburbanites (Swanson, 1996; Savitch and Vogel, 2004).

Thirdly, although metropolitan governments perform system maintenance functions well (e.g., water supply, sewerage treatment and transportation), they focus on the growing suburbanising periphery, which frequently lacks infrastructure, rather than the urban core (Williams, 1971). Fourthly, metropolitan governments scarcely and at best only partially address the unequal access to suburban lifestyles that is often promoted as a major rationale for establishing the metropolitan government in the first place (Harrigan, 1996). For example, while the seven-county Minneapolis–St. Paul

Metropolitan Council did begin some revenue sharing on new development, less than half of the new taxes go to other localities in the region, which is an insignificant fraction of local budgets. Also, the Metropolitan Council's experiment with fair share housing has not altered racial polarisation within the Twin Cities region and shows no marked diversion from similar areas without metropolitan government.

The public choice school alternative

The Public Choice School traces its roots to Charles Tiebout's (1956) classic article, 'A pure theory of local expenditures' and is elaborated by Vincent Ostrom and colleagues' (1961) 'The organization of government in metropolitan areas: a theoretical inquiry.' For public choice scholars, fragmentation of local government is a virtue rather than a vice to be corrected. The public choice school relies on the market as the organising mechanism to provide and coordinate basic public services in the metropolitan area. Local government fragmentation leads local governments to compete for residents and businesses and thus encourages them to keep taxes low, provide efficient low-cost public services and be responsive to citizens. The market disciplines local government leaders. The danger is that misguided reform, for example city–county consolidation, leads to over-centralisation, which undermines democratic self-governance. Fred Siegel (1997) argues that liberal big city mayors engaged in profligate spending led to bloated city bureaucracies, poor services and high taxes. Eventually, citizens and businesses revolted by *exiting* the community (see Hirschman, 1970). Over time, declining populations and business disinvestment led voters to select more conservative and fiscally responsible mayors who responded by privatising services, reducing liberal excess and cutting spending, leading to better and more efficient services to recapture growth by luring back citizens and businesses and thus saving their cities.

There are a number of criticisms of the public choice school. First, critics charge that it disregards the lack of *equity* in the finance and distribution of urban services (Warren et al., 1992). Allowing numerous and privileged suburban municipalities permits middle- and upper-class residents to escape their moral responsibility to contribute to the core city's fiscal, economic and social well-being. Local autonomy and zoning authority allows the newly incorporated suburban cities to engage in exclusionary zoning practices, creating affluent communities with only large, single family homes. As Anthony Downs (1994) explains, these small cities put into place a number of regulations regarding building materials, minimum lot size, minimum square footage and minimum setbacks, which increase housing costs. No space is provided for multi-family housing, limiting the ability of the poor to move to these communities. And suburbanites fail to contribute to the cost of providing expensive infrastructure and services in the urban core. (Few cities in the US have an income or commuter tax.)

It is obvious that under public choice assumptions, low-income residents lack the resources to move to the suburbs and so 'exit' is not an option for them. Public choice has not only failed to take account of its upper-middle-class assumptions, but rather egregiously ignores those who cannot afford to move. Its class bias also assumes that 'places' can be exchanged, like poker chips on a gambler's table and disregards the emotive that 'place' holds for those who lack mobility, particularly blue collar workers, the elderly and ethnic minorities who rely on neighbours and local institutions for daily needs .

Secondly, many point out that the fragmented metropolis can hardly be viewed as having an *efficient* arrangement for providing public services. Although local governments do selectively cooperate to create metropolitan-wide special districts and interlocal government agreements to gain the benefits of economies of scale, there is little overarching coordination. Critics would also point out that without a strong body making tough decisions over authoritative allocation of values, any meaningful metropolitan cooperation is not possible (Norris, 2001). Metropolitan cooperation, where it occurs, tends to be limited to non-controversial issues and weak. Thus, local governments will work together on purchasing cooperatives but compete on business attraction (Savitch and Vogel, 1996). Thirdly, Lyons and colleagues (1992) find citizens do not behave in ways the Tiebout model suggests. Citizens do not have information about the alternative tax and services provided by localities when making location choices. This calls into question the underlying theoretical assumption of the public choice model.

New regionalism

Urbanists have been rethinking the nature of metropolitan governance over the last decade. In the past, scholars called for metropolitan cities or the establishment of metropolitan *government* as a solution to functional and territorial fragmentation of local government in the metropolis. Metropolitan *government*, which stressed formal, vertical institutions, was viewed as a way to enhance efficiency, effectiveness, accountability and equity. Now scholars talk of metropolitan *governance*, which stresses informal horizontal networks and they are more concerned with reducing disparities between the central cities and suburbs. Many of these studies are lumped together under the label 'new regionalism', reflecting the development of a new paradigm of metropolitan governance and growing consensus between followers of public choice and metropolitan government advocates.

Roger Parks and Ronald Oakerson rescue public choice with their reformulation of public choice as *local public economies* (1989, 2000). They distinguish production from provision of public services so that a local government may provide for garbage collection (provision) but then contract out for the service with private vendors (production) to gain efficiencies and economies of scale without actually consolidating the service or governments. Polycentrism or decentralisation allows citizens and officials to find the right scale to provide services while promoting competition to ensure cost-effective and efficient services. An ongoing local constitutional process occurs over changes in boundaries, services and institutional processes so that a local system of 'governance' is created and evolves over time to meet citizens' needs. Parks and Oakerson (2000) find that metropolitan reformers fail to appreciate that there is a 'complex system' of local governance in the metropolitan area. These authors emphasise that a *new regionalism* needs to be matched with a *new localism*. By this they mean that getting bigger also requires getting smaller. Neighbourhood residents need greater control over the quality and quantity of services they receive. Unfortunately, the evolving complex system of metropolitan governance has not been able to reduce the growing disparities between central city and suburban residents in the US (Altshuler et al., 1999).

Although many advocates of metropolitan government still favour strong metropolitan government, they have increasingly recognised the political obstacles (Downs, 1994). Metropolitan or regional governments are squeezed between higher and lower governmental levels making them vulnerable to attack from above and below. In the 1990s, there was a worldwide retreat from metropolitan governments, most apparent in the disbandment of the Greater London Council (Sharpe, 1995). Even highly successful models, such as that of Toronto's federated metropolitan government, struggled. The continuing outward spread of the metropolis rendered the existing boundaries inadequate for regional policy making (Feldman, 1995).

New regionalism developed in the 1990s as urbanists increasingly recognised the interdependence of the city and suburbs (see Savitch et al., 1993; Barnes and Ledebur, 1994). The population continued to spread outwards to suburbs, exurbs and edge cities. New regionalists recognised that the city-region, not the city, was the relevant unit for competing in the world economy. For new regionalists, the urban crisis today revolves around the racial, economic and social disparities between cities, including older inner ring suburbs, and newer more outlying suburbs (Rusk, 1993; Orfield, 1997; Altshuler et al., 1999).

The new regionalist policy agenda calls for reducing social, economic and fiscal disparities between the core cities and their suburbs. Thus, new regionalists favour tax sharing among local governments to ensure an adequate tax base for localities, affordable housing in the suburbs to reduce segregation and address the spatial mismatch in jobs and residence, and smart growth policies to stop federal, state and local governments from investing resources to service growth that promotes sprawl and channel growth back to the central city. New regionalists call for more resources and autonomy for local governments to address their problems and to structure intergovernmental relations in such a way as to achieve new regionalist ends (Savitch and Vogel, 2000a).

Some areas, such as Louisville in the 1980s and 1990s, Washington DC and Pittsburgh achieved a modicum of coordination through mutual adjustment. This may take the form of interlocal government agreements or public–private partnerships. In Louisville, for example, the city and county negotiated a comprehensive compact to share tax revenue, place a moratorium on new municipal incorporations and annexation, and jointly fund and manage a number of services including public transit, libraries and sewers (Savitch and Vogel, 2000b). This is a problem-oriented approach rather than a structuralist approach.[1]

There are some divisions among new regionalists. For example, former Albuquerque Mayor David Rusk (1993) believes central cities are not sustainable without city–county consolidation. He argues that consolidation will lead to more regional equity as the new metropolitan governments promote affordable housing in the suburbs and deconcentrated poverty in the central city. Leading urbanists Peter Dreier, John Mollenkopf and Todd Swanstrom (2004) view regionalism as essential to saving the cities and view the Louisville case positively. Savitch and Vogel (2004) are less sanguine about city–county consolidation as a means to promote equity. Studying the Louisville case, they point out consolidated cities are dominated by suburban constituencies and minority dilution undermines the power of inner city black populations, which have gained political power with the civil rights movement. These authors point out those rigid types of regionalism like city–county consolidation cannot accommodate development beyond the newly merged area. Consolidated government is often frozen by static boundaries and inflexible governmental institutions. Savitch and Vogel (2000b) argue that a new regionalism agenda can be further advanced by focusing less on structural reform and more on enhancing governance arrangements such as compacts, federations and cooperative agreements.

New regionalists have sought to identify empirical reference points to consider whether new regionalism may succeed where metropolitan government and public choice has not. The metropolitan government school approach of consolidation or large-scale metropolitan government has little relevance to the problems confronting metropolitan regions today. Similarly, the public choice school offers little help to policymakers or scholars seeking to address urban ills. Greater reliance on markets does not mean the lot of the poor is improved or lead to government cooperation in the metropolitan region. Thus, new regionalists focused on establishing a set of real world models of metropolitan governance. New regionalists and critics then explored whether these models were effective at reducing the growing urban–suburban disparities, enhancing regional growth policies to reduce sprawl, producing affordable housing in the suburbs, and leading to a more competitive city in the world economy.

The new regionalism record has been disappointing. The new regionalism agenda has not been fully embraced and is unproven in practice (Lefèvre, 1998; Frisken and Norris, 2001; Norris, 2001; Vogel and Nezelkewicz, 2002). Louisville probably represented the most far-reaching experiment with its compact in the 1980s and 1990s. However, civic leaders and reformers favoured outright city–county consolidation and the compact was not renewed. Moreover, the larger metropolitan region – the remaining counties in the metropolitan area – were not integrated into a regional decision-making framework, at least not in a meaningful way (Vogel and Nezelkewicz, 2002). Other examples of mutual adjustment, such as Washington DC and Pittsburgh, and even those with formal metropolitan government, such as Portland and Minneapolis St. Paul, have rather weak regionalism institutional arrangements and policies. David Imbroscio (2006) suggests that the 'inside game' of community development has been abandoned without evidence that an 'outside game' (regionalism) will bring greater gains to the poor and minorities in the city.

There is little evidence that the new regionalism will reduce disparities between the cities and suburbs (Altshuler et al., 1999). Although there has been much discussion of new metropolitan governance systems, the rhetoric far exceeds their performance (Lefèvre, 1998). Further, Neil Brenner (2002) argued that new regionalists were misunderstanding the larger point about new regional dynamics. He argued that new regionalism reflected a 'postfordist urban restructuring and neoliberal (national and local) state retrenchment' rather than experimentation over new forms of regional governance to realise local autonomy and ameliorate the urban crisis (2002: 3).

Rescaling and reterritorialisation: extending new regionalism

Over time, new regionalism has been recast into a broader theoretical framing and we label that *rescaling and reterritorialisation* to distinguish it from the earlier new regionalism. The city-region remains the focal point. Scholars observe 'a series of distinctive phenomena that we might generally refer to as "city-regions" are indeed making their appearance as major elements of the current world scene, and that the advent is intrinsically related to intensifying levels of globalization' (Scott, 2001: xiv). Allen Scott explains that new regionalism 'is rooted in a series of dense nodes of human labor and communal life scattered across the world' (2001: 1).

> These nodes constitute distinctive subnational (i.e. regional) social transformations due to the impacts of globalization. Many of them are foci of significant new experiments in local political mobilization and reorganization as different social groups within them strive to deal with the stresses and strains to which they are increasingly subject as a result of globalization. Many of them, too, are now starting to take on definite identity and force as economic and political actors on the world stage. The new regionalism, then, differs in the first instance from an older regionalism in which the individual regions within any national territory were apt to be much more subservient to the dictates (but also more shielded from outside turbulence by the protective cloak) of the central state. (2001: 1)

Neil Brenner's (2004) *New State Spaces* proposes a more dramatic and grand theory to account for the new regionalism. Brenner argues that at the meso-level, we are witnessing the restructuring of the modern state from the 1980s to the present, following the crisis and failures of Keynesian economics in the 1970s. He theorises that modern capitalism requires a reconstituted state scale around the city-region. The resultant new regionalism experiments are responses to these pressures. Western Europe forms the backdrop to consider how and why these changes are occurring.

The main critique of the rescaling and reterritorialisation paradigm, at least as presented by Brenner, is that it has a strong tendency towards economic determinism and is highly abstract (Beauregard, 2006). As the argument is currently presented, this kind of economic determinism robs reterritorialisation of any political will and by some empirical accounts is not accurate (Savitch, 1988). In addressing the broader features of economic change and their consequences for the modern state, there is an 'absence of politics' (Le Galès, 2006) in the same way that Sassen (2001) articulates a theory of global cities in New York, London and Tokyo without specifically articulating the politics of creating global cities and the points at which there was political choice and human agency leading to global city formation.

The reconstitution of the modern state can be observed in the territorial review studies undertaken by the Organisation for Economic Co-operation and Development (OECD, 2007) over the last decade. OECD is responding to the shift from a

> managerial mode of governance which is primarily concerned with effective provision of social welfare services to citizens to that of entrepreneurialism, strongly characterised by a pro-economic growth strategic approach, risk-taking, innovation and an orientation toward the private-sector. (2007: 3)

OECD recommendations include deregulation, political decentralisation and privatisation, alongside greater metropolitan and regional decision-making capacity to enhance the economic competitiveness of city-regions in the world economy. What is most striking is the explicit substitution of entrepreneurialism and facilitating the market and rejection of redistributive values.

There are a number of scholars who point to *reterritorialisation* to highlight that territory and politics are being rescaled within nations with evidence of a shift from national to regional and local levels (Keating, 2001). There is also a rescaling process within metropolitan cities to create or strengthen metropolitan decision-making capacity and to shift more local services downwards to new or reinvigorated lower units (Stoker, 2004; Denters and Rose, 2005). At the local and regional levels, this urban restructuring is leading to new governance arrangements for metropolitan areas (Hoffmann-Martinot and Sellers, 2005).

The reterritorialisation process is primarily aimed at enhancing the economic competitiveness of world cities (Scott, 2001). Regional government played a major role in the development of global cities both in terms of redesigning the city to meet the needs of global capital and in enhancing economic competitiveness through infrastructure development and government policies (Savitch, 1988; Fainstein, 1994). Changing the territorial boundaries and institutional arrangements of governance for metropolitan cities is viewed as integrally related to leadership capacity and development strategy and therefore the competitiveness of the city in the world economy. This is illustrated by comparing recent reforms in Toronto and London.

The former city of Toronto and Metro Toronto were amalgamated in 1998 into the new city of Toronto. The Greater Toronto Area (GTA) taskforce was set up because of concerns that Toronto was losing its economic competitiveness. The taskforce pointed to the city-region as the relevant economic unit for competing in the world economy. Since the region had grown beyond the existing Toronto Metro boundaries, the taskforce recommended a new regional governance arrangement for the GTA. However, the taskforce believed that a large centralised and hierarchical, metropolitan government would be inefficient and impractical. Rather, the taskforce focused on proposing a looser overarching governance arrangement while leaving existing local governments in place.

Originally, the taskforce was set up in 1995 by the Ontario New Democratic Party (NDP), a left-leaning labour oriented party. However, shortly afterwards, the Progressive Conservative party came into power. The new government rejected the taskforce recommendations and instead proposed amalgamation of the existing Toronto Metro with the cities in its boundary, the largest being Toronto. The remaining GTA governments were excluded from the amalgamation. Thus, the federative model was abandoned and no new overarching regional government was created. The amalgamation was imposed by the Province and occurred even though there was significant local opposition (Horak, 1998; Sancton, 2000).

Clearly, reterritorialisation in Toronto resulted from the interplay of politics and economics. Many believe the Conservative government sought to punish the progresssive regime in Toronto that opposed it. Initially, Premier Mike Harris proposed eliminating the Metro tier and leaving the municipalities in place. The concerns voiced in the Provincial elections were the need to save money, reduce intense inter-local conflict and perceived Metro incompetence. However, the Tory government found that eliminating Metro was impractical since it accounted for about 70 percent of local expenditures in its role as regional service provider. If Metro was dismantled, then an alternative would be needed such as special districts. Therefore, the province turned to amalgamation and eliminated the lower-tier municipalities. The rest of the region that had been the original GTA taskforce concern was left out of the equation since the Conservative government drew much of its support from there and did not wish to antagonise its core electroral constituency, which was vigorously opposed to being incorporated into the new city of Toronto (Vogel, 2007).

After a decade of turmoil and scandal, the new city of Toronto appears to be stabilising (Vogel, 2007). The city under a progressive mayor, David Miller, and province, under a Liberal Ontario premier, McGinty, have recently agreed on a new city charter with greater powers for the city including stronger powers for the mayor. The rationale for the original amalgamation and the new charter are to enhance the competitiveness of the city of Toronto in the world economy. However, the final result is a throwback to the progressive regionalism of the mid-twentieth century. A short-lived experiment with a Greater Toronto Services Board (GTSB) would have tied the amalgamated city into a common assembly with the neighbouring regional governments. This plan was aborted after a two-year experiment. The suburban counties with a more conservative ideology and party base balked at sharing resources and decision-making with the more radical city of Toronto.

A contrasting case is London. In 1986, the Greater London Council (GLC) was abolished after conflicting with Prime Minister Margaret Thatcher's Conservative revolution (Sharpe, 1995). In 1997, Tony Blair ran on a New Labour platform including the return of some form of government for greater London. The Greater London Authority (GLA) was established in 1999 including both a strong executive mayor and metropolitan assembly. Elections for the new government were held in 2000. At the time of the demise of the GLC, the central government directly assumed responsibility for strategic direction for London. The restoration of a regional government for London is a major step towards devolution. However, the central government continues to play a strong hand in regional and development policy in London. The boroughs also remain strong. This leads to a new regional politics playing out as the GLA seeks greater latitude from central control without antagonising the boroughs. The GLA has three strategic policy areas under its domain: traffic and transport policy, crime and policing, and economic development. Former Mayor Ken Livingstone surprised even his critics with a number of early successes. At the same time the GLA was being reborn, the British government was pursuing a broad set of policies aimed at promoting greater devolution. Initially, these efforts focused on strengthening regions for economic development. More recently, the creation of regional assemblies in Northern Ireland, Scotland and Wales has led to dramatic devolution.

Scholars are somewhat ambivalent about whether the new London governance arrangements actually represent significant devolution. Thornley (2003) and Tomaney (2002) highlight the role of an elected mayor in pursuing an independent metropolitan strategy sometimes at odds with the central government and ministries. However, many point to the very limited authority of the GLA and the mayor especially compared to other world cities (Travers, 2002; 2004; Hambleton and Sweeting, 2004; Newman and Thornley, 2005).

─────── **The regional challenge and future directions for research** ───────

Today, metropolitan and regional scholars continue to explore old regionalism questions while adding new regionalism ones to the mix. However, research is less likely to be framed in the traditional old style metropolitan government or public choice school language (Campbell and Durning, 2000). Research questions include:

1 Does local government fragmentation lead to less efficient and effective public services?
2 Does metropolitan government lead to fewer disparities between central cities and suburbs on race, class and income?
3 Under what conditions can boundaries of government be extended, metropolitan government created, or interlocal cooperation fostered?
4 What is driving the rescaling and reterritorialisation processes and what are the implications for local democracy?

The most extensive set of answers to the first two questions was provided by The Committee on Improving the Future of US Cities Through Improved Metropolitan Area Governance under the National Academy of Sciences (Altshuler et al., 1999). The committee concluded: 'The preponderance of evidence indicates that small local governments (and thus metropolitan areas characterised by fragmentation) are more efficient for labor-intensive services (because of economies of scale) and for certain overhead functions' (1999: 106). The committee also concluded that 'consolidation has not reduced costs ... [and] may have even increased local expenditures' (1999: 106). The committee found no evidence that metropolitan reform would have a 'significant impact on redistributing income or on addressing the problems of the poor or racial minorities' (1999: 106–7).

For example, a symposium in *Public Administration Quarterly* (Campbell and Durning, 2000) focused on 'Is city–county consolidation good policy?' and sought to provide contemporary answers to the question of whether metropolitan consolidation led to lower costs, greater efficiency and more effective public services. This symposium suggested that 'future research on consolidation should not focus on confirming or disconfirming the two dominant models' (metropolitan government and public choice). For these scholars, the 'key research question is not whether city–county consolidation is good public policy in general but whether it is a good idea for a specific set of governments that are considering merger' (2000: 139).

Focusing upon the third question on the likelihood of adopting metropolitan reform, Suzanne Leland and Kurt Thurmaier (2004) tested the long-accepted classic Rosenbaum and Kammerer (1974) *power deflation* model to account for metropolitan reform. Under the model, a local government system fails to respond to a severe crisis leading to delegitimation. Then, an *accelerator* such as a scandal leads to a collapse of the old order and its replacement by a new one. They led a team of scholars carrying out a series of case studies to test the conventional wisdom. They found the thesis was not supported. They concluded that in the contemporary era, those places that linked city–county consolidation and by implication metropolitan reform, to enhanced economic development were more likely to be successful. Thus, the reform agenda they believe has shifted from efficiency to economic development. Alternatively, Richard Feiock and Jered Carr (2001) point to a political logic rather than an economic logic to explain successful metropolitan reform (see also Feiock et al., 2006)[3].

New regionalists emphasise that metropolitan governance arrangements are the result of a long-term negotiated process of structuring governance among and between local, state/provincial and central governments and private actors (Savitch and Vogel, 2000a; Parks and Oakerson, 2000). Single over-arching metropolitan governments are unlikely to be created today and existing ones must struggle to connect to the ever-expanding regional scale. Thus, governance, strategic decision-making and intergovernmental management become central concerns.

The fourth question has been most vigorously pressed by Neil Brenner (2002) who argues that the modern capitalist state is reorganising around the city-region. The problem for scholars is how to objectively discern the factors driving rescaling and reterritorialisation and the difficulty of inferring motives. For example, is rescaling driven by local civic elites operating on neo-liberal prescriptions such as following the advice of OECD, or is it the force of global capital with little local choice? Grand theory tends to push political choice to the side but urbanists have long pointed to the importance of human choice, even if circumscribed by larger economic forces. The challenge for scholars is to design studies that link these separate research questions together.

Conclusion

Historically, the field has been dominated by two normative theories about the way to finance and provide services in the metropolis. In the nineteenth and twentieth centuries, proponents of *metropolitan government* sought to expand the city's territorial boundaries through annexation or consolidation to create a metropolitan city. Local government fragmentation was viewed as an impediment to efficient and effective government services leading to waste and duplication. In the mid-twentieth century, the *public choice* school challenged the need for metropolitan government. Public choice scholars pointed to the lack of empirical evidence to support metropolitan reform assumptions. The public choice perspective offered an alternative market model identifying fragmentation as a virtue leading to greater competition among localities to provide high quality services and meet the needs of citizens and businesses.

Metropolitan government advocates responded that poor residents had little choice about where to reside. They pointed to the fragmented system of local government which locked low-income residents in the central city with inferior services and declining revenues while more affluent residents could flee to the suburbs and escape responsibility for inner city problems. Public choice critics countered that empirical evidence contradicted reform assumptions that centralisation increases efficiency.

In the mid-twentieth century, the metropolitan government school was modified to emphasise the benefits of two-tiered metropolitan government. In the 1980s, a more nuanced public choice perspective evolved in the US under the label *local public economies*. This view acknowledged the critique that the public choice perspective did not adequately address inequalities resulting from the fragmented system of local government.

There has been some convergence among adherents of the two main theoretical perspectives on two key issues. First, the rationale for metropolitan government focuses less on the criteria of efficiency and more on enhancing economic competitiveness of the city-region. Scholars and reformers frequently cite globalisation as a factor stimulating metropolitan reform. Secondly, metropolitan reform proposals focus more on structuring a system of governance rather than a centralised metropolitan government. Today, scholars and practitioners alike tend to frame their analysis in the language of *new regionalism* or *rescaling the city* rather than the more traditional language of metropolitan government. However, the central issues remain about the best way to organise the system of metropolitan governance and its consequences. There is also a disjuncture between scholars and practitioners, with the former finding little compelling evidence to support reform prescriptions while the latter often accept on faith the benefits of reform.

The local public economies research agenda (Parks and Oakerson, 2000) is now indistinguishable from the new regionalism research agenda (Savitch and Vogel, 2002a) except for the language employed. Most excitingly, the idea of reterritorialisation offers scholars an opportunity to account for agency in urban politics. Thus, linking territory and power contains a host of possibilities for explaining how cities are being shaped for future generations. This has the potential to help revitalise the field of urban politics and propel it back into the mainstream of political science.

Notes

1 The other two approaches for local metropolises to address the regional agenda identified by Savitch and Vogel (1996) were avoidance and conflict and instituting formal metropolitan government. St. Louis, New York and Los Angeles are characterised by the avoidance and conflict pattern with little evidence of regional collaboration among local governments. The third pattern, metropolitan government, exists in a small number of US cases such as Minneapolis–St. Paul and Portland, or with respect to city–county consolidation, in Nashville, Jacksonville, Indianapolis, and most recently Louisville. Savitch and Vogel view Louisville as an aberration and are sceptical that there will be more such cases. Internationally, London metropolitan government has been reestablished but in a much looser form and perhaps representing a hybrid of mutual adjustment and metropolitan government.
2 This was not anticipated by the Ministry of Municipal Affairs. In saving the Metro tier, the Minister had not realised that the lower tier would have to be sacrificed (Vogel, 2007).
3 Feiock and colleagues emphasise the structure of the argument (heresthetics) to explain the success of some mergers.

References

Altshuler, Alan, Morrill, William, Wolman, Harold and Mitchell, Faith (eds) (1999) *Governance and Opportunity in Metropolitan America*. Washington, DC: National Academy Press.
Barlow, I.M. (1991) *Metropolitan Government*. New York: Routledge.
Barnes, William R. and Ledebur, Larry C. (1994) *Local Economies: The U.S. Common Market of Local Economic Regions*. Washington, DC: National League of Cities.
Beard, Charles (1923) *The Administration and Politics of Tokyo*. New York: Macmillan.
Beauregard, Robert A. (2006) 'Book review: *New State Spaces: Urban Governance and the Rescaling of Statehood*,' *Urban Affairs Review*, 41: 416–18.
Benton, Edwin J. and Gamble, Darwin (1983) 'City/county consolidation and economies of scale: evidence from a time-series analysis in Jacksonville, Florida,' *Social Science Quarterly*, 65: 190–8.
Bish, L. Robert and Ostrom, Vincent (1979) *Understanding Urban Government: Metropolitan Reform Reconsidered*. Washington, DC: America Enterprise Institute for Policy Research.
Brenner, Neil (2002) 'Decoding the newest 'metropolitan regionalism' in the USA: a critical overview,' *Cities*, 19 (1): 3–21.
Brenner, Neil (2004) *New State Spaces: Urban Governance and the Rescaling of Statehood*. Oxford: Oxford University Press.
Campbell, Richard W. and Durning, Dan (2000) 'Is city-county consolidation good policy? A symposium,' *Public Administration Quarterly*, 24: 133–9.
Condrey, Stephen (1994) 'Organizational and personnel impacts on local government consolidation: Athens-Clarke County, Georgia,' *Journal of Urban Affairs*, 16 (4): 371–83.
Denters, S.A.H. and Rose, Lawrence (eds) (2005) *Comparing Local Governance: Trends and Developments*. New York: Palgrave Macmillan.
Downs, Anthony (1994) *New Visons for Metropolitan America*. Washington, DC: Brookings.
Dreier, Peter, Mollenkopf, John and Swanstrom, Todd (2004) *Place Matters Metropolitics for the Twenty-first Century*, 2nd edn. Lawrence, KS: University Press of Kansas.

Fainstein, Susan (1994) *The City Builders: Property, Politics and Planning in London and New York.* Cambridge, MA: Blackwell.

Feiock, Richard C. and Carr, Jered B. (2001) 'Incentives, entrepreneurs, and boundary change: a collective action framework', *Urban Affairs Review*, 36: 382–405.

Feiock, Richard C., Carr, Jered B. and Johnson, Linda S. (2006) 'Structuring the debate on consolidation: a response to Leland and Thurmaier', *Public Administration Review*, 66 (2): 274–8.

Feldman, Lionel D. (1995) 'Metro Toronto: old battles – new challenges', in L.J. Sharpe, *The Government of World Cities: The Future of the Metro Model.* New York: John Wiley and Sons.

Frisken, Frances and Norris, Don (2001) 'Regionalism reconsidered', *Journal of Urban Affairs*, 23: 467–78.

Greer, Scott (1962) *The Emerging City.* New York: Free Press.

Hambleton, R. and Sweeting, D. (2004) 'U.S.-style leadership for English local government?,' *Public Administration Review*, 64 (4): 474–88.

Harrigan, John (1996) 'Minneapolis–St. Paul: Structuring metropolitan government', in H.V. Savitch and Ronald Vogel (eds), *Regional Politics: America in a Post-city Age.* Thousand Oaks, CA: Sage. pp. 206–28.

Hirschman, Albert O. (1970) *Exit, Voice, and Loyalty.* Cambridge, MA: Harvard University Press.

Hoffman-Martinot, Vincent and Sellers, Jefferey (eds) (2005) *Metropolitanization and Political Change.* Wiesbaden: VS Verlag.

Horak, Martin (1998) *The Power of Local Identity: CSLD and the Anti-Amalgamation Mobilization in Toronto.* Toronto: Centre for Urban and Community Studies.

Horan, F. James and Taylor, G. Thomas (1977) *Experiments in Metropolitan Government.* New York: Praeger.

Imbroscio, David L. (2006) 'Shaming the inside game: a critique of the liberal expansionist approach to addressing urban problems,' *Urban Affairs Review*, 42 (2): 224–48.

Jones, V. (1942) *Metropolitan Government.* Chicago: University of Chicago Press.

Keating, Michael (1995) 'Size, efficiency, and democracy: consolidation, fragmentation, and public choice', in David Judge, Gerry Stoker and Harold Wolman (eds), *Theories of Urban Politics.* Thousand Oaks, CA: Sage.

Keating, Michael (2001) 'Governing cities and regions: territorial restructuring in a global age', in Allen J. Scott (ed.), *Global City-Regions: Trends, Theory, Policy.* Oxford: Oxford University Press. pp. 371–90.

Keating, Michael, Loughlin, John and Deschouwer, Kris (2003) *Culture, Institutions, and Economic Development.* Cheltenham, UK/Northampton, MA: Edward Elgar.

Le Galès, Patrick (2006) 'New state space in Western Europe?,' *International Journal of Urban and Regional Research*, 30 (3): 717–21.

Lefèvre, Christian (1998) 'Metropolitan government and governance in western countries: a critical review,' *International Journal of Urban and Regional Research*, 22 (1): 9–25.

Leland, Suzanne M. and Thurmaier, Kurt M. (2004) *Case Studies of City-County Consolidation: Reshaping the Local Government Landscape.* Armonk, Y. M.E. Sharpe.

Lyons, W.E., Lowery, David and De Hoog, Ruth Hoogland (1992) *The Politics of Dissatisfaction: Citizens, Services, and Urban Institutions.* Armonk, NY: M.E. Sharpe.

Maxey, C. (1992) 'The political integration of metropolitan communities', *National Municipal Review*, 11 (8): 229–52.

Molotch, Harvey (1976) 'The city as growth machine: toward a political economy of place', *American Journal of Sociology*, 82: 309–32.

Newman, P. and Thornley, A. (2005) *Planning World Cities: Globalization and Urban Politics.* Houndmills, Basingstoke, Hampshire: Palgrave.

Norris, Donald F. (2001) 'Whither metropolitan governance', *Urban Affairs Review*, 36 (4): 532–50.

Orfield, Myron (1997) *Metropolitics.* Washington, DC: Brookings Institution Press.

Organisation for Economic Co-operation and Development (OECD) (2007) *Competitive Cities: A New Entrepreneurial Paradigm in Spatial Development.* Paris: OECD.

Ostrom, Elinor (2000) 'The danger of self-evident truths', *PS: Political Science and Politics*, 33 (1): 33–44.

Ostrom, Vincent, Tiebout, Charles and Warren, Robert (1961) 'The organization of government in metropolitan areas: a theoretical inquiry', *American Political Science Review*, 55: 831–42.

Parks, Roger, and Oakerson, Ronald (1989) 'Metropolitan organization and governance – a local public economy approach', *Urban Affairs Quarterly*, 25 (1): 18–29.

Parks, Roger and Oakerson, Ronald (2000) 'Regionalism, localism, and metropolitan governance: suggestions from the research programme on local public economies', *State and Local Government Review*, 32: 169–79.

Powell, John (2000) 'Addressing regional dilemmas for minority communities' in Bruce Katz (ed.), *Reflections on Regionalism*. Washington, DC: The Brookings Institution.

Robson, William A. (1939) *The Government and Misgovernment of London*. G. Allen & Unwin Ltd.

Rosenbaum, W.A, and Kammerer, G.A. (1974) *Against Long Odds*. Beverly Hills, CA: Sage.

Rusk, David (1993) *Cities without Suburbs*. Washington, DC: Woodrow Wilson Center Press.

Sancton, Andrew (2000) *Merger Mania: The Assault on Local Government*. Westmount, Quebec: Price-Patterson Ltd.

Sassen, Saskia (2001) *The Global City: New York, London, Tokyo*. Princeton, NJ: Princeton University Press.

Savitch, H.V. (1988) *Post-Industrial Cities: Politics and Planning in New York, Paris, and London*. Princeton, NJ: Princeton University Press.

Savitch, H.V. and Vogel, Ronald K. (eds) (1996) *Regional Politics: America in a Post-city Age*. Thousand Oaks, CA: Sage.

Savitch, H.V. and Vogel, Ronald K. (2000a) 'Paths to the new regionalism', *State and Local Government Review*, 32 (3): 158–68.

Savitch, H.V. and Vogel, Ronald K. (2000b) 'Metropolitan consolidation versus metropolitan governance in Louisville', *State and Local Government Review*, 32 (3): 198–212.

Savitch, H.V. and Vogel, Ronald K. (2004) 'Suburbs without a city: power and city–county consolidation,' *Urban Affairs Review*, 39 (6): 758–90.

Savitch, H.V., Collins, David, Sanders, Daniel and Markham, John (1993) 'Ties that bind: central cities, suburbs, and the new metropolitan region', *Economic Development Quarterly*, 7 (4): 341–57.

Scott, A.J. (ed.) (2001) *Global City-Regions: Trends, Theory, Policy*. Oxford: Oxford University Press.

Self, Peter (1982) *Planning the Urban Region: A Comparative Study of Policies and Organizations*. Tuscaloosa, AL: University of Alabama Press.

Sharpe, L.J. (ed.) (1995) *The Government of World Cities: The Future of the Metro Model*. New York: John Wiley.

Siegel, Fred (1997) *The Future Once Happened Here: New York, D.C., L.A. and the Fate of America's Big Cities*. New York: Free Press.

Stephens, G. Ross and Wikstrom, Nelson (2000) *Metropolitan Government and Governance*. Oxford: Oxford University Press.

Stoker, G. (2004) *Transforming Local Governance: From Thatcherism to New Labour*. New York: Palgrave Macmillan.

Studenski, P. (1930) *The Government of Metropolitan Areas in the United States*. New York: National Municipal League.

Swanson, Bert (1996) 'Jacksonville consolidation and regional governance', in H.V. Savitch and Ronald K. Vogel (eds), *Regional Politics: America in a Post-city Age*. Thousand Oaks, CA: Sage.

Thornley, A. (2003) 'London: institutional turbulence but enduring nation-state control', in W. Salet, A. Thornley. and A. Kreukels (eds), *Metropolitan Governance and Spatial Planning*. London: Spon Press. pp. 41–56.

Tiebout, Charles M. (1956) 'A pure theory of local expenditures', *Journal of Political Economy*, 64: 416–24.

Tomaney, J. (2002) 'The new governnance of London: a case of post-democracy', *City* 5 (2): 225–48.

Travers, T. (2002) 'Decentralization London-style: the GLA and London governance', *Regional Studies*, 36 (7): 779–88.

Travers, T. (2004) *The Politics of London: Governing the Ungovernable City*. Houndmills, Basingstoke, Hampshire: Palgrave.

US Advisory Commission on Intergovernmental Relations (ACIR) (1976) *Improving Urban America: A Challenge to Federalism.* Washington, DC: ACIR, M-107, September.

Vogel, Ronald K. (2007) 'Rescaling the city: a comparative perspective of metropolitan reform and regionalism in Toronto and Tokyo', in Jean-Pierre Collin and Mélanie Robertson (eds), *Governing Metropolises: Profiles of Issues and Experiments on Four Continents.* Sainte-Foy (Quebec City): Presses de l'Université Laval. pp. 259–82.

Vogel, Ronald K. and Harrigan, John J. (2007) *Political Change in the Metropolis.* New York: Longman.

Vogel, Ronald K. and Nezelkewicz, Norman (2002) 'Metropolitan planning organizations and the new regionalism: the case of Louisville', *Publius: the Journal of Federalism,* 32 (1): 107–29.

Warren, Robert, Rosentraub, Mark S. and Weschler, Louis F. (1992) 'Building urban governance: an agenda for the 1990s', *Journal of Urban Affairs,* 14 (3): 399–422.

Williams, Oliver (1971) *Metropolitan Political Analysis: A Social Access Approach.* New York: Free Press.

Wood, Robert C. (1958) 'The new metropolises: green belt, grass roots versus gargantua', *American Political Science Review,* 52: 108–22.

Wood, Robert C. (1961) *1400 Governments: The Political Economy of the New York Metropolitan Region.* Cambridge, MA: Harvard University Press.

8

URBAN POLITICAL LEADERSHIP

Stephen Greasley and Gerry Stoker

The prominence of 'leadership' in discussions of local democracy is associated with a view of the political process that is more expansive than the calculus of interest and the technocratic delivery of services. Those who write about leadership also tend to be interested in vision and creativity and the legacies, for good and ill, that identifiable individuals leave on the urban landscape. Because of the nebulous nature of concepts such as vision and creativity, and despite the importance of leadership, theoretical developments have been slow in coming. Over a decade ago, in the first edition of this book, Clarence Stone characterised the study of political leadership in cities as *ad hoc* and 'embedded in various biographies'. He argued that, although the focus on personal attributes makes theoretical development and systematic empirical work difficult, the study of individual leaders was valuable, 'elusive as the personal may be as a research target, its importance nevertheless makes leadership a fitting topic of study, more so than the formal structure of government' (1995: 96). At the time that Stone was writing, there was discussion in the air of reform to English local government allowing greater individual power to council leaders in the hope that this would facilitate a more visible and proactive style of leadership in English cities. Sounding a note of caution, he argued that stronger leadership may not follow from the establishment of directly elected mayors or from strengthening the formal powers of leaders (1995: 114).

Ten years on and the relationship between the formal structure of a local government system and the styles of leadership it produces continues to be a matter of theoretical, empirical and policy discussion fuelled, in part, by a reform agenda in Europe which seems to favour stronger individual local leadership. In England, reforms have been tentative when the existing structures of local government are considered but radical in the establishment of a directly elected mayor to lead the new Greater London Authority (GLA). The perceived success of the London mayor has led policy-makers in national government to strengthen GLA mayoral powers *vis-à-vis* the London boroughs, and the indications are that they will return to the issue of strengthening leadership in English local government as a whole in the imminent (at the time of writing) local government white paper. Across Europe as well, there have been moves to adopt elected mayors for local government or to strengthen executive political leadership in other ways (Borraz and John, 2004; Elcock, 2006).

Whilst developments in the structure of local government in Europe have strengthened the position of leaders, a significant research effort has been devoted to understanding the impact of institutional factors on leadership styles. This research has primarily focused on individual countries, for example in England (Stoker et al., 2004; John and Gains, 2005), but there have been attempts at cross-national comparison (Mouritzen and Svara, 2002). There has also been debate about what lies behind the European trend, if it is indeed a trend (Borraz and John, 2004).

In the following section, we review some of the attempts to study urban political leadership. They have largely relied on three sets of factors: contextual influences on the way leaders perform; the characteristics, skills and capacities of individuals in leadership positions; and the distribution of decision-making powers within the organisations of local government (see Lowndes and Leach, 2004). It would be hard to argue that any one of these sets of factors is irrelevant but a comparative assessment of their importance runs into methodological problems. Look at specific policy decisions and how they are made and individual factors will dominate; look at patterns of leadership style over a larger number of cases and individual factors start to fade. Human agency operates in the context of more general forces which are revealed only with fairly large scale comparison over a period of time. A good example is the reform trend across Europe towards stronger leadership in local government, which is discussed by Borraz and John (2004). No doubt each reform process is a complex balance of interests, whims and individual views, and yet they all appear to move in the same direction. We conclude the chapter with a discussion of the various explanations that have been offered for these changes.

Political leadership

Although political leadership, and other types of leadership, are exercised by people in a variety of positions across any given town or city, in this chapter we are only concerned with those people at the top of cities' and towns' formal political structures. The key distinction between political office holders and other types of political leadership (challengers, interest group and social movement leaders) is that the first group has influence over public resources and hence has accountability and power relations with all the citizens within the area.

Leach et al. (2005) identify the tasks for local political leaders which they believe to be relevant in all contexts: maintaining political support; developing policy direction; representing and defending the authority's goals in negotiation with other bodies; and ensuring task accomplishment. There are, of course, other tasks that might also be important, for example trying to engage the public, institutional development or managing community conflict. Whatever the exact mix of leadership functions, there are three broad factors that are often used to try to account for how leaders might set about their roles – the context in which they operate, the personal skills and capabilities which they bring to their role and the institutional structure in which they find themselves.

The context of urban political leadership

Context is used in two ways in social explanation: one is to argue that local context exerts such a strong influence that any generalising theories are suspect, as are structural reform efforts based on generalised theories. The danger with this view is that 'context' then becomes a container for all the variation and facets in the world that cannot be explained by explicitly conceptualised variables – it is more a measure of ignorance than an alternative explanation. Lowndes and Leach (2004) avoid this trap by presenting an explicit framework for analysing the influence of local context on reforms of political management in English local government; the most important element they identify is local political and organisational culture. Following March and Olsen (1989), they argue that behaviour in institutions, and in this case the role of leaders, is shaped by views of what is appropriate that are themselves conditioned by organisational history. Whilst we do not deny that culture may exert an important influence over individual behaviour, further research is required to examine just how important this influence is relative to the influences of structural features and individual interests.

First, there is a problem of misattribution. From our experience of speaking with leaders in local government, the way they define their role has to do with what they think the opportunities and costs are – i.e. how much resistance they will face – as well as what they believe to be appropriate – conflicting goals and the balance of power as well as informal rules and the logic of appropriateness. This response then raises the question of exactly how stable organisational traditions actually are. Might it not be the case that those traditions that survive are the ones that have not come into conflict with powerful actors' interests?

Secondly, there is the potential to confuse local political culture with local authority political culture. Many of the mayoral elections in England have demonstrated exactly how great the gap is between these two elements. Given the opportunity to vote, all at the same time on who should hold the most important political position, a number of electorates have broken with party (sometimes one-party) dominance and voted in independent candidates.

Ironically, the second use of context leads to the opposite conclusion: that 'context' is so strong, and uniform, that there is effectively no variation and urban political leadership is largely epiphenomenal. The powers at work in the global capitalist economy, or more prosaically within central–local governmental relations, are such that there is little scope for choice. Sites (1997), in a study of three New York mayors – Koch, Dinkins and Giuliani – whose policy rhetoric varied quite markedly, still finds that the content of policy showed significant continuities. Development policy favoured market interests under each of the mayors, who despite their different visions of what city governance should be, were all constrained by economic restructuring and fiscal problems.

But whilst it is true that, as Yates (1977) predicted, the conditions that previously supported 'boss' style leaders no longer pertain in American and European cities, leaders who act as brokers may still achieve significant goals, although clearly their room for manoeuvre is limited by the interests of groups that they have to deal with. Identifying and analysing cities' scope to select different policy approaches were key aims in the development of the urban regime concept, as discussed in Karen Mossberger's chapter.

Individual factors in urban political leadership

As the earlier quote from Stone suggests, much of the research on the varying performance of leaders has focused on individual factors and this is the second approach we discuss. He argues that variation in individual attributes is worth examining because 'leadership study is about human agency and its role in social causation' (1995: 105). One does not have to take the 'general on horseback' approach to urban political leadership in order to allow that personal characteristics have a role to play and that there is an 'interpretive space' in which leaders can move (Leach et al., 2005; Chapter 7).

A number of attributes or capabilities have been suggested as important for explaining leadership performance. Leach et al.'s (2005) research on English councils is one of the few projects that has used a systematic methodology for assessing the capabilities of lead politicians (their study included cabinet members as well as the mayor or leader of the council). Using responses to self-assessment questionnaires, they found that councillors in leadership positions rated themselves more highly than other councillors with regard to four general capabilities: 'personal effectiveness', 'strategic direction', 'political intelligence' and 'organisational mobilisation',

Stone's chapter in the first edition of this book took a different approach, using case studies of prominent local leaders in the United States to draw conclusions about the influence of individual attributes on local politics. Curley, in Boston in the early part of the twentieth century, advocated the interests of immigrants and minorities but his use of the 'politics of division' unintentionally set the pattern of group rivalries which was later expressed in anti-Semitism and anti-black sentiments (Stone, 1995: 101–2). La Guardia, leading New York also in the early twentieth century, is given a more positive assessment. He was successful in expanding the merit system of appointments and based his progressive agenda on common interests rather than group resentments and competition. Daley's long tenure as mayor of Chicago was paternalistic and whilst it produced significant redevelopment, this was achieved by largely going with the grain of powerful interests in the city. Harold Washington's much shorter period as Chicago mayor, in Stone's view, addressed more fundamental issues, reforming city government and engaging a wide coalition of community groups.

In assessing the impact of different mayors, Stone proposes we use a counterfactual method – what is different now because of the actions of the leader? There are three elements to consider: the amount of resistance that a mayor has to overcome to achieve goals; whether the mayor supported an expansive understanding of citizens' roles; and, whether a mayor's values are institutionalised in a way that makes a long-term difference to the governance of a city. Curley, although an advocate of deprived groups, was undermined by desire for personal wealth and ambition for higher office. Daley had little redistributive impact, nor a great impact on the way citizens engaged with government. La Guardia's and Washington's achievements are judged more favourably; their redistributive efforts were still constrained but had greater scope than the other two mayors. They both also had a greater impact on community groups and on reforming the instruments of government. In a downbeat summing up, Stone claims that, often as a result of personal ambition, mayors try to avoid the difficult tasks; instead they select quick successes and try to limit the impact of citizen involvement (1995: 110). The handling of different and sometimes conflicting aims is, in the view of Stone, a reflection of character and this helps to explain why the opportunities of the mayoral office are often not fully utilised. This explanation of the limits of mayoral activism contrasts with the account offered by Sites (1997). Stone, whilst recognising that contextual factors certainly impose costs on certain types of agenda, still insists these are costs that leaders could choose to bear. For Stone, it is the personal attributes of mayors, their leadership qualities, that are crucial for explaining whether they tackle the important but politically costly issues.

Institutional form and urban political leadership

None of the authors who have examined individual attributes have argued that they operate in a vacuum, and the final approach tries to assess the influence of institutional structure on leadership styles. There has been considerable interest in this question recently – one of the most comprehensive studies, conducted by Mouritzen and Svara (2002), compared the style of leaders cross-nationally to try to assess the influence of different institutional forms of local government on leadership activity. Borraz and John (2004) have tried to tie together changes in European local leadership and assess some of the explanations which have been offered. Other studies have focused on single countries examining how the reform of local government is affecting local leadership (Cusack, 1999; Lowndes and Leach, 2004; Stoker et al., 2004).

Mouritzen and Svara (2002) use a fourfold categorisation for national systems of local government based on the balance between three organising principles of local government – the *layman rule* that elected citizens should be intensively involved in decision-making; *political leadership* with power to give direction to government; and *professionalism* provided by appointed officials with specific expertise. The *strong mayor* systems give significant formal and informal power to the elected mayor, with politicians largely ascendant relative to professional bureaucrats. In the *committee-leader* form, whilst there is still a political leader, executive functions are shared with professionals and collegiate bodies. In the *collective* form, there is one collegiate body of elected politicians where executive power rests. Finally, in the *council-manager* form, executive functions are given to a professional bureaucrat, appointed by the council. In this form, there is little involvement of politicians in administrative matters. The local government systems of 14 countries were allocated to a category (with the exception of the United States which is split between *strong mayor* and *council-manager*). The study then related these different types of structure to the role that political leaders adopt based on the assessments of local government CEOs. This relationship is not, as the authors note (2002: 67), automatic; rather it is about setting the overall parameters. They find little relation between the form of government and the public leadership role of leaders and whether or not they adopt a proactive approach – a clear relation with policy leadership. But it is party leadership that is most closely related to the forms of government identified. Leaders in collective or council-manager forms are found to be less likely to bring party concerns into their role – strong mayor and leader-committee forms are more likely.

Of course, not all countries have a single unique structure for political management shared across all authorities. Cusack (1999) exploits variation in German local government structure to compare strong mayoral authorities with more collectivist approaches, and Greasley and Stoker (2006) have similarly exploited the different forms of English local government to draw conclusions about the relation between institutional structure and leadership styles. Cusack (1999) used a veto-player model to conceptualise the extent to which institutional structure supported strong leadership. In the authorities with strong mayoral systems, there are fewer veto players – people or groups of people with the ability to block policy change or reform – thus giving the leader greater opportunities to change direction and to implement changes. Cusack's study found that measures of the concentration of decision-making power had a positive association with citizens' reported satisfaction with local government.

The veto player approach was also used by Greasley and Stoker (2006) to frame a study of leadership in English local government. As a result of the reforms of the Local Government Act 2000, there are four types of structure in English local authorities: mayor-council manager; mayor-cabinet; leader-cabinet; and streamlined-committee. The last of these is only permitted in authorities with populations of less than 85,000 and there is only one council that has adopted the mayor-council manager. This institutional variation allows some opportunity to assess the impact of formal rules on leader roles but the comparison is limited by the fact that there are only 12 mayoral authorities.

Two overarching questions were used to draw out the key differences between mayoral constitutional arrangements and others. The first question asks how free, according to formal organisational rules, are leaders to take decisions? The second set of questions relates to a leader's relationship with her 'followers'. How much scope for creativity do followers allow to those in leadership positions, and how much time are leaders given to show that their policies are having a positive impact? This second set of questions tries to explore whether leaders have the opportunity to shape the interests and preferences of followers, through persuasion and the articulation of a common vision, or on the other hand, whether they operate in a context where followers have 'hardened' preferences and closely monitor leaders' adherence to them. This reflects Jones' (1989) distinction between 'newtonian' leadership where the essential task is to balance the immutable interests of groups and individuals, and 'biological' leadership where part of the leadership role is to develop innovative and new ideas which followers may not have previously considered.

The institutional position of English elected mayors when compared to council leaders allows them greater decision-making power. In addition, mayors are likely to face a different type of monitoring by followers because they rely on the public at large to put them and keep them in position, whereas for council leaders this process is mediated by other councillors. In addition, mayors serve a four-year term where leaders have to be re-elected to that position by their fellow councillors annually. These institutional features of the mayoral system, it was argued, should allow a greater space for mayors to develop and implement new policies when compared with leaders in leader-cabinet models. A set of questions was posed to councillors, officers and stakeholders in a selection of mayoral authorities and authorities with other systems. In mayoral authorities, respondents were more likely to agree that over the previous two years, decision-making had speeded up, the role of the leader had become stronger and his or her public profile had increased. They were also more inclined to agree that the public had become more involved in decision-making and that the council's relations with partners had improved. These findings suggest, that in the view of the respondents, elected mayors are in a better position to deliver a coherent agenda and are more likely to promote their agenda outside the council, rather than being dominated by parties or other elected members.

Mullin et al. (2004) use a comparative study of mayors in three Californian cities to assess the influence of reform of the mayoral role on leadership styles and conclude that whilst institutional structure does not determine mayors' effectiveness or leadership styles, they do influence the success of mayors by changing the constraints and opportunities. Morgan and Watson (1995), also comparing mayoral powers in the United States, found little evidence that mayoral power influenced per capita spending (minus intergovernmental transfers) and conclude that the environmental factors, discussed earlier, swamp any mayoral autonomy created by constitutional construction.

All of the institutional approaches discussed have tried to grasp two dimensions of leaders' positions and how they interact, their relationship *vis-à-vis* the council or other elements of the institution and their position relative to other actors in their area. Sweeting's (2003) assessment of the strength of the new London mayor explicitly conceptualises these two dimensions. The internal relationship is a reflection of a mayor's control over the budget, control over policy, power to appoint senior staff, the direction of authority and accountability, and the existence of other elected officials or bodies covering the jurisdiction. Whilst being strong with respect to the council, Ken Livingstone was judged, early in his tenure, to be fairly isolated with respect to other important actors outside the GLA. At the time Sweeting was writing, Livingstone's influence within the Labour government was limited by the fact that he had left the party in order to stand against its official candidate for London mayor. In addition, a court case over the way that the underground system was to be run, which the mayor lost, put him at loggerheads with the national government. Since then, Livingstone has rejoined the Labour party and a more conciliatory relationship with national government has developed. It is clear from Sweeting's analysis that national government has a dominant legal position with respect to the mayoral office as well as providing the lion's share of the GLA's funding. Livingstone's later strategy of working with the centre reflects this position. We have to be careful, however, when concluding that national funding weakens the position of the London mayor. Drawing on the lessons from Sites' (1997) research in New York, we might equally conclude that national funding provides a buffer against the dominating economic interests that faced Koch, Dinkins and Giuliani.

Individuals, context and institutions

How do these different factors – contextual, individual and institutional – fit together? A difficulty in synthesising or assessing the comparative weight of these factors is that researchers are often asking different questions and applying different methods. Institutional forms are most likely to show their influence where there are a moderate or large number of cases, studied over a period of time, with important variation in institutional factors studied (Mullins et al., 2004 is an exception). When a small number of case studies with limited timescales are used, institutional factors are more likely to appear swamped by the contingencies of everyday decision-making.

Stone's (1995) assessment that personal factors are a more fitting object of study than the formal structure of government is supported with evidence from a small number of mayors in relatively similar institutional structures, compared to say the variation found across countries or the variation implied by advocates of reform. In addition, the biographical method faces serious questions about the extent to which findings can be generalised. There is likely to be bias in the historical material available with high profile and controversial mayors in large cities leaving a greater historical trail than the less prominent leaders.

In larger scale research (Cusack, 1999; Mouritzen and Svara, 2002; Greasley and Stoker, 2006), institutional factors do appear to surface in varying degrees. There are problems, however, with these studies. Conclusions drawn from the study of the influence of English mayoral systems are limited by the small number of mayoral authorities available for comparison and some bias may enter the analysis because the mayoral systems in England were largely adopted in response to previous organisational crises. It may then be no surprise that they show more marked change. This question of attribution of causality is a problem for all empirical analyses of the impact of institutional factors. If the selection of institutional form reflects some underlying cultural variables (as suggested by Mouritzen and Svara, 2002), it may be that it is these underlying influences that account for variation identified in leadership roles rather than the formal organisational rules. This is effectively another version of the 'local context' argument described earlier and if valid would have fairly damaging implications for institutional reform agendas. There are reasons for thinking this issue is not too important; see for example our earlier point about the difference between local political culture and local authority political culture. Very few people would argue that the party dominance of English local political institutions reflects a fondness for party politics in the wider citizenry. Indeed, a cultural shift away from right–left politics is one of the explanations that has been mooted for the European trend to strengthening local leadership (see discussion below).

A more serious problem with the larger scale institutional studies discussed is that they are unable to shed any light on some of the most important parts of leadership, i.e. the reasons we were interested in leadership in the first place – the vision and creativity of politics. That, however, is not a criticism of the validity of their findings but rather an acceptance that they can only answer the question that they are asking. A final concern with some of the institutional analyses is that they measure the impact of formal structures on the perceived styles of leaders rather than their ability to effect change. Morgan and Watson (1995) found no effect from mayoral strength on local government expenditure in the round. Although it is not clear that this aggregate assessment of leader impact on budgets is the most appropriate measure, especially if transferred to English local authorities, it is a useful reminder to researchers that style of leadership is not the end point of analysis.

There is another methodological question that is highlighted by debates about the impact of institutional reform on leadership style. Lowndes and Leach (2004) argue that the diversity of response to the political management reforms in England is a sign of their limited impact. This reveals a deterministic approach to social causation: 'a wider range of formal powers did not *necessarily* produce proactive individualistic exploitation of those powers' (2004: 573, emphasis added). Probabilistic versions of social explanation are less concerned about the diversity of response to reform – they expect there to be a distribution with an upper tail and a lower tail. The standard applied to reforms is whether they have made particular types of leadership more likely, rather than whether they necessarily produce proactive leadership.

We have said little in this section about the relevance of general shared context on the role that leaders play. The reason is that it is a key element in attempts to explain the European trend to stronger local leadership, to which we now turn.

Trends in European urban leadership

A European trend towards strengthening the leadership powers of local politicians has been noted in the research literature (Borraz and John, 2004; Elcock, 2006). This is evidenced by reform in England, Germany (Cusack, 1999), Italy, Norway, France and Spain (Borraz and John, 2004). Inevitably, a number of explanations have been proposed for this trend and Borraz and John (2004) weigh up their credentials. They argue that 'mimetism' or transfer from one country to another has not played an important role as yet but that competitive pressures may still lead to wider adoption of forms of stronger leadership. Likewise, despite the fact that some urban political leaders are performing on the European stage, Borraz and John find no strong evidence for linking the reform trend to a general Europeanisation argument.

The three interrelated factors that are picked out as important shared contextual influences are a common legitimacy crisis across European democracies that has seen falling participation in the formal accountability mechanisms of government, a political culture that has shifted away from left–right polarities and loyalty to political parties, and changes in the institutional structures of governance that require local governments to manage and negotiate networks of organisations in order to deliver both the traditional services of the welfare state and to pursue regeneration agendas. Reforms which support individualised leadership might address these problems by making decision-making structures simpler, clarifying who is to be held accountable for decisions, weakening the influence of party groups on leadership and providing a focus for a local government's relations with networks and stakeholders. There appears to be little strong evidence either way on the effectiveness of this strategy.

There is little evidence to support the claim that the mayoral system has increased turnout, although in England it has certainly had electoral implications. A number of the first cohort of mayors would have been extremely unlikely to find themselves leading their councils if the allocation of that position had been mediated by the wider group of councillors. There is also evidence that directly elected mayors have greater name recognition for the public than leaders in other forms (Randle, 2004). Borraz and John (2004) also find little evidence that electoral turnout has increased in the other reforming European countries they discuss.

What is interesting from the perspective of this chapter is that the 'solution' that reformers have chosen is to strengthen the role of leader or mayor *vis-à-vis* their council or assembly. It is not at all clear that reforming the structures of political management is the best way to respond to these challenges. As Borraz and John (2004) point out, the reforms in Europe have not been matched with greater resources for leaders and mayors with which to pursue locally defined objectives. The position of leaders *vis-à-vis* their council may in fact be the least of their problems.

Local leaders in all types of system have to resolve, or at least manage, tensions between the formal elected office as the key local institution of legitimacy and the fact that most of the resources required to deliver electoral promises are beyond political leaders' direct control. Directly elected mayors have found themselves in a system where they are the centre of legitimacy and accountability but they have limited resources with which to deliver on policy agendas, very much as Sweeting's (2003) analysis of the London mayorality highlights.

Conclusion

The study of urban political leadership, like many of the theories discussed in this book, inevitably leads into fairly difficult questions about the impact individuals' actions may have on a complex social system and on the contested encounter between theory and evidence. In the case of political leadership, perhaps more so than any of the other theories in the book, reformers and policy-makers are deeply engaged in these debates and in shaping the futures of local government based on assumptions about the scope for leadership to make a difference.

Over the last decade of research and policy, the key questions are not hard to identify:

* Does leadership make any difference to the outcomes of city government?
* If so, do formal structures make a difference to how leaders play their role?
* If so, is it possible to reform these structures in a way that will, overall, make visible and effective leadership more likely?
* If so, is it the best way to address the problems facing local democracy?

The first question is really a subset of the 'why does urban politics matter' question tackled by John in Chapter 1. The second and third questions receive a qualified yes from the research discussed here. Formal structures can both make it more possible for mayors to push agendas through their council and can increase the likelihood that mayors will orient themselves more to the citizens as a whole than to other members of the council.

Is strengthening leadership the best way to address the problems of local democracy? There appears to be little impact of reform on formal participation through voting (Borraz and John, 2004), but falling participation is a problem which extends well beyond local government. In England at least, reforms appear to have greatly weakened the influence of party politics in a number of the mayoral authorities, and brought in a group of independent leaders who may be less inclined to define themselves with reference to a left–right continuum. Are leaders who are stronger in relation to their council in a better position to articulate a policy agenda and mobilise fragmented resources to pursue it? That question is far more difficult to answer but is likely to become more important, particularly if a European trend towards strong leadership of weak local government continues.

--------------------------------- **References** ---------------------------------

Cusack, T. (1999) 'Social capital, institutional structures, and democratic performance: a comparative study of German local governments', *European Journal of Political Research*, 35 (1): 1–34.

Elcock, H. (2006) 'Comparing elected mayors'. Paper presented to the PSA annual conference, University of Reading.

Greasley, S. and Stoker, G. (2006) 'Understanding the dynamics of political leadership: reflections drawn from the experience of urban mayors in England'. IPEG, Working Paper, University of Manchester.

John, P. and Gains, F. (2005) *Political Leadership and the New Council Constitutions*. London: ODPM.

Jones, B. (1989) 'Causation, constraint and political leadership', in B. Jones (ed.), *Leadership and Politics: New Perspectives in Political Science*. Kansas: University Press of Kansas. pp. 3–14.

Leach, S., Hartley, J., Lowndes, V., Wilson, D. and Downe, J. (2005) *Local Political Leadership in England and Wales*. York: Joseph Rowntree Foundation.

Lowndes, V. and Leach, S. (2004) 'Understanding local political leadership: constitutions, contexts and capabilities', *Local Government Studies*, 30 (4): 557–75.

March, J. and Olsen, J. (1989) *Rediscovering Institutions*. New York: Free Press.

Morgan, D. and Watson, S. (1995) 'The effects of mayoral power on urban fiscal policy', *Policy Studies Journal*, 23 (2) : 231–43.

Mouritzen, P. and Svara, J. (2002) *Leadership at the Apex: Politicians and Administrators in Western Local Government*. Pittsburgh: University of Pittsburgh Press.

Mullin, M., Peele, G. and Cain, B. (2004) 'City Caesars? Institutional structure and mayoral success in three California cities', *Urban Affairs Review*, 40 (1): 19–43.

Randle, A. (2004) *Mayors' Mid-term*. London: New Local Government Network.

Sites, W. (1997) 'The limits of urban regime theory: New York city under Koch, Dinkins and Giuliani', *Urban Affairs Review*, 32 (4): 536–57.

Stoker, G., Gains, F., Greasley, S., John, P. and Rao, N. (2004) *Operating the New Council Constitutions in English Local Authorities*. London: ODPM.

Stone, C. (1995) 'Political leadership in urban politics', in D., Judge, G. Stoker and M. Wolman (eds), *Theories of Urban Politics*, 1st edn. London: Sage. pp. 96–116.

Sweeting, D. (2003) 'How strong is the mayor of London?', *Policy and Politics*, 31 (4): 465–78.

Yates, D. (1977) *The Ungovernable City*. Cambridge, MA: MIT Press.

9

GOVERNANCE AND THE URBAN
BUREAUCRACY

Anne Mette Kjaer

Over the last two decades the term 'governance' was applied to denote a change in public administration from a set-up focusing on hierarchy and clear demarcation lines between politics and administration, and between the state and society, to an organisational set-up emphasising networks and the overlapping roles of politicians and administrators as well as of state and society actors. This is no less the case in the local state where the change has been described as a move from 'local government' to 'community governance' (Stoker, 1999). Urban Governance Theory thus highlights changes in urban bureaucracy such as the move towards a blurring of public–private boundaries, the rise of an increasing number of governance networks, and a greater inclusion of actors other than the local state in the pursuit of community goals (Pierre, 2005).

Urban Governance Theory has so far been mainly a European approach. In America, issues of network governance have been addressed through other frameworks, such as Urban Regime Theory. However, in recent years, the approach has become more common in the American academia as well, as reflected in the influential volume by Goldsmith and Eggers, *Governing by Network* (2004). Urban Governance Theory has strengths and weaknesses. It allows the observer to look beyond the institutions of the local state to find arrangements of varying degrees of formality and including varying types of actors (Pierre, 2005). Governance theory gives us an analytical lens through which we can examine how various coordinating set-ups promote varying degrees of efficiency, synergy, inclusion and empowerment. The weaknesses of governance theory are that it often fails to focus on issues of power, conflict and interests. In addition, governance theory could be of more guidance in identifying the institutional underpinnings that promote cases of good urban governance. As Pierre (2005) argues, studies in urban governance often fail to uncover the extent to which institutional and normative variation explains differences in the urban governance process.

The purpose of this chapter is to discuss the strengths and weaknesses of a governance lens when analysing changes in urban bureaucracy. The chapter suggests ways to better incorporate notions of power, conflict and interests into governance theory by arguing that governance theory could draw more upon political economy approaches such as that used in urban regime theory (see Karen Mossberger's contribution to this volume). The chapter is organised in three sections, of which the first gives an account of strengths and weaknesses by sketching how key issues are viewed in the old public administration, the new public management and in governance theory. The second section gives illustrations of how the strengths and weaknesses have real consequences for the conclusions we draw when studying urban organisational change and thus indirectly also for the policy implications that may be drawn from research. The final section suggests ways in which governance theory could draw upon notions of power and interests found in political economy approaches and upon institutionalists' focus on informal norms and patterns of behaviour.

Theorising changes in the urban bureaucracy

The changes in both urban and national bureaucracy over the last decades have been described as a shift from 'government' to 'governance' (Rhodes, 1997; Stoker, 1999) or as a move from the 'old governance' to the 'new governance' (Peters, 2000). 'Government' or 'old governance' refers to steering capacity and rests on a theoretical model that was originally based on Max Weber's theories of the modern bureaucracy. In Weber's model (Weber, 1978), organisations are hierarchical, public officials are recruited on merit, and there is a clear separation between the private and public spheres. The model began to lose ground during the postwar period with the expansion of the welfare state and of the number and rising complexity of state functions.

The Reagan and Thatcher era of the 1980s was characterised by an array of new public management reforms that were, if not global, then at least very widespread in geographical scope (Pollitt and Bouckaert, 2000: 24). Although there is no agreed-upon definition of new public management, most observers seem to agree that it entails at least seven aspects (Peters and Wright, 1996; Rhodes, 1997; Kjaer, 2004a): the transfer of private sector management principles to the public sector, such as hands-off, professional management; explicit standards and measures of performance; managing by results and value for money; privatisation; agencification; competition; decentralisation; and citizen empowerment. User committees in schools or daycare centres are examples of institutions set up in order to enhance parental influence on a public service.

The wave of new public management reforms can be seen as a forerunner for the emergence of the concept of governance in the 1990s. The 'new governance', as Guy Peters (2000) calls it, is associated with the rise of networks and the blurring of public–private boundaries. It thus departs from traditional Weberian notions of hierarchy. Governance theory often emphasises a move of power away from the central

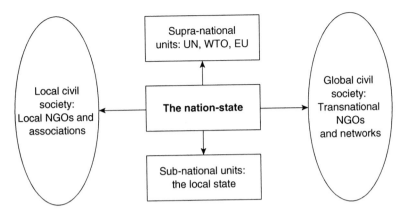

Figure 9.1   Authority migration

state upwards, towards supra-national units, and downwards towards decentralised units of governance. This movement of power within a political system has been termed authority migration (Gerber and Kollman, 2004). However, governance theory also focuses on a move outwards towards non-governmental actors locally as well as globally, a move that could arguably be termed authority migration as well (see Figure 9.1). Authority migration denotes a phenomenon in which the central state's capacity to steer deteriorates at the same time as other organisations and actors gain importance in governance processes. The third theoretical model may thus be called governance theory, the new governance, or, as it has also been termed, the governance 'orthodoxy' (Marinetto, 2003; Davies, 2005).

The three theoretical models of bureaucracy have different assumptions about efficiency, democracy, power, the role of the local state, and the role of the urban bureaucrat.

In Table 9.1, the assumptions in theories of governance are contrasted with the assumptions in old and new public management. There is a potential tension between efficiency and democracy that is addressed in different ways by the three theoretical positions. In the traditional model of public administration, the tension is solved by a model in which a bureaucracy, based on hierarchy, merit recruitment, and good pay and promotion systems, is controlled by an elected representative body. Efficiency is secured through an instrumental and technically competent bureaucracy for which the central mechanisms for coordination are command and control (Rhodes, 1999). The role of the urban bureaucrat in a traditional hierarchy is thus the technocrat: a neutral implementer of decisions taken in the city council.

The notion of power in the traditional model is one of A being able to get B to do something B would not otherwise have done (Lukes, 1974). Power is thus identifiable, visible and located in the centre of government, and this renders democratic control possible. In this model, the state provides overall direction by implementing policies that are in line with what elected bodies have identified as the national or

Table 9.1 Assumptions in the old public administration, the new public management and governance theory

Key concepts in governance theory	Assumption in the old public administration	Assumption in the new public management	Assumptions in governance theory
Efficiency	Secured through the bureaucratic hierarchy	Secured through competition	Secured through cooperation and partnerships
Democracy	Secured through elected parliaments. Separation of politics and administration	Aggregation of individual preferences defined by politicians. Separation of politics and management	Secured through participation. No analytical separation of politics and implementation processes
Power	Is visible and located in the centre of government	Is dispersed in the marketplace and therefore unproblematic	Is fragmented and/or shared in consensus building networks
The role of the local state	The state as steering and control mechanism	The state provides an enabling environment for the market	The state facilitates network governance
The role of the urban bureaucrat	Technocrat, driven by prospects of predictable career	Competitive employee, driven by incentives of performance pay	Mediator and networker, driven partly by prospects of self-development in a dynamic working environment

community interest. The main weaknesses in the model are that with an increasing number of functions, the exercise of public authority may sometimes happen beyond the legislatures' reach. Accountability chains become longer with the development of the modern welfare state (Day and Klein, 1987). Efficiency may be adversely affected by too much political intervention or by bureaucratic rigidity that arise from following standard operating procedures. In addition, public choice theorists have argued that efficiency is undermined by bureaucrats wanting to always maximise budgets and, where larger budget allocations are not possible, they strive to minimise their efforts, or in other words, maximise slack (Niskanen, 1994).

The arguments by public choice theorists led to theories of new public management that were based in economic analysis and used economic assumptions of individual behaviour, such as that of utility-maximisation, in the study of public organisations. In the new public management, the trade-off between efficiency and democracy is solved by the reliance upon competition as the way to ensure efficiency and by delimiting the role of politicians to that of aggregating individual preferences. Power is not in focus in new public management theory but there is an implicit assumption that it is not necessary to focus on power since it will be dispersed and therefore lie in a plurality of hands in the market. The state should steer, not row (Osborne and Gaebler, 1992). In the model, state power would be a problem if the state intervened too much and in unilateral ways; hence the state should constitute no more than an enabling environment for the market. The role of the public bureaucrat is seen as one of neutral efficiency, driven by the benefits of performance pay. Performing better according to certain set criteria, such as a certain number of tasks done, or a certain number of clients dealt with, means receiving pay bonuses. New management ideas, as represented in the American best-seller *Reinventing Government* by Osborne and Gaebler (1992), inspired policy reforms in many countries, not least in the US with the Clinton administration's policy of 'creating a government that works better and costs less' (Gore, 1993; Pollitt and Bouckaert, 2000: 31).

The weaknesses of the new public management model have been pointed at by scholars focusing on the inequity that market solutions may lead to. The consequence of viewing power mainly as state intervention is that power relations in society are overlooked (Shapiro, 2004). Additionally, identifying public goals may not be only a matter of aggregating individual preferences. What really is in the interest of a local political community can be lost out of sight. Therefore, a democratic deficit may be argued to characterise the model (Kjaer, 2004a; Stoker, 2004).

Governance theory gained ground partly as a critique of the NPM, and partly as a near global trend towards a renewed focus on the role of civil society in the pursuit of public goals. Governance theorists argue that due to the complexity of the challenges local communities face today, the local state cannot just leave it to markets to solve social, economic or environmental problems. Local managers have to mobilise citizens and include local knowledge in public policies (Lowndes and Sullivan, 2004; Stoker, 2005). The urban bureaucracy should not be a closed hierarchy, and neither should it be a hands-off enabling framework. Rather, it should be innovative, it should encourage participation and identify new partners, it should be organised horizontally and be open to interaction and with community members.

In governance theory, there is an understanding that rather than being at odds, efficiency and democracy are mutually reinforcing. The reason is that if consensus has been reached around a public policy, its implementation is smooth, since the policy is either passively accepted or, most likely, actively endorsed by the citizenry. Governance theory assumes that there are multiple sources of legitimacy, e.g. legitimacy does not only emerge from having followed democratic election procedures but also from having involved key stakeholders in the formulation or implementation of a policy. And cooperation from stakeholders ensures a higher degree of efficiency. In the words of Gerry Stoker (2003: 9), 'to launch a waste recycling scheme or change driving habits requires an extensive dialogue and high levels of trust between the public and authorities'. Citizen participation in implementation processes thus ensures efficiency. In that sense, governance theory does not see a trade-off between efficiency and democracy, and it assumes certain levels of trust and reciprocity in order to achieve public goals.

Power tends to be rather overlooked in (anglo-)governance theory (Marinetto, 2003; Davies, 2005). There is an implicit assumption that participation and inclusion will overcome the fact that the ability of civil society groups or individuals to promote their interests may vary. Participation is thus, in a sense, assumed to automatically create consensus. Participatory governance promotes win–win situations in which all parties gain from active community involvement. State–society synergy emerges where local communities are engaged, through what Elinor Ostrom (1996) terms co-production, with local authorities, in constructing sewage systems or making irrigation systems work, or improving health care (Evans, 1996; Ostrom, 1996; Tendler, 1997). The fact that network-actors may not be equally endowed with resources or that their interests may conflict is rarely systematically addressed (Davies, 2005). Thus, some observers have called for analysis of the underlying tensions in capitalist economies that may lead to governance failure (Jessop, 1998).

In a framework of co-production, the local state not only provides an enabling framework for participation through guaranteeing basic rights, it also directly encourages participation through initiating new development projects. The role of the state is thus to facilitate network governance, to mobilise citizens through public meetings or the media and in other ways work for more inclusion. The role of the urban bureaucrat in governance theory is different from the other models. The urban manager must know how to mobilise communities and to involve them in pursuit of community goals in, e.g. health care, urban regeneration and neighbourhood renewal, or crime prevention. Governance theorists therefore refer to the public manager as someone who participates in networks spanning the public–private divide. It is someone who relates outwards from the organisation as much as inwards within the bureaucracy, and it is someone who is driven as much by the response she/he gets from the public as by pay and promotion. Communication skills and the ability to deal with the press enter as important qualifications, and good networking and negotiating skills are also necessary. As Christopher Pollitt (2003: 42) has recently put it: 'Civil servants must learn to communicate faster, earlier and with a wider range of stakeholders. They need to acquire new skills, and the systems which recruit, train, appraise, audit and reward them all require adjustment'. In other words, technical competence is no longer enough, as social competence matters too. Moreover, Gerry Stoker (2004) emphasises that urban managers in a governance environment must acquire the capacity to manage change, to create the momentum for change, to champion its delivery and sustain its impact.

There is no common definition of governance in governance theory, but it may be referred to broadly as the setting, application and enforcement of the rules of the political game (Kjær, 2004a: 12). Whereas some governance theorists, such as Rod Rhodes (1997), would prefer a narrower definition referring only to inter-organisational networks, the broader definition is useful because it covers many different substantial governance perceptions. However, the definition risks being too general and may be prone to what Giovanni Sartori (1970) has termed 'conceptual stretching'. Sartori argues that the more globalised the world becomes, the more political scientists have resorted to vague amorphous concepts in order to make them applicable worldwide (1970: 1034). In that way, we may gain extensive coverage but lose precision. One of the central requirements for effective comparative analysis, therefore, is to develop concepts that can travel and still have substantial meaning and validity (Sartori, 1970; Peters, 2000; Kjaer, 2004b). In order to meet the travelling test, governance may be identified with different organisational set-ups. A set-up relying on public–private partnerships, or on inter-organisational networks, may be one form of governance. An urban regime is yet another sub-type of governance, i.e. another value on the dependent variable (Pierre, 2005; see Karen Mossberger, this volume). 'The enabling state' as the term emerged in Britain in the 1990s is also a sub-type of governance. The enabling state refers to a process of redefining state functions so that a core of policy-making remains at the centre while delivery functions become decentralised, contracted out or left to special purpose bodies (Deakin and Walsh, 1996; Gilbert, 2005). The British New Labour government's strategy of devolving governance, setting up regional assemblies, and elected mayors for towns and cities, drew upon the notion of the enabling state (Stoker, 2002). This may be termed a case of transatlantic policy transfer, since the notion of the enabling state was coined in America. The role of government in governance is therefore an empirical as much as a theoretical question.

Illustrations of the strengths and weaknesses of governance theory

The literature on the changes in local government has been replete with references to such ideas as power-sharing, networking and partnering; all to create win–win situations. These elements have a positive connotation and refer to the good side of the changes: that implementation of policy decisions in many cases have improved, that an increasing number of actors are included in the pursuit of collective goals, and that actors are empowered through their participation. On the other hand, the fragmentation and the emergence of quite autonomous and closed policy networks constitute the flip side of the coin: identifying power becomes more complex and, therefore, holding the exercisers of power responsible through institutions of public accountability is rendered more of a challenge. In addition, the assumptions about the norms and institutions underpinning governance networks may not always be met in practice. Governance theory arguably needs a tool for identifying the norms that are assumed necessary in order to sustain fruitful public–private cooperation.

This section will illustrate how an analytical lens excluding notions of power, conflict, interests and norms might lead us to draw overly optimistic conclusions about the feasibility of governing through networks. The section will thus give examples of types of institutional set-ups that at the same time reflect changes in the urban bureaucracy and pose challenges for governance theory. Examples of such set-ups may be found in various types of joined-up government, in public–private partnerships or other policy networks, or in the existence of special purpose bodies such as quangos.

Joined-up government is a key theme for New Labour in the UK. It is used in the Cabinet Office Paper 'Wiring it up', a part of the modernising government initiative (Cabinet Office, 2000; Ling, 2002; Pollitt, 2003). Vernon Bogdanor (2005: 1) defines joining up as:

relating to, or designating a political strategy which seeks to coordinate the development and implementation of policies across government departments and agencies, especially with the aim of addressing complex social problems, such as social exclusion and poverty, in a comprehensive, integrated way.

Joined-up government is a strategy which seeks to bring together not only government departments and agencies, but also a range of private and voluntary bodies, working across organisational boundaries toward a common goal (ibid; see also Ling, 2002). A public–private partnership is one type of joined-up government as it refers to a strategic alliance between two or more actors from some combination of the public sector, business and/or civil society. The interests of the partners may differ but they collaborate to solve a common problem through the sharing of risks, responsibilities, resources and competencies for mutual benefit for all collaborating parties. Voluntarism, mutuality and reciprocity are thus crucial to a functioning partnership (Googins and Rochlin, 2000; Joergensen, 2005). The New Labour sees multi-agency partnerships as key instruments for achieving joined-up government and democratic renewal at the local level (Lowndes and Sullivan, 2004: 55).

An example of a public–private partnership is the regional partnership for economic development in South Wales which has become 'an independent executive composed of all the regional stakeholders' (Morgan et al., 1999). Morgan, Rees and Garmise's research suggests that for a public–private partnership to work according to its purpose, a sense of equality among the parties is necessary. In the case of South Wales Regional Development, it seemed that local players were brought in as partners in a top-down fashion so as to exclude junior players from key decisions. In the South Wales partnership, 'many of the partners see partnership in a horizontal sense in which equal partners work towards common ends. Central government has been tending to see partnership in vertical terms in which the Welsh Office plays the decisive role' (1999: 182). The Welsh Office seemed to only delegate responsibility to its own quangos which were unaccountable to the community, 'so much mistrust exists between the regional development partners, especially local authorities and the Welsh Office' (1999: 184). The Business connection in South Wales was apparently unsuccessful. There were no inquiries from businesses due to lack of guidance on networks from the Welsh Office.

The findings of Morgan, Rees and Garmise suggest that it can be difficult to impose a public–private partnership where no prior informal links or norms of reciprocity existed. In addition, when implemented in a top-down fashion, public–private partnerships may reinforce vertical networks rather than nurturing horizontal ones – and vertical networks cannot sustain trust; on the contrary, they may give rise to distrust and potentially aggravate conflict. The case illustrates that setting up public–private partnerships does not automatically enhance efficiency and effectiveness – in this case, regional economic development. The case also serves to illustrate that the model of urban bureaucracy on which governance theory rests cannot be universally applied because its assumptions about the normative underpinnings of collaborative arrangements, such as trust and reciprocity, are not always met. In this case, the way the Welsh Office considered partners as subordinate players gave ground to mistrust and scepticism. Governance theory should thus be better able to identify and explain why collaborative arrangements succeed in some cities or regions and fail in others.

Another example of a partly failed strategy based on governance assumptions can be found in Danish nature policy. The EU Habitats directive on the conservation of natural habitats and wild flora and fauna compels member states to identify special areas of conservation. In Denmark, the identification of these areas occurs through collaboration between central government, the regions and experts. The government has suggested that some of these areas should be designated as national parks, and it was decided that the establishment of national parks should be entirely voluntary and should occur through a process of incorporation of as many individuals and groups from civil society as possible. The policy is thus based on the governance-notion of consensus-creation through voluntary networks and participation. The results from the pilot projects show that although many actors became included in the process, a series of problems arose relating to the assumptions about consensus and win–win situations (Agger, 2004; Hansen et al., 2005). The problems had to do with both the character of the policy networks involved – in other words, who participated – and the issue of power and interests: did the interests conflict and was it possible to reach consensus?

In relation to the character of the network, the networks in most pilot projects were quite narrow, although broad participation was encouraged and public meetings were held in which citizens and NGOs were encouraged to sign up for voluntary working groups focusing on such themes as nature and geology, culture and rural development, farming and forestry or outdoor life and tourism. Although many people did sign up at the meetings, in one pilot project it was reported that participation in the working groups decreased rapidly as many lay people felt excluded because of their own lack of technical knowledge. In another pilot project, it was reported that the participants were the usual suspects, mostly men aged 45–50 and mostly experts. The general experience from the pilot projects was that participation was not as broad-based and inclusive as expected. Networks involving many stakeholders may be successful at setting agendas and carrying out decisions that are beneficial to a community but they may also be good at exclusion through their strong intra-network ties (Granovetter, 1973). They may be modern versions of the old boy network where you need to pay attention to who is not invited to participate, as a director of a voluntary sector group tells Barbara Reid (1999: 142) in her study of housing policy. Along the same lines, Davies (2005: 329) points to a tendency characterising most open networks to gradually become more closed, more resembling what Rhodes (1997) has called policy communities, as powerful interests gain control of the agenda.

With regard to conflicting interests, none of the pilot projects succeeded in reaching a consensus on the setting up of a national park. This was mainly due to the fact that farmers were against the whole idea of a national park due to their fear that it would impinge on their use of the land. In one region, a recommendation based on agreement was indeed made but only after the farmers had withdrawn from the project. Since unanimity was a precondition, the establishment of the national park proved infeasible. Hence, in the case of nature conservation, agricultural interests are often in conflict with the interests of the local community as such. Organisational solutions based on voluntary consensus, trust and reciprocity among involved stake-holders are probably not feasible. When the assumptions of trust and reciprocity do not hold, a strategy which depends on them may give urban professionals an impossible task of mobilising a community where the conditions for inclusion and participation are not present. Strategies based on the governance model in a context of conflicting interests are not likely to have a successful outcome. In such a situation, some sort of hierarchical intervention to alter the form of participation may be necessary. In the case of national parks, a national assessment team recommended that measures be found to promote trust between farmers and authorities.

The illustration is in line with Davies' (2005) argument that collaborative horizontal set-ups may fail to create consensus due to the underlying tensions in market economies and therefore they will require hierarchical intervention. Davies (2005) sketches the dilemma that failure of the consensual model calls for government intervention, but that central control may inhibit the vital deliberative city. The dilemma is not immediately solvable but calls for more analysis into how democracy can be strengthened through increased representation and deliberation. It also calls for more work on how hierarchy, network and market solutions may best be combined. As Hirst (2000) has argued, the old model, based on representative democracy and bureaucratic hierarchy, was designed to settle conflicts, while networks were not. Stoker (2004) distinguishes between divisible and in-divisible conflicts. Divisible conflicts are about distributional issues, and in-divisible conflicts are more deep-seated socio-economic or ideological conflicts. Networks may be able to solve divisible conflicts, but they are given an impossible job if they are to solve in-divisible conflicts. In the latter case, solutions based on the traditional Weberian model or on more deliberative models may prove more successful.

A final illustration of weaknesses in governance theory can be found in the challenge to the theory posed by the existence of special purpose bodies, such as quangos. Although quangos are usually cooperating with other organisations or actors, their semi-autonomous status may put them beyond democratic control, and the solution may not be more networking. The term quango refers to organisations that are situated somewhere between 'government departments and private society', as Barker (1994) puts it, and it is based on the American term 'quasi-non-government organisation'. A quango may also be termed a special-purpose body; an organ in the so-called grey zone between private and public (Greve, 1996; Rhodes, 1997). Although quangos have existed for as long as 200 years (such as the Board of Trade in Britain), there is a consensus that since the 1980s, many countries, implementing the new public management, have experienced an 'explosion of quangos' (Greve et al., 1999). Quangos are deliberately designed to be removed from the urban bureaucracy to enjoy semi-autonomous legal and/or financial status, such as the UK learning and skills councils. They have been criticised as a way of bypassing local government since they are set up with semi-autonomous status, thus, in the words of Rod Rhodes (1997: 14), 'substituting private government for public accountability'.

The challenge for local governments has been described as being how to obtain influence on the quangos (Painter et al., 1996). The UK Local Government

Management Board in 1996 reported on two surveys – one of local authorities, one of local communities – regarding their perception of local quangos (or non-elected agencies, as the report prefers to call them). The principal findings showed that local authorities were of the opinion that the quality of services may have improved with the rise of quangos but that this had occurred at the cost of accountability (Painter et al., 1996: 5). On matters such as openness, transparency, information to the public and appointments, the local authorities' assessment was mainly negative. The survey of user groups and community organisations also showed negative perceptions. Local communities felt the quangos were highly secretive, for example, in holding closed meetings, making inadequate provision for consultation, being reluctant to divulge information and discouraging partici-pation. A common observation was that few councillors or local officers were appointed to local quangos' boards. There was large-scale support among the local authorities for attempting to increase the amount of influence local authorities had on their functioning. Although not considered feasible, the most desirable reform proposal was to reabsorb the local quangos into local government. The local com-munities thought that local government was far more likely than quangos to con-sider equity in the delivery of services, and they also thought the local authorities were most likely to provide efficient and quality service delivery. Thus, in this respect, 'the user groups/community organisations seemed more upbeat on local governments' behalf than local government itself' (1996: 9).

Governance theory emphasises, as mentioned, the benefits of inclusion and empowerment through participation in networks. The policy recommendation in response to 'the quango challenge' would be one of encouraging the quangos to be more open and cooperative, to relate more to the surroundings, to be more trans-parent and be more involved in networks. However, as the example above demon-strates, this may not be a realistic recommendation with regard to most quangos because their semi-autonomous status does not encourage a network solution. Hence, a more feasible solution may be to subject quangos to other types of democ-ratic control. These types may be the traditional type based on representative democ-racy where quangos would be subjected to the control of a popularly elected council. It may also be of a more deliberative kind where the quangos by law would have to be subjected to public hearings. In either type, the urban manager would need to cooperate closely with elected bodies in order to hold quangos to account.

A deliberative forum is a formal public hearing where a representative group of the population is invited to debate a public issue. It combines two central elements of a democratic process: representation and deliberation. Deliberative democracy cannot replace representative democracy, but in a situation where semi-autonomous bodies or closed policy networks are beyond democratic control, it may strengthen public debate and attention to the quangos, forcing them not to ignore the community's interests. Deliberative democracy may serve to strengthen a public space in which individuals act as citizens considering the common good, and thereby provide a counterweight to the networks, in which individuals act as users, clients or cus-tomers, considering their own particular interests rather than the public good (Kjaer,

2004a: 57). Democratising urban politics in a deliberative direction would mean that the urban bureaucracy would face demands of increasing transparency. The urban bureaucrat has been much less in focus than the elected councillor when discussing the democratic challenges posed by policy networks. But new governance arrangements, or what Stoker (2005) has termed 'networked community governance', may require the urban manager to take part in deliberation, for example to become co-decision maker in the context of partnership working rather than merely acting as adviser, and to be someone who relates to media, who thinks about how to present ideas, problems and dilemmas in the delivery of public service to the community. Urban bureaucrats may, as Ling (2002) notices, provide resistance to change since their roles are being redefined, but in many cases, they are themselves frontrunners, contributing to the redefinition of their roles. When service delivery becomes more complex, when accountability becomes harder to place, transparency and the role of the urban bureaucracy become important. Open meetings, minutes on websites and more inclusion are all measures to increase transparency in the new governance.

In sum, the illustrations show that there may be a need for governance theory to better incorporate notions of power, interests and democratic control. Jonathan Davies (2005: 318) argues that while the governance orthodoxy does not deny that conflict can potentially undermine governance networks or partnerships, the orthodoxy cannot explain how conflict is managed or overcome, or what should happen when it can't be. There may also be a need for more institutional analysis, especially with regard to identifying the informal norms and patterns of behaviour that may be necessary to sustain cooperative networks. The next task, then, is to outline how these aspects can be better incorporated.

Implications for governance theory

A first step in strengthening governance theory so as to better explain variations in governance, and to explain governance failure (Jessop, 1998), is to recognise that governance is basically the handling of rules through which public policies are pursued. Understood in this way, governance may take the form of networking, but it may also rely on hierarchy or on market mechanisms. Therefore, a first step is to recognise that the concept of authority migration described earlier is not absolute: the role of government in governance is an empirical question. Having taken this step, the next is to better theorise what rules of governance can be applied when and in which particular context. As demonstrated, network solutions are not always adequate and it is too soon to entirely abandon the state hierarchy. Networks also exist in the shadow of hierarchy (Scharpf, 1994). As Davies (2005: 319) has formulated it, 'to question the orthodox model of governance is not to suggest that the state is a rational, homogenous entity capable of securing perfect compliance. Rather, it is to exercise caution about the extent to which networks function without command structures'. There is a need for a better understanding of the conditions under which collaborative arrangements such as governance networks and partnership work. Such an understanding may allow us to answer questions such as:

* Under what conditions, if at all, may collaborative networks in the pursuit of public goals work without hierarchy? E.g. if members of networks are basically unequal, as in American urban regimes and partnerships for economic development (Squires, 1989), can they reach outcomes satisfactory to the community as such? If they can't, is there a need for intervention by the centre, or is it possible to build up trust among members on a local scale without central intervention?
* What measures may alleviate or create consensus between conflicting interests? When are conflicts in-divisible? What, if anything, can urban managers do to solve conflicts and if they cannot be solved, does the urban bureaucracy then revert to a more traditional top-down role?
* What are the causes of varying success of governance strategies? When and how have urban managers successfully intervened or participated in governance networks?
* Under what conditions do strategies based on participation and devolution end with centralising tendencies and hierarchical intervention? – and if so, to what extent is the culture and practice of the city government bureaucrat responsible?

In order to answer these questions, governance theory could draw upon political economy approaches as they are found in urban regime theory (Mossberger, this volume; Mossberger and Stoker, 1998; Imbroscio, 2003) and other institutionalist approaches (Ostrom, 1990, 1991; Lowndes, 2005).

Urban regime theory is similar to urban governance theory in some ways, for example in its focus on informal public–private cooperation. It is also different. For example, it focuses more on agenda-setting coalitions, operating on the input side of policy-making, whereas urban governance theory tends to focus more on policy-implementing networks, i.e. on policy and public service delivery. In urban regime theory, the focus is on interactions between social groups and elected councillors rather than with urban managers. Another difference is that urban regimes are typically established by societal actors whereas governance networks are often set up through government engineering. Urban regime theory can contribute to governance theory because it situates regimes within a political economy rather than a pluralist framework (Imbroscio, 1998; Mossberger and Stoker, 1998: 829). This means that business interests are incorporated. Although business is not by definition a part of governance networks, the idea of placing network analysis within a political economy context makes sense, because it brings in issues of power and inequality. Early urban regime theory, e.g. Stone (1980), has pointed to the fact that the socio-economic system confers advantages and disadvantages on groups in ways that predispose urban officials to favour some interests, notably business, at the expense of others. Others (notably Lowi, 1979) have referred to the same phenomenon as 'state capture' to describe how the local state is dominated by powerful interest groups. While state capture may particularly characterise the United States where local governments depend much on locally generated revenue, the phenomenon could very well occur in relation to new policy networks. However, the notion of state capture is conspicuous for its absence in the governance literature.

Placing network analysis within the traditions of political economy allows us to launch a mapping of the interests at stake and to make assumptions about their impact and whether equitable networking will be feasible in a specific context. For instance, an interest group may be against an organisational set-up that it perceives will promote a policy that is unwanted by the group. At the same time, the actors who may benefit from the policy change may be less well organised, the interests may be spread over a large part of the population and hence more difficult to mobilise, or the ones who would benefit from the policy change may be unaware of future benefits from the change (Wilson, 1989; Haggard and Kaufman, 1992). In the case of nature politics described above, landowners' interests blocked consensus-creation and hence the networks did not lead to the expected results. In the case of the Welsh Office, city managers may have had an interest in retaining control and therefore did not treat others as equal partners in the network. An interest-mapping exercise would allow for what Bob Jessop (1995, 2002) has termed 'meta-governance': to not only govern networks, but to be able to choose between various solutions, such as hierarchy, market or network. And it would allow for realistic considerations of the kind of partnerships that are feasible and of the kind of consensus that can be reached, for instance, through network management or through compensation measures (Haggard and Kaufman, 1992; Kickert et al., 1999).

Finally, governance theory is, arguably, grounded in institutionalism (see Lowndes, this volume), since governance is about the way political actors affect formal and informal rules, norms and patterns of behaviour (Kjaer, 2004a). Institutions are often path-dependent and change only gradually (Putnam, 1995; Lowndes, 2005). However, most consensual strategies based on governance assumptions seem to take for granted that certain norms of trust and reciprocity exist or can be built through networks. Even if it is recognised that the lack of trust may undermine cooperation, we need to know more about how lack of trust may be ameliorated. Thus, a careful analysis of the degree of formal and informal institutions in a region, especially between key stakeholders in a certain policy area, would be a tool to discuss the feasibility of a strategy based on collaborative arrangements between equal partners. Combined with a thorough mapping of interests, such analysis could give governance theory better tools to explain success and failure in urban governance.

References

Agger, Peder (2004) 'Tanker om fremtidige udfordringer til planlægningen' (future challenges to planning). Paper presented at the Open Land conference: where is management headed? June, Fåborg.

Barker, Anthony (ed.) (1982) *Quangos in Britain*. Oxford: Oxford University Press.

Bogdanor, Vernon (2005) *Joined-up Government*. Oxford: Oxford University Press.

Cabinet Office (2000) 'Wiring it up – Whitehalls management of cross-cutting policies and services'. Performance and innovation unit report, January, London.

Davies, Jonathan (2005) 'Local governance and the dialectics of hierarchy, market and network', *Policy Studies*, 26 (3, 4): 311–35.

Day, Patricia and Klein, Rudolf (1987) *Accountabilities: Five Public Services*. London: Tavistock Publications.

Deakin, Nicholas and Walsh, Kieron (1996) 'The enabling state: the role of markets and contracts', *Public Administration*, 74 (1): 33.

Evans, Peter (1996) 'Government action, social capital and development: reviewing the evidence on synergy', *World Development*, 24 (6): 1119–32.

Gerber, Elisabeth R. and Kollman, Ken (2004) 'Authority migration: defining an emerging research agenda', July, 397–401. PS-political science Online. www.apsanet.org

Gilbert, Neil (2005) '"The Enabling state?" – from public to private responsibility for social protection, pathways and pitfalls', OECD social, employment and migration working papers, no. 26.

Goldsmith, Stephen and Eggers, William (2004) *Governing by Network. The New Shape of the Public Sector*. Washington, DC: Brookings Institution Press.

Googins, Bradley K. and Rochlin, Steven A. (2000) 'Creating the partnership society: understanding the rhetoric and reality of cross-sectoral partnerships', *Business and Society Review*, 105 (1): 127–44.

Gore, Al (1993) *Creating a Government that Works Better and Costs Less. Report of the National Performance Review*. Washington, DC: US Government Printer.

Granovetter, Mark (1973) 'The strength of weak ties', *American Journal of Sociology*, 78 (6): 1360–80.

Greve, Carsten (1996) *Den grå zone (The Grey Zone)*. Copenhagen: Department of Political Science.

Greve, Carsten, Flinders, Mathew and van Thiel, Sandra (1999) 'Quangos: what's in a name? Defining Quangos from a comparative perspective', *Governance*, 12 (2): 129–45.

Haggard, Stephan and Kaufman, Robert R. (eds) (1992) *The Politics of Economic Adjustment*. Princeton: Princeton University Press.

Hansen, H.P., Clausen, L.T. and Esben, T. (2005) 'Democracy and sustainability – a challenge to modern nature conservation'. Paper presented at the 11th International Symposium on Society and Resource Management, Ostersud, Sweden, June.

Hirst, Paul (2000) 'Democracy and governance', in Jon Pierre (ed.), *Debating Governance: Authority, Steering and Democracy*. Oxford: Oxford University Press.

Imbroscio, David L. (1998) 'Reformulating urban regime theory: the division of labor between state and market reconsidered', *Journal of Urban Affairs*, 20 (3): 233–48.

Jessop, Bob (1998) 'The rise of governance and the risk of failure: the case of economic development', *International Social Science Journal*, 50 (155): 29–46.

Jessop, Bob (2002) 'Governance and Meta-governance: On Reflexivity, Requisite Variety, and Requisite Irony', The Department of Sociology, Lancaster University.

Joergensen, Mette (2006) 'Evaluating cross-sector partnerships.' Paper presented at the Public-private partnerships in the post WSSD-era conference, Copenhagen Business School, August.

Kickert, Walter J.M., Klijn, Erik Hans and Koppenjan, Joop F.M. (1999) *Managing Complex Networks: Strategies for the Public Sector*. London: Sage Publications.

Kjær, Anne Mette (2004a) *Governance*. Cambridge: Polity Press.

Kjær, Anne Mette (2004b) 'Does governance have a travelling problem?' Paper contribution to the workshop 'The area studies controversy and the challenge to political sciences', Vægtergaarden, Djursland, December 2–3.

Ling, Tom (2002) 'Delivering joined-up government in the UK: dimensions, issues and problems', *Public Administration*, 80 (4): 615–42.

Lowi, Theodore (1979) *The End of Liberalism: The Second Republic of the United States*. New York: W.W. Norton and Company.

Lowndes, Vivien (2005) 'Something old, something new, something borrowed … how institutions change (and stay the same) in local governance', *Policy Studies*, 26 (3, 4): 291–309.

Lowndes, Vivien and Helen Sullivan (2004) 'Like a horse and carriage or a fish on a bicycle: how well do local partnerships and public participation go together?', *Local Government Studies*, 30 (1): 51–73.

Lukes, Steven (1974) *Power: A Radical View*. Basingstoke: MacMillan.

Marinetto, Mike (2003) 'Governing beyond the centre: a critique of the anglo-governance school', *Political Studies*, 51 (3): 592–608.

Morgan, K., Rees, G. and Garmise, S. (1999) 'Networking for local economic development', in G. Stoker (ed.), *The New Management of British Local Level Governance*. Basingstoke: Palgrave.

Niskanen, William A. Jr. (1994) *Bureaucracy and Public Economics*. Cheltenham: Edwin Elgar.

Osborne, David and Gaebler, Ted (1992) *Reinventing Government: How the Entrepreneurial Spirit is Transforming the Public Sector.* Reading, MA: Addison-Wesley Publishing.

Ostrom, Elinor (1990) *Governing the Commons: The Evolution of Institutions for Collective Action.* Cambridge: Cambridge University Press.

Ostrom, Elinor (1991) 'Rational choice theory and institutional analysis: toward complementarity', *American Political Science Review,* 85 (1): 237–43.

Painter, Chris, Rouse, J., Isaac-Henry, K. and Munk, L. (1996) 'Changing local governance: local authorities and non-elected agencies', Local Government Management Board research report.

Peters, Guy B. (2000) 'Governance and comparative politics', in Jon Pierre (ed.), *Debating Governance: Authority, Steering, and Democracy.* Oxford: Oxford University Press.

Peters, Guy and Wright, Vincent (1996) 'Public policy and administration, old and new', in Robert E. Goodin and Hans-Dieter Klingemann (eds), *A New Handbook of Political Science.* Oxford: Oxford University Press.

Pierre, Jon (2005) 'Comparative urban governance: uncovering complex causalities', *Urban Affairs Review,* 40 (4): 446–62.

Pierre, Jon and Peters, Guy (2000) *Governance, Politics and the State.* New York: St. Martins Press.

Pollitt, Christopher (2003) 'Joined-up government: a survey', *Political Studies Review,* 1: 34–49.

Pollitt, Christopher and Bouckaert, Geert (2000) *Public Management Reform: A Comparative Analysis.* Oxford: Oxford University Press.

Putnam, Robert D. (1994) *Making Democracy Work: Civic Traditions in Modern Italy.* Princeton, NJ: Princeton University Press.

Reid, Barbara (1999) 'Reframing the delivery of local housing services: networks and the new competition', in Gerry Stoker (ed.), *The New Management of British Local Level Governance.* Basingstoke: Palgrave.

Rhodes, R.A.W. (1997) *Understanding Governance: Policy Networks, Governance, Reflexivity and Accountability.* Buckingham: Open University Press.

Rhodes, R.A.W. (2000) *Governance: and Public Administration.* Jon Pierre (ed.), *Debating Governance: Authority, Steering, and Democracy.* Oxford: Oxford University Press.

Sartori, Giovanni (1970) 'Concept misformation in comparative politics', *The American Political Science Review,* 64 (4): 1033–53.

Scharpf, Fritz W. (1994) 'Games real actors could play: positive and negative coordination in embedded negotiations', *Journal of Theoretical Politics,* 6 (1): 27–53.

Shapiro, Ian (2004) 'Power and democracy', in Fredrik Engelstad and Øyvind Østerud (eds), *Power and Democracy: Critical Interventions.* Aldershot: Ashgate.

Squires, Gregory (ed.) (1989) *Unequal Partnerships. The Political Economy of Urban Redevelopment in Postwar America.* New Brunswick: Rutgers University Press.

Stoker, Gerry (ed.) (1999) *The New Management of British Local Level Governance.* Basingstoke: Palgrave.

Stoker, Gerry (2002) 'Life is a lottery: New Labour's strategy for the reform of devolved governance', *Public Administration,* 80 (3): 417–34.

Stoker, Gerry (2003) 'Joined up public services. A briefing note for IPEG's public service cluster', Working Paper, at www.ipeg.org.uk

Stoker, Gerry (2004) 'Distributing democracy: seeking a better fit for all tiers of government', Working Paper, at www.ipeg.org.uk

Stoker, Gerry (2005) 'New localism, participation and networked community governance', Working Paper, at www.ipeg.org.uk

Stone, Clarence N. (1980) 'Systemic power in community decision making: a restatement of stratification theory', *The American Political Science Review,* 74 (4): 978–90.

Tendler, Judith (1997) *Good Government in the Tropics.* Baltimore and London: The Johns Hopkins University Press.

Weber, Max (1978) *Economy and Society. An Outline of Interpretive Sociology,* edited by Guenther Roth and Claus Wittich. Berkeley: University of California Press.

Wilson, James Q. (1989) *Bureaucracy: What Government Agencies Do and Why They Do it.* New York: Basic Books.

10

GLOBALISATION AND URBAN ISSUES IN THE NON-WESTERN WORLD

Richard Stren

Powerful global influences are increasingly impacting cities in the non-Western or developing world. Theories of why and how this process is playing out are legion, but – and this is the main argument of this chapter – few of them incorporate the political as an element worthy of explanation or sustained analysis. In this chapter, we will look at some of the main approaches to the social science study of urbanisation in Africa, Asia and Latin America; and as we do so, we will attempt to excavate political arguments and to interrogate some of the reasons why 'politics' has such a limited and implicit presence in this literature.

——— Global urbanisation: from demography to politics to organised crime ———

For those interested in the world-wide social revolution that we call urbanisation, the first step in confronting the complexities of this phenomenon is to consult aggregate demographic statistics. For large cities everywhere, the standard comparative text for this purpose is the meticulously edited *World Urbanization Prospects* (WUP), produced every year in updated form by the Population Division of the United Nations Department of Economic and Social Affairs. We learn in this report that, for example, by sometime in 2007, half the world's population will live in urban areas; that cities in the developing world are expected to grow approximately four times faster (at 2.2 percent annually) over 2005–2030, than cities in the more developed countries (at 0.5 percent annually); that Africa and Asia were the least urbanised areas in the world (at 38 percent and 40 percent, respectively) in 2005, but by 2030 almost 7 of every 10 urban residents in the world will be living in Africa and Asia (with 51 percent and 54 percent urban, respectively); and that megacities – cities with populations of 10 million or more – numbered 20 in 2005, and of these 20, 3 were in developed countries, and 17 were in developing or transitional countries (United Nations, 2006).

Two major trends

International migration Two major trends are not revealed in the UN figures. One is the growing importance of international migration. For Canada and the United States, for example, overseas immigration (now mainly from developing countries) is a major factor in urban growth (Bourne and Simmons, 2004). Alternatively, one can examine cities from the point of view of the migrant communities themselves. Thus, Lisa Benton-Short and her colleagues look at the proportion of foreign-born (or immigrants) living in major cities around the world (Benton-Short et al., 2005). As they argue, cities are constantly being ranked against each other according to essentially economic and commercial criteria. But because of globalisation, 'rates of migration have accelerated and the diversity of origin points has increased' (2005: 947). For Michael Peter Smith, a leading theorist of global urban phenomena, these international population flows and their continuing connections with country of origin are a central part of 'transnational urbanism', a concept which he prefers to use rather than globalisation (Smith, 2001).

The study of the *political* effects of these major immigration flows from developing countries to cities in more developed regions is in its infancy. Collections of city-level case studies help to establish the locality and significance of issues emanating from immigration (Marcuse and van Kempen, 2000; Balbo, 2005) A classic study of Miami, by Alexandro Portes and Alex Stepick (two sociologists) has set a high standard of research and analysis. Writing in the early 1990s, by which time Miami was dominated politically by the Hispanic (Cuban) population, the authors survey the process by which this political transformation from a southern white dominated city to a Hispanic 'enclave' city took place (Portes and Stepick, 1993). As the population of the area became majority Hispanic by 1990 (Portes and Stepick, 1993: 211), political control over both the county and the city governments was taken over by Hispanics.

The strength of the Cubans as a political force in South Florida is attributed by Portes and Stepick to the gradual creation of a 'moral community' based on a common experience of hardship in, and escape from Cuba. It was reinforced by 'the social capital on which their collective business advancement was cemented' (Portes and Stepick, 1993: 140). The extreme right-wing and superpatriotic attitudes of many in this community, however, set them at odds with other communities (such as other Hispanic groups, local liberals, and the African-American community) in the area. In a distinction made famous by Robert Putnam, the Cubans in Miami-Dade County have 'bonding' (or exclusive) social capital, rather than 'bridging' (or inclusive) social capital (Putnam, 2000: Chapter 1). Extending the notion of bridging social capital to a comparative study of three cities, Blair Ruble develops the concept of what he calls 'diversity capital'. Essentially, this means the ability of a group (or groups) to parlay social and cultural differences into policies and institutions that unite, rather than further divide large cities. Looking at different immigrant groups in Washington, Montreal and Kyiv, Ruble shows how transnational communities help to shift the political discourse from confrontation to more pragmatic local issues (Ruble, 2005). We are reminded again of the injunctions of Smith, as illustrated in his analysis of the daily and political experiences of Mexicans and Koreans in Los Angeles, not to forget the important role of local agency in the transnational process (Smith, 2001, Chapter 4).

The growing power of cities   The second trend has to do with the increasing power and economic influence of cities – particularly large, metropolitan regions. In the United States, a detailed study has shown that the 361 metropolitan area economies are responsible for 86 percent of the total GDP of the whole country. If it were a country, for example, the metropolitan region of New York would have the tenth largest economy in the world (US Conference of Mayors, 2007: 12). In proportion to their populations – which are already very large – metropolitan areas around the world make a very important contribution to the economies of their respective countries.

In most countries, metropolitan areas are comprised of a number of clustered, multi-centred cities, a large total population (normally over 1 million) and a complex and usually very fragmented governance system (Ruble et al., 2001; Laquian, 2005). As they grow in size, these metropolitan areas have in many cases become regions – a step higher in the geographical lexicon than 'areas' or 'agglomerations'. These regions can be very large indeed, rivaling provinces or states as second orders of social and political organisation, even though in most cases their formal political status is unclear. From the more traditionally structured 'global city regions' of London, Mexico City or Emilia-Romagna (Scott, 2001) to the huge, sprawling 'desakota regions' of Southeast Asia that mix rural and urban settlements and modern and traditional economic activities, new forms of spatial and social organisation are emerging.

The governance structures of these city regions are almost always contested and transitory, but most of the larger regions enjoy (or experience) a very fragmented institutional and decisional structure. With the exception of China, which has elevated five major cities (Shanghai, Beijing, Gwangzhou, Tianjin and Chongqing) to virtual provincial status with mayors appointed by the central government; and South Africa – which through a powerful Municipal Demarcation Board in 2000 created six single-tier metropolitan areas in which regional economic and political boundaries were more or less coterminous (Cameron, 2005) – most large cities in developing countries (and most in North America and Europe as well) are governed through extremely localised and incoherent structures (Islam, 2003; Montgomery et al., 2003: Chapter 9; Segbers, 2007).

Urban fragmentation: a strengthening international pattern?

Local political incoherence and fragmentation are challenges in almost all large jurisdictions. For developing countries, there is little scholarly discussion of this phenomenon except expression of the opinion that it ought to be dealt with by the government. Nevertheless, it seems logical to assume that, with widespread decentralisation (Manor, 1999) and democratisation (Huntington, 1991; Handelman and Tessler, 1999) as important processes in developing countries over the last two decades, the same jurisdictional incoherence might be expected to obtain in the new metropolitan areas of Africa, Asia and Latin America. Such consequences would be amplified by two additional – but very powerful – factors: the fragmentation of infra-structure, and the increasing polarisation of class and income. Both are at least partly a result of 'globalisation effects' in large cities. These two factors are central to a great deal of theorising about cities in developing countries.

Infrastructural fragmentation   Ecological fragmentation has long been a 'fact on the ground' for cities in developing countries. Thus, Marcello Balbo points out that, although Western industrial cities are characterised by a certain coherence that is amenable to master planning, almost all cities in developing countries are more com-plex, both spatially and socially:

> ... the city of the Third World is a city of fragments, where urbanization takes place in leaps and bounds, creating a continuously discontinuous pattern. In the fragmented city, physical environment, services, income, cultural values and institutional systems can vary markedly from neighbourhood to neighbourhood, often from street to street. (Balbo, 1993: 24)

How well does this picture accord with reality? Cities in developing countries vary enormously, but as Stephen Graham and Simon Marvin have argued, the urban world of the last decade has been witness to a 'splintering urbanism' in which 'stan-dardised public or private infrastructure monopolies ... laid out to offer broadly sim-ilar services at relatively equal user charges over cities and regions, are receding as hegemonic forms of infrastructure management' (Graham and Marvin, 2001: 383). A major factor behind these changes in developing country cities is the inability of service providers to keep pace with demographic growth. But two more general fac-tors include 'the widespread retreat of the idea that networked services are "public" services that should be available to all at standard tariffs' (2001: 96), and the perva-siveness of the notion that all forms of ownership (public, private and non-profit) should compete for the supply of local services.

That *any* level of private provision of local urban services should be acceptable has encountered a great deal of criticism, both theoretical and political. This is a com-plex subject, for which there is an enormous literature in economics, geography and political science. Basically, since the 1970s, neo-liberal ideas of the proper function of the local state have led – in many developing countries – to policies which have resulted in an increasing emphasis on cost recovery in the provision of such local services as water, electricity, sanitary services and waste disposal. In his history of neoliberalism, David Harvey observes that, as the locus of social policy is drawn away from collective decision-making institutions, and 'given the neo-liberal suspi-cion of democracy', a means needed to be found to connect the state to new processes of capital accumulation. One response, says Harvey, was the notion of 'public–private partnerships' (Harvey, 2005: 76).

The versions and urban service dimensions of public–private partnerships are effec-tively discussed by Richard Batley (2001). He cautions against 'a naive belief in pri-vatisation' under all conditions. But he shows, nevertheless, that privatisation operates better with some services (for example, solid waste collection) than others (for example, water), according to the degree to which the service in question is a private, rather than a pure public good, where users cannot easily be charged and non-users excluded. Laïla Smith, writing about water distribution policies in Cape Town, South Africa, argues that water is a 'merit good' since its distribution generates positive externalities and is a benefit to the collective interest (Smith, 2004). Her research in Cape Town shows that as more stringent cost-recovery methods were applied to the poor households that had previously obtained water free of charge, more water cutoffs took place and more 'repeated acts of civil society disobedience' took place in low-income areas of the city (Smith, 2004: 391). Local resistance to service charges for water and electricity in South Africa has been well documented (Bond, 2000: Part II; Ballard et al., 2006), as the South African government attempts to achieve some balance between efficiency and equity.

In Latin America, the most dramatic case of a local protest took place in Cochabamba, Bolivia during the period from 1999 to 2000. In 1999, a consortium jointly owned by the multinational firms Bechtel and United Utilities took over the city's water system, and promptly raised water rates in increments up to 200 percent higher than previous levels. These rate increases were especially burdensome for the very poor, many of whom live in the higher elevations of the city and have always suffered from low water pressure and uneven supply. The rate hikes, coming before the concessionary company had extended the service network or visibly improved service provision, led to massive demonstrations and city-wide blockades in a protest movement that was ultimately aimed against the whole political establishment responsible for the deal. While arguments in favour of water privatisation emphasise the importance of attracting capital to improve production and distribution facilities, the social protest movement literature stresses the underlying inequalities in local (and ultimately national) societies as the basis of the water problems of the poor (Olivera with Lewis, 2004). A variation on this approach is the political ecology approach, developed effectively by the geographer Erik Swyngedouw on the politics of water distribution in Guayaquil, Ecuador. In telling the complex story of how the water vendors (*tanqueros*) – who purchase water from a privatised company – maintain prices and profit levels in supplying the poorest segment of the city's population, Swyngedouw shows how the process reinforces political and social inequality (Swyngedouw, 2004).

Socioeconomic fragmentation Partly as a result of the external influences relating to globalisation, many observers of cities in the developing world have commented on increasing socioeconomic differentiation during the decade of the 1990s. Alan Gilbert, writing about Latin American cities toward the end of the 1990s, claims that these cities 'remain highly segregated' (Gilbert, 1996: 91). And there is no sign that residential segregation (between the rich and poor) is declining: 'indeed in some respects there is greater polarization' between rich and poor (Gilbert, 1996: 3). Examples abound in many parts of the developing world (Marcuse and van Kempen, 2000; Gugler, 2004; Murray, 2004).

But Sao Paulo, the commercial capital of Brazil, has the dubious distinction of having elicited perhaps the most provocative and extensive literature on urban inequality.

Teresa Caldeira, a Brazilian planner/anthropologist, has exhaustively described the development of social and spatial segregation in Sao Paulo from the early twentieth century to the present. Caldeira's close study of a rapidly growing suburban neighbourhood (Morumbi) shows that fear of violence and crime is a pervasive subject in everyday conversation. The fear of crime is, however, common throughout all social groups of the city, as 'people from all social classes fortify their homes, change their habits, and end up transforming the city and its public areas'. The result is a city made up of 'fortified fragments' from which the poor and marginalised are physically excluded (Caldeira, 2000). 'Territorial exclusion', argues a senior Brazilian planner, effects the poor most severely (Rolnick, 1999), and leads to resentment and anger when infrastructure, services and well-paid employment are not easily available in many peripheral areas. Sao Paulo recorded 11,455 homicides in 1999, dwarfing the numbers for other large cities; in the same year, New York registered 667 homicides (Manso et al., 2005: 1).

For complex reasons, the homicide rate in Sao Paulo began to decline after 2000. But it has been an important issue in local politics in that city – as well as in Rio de Janeiro – for some time. Fear of crime is a constant theme in local politics both in Brazil and other Latin American countries (Rotker, 2002). It has also been recorded at high levels through a survey in Nairobi, Kenya, and through a national survey in South Africa (UN-HABITAT, 2007: 73). A study of Diadema, a peripheral municipality in the Sao Paulo region with the highest murder rate in Brazil – at 141 per 100,000 in 1999 – shows how a combination of community work, political organisation and the expansion of commerce into previously dangerous areas was able to reduce the level of violence to a more tolerable level. In 2003, the homicide rate had declined to 74 per 100,000; still, this was 50 percent larger than the overall rate for greater Sao Paulo in the same year. In 2004, the reelected mayor of the city (a member of the Worker's Party) focused his campaign on 'the reduction of violence, proclaimed on billboards and streamers on the main avenues' of the town (Manso et al., 2005: 6). In studies of urban violence in the developing world, a central theme is that globalisation is closely related to the spread of organised criminal gangs. In the words of a major UN report, '[t]hese groups thrive in political and social contexts where traditional values have given way to "a mentality of individual advancement at any price". Fed by market forces, and especially by globalisation, organised crime groups have adapted to changing economic and social conditions faster than the abilities of most states to constrain them' (UN-HABITAT, 2007: 60).

World cities, global cities and ordinary cities: the representation of the global south

With the development of new and more extensive processes of global economic, social and political relations, scholars in the urban field have developed new ways to classify and categorise cities. The literature on this subject is vast, particularly in the disciplines of geography, planning and sociology. In the early stages of this research, John Friedmann and Goetz Wolff (1982) drew our attention to what they called 'world cities'. Developing this notion further several years later, Friedmann proposed what he called 'the world city hypothesis'. By this, he advanced seven hypotheses about major cities involved in global economic relations, hypotheses that placed cities in a hierarchy according to their importance for capital accumulation, their production and employment sectors, and their importance as points of destination for international migration. In a table and diagram, Friedmann sketched out a 'hierarchy' of 30 cities, placing them in four categories, according to whether they were primary or secondary cities in either 'core' countries, or 'semi-peripheral' countries. The primary cities in the 'core' countries were London, Paris, New York, Los Angeles and Tokyo. Other cities occupied a more secondary status in the world system (Friedmann, 1986). In this influential categorisation, the characteristics and dynamics of the cities in the system are defined largely by their relative economic positions; but except for the relative importance of core and semi-peripheral countries, political elements are absent in this discussion. In his reply to the discussions and papers at a symposium dedicated to his work, Friedmann observed that, if the 'emerging world city paradigm' allows the integration of many research streams into a single meta-narrative, the 'counter-narrative' to this statement is the 'excluded two-thirds of humanity' that is not incorporated into the relationships established by the world city system (Friedmann, 1995: 43–4).

Side by side with Friedmann's 'world cities' model is the 'global cities' model of Saskia Sassen. While there is a family resemblance between the two models, Sassen's cities are the very highest 'command points in the organisation of the world economy ... as key locations for finance and for specialized service firms, which have replaced manufacturing as the leading economic sectors ... [and]as sites of production, including the production of innovations ... ' (Sassen, 1991: 3). As such, says Sassen, they represent a new model of urbanisation never seen before. Sassen's major book lists five examples of this 'new type of city' – New York, London, Tokyo, Frankfurt and Paris. Her book focuses on the first three. Her studies deal in detail with the development of the financial industry and its ancillaries (accountancy, law, insurance and the like), and the parallel and consequential social polarisation and spatial fragmentation that takes place in the individual global cities themselves. In the Epilogue to the second edition of *The Global Cities*, Sassen says that she agrees with her critics (for example, Logan (2000), Marcuse and van Kempen (2000) and Smith (2001)) that globalisation is a confusing and complex process, that is not the 'sole cause' of social and spatial polarisation in global cities, and that the impact of globalisation varies across cities and countries because of the differential role of the state (Sassen, 2001).

Granted, globalisation may not account for everything. But as other, related studies show, international capital, technological and human capital flows are profoundly changing a wide range of cities – and city regions — in both the north and the south (Marcuse and van Kempen, 2000; Scott, 2001; Gugler, 2004; Balbo, 2005; Sassen, 2007). In an excellent collection of studies of the politics of planning in four major 'global city regions' (Johannesburg, Mumbai/Bombay, Sao Paulo and Shanghai), Simon Raiser and Krister Volkmann observe how the cases have evolved in the context of globalisation.

This has set in motion similar trends, which influence current urban and regional develop-ment in powerful ways. Most notable of these is the development of districts with privi-leged access to global networks next to districts that are only precariously serviced and rely mainly on informal structures. At the same time, the four city regions are characterised by a unique local context, which derives from long-standing cultural specifics as well as more recent history, including apartheid, military rule, and a socialist state-economy. (2007: 31)

For researchers, correctly situating the specific and contextual 'facts' of a particu-lar local case in the context of the most powerful general factors is not only delicate and demanding, but one of the most important methodological challenges in the comparative urban field.

Some major limitations of the world cities/global cities literature are addressed by Jennifer Robinson. Taking off from the notion of 'ordinary cities' earlier proposed by Ash Amin and Stephen Graham, Robinson argues that, far from the lofty hierarchies of 'world cities' and 'global cities', 'all cities, from Los Angeles to Lagos, from Johannesburg to Jakarta, would be better off for being understood as ordinary' (Robinson, 2006: 171). Her first point is that, by designating and ranking cities according to certain outstand-ing, even exceptional characteristics (such as having the highest levels of corporate headquarters, stock market transactions and international airline landings), many other important qualities and processes associated with these cities – such as politics – are ignored. For example, local political characteristics are almost fully ignored in this literature, and the nature of the criteria – which are predominantly economic – ensures that most cities in Asia, Africa and Latin America are totally left out of the discussion. Comparative information on aspects of local governance (defined as the relationship between the local state and civil society) could be extremely revealing, but is rarely developed outside World Bank documents – and these documents generally focus on the effectiveness of state institutions (Léautier, 2006).

A second point that Robinson makes is that comparative urban studies involving theories or major concepts almost always start and end with the experiences of cities in the 'global north'. She cites a work by Dipesh Chakrabarty (2000) who argues that, in historical scholarship on the post-colonial south, Europe acts 'as a silent referent'. Chakrabarty goes on to say that, although 'third-world historians feel a need to refer to works in European history, historians of Europe do not feel any need to recipro-cate' (2000: 28). A very similar pattern, says Robinson, obtains in geography with respect to studies of post-colonial Africa, Asia and Latin America. Also 'the publish-ing industry strongly privileges the markets of wealthy countries in making decisions about what sorts of books to publish' (Robinson, 2006: 169).

One partial explanation for this imbalance in the field of urban studies may be the notion of 'disciplinary clusters'. On the basis of a large-scale survey of published urban research in 41 countries of the global south from the 1960s to the mid-1990s, the Global Urban Research Initiative project concluded that urban work in the three major regions of the developing world was dominated by different disciplinary clus-ters: in Latin America, the dominant disciplines were (and still are) sociology and architecture/urban planning; in Asia, geographers, economists and urban/regional planners are the major researchers; and in Africa, urban geographers are the most prominent, with a sprinkling of sociologists and political scientists (Stren, 1995). In North America and Europe, where there is a much more balanced distribution of disciplinary research among the major social science disciplines and planning, political science has a more substantial role to play. At a more general level, these relationships may only reinforce – in one interpretation – the construction of what Arturo Escobar calls 'developmentalism', or the simplification, from the point of view of Europe and North America, of the problems and cultural complexities of nations and regions of the global south into a replicable strategy for dealing with economic development and change. To put it another way:

> what is at stake is the process by which, in the history of the modern West, non-European areas have been systematically organised into, and transformed according to, European constructs. Representations of Asia, Africa, and Latin America as Third World and underdeveloped are the heirs of an illustrious genealogy of Western conceptions about those parts of the world. (Escobar, 1995: 7)

Thus, typical European urban planning constructs such as 'master planning', 'neighbourhood' and even 'community' can take on a very different meaning when applied to urban settlements in the global south, particularly very poor settlements. Master planning, in particular, as a model for the planning of new towns and capital cities in tropical countries, has encountered a number of severe challenges in the face of poverty and weak state machinery (Holston, 1989; Scott, 1998; Montgomery et al., 2003: Chapter 2).

International organisations and urban politics in the global south: the local becomes political

From the early 1970s, international development agencies have taken a direct interest in issues of planning, services and infrastructure for cities of developing countries. The two major multilateral organisations involved have always been the World Bank (formed out of the Bretton Woods agreements in 1944), and the United Nations Centre for Human Settlements (UNCHS), which became UN-HABITAT (a higher level in the UN system) in January 2002. UN-HABITAT, which in principle works in all countries (but undertakes projects largely in the developing world), has fewer projects and a much lower level of available resources than the Bank, but it focuses almost entirely on the urban field. In many of their projects, these organisations make an attempt to relate theories of urban development to practical work on the ground. There is, nevertheless, a scholarly literature critical of their activities, particularly those of the Bank, and even its urban programmes (Osmont, 1995; Bond, 2005; Ramsamy, 2006), but much of the work of these agencies is protected by rules of confidentiality, so that those who know the most – often scholars in developing countries – write the least. Politics – or local politics – as an object of study or reflection by these international agencies is virtually absent from work that they support.

A world of squatters?

The focus of a great deal of the work of the international community – including the World Bank and UN-HABITAT– has been on urban poverty. While rural poverty has been a traditional concern of assistance programmes for many years, the emphasis on urban poverty has been reinforced by the inclusion of this theme in the United Nation's important list of Millennium Development Goals (MDGs).[1] Within the seventh goal to achieve sustainable development is what is known as 'Target 11': 'Achieve significant improvement in lives of at least 100 million slum dwellers, by 2020'. Two major books have focused on the condition of the urban poor in developing countries. Appearing in 2005, Robert Neuwirth's *Shadow Cities: A Billion Squatters, A New Urban World* is dedicated to 'squatters everywhere'. Based on having lived for several months each time in four urban squatter areas on four continents (in Brazil, Kenya, Turkey and India), Neuwirth (an American reporter previously living in Brooklyn) tells the human stories of struggle and survival among the people he got to know. He is overwhelmed by the magnitude of the problem, but he sees these urban spaces as the cities of the future.

Who – or what – is responsible for this situation of poverty, insecurity and intolerable day-to-day living conditions for so many? Neuwirth's answer is part of his descriptive narrative: governments (and local police) are corrupt, international agencies such as UN-HABITAT are well-meaning but incompetent and out of touch with reality on the ground, the media regularly report squatter areas incorrectly as if they are dominated by crime, and legal institutions protect the most powerful private interests. In the end, he suggests, this hardly matters. The squatters themselves by their numbers, and by their fierce and determined energy, are building a new urban world, just as so many of them did in earlier years in American cities such as Chicago, San Francisco and New York (Neuwirth, 2005).

A planet of slums?

Echoing many of the same sentiments but with a decidedly sharper political voice is the important book by the urban journalist Mike Davis, *Planet of Slums* (2006). Based on an original article written earlier (Davis, 2004), itself a commentary on the UN HABITAT report, *The Challenge of Slums* (2003), the book is an indictment of the inability (or deliberate avoidance), on the part of governments in both the north and the south, to improve the lives and life chances of increasing numbers of poor and destitute people living in more than 200,000 slums around the world (Davis, 2006: 26). 'The principal function of the third world urban edge' is, he says, 'as a human dump' (Davis, 2006: 47). Responsibility for the current situation (notwithstanding the role played by colonialism in creating the framework for dysfunctional urban development in the first place) is placed on the international financial institutions (especially the World Bank and the IMF) for having promoted harsh structural adjustment programmes (SAPs) during the 1980s – programmes that reduced social expenditures and government employment in the cities in particular. Currently 'fashionable' solutions to the spreading problem of urban poverty and informality in so many countries – such as land titling in informal settlements (De Soto, 2000), microfinance and the MDGs (see above) – are dismissed by Davis as window-dressing at best, or more concretely (as in the case of land titling and MDGs) as, respectively, a 'bootstrap model of capitalism ... especially popular because of the simplicity of the recipe' (Davis, 2006: 179) and 'the last gasp of development idealism' (Davis, 2006: 200).

The murky category of 'informal' or the 'informal sector' has bedevilled much social science writing on cities in developing countries. First developed conceptually by the anthropologist Keith Hart (1973) in his study of migrant economic activities in Ghana in the early 1970s, the informal sector was officially defined and legitimised by the International Labour Organisation and became a central conceptual tool of economic analysis of cities during the 1970s and 1980s. By the early part of the current decade, however, economists writing on behalf of the National Research Council in the US could state that both formal and informal sectors in developing countries they surveyed had become increasingly heterogeneous. As a result:

no insurmountable barriers appear to divide these two sectors. If this view is correct, then the terms 'formal' and 'informal' are now useful mainly as evocative labels that suggest general characteristics, rather than being descriptive of deep-seated market rigidities and dualisms ... the root causes of urban inequalities must be sought in the opportunities and constraints that can be found in both sectors. (Montgomery et al., 2003: 339–40)

The urban poor and the question of agency

A central issue in the political literature on the growing numbers of urban poor in developing countries is agency. To what extent are the forces impinging on the poor so powerful as to extinguish all possibility of political response at the local level? Do the poor have any 'voice' in this massive scenario? Since much of the social science literature on cities outside North America and Europe is written by geographers, planners and sociologists, the role of the political is often approached either indirectly (as in accounts that emphasise structural factors that impinge upon the poor, or upon cities in general), or not at all. 'Policy' – a political category if ever there was one – is usually presented as an idealised solution to a set of problems or structural contradictions, whereas the political requirements for such a policy, or policies to be put in place, are rarely if ever specified (but see Devas, 2002). For the most part, we have an array of unrelated case studies. Within this group of otherwise unconnected works, some writers have focused on the politics of local planning and employment issues, with an emphasis on new civil society groupings and the struggle over new public spaces in a neo-democratic setting (Graham and Jacobi, 2002; Winchester et al., 2003; Mitlin and Satterthwaite, 2004: Part III; Cross and Morales, 2007), while others have looked at the sociological conditions for new political alliances and influences within the informal urban economy itself (Simone, 2004). Two outstanding collections of essays on urban informal politics and organisation in Africa are the product of the Nordic Africa Institute in Uppsala. Both these collections consider both the international forces creating and enhancing urban informality, as well as the response to these conditions by local people in an almost bewildering variety of ways (Tostensen et al., 2001; Hansen and Vaa, 2004).

In the myriad case studies of the relationship between the state (or its absence), and the inhabitants of the urban informal sector, politics is never far from the surface. But it is rarely specified as a central variable. Standing out as a brilliant and very promising exception to this muting of the political in the everyday lives of the urban poor is the approach of Asef Bayat, who goes beyond earlier notions of the 'passive poor' and the 'culture of poverty' (Lewis, 1961), the 'integration of marginality' thesis of Janice Perlman (1976), the 'survival strategy' approach, and the 'political mobilization of the poor' approach of the social movement theorists such as Manuel Castells (1983), to suggest a new perspective: 'the quiet encroachment of the ordinary'. In this formulation, poor households in the informal sector push against public restrictions to set up trading places on the sidewalks, to erect 'illegal' houses in local materials on previously unoccupied land, or to work as traditional doctors, 'street lawyers' or transport operators in the popular settlements – all in formal contradiction of city regulations and often in violation of the monopoly rights of large formal urban businesses. While mass actions of this nature do not start as political actions, they verge into political domains when – as so often happens – urban administrations attempt to regulate or remove them (Bayat, 2004). Understanding and theorising the politics of this sector will be a major challenge for researchers for many years.

Futures for comparative urban research

As we have suggested in this chapter, comparative research on urban politics in developing countries is still very thin. There are three approaches to this challenge that are likely to have some traction in coming years.

In terms of research methodologies, case studies of particular cities, or neighbourhoods in cities – in relation to some conceptual or theoretical question – are likely to continue to be the most common. Large-scale multi-city studies will be rare, especially since international agencies (who often provide funding for international work) do not normally favour cross-regional work, and practical or current policy questions are best addressed in a local context. But as more case studies are accumulated, comparative work can be undertaken using secondary research methods.

A second trend is likely to be more studies which link, and compare, cities in the 'north' and the 'south'. Linkages are increasingly formed by trade (including tourism) and the movement of people, but they will be reinforced by the connections between municipal governments themselves (sometimes called 'decentralized cooperation'), and by the relationships established by the spread of specialised office functions of multinational corporations. So far, few studies compare cities in different regions of the south, but this is likely to increase in frequency as major countries (such as South Africa, India, China and Brazil) develop cultural and commercial interests in other southern regions.

Finally, we can speculate on theoretical approaches to comparative urban politics. Critical, post-colonial studies, which are increasingly important in anthropology and geography, will probably become more significant in political science over the next decade. Issues such as gentrification and the marginalisation of the poor, the environmental cost burden of urban growth in developing countries, and the deeper understanding of urban political questions that may be apprehended through such concepts as multilevel governance, governability, and social sustainability may also generate research studies. As the growing importance (socially and economically) of cities is recognised, urban political studies will undoubtedly gain more traction in the comparative field. Just as political studies have followed urbanisation patterns in the United States and Western Europe, the force of practical issues – such as dealing with poverty, disease, inequity, social diversity and infrastructural scarcity – will demand imaginative ideas that can help us to understand the complex politics of urban development of 80 percent of the world's population.

For the future of urban political studies in developing countries, there is nowhere to go but up.

Note

1   At the United Nations Millennium Summit in September 2000, world leaders agreed to a set of eight measurable goals and targets relating to various aspects of social, economic and environmental development. They can be accessed at http://www.un.org/millennium goals/

References

Balbo, Marcello (1993) 'Urban planning and the fragmented city of developing countries', *Third World Planning Review*, 15 (1): 23–35.

Balbo, Marcello (ed.) (2005) *International Migrants and the City*. Nairobi and Venice: UN-HABITAT and the Università Iuav di Venezia.

Ballard, Richard, Habib, Adam and Valodia, Imraan (eds) (2006) *Voices of Protest. Social Movements in Post-Apartheid South Africa*. Scottsville, South Africa: University of KwaZulu-Natal Press.

Batley, Richard (2001) 'Public-private partnerships for urban services', in Mila Freire and Richard Stren (eds), *The Challenge of Urban Government. Policies and Practices*. Washington: World Bank Institute; and Toronto: Centre for Urban and Community Studies. pp. 199–214.

Bayat, Asef (2004) 'Globalization and the politics of the informals in the global south', in Ananya Roy and Nezar Alsayyad (eds), *Urban Informality. Transnational Perspectives from the Middle East, Latin America, and South Asia*. Lanham, MD: Lexington Books. pp. 79–102.

Benton-Short, Lisa, Price, Marie D. and Friedman, Samantha (2005) 'Globalization from below: the ranking of global immigrant cities', *International Journal of Urban and Regional Research*, 29 (4): 945–59.

Bond, Patrick (2000) *Cities of Gold. Townships of Coal. Essays on South Africa's New Urban Crisis*. Trenton, NJ: Africa World Press.

Bond, Patrick (2005) 'Globalisation/commodification or deglobalisation/decommodification in urban South Africa', *Policy Studies*, 26 (3): 337–58.

Bourne, Larry S. and Simmons, Jim (2004) 'The conceptualization and analysis of urban systems: a North American perspective', in Tony Champion and Graeme Hugo (eds), *New Forms of Urbanization. Beyond the Urban-Rural Dichotomy*. Aldershot: Ashgate. pp. 249–67.

Caldeira, Teresa (2000) *City of Walls: Crime, Segregation, and Citizenship in Sao Paulo*. Berkeley: University of California Press.

Cameron, Robert (2005) 'Metropolitan restructuring (and more restructuring) in South Africa', *Public Administration and Development*, 25 (4): 329–39.

Castells, Manuel (1983) *The City and the Grassroots*. Berkeley: University of California Press.

Chakrabarty, Dipesh (2000) *Provincializing Europe: Postcolonial Thought and Historical Difference*. Princeton: Princeton University Press.

Cross, John and Morales, Alfonso (eds) (2007) *Street Entrepreneurs. People, Place and Politics in Local and Global Perspective*. London: Routledge.

Davis, Mike (2004) 'Planet of Slums', *New Left Review*, 26 (March/April): 5–34.

Davis, Mike (2006) *Planet of Slums*. London: Verso.

De Soto, Hernando (2000) *The Mystery of Capital. Why Capitalism Triumphs in the West and Fails Everywhere Else*. New York: Basic Books.

Devas, Nick with Amis, Philip, Beall, Jo, Grant, Ursula, Mitlin, Diana, Nunan, Fiona and Rakodi, Carole (2002) *Urban Governance, Voice and Poverty in the Developing World*. London: Earthscan.

Escobar, Arturo (1995) *Encountering Development. The Making and Unmaking of the Third World*. Princeton: Princeton University Press.

Friedmann, John (1986) 'The world city hypothesis', *Development and Change*, 17 (1): 69–84.

Friedmann, John (1995) 'Where we stand: a decade of world city research', in Paul Knox and Peter Taylor (eds), *World Cities in a World System*. Cambridge: Cambridge Univesity Press. pp. 21–47.

Friedmann, John and Wolff, Goetz (1982) 'World city formation: an agenda for research and action', *International Journal of Urban and Regional Research*, 6 (3): 309–44.

Gilbert, Alan (1996) 'Land, housing and infrastructure in Latin America's major cities', in Alan Gilbert (ed.), *The Mega-City in Latin America*. Tokyo: United Nations University Press. pp. 73–109.

Graham, Lawrence and Jacobi, Pedro (2002) 'Sao Paulo: tensions between clientelism and participatory democracy', in David J. Myers and Henry A. Dietz (eds), *Capital City Politics in Latin America*. Boulder, CO: Lynn Rienner. pp. 297–324.

Graham, Stephen and Marvin, Simon (2001) *Splintering Urbanism: Networked Infrastructures, Technological Mobilities and the Urban Condition*. London: Routledge.

Gugler, Josef (ed.) (2004) *World Cities Beyond the West. Globalization, Development and Inequality*. New York: Oxford.

Handelman, Howard and Tessler, Mark (eds) (1999) *Democracy and its Limits. Lessons from Asia, Latin America, and the Middle East*. Notre Dame, IN: University of Notre Dame Press.

Hansen, Karen Tranberg and Vaa, Mariken (2004) *Reconsidering Informality. Perspectives from Urban Africa*. Uppsala: Nordic Africa Institute.

Hart, Keith (1973) 'Informal income opportunities and urban employment in Ghana', *Journal of Modern African Studies*, 11 (1): 61–89.

Harvey, David (2005) *A Brief History of Neoliberalism*. Oxford: Oxford University Press.

Holston, James (1989) *The Modernist City. An Anthropological Critique of Brasília*. Chicago: University of Chicago Press.

Huntington, Samuel (1991) *The Third Wave*. Norman, OK: University of Oklahoma Press.

Islam, Nasrul (2003) 'Reforming governance in Dhaka, Bangladesh', in Patricia McCarney and Richard Stren (eds) *Governance on the Ground. Innovations and Discontinuities in Cities of the Developing World*. Baltimore and Washington: The Johns Hopkins University Press and The Woodrow Wilson Center Press. pp. 194–219.

Laquian, Aprodicio (2005) *Beyond Metropolis. The Planning and Governance of Asia's Mega-urban Regions*. Baltimore: Johns Hopkins University Press.

Léautier, Frannie A. (ed.) (2006) *Cities in a Globalizing World. Governance, Performance and Sustainability*. Washington: The World Bank.

Lewis, Oscar (1961) *The Children of Sanchez. Autobiography of a Mexican Family*. New York: Random House.

Logan, John R. (2000) 'Still a global city: the racial and ethnic segmentation of New York', in Peter Marcuse and Ronald van Kempen (eds), *Globalizing Cities. A New Spatial Order?* Oxford: Blackwell. pp. 158–85.

Manor, James (1999) *The Political Economy of Democratic Decentralization.* Washington: The World Bank.

Manso, Bruno Paes, Faria, Maryluci de Araújo and Gall, Norman (2005) *Diadema. Democracy 3. Frontier Violence and Civilization in Sao Paulo's Periphery.* Sao Paulo: Fernand Braudel Institute of World Economics, Braudel Papers No. 36.

Marcuse, Peter and van Kempen, Ronald (eds) (2000) *Globalizing Cities. A New Spatial Order?* Oxford: Blackwell.

Mitlin, Diana and Satterthwaite, David (eds) (2004) *Empowering Squatter Citizens. Local Government, Civil Society and Urban Poverty Reduction.* London: Earthscan.

Montgomery, Mark, Stren, Richard Cohen, Barney and Reed, Holly (eds) (2003) *Cities Transformed.* Washington: National Academies Press.

Murray, Martin J. (2004) 'The spatial dynamics of postmodern urbanism: social polarisation and fragmentation in Sao Paulo and Johannesburg', *Journal of Contemporary African Studies*, 22 (2) (May): 139–64.

Neuwirth, Robert (2005) *Shadow Cities.* New York: Routledge.

Olivera, Oscar (in collaboration with Tom Lewis) (2004) *¡Cochabamba! Water War in Bolivia.* Cambridge, MA: South End Press.

Osmont, Annik (1995) *La Banque mondiale et les villes.* Paris: Karthala.

Perlman, Janice (1976) *The Myth of Marginality. Urban Poverty and Politics in Rio de Janeiro.* Berkeley: University of California Press.

Portes, Alejandro and Stepick, Alex (1993) *City on the Edge. The Transformation of Miami.* Berkeley: University of California Press.

Putnam, Robert (2000) *Bowling Alone. The Collapse and Revival of American Community.* New York: Simon and Schuster.

Raiser, Simon and Volkmann, Krister (2007) 'City regions between their legacies and the global context', in K. Segbers (ed.), *The Making of Global City Regions.* Baltimore Johns Hopkins University Press. pp. 27–31.

Ramsamy, Edward (2006) *The World Bank and Urban Development. From Projects to Policy.* London: Routledge.

Robinson, Jennifer (2006) *Ordinary Cities. Between Modernity and Development.* London: Routledge.

Rolnick, Raquel (1999) 'Territorial exclusion and violence: the case of Sao Paulo, Brazil'. Comparative Urban Studies Occasional Papers Series, No. 26, Woodrow Wilson International Center for Scholars, Washington, DC.

Rotker, Susana (ed.) (2002) *Citizens of Fear. Urban Violence in Latin America.* New Brunswick, NJ: Rutgers University Press.

Ruble, Blair (2005) *Creating Diversity Capital. Transnational Migrants in Montreal, Washington, and Kyiv.* Baltimore: Johns Hopkins University Press.

Ruble, Blair, Stren, Richard, Tulchin, Joseph and Varat, Diana (eds) (2001) *Urban Governance Around the World.* Washington: Woodrow Wilson International Center for Scholars, Comparative Urban Studies Project.

Sassen, Saskia (1991) *The Global City.* Princeton: Princeton University Press.

Sassen, Saskia (2001) *The Global City,* 2nd edn. Princeton: Princeton University Press.

Sassen, Saskia (ed.) (2007) *Deciphering the Global. Its Scales, Spaces and Subjects.* New York: Routledge.

Scott, Allen J. (ed.) (2001) *Global City-Regions. Trends, Theory, Policy.* New York: Oxford University Press.

Scott, James C. (1998) *Seeing Like a State. How Certain Schemes to Improve the Human Condition have Failed.* New Haven: Yale University Press.

Segbers, Klaus (ed.) (2007) *The Making of Global City Regions. Johannesburg, Mumbai/Bombay, Sao Paulo, and Shanghai.* Baltimore: Johns Hopkins University Press.

Simone, Abdoumaliq (2004) *For the City Yet to Come. Changing African Life in Sour Cities.* Durham: Duke University Press.

Smith, Laïla (2004) 'The murky waters of the second wave of neoliberalism: corporatization as a service delivery model in Cape Town', *Geoforum*, 35 (3): 375–93.

Smith, Michael Peter (2001) *Transnational Urbanism. Locating Globalization.* Oxford: Blackwell.

Stren, Richard (1995) 'Major urban research themes for the 1990s: an introduction', in Richard Stren and Judith Bell (eds), *Urban Research in the Developing World. Perspectives on the City.* Toronto: University of Toronto, Centre for Urban and Community Studies. pp. 1–17.

Swyngedouw, Erik (2004) *Social Power and the Urbanization of Water.* Oxford: Oxford University Press.

Tostensen, Arne, Tvedten, Inge and Vaa, Mariken (eds) (2001) *Associational Life in African Cities. Popular Responses to the Urban Crisis.* Uppsala: Nordic Africa Institute.

UN-HABITAT (2003) *The Challenge of Slums. Global Report on Human Settlements 2003.* London: Earthscan.

UN-HABITAT (2007) *Enhancing Urban Safety and Security. Global Report on Human Settlements 2007.* London: Earthscan.

United Nations (2006) *World Population Prospects. The 2006 Revision, Highlights.* Accessed 1 July 2007 at:http://www.un.org/esa/population/publications/WUP2005/ 2005WUPHighlights _Final_Report.pdf

United States Conference of Mayors (2007) *U.S. Metro Economies. Gross Metropolitan Product with Housing Update.* Lexington, MA: Global Insight. Accessed 1 July 2007 at: http://www.city-mayors.com/statistics/richest-cities-2005.html

Winchester, Lucy, Cáceres, Teresa and Rodriguez, Alfredo (2003) 'Bellavista: local political activism in defense of a barrio', in Patricia McCarney and Richard Stren (eds), *Governance on the Ground. Innovations and Discontinuities in Cities of the Developing World.* Baltimore and Washington: The Johns Hopkins University Press and The Woodrow Wilson Center Press. pp. 83–110.

Part IV

CITIZENS

11

POVERTY, INEQUALITY AND SOCIAL EXCLUSION[1]

Mara S. Sidney

Since the era of industrialisation, North American and European cities have been home to significant populations of poor people. Although poverty certainly exists in rural areas, it is linked in the modern imagination to images of urban life, from Jacob Riis's 1890 portrayal of tenement life in *How the Other Half Lives*, to the numerous images of urban ghettos that appear on any given day in contemporary newspapers and on television. Cities, of course, are also home to many of a society's wealthy people, thus making social inequality and stratification visible because of the density and proximity of urban life. Think of Dickens' numerous portraits of wealthy industrialists alongside indigent waifs or workers, or contemporary images of gentrified neighbourhoods where luxury shops and patrons share city blocks with the homeless. Certainly in the twentieth century and into the present, questions and concerns about poor people underlie and motivate much urban research and urban reform efforts. As scholars consider the position and experiences of poor people in cities, they also raise questions central to the field of political science about democracy, equality and social justice.

Theories of urban politics have long addressed the marginal position of poor people. Some theories focus on the marginal representation and voice of the poor within city government, examining the mechanisms that exclude the poor from influence, as well as the moments when some degree of voice has been achieved. Other theories focus on the control of urban land and other forms of capital, examining how private and public sector actors together exclude or displace the poor from urban space and urban planning processes. Research also focuses on institutions and movements to resist this exclusion, whether through grassroots-based community development or cooperative ownership arrangements. In the past decade, social exclusion has emerged as a concept through which to study aspects of urban life, drawing attention to the multiple dimensions of marginalisation that characterise the lives of the poor. This chapter reviews components of three theoretical approaches to the poor in urban politics, considers some cross-cutting themes, and offers suggestions for further development of urban political theory.

Poverty and inequality in cities

Although on a global scale, a greater share of poor people still live in rural areas, the share of the world's poor living in cities is growing, and the United Nations predicts it will exceed 50 percent within decades (UN-Habitat, 2006). Poverty is increasing in cities, and becoming more severe; as the United Nations Human Settlement Programme reports, 'there are now higher numbers of the "poorest of the poor" in urban centres throughout the world than at any previous time ...' (2003: 29). UN-Habitat estimates that, worldwide, one of three city dwellers lives in slum conditions (see Stren, this volume). While it used to be the case that the urban poor fared marginally better than the rural poor, this is no longer true. According to UN reports, impoverished people in cities face multiple dimensions of deprivation, from high mortality rates and low access to health care, to sub-standard living conditions and insecure housing arrangements, to lack of access to education and employment. Because of the increasing poor population in cities throughout the world, and the economic importance of cities within national economies and the global economic system, UN-Habitat argues for a range of anti-poverty programmes targeted to cities: 'The global fight against poverty is dependent on how well cities perform' (2006: 46).

North American and European metropolitan areas also house significant shares of their nations' poor. In the United States, the urban poverty rate has long been higher than that in the suburbs, and neighbourhoods of concentrated poverty cluster in central cities. The average urban poverty rate was 16.4 in 1999, with the suburban poverty rate at 10.3 percent (Dreier et al., 2001: 38). In 2000, a study found that one in eight US cities was burdened by at least two of the following characteristics: unemployment at least 50 percent higher than the national average, a poverty rate of at least 20 percent, and population loss of more than 5 percent since 1980 (2001: 16). Within US cities, poor and affluent families tend to live in different neighbourhoods. Whereas the spatial concentration of poverty rose from 1970 to 1990 in US metropolitan areas, it declined in many places during the 1990s (Jargowsky, 2003). By 2000, about 8 million people lived in high-poverty neighbourhoods whereas 10 million had ten years earlier (2001: 4). These changes were particular to the South and the Midwest, whereas the population of high-poverty regions in the Northeast remained about the same, and that in the West increased (2001: 5). Nonetheless, the absolute number of people in poverty rose throughout the 1990s.

European cities have also seen growing numbers of the poor, but poverty tends to be less concentrated than in the United States (LeGales, 2002). LeGales describes a resurgence of poverty in Europe over the last 20 years, emerging from economic restructuring, the fragility of social bonds and the decline of social policies. Poverty is measured differently in European countries than in the United States, so figures are not directly comparable, but a study of 58 cities found that 23 percent, on average, of the population was financially poor.

Defining poverty and exclusion

Urban scholars conceptualise poverty in different ways, partly due to different national systems of measuring it. They use national census data on income levels and poverty thresholds as one indicator of the extent of poverty in a place, but also reflect on the limitations of these types of measures. For example, they might note that the US poverty rate tends to underestimate poverty because it is calculated based on the Department of Agriculture's minimum food budget multiplied by three, irrespective of regional differences in cost of living and because it incorporates outdated assumptions about family expenditures (Dreier et al., 2001: 17). Some scholars document low-income populations by using income data relative to the median income; thus they might examine the portion of households earning 20 percent, 40 percent or 60 percent of the area median income as a way to specify a population. In general, scholars examining the role of the poor in political or policy processes define poverty more loosely because they focus on mobilisation, advocacy and other political processes within a city on behalf of the disadvantaged. Either explicitly or implicitly, they acknowledge and examine the social and political consequences of poverty, thereby linking what Europeans call 'income poverty' to other forms of disadvantage.

European scholars studying social exclusion are likely to see income as one of a cluster of conditions mutually reinforcing one another. That is, social exclusion denotes how people are 'disconnected from mainstream society in ways that [go] beyond poverty – for example non-participation in politics, poor health, and geographic isolation' (Davies, 2005: 4). The concept can direct attention to an array of 'linked problems such as unemployment, discrimination, poor skills, low incomes, poor housing, high crime, bad health and family breakdown' (2005: 5) and to the mechanisms that produce these problems.

The poor in theories of urban politics

In general, urban politics scholars working in North American and European contexts observe and assume that poor people and their advocates will have limited power in the political world, stemming from their systemic social disadvantage in capitalist societies and liberal political systems. Broadly, three types of theoretical approaches encompass much of the scholarship on urban politics and the poor. One approach emphasises the role of politics in shaping the prospects for the poor, a second the role of the economy. A third uses a problem-centred lens, considering how multiple macro- and micro-level political, economic and social forces simultaneously produce a particular kind of urban problem.

Politics first

The pluralist approach to urban politics, developed by Dahl, was perhaps the least pessimistic about the prospects for the poor to influence political processes. Its emphasis on the fragmentation of policy arenas within the city, and the observation that no group is permanently excluded, nor has inequalities that cumulate across policy arenas, led to the assertion that the poor could influence particular policy arenas at particular points in time (Judge, 1995). Pluralism rejected the idea of a ruling elite who influenced all spheres of decision-making. Yet urban scholars have long discounted many of pluralism's core assumptions by drawing attention to the second and third faces of power (e.g. the issues that never get onto a city's policy agenda, and the structural and cultural constraints of the social, political and economic systems) (Judge, 1995).

Regime theory is now the dominant theoretical approach focusing on political relationships in cities to explain responsiveness to low-income people (see Mossberger, this volume). Its attention on coordination of multiple actors as the primary governance task envisions an avenue toward inclusion, albeit tempered with realism that, especially in the US context, resources needed to support the needs of the poor are not typically present (Stone, 1993; Stoker, 1995). In his typology of regimes, Stone includes the 'lower-class opportunity expansion regime' (1993), focused on 'enriched education and job training, improved transportation access, and enlarged opportunities for business and home ownership' (1993: 20). While the full-blown lower-class opportunity expansion regime may remain in the realm of theory, Stone's and colleagues' work focuses on identifying and understanding governing regimes where steps toward this ideal have been attempted and in some cases, where there is evidence of modest success. The study of regimes directs attention to regime membership and posits that regime priorities will vary depending on who takes part, with what resources. As such, Stone rejects the premise that the growth imperative dictates that urban regimes should be expected always and primarily to focus on physical development. If regime partners advance social concerns, and have some level of resources, then broader agendas can result. In particular, prospects for responding to the urban poor hinge on links between government and non-profits, and whether together with the business sector, these actors can mobilise adequate resources for a wider agenda.

Community organising represents an important and commonly used strategy through which low-income people and their advocates pursue policy changes and influence at City Hall. Recent scholarship on community organising considers the impact of broad social, economic and political changes on its methods, goals and prospects for success. For example, under conditions of a globalised and restructured economy, community-based groups advocating for the poor are more likely to engage in living wage campaigns and to turn to social service provision (Orr, 2007). As local elite power structures become more fragmented, organisers face the challenge of finding targets with the power to make change; increasing fragmentation of the civic sector also makes mobilisation and coalition-building more difficult. Orr and the authors in his edited volume suggest that while small victories do improve the daily lives of disadvantaged people, these changes do not add up to broad progressive agendas in city government, or to real inclusion of poor people's advocates in the local power structure.

Ferman's work on neighbourhood politics in Chicago and Pittsburgh speaks to this problem by pointing to the importance of institutionalising progressive neighbourhood agendas (1996). Her work suggests that elected officials (e.g. reform or populist mayors) do not always take steps to institutionalise change, but that when they do, neighbourhood voice can be incorporated into city governance; this occurs in Pittsburgh through regular funding of neighbourhood-based groups and community development corporations, neighbourhood-oriented planning in city agencies, and regular communication and consultation about local development. Nonetheless, Ferman echoes other researchers when she finds that institutionalisation occurs for a narrow band of reforms – unidimensionally around local economic development, rather than for a broad set of progressive measures across multiple policy issues (see also Fagotto and Fung, 2006 on the Minneapolis Neighborhood Revitalisation Program).

While studies of organising document the emergence of new groups to meet new issues (see Rabrenovic, this volume), or to address issues that existing groups will not take up, many works also chart a historical trajectory of organising that serves to build capacity and generate leaders, even as groups adapt to changes in the urban context. Thus, numerous works point to the beginnings of organising in Alinsky-style or other sorts of protest groups post-Second World War, joined later by neighbourhood-based mobilisation against federally funded urban renewal projects. From there, groups often began to engage in neighbourhood development, using models of community non-profit development. In some places, these organisations became launching pads for political careers, as neighbourhood leaders ran for city council or for mayor.

In sum, 'politics first' approaches to the place of the poor in urban politics focus on political relationships and regimes that govern policy-making and implementation in cities and mobilisation of poor people through strategies such as community organising. These studies identify the structural constraints and opportunities within which actors manoeuvre to pursue their goals, and the achievements and limits of these efforts.

Economics first

Most pessimistic about prospects of the poor have been elite theories and related political economy and Marxist approaches such as 'the growth machine' and 'city trenches'. Each asserts that a business-dominated local elite exercises power to advance its interests, at the expense of the poor. Scholars challenge the ideology of value-free development (that growth is good for all), asserting that low-income groups bear the costs of growth (Harding, 1995). Thus, Logan and Molotch develop the concept of a local growth machine, analysing which elite actors take part, and how their actions privilege the exchange values of land rather than the use values held by lower income renters. They depict a city in which the poor may resist displacement, but ultimately are likely to fail, and to be pushed from neighbourhood to neighbourhood as the growth machine expands its reach, discovering new sites within the city and perhaps abandoning others (Logan and Molotch, 1987).

Katznelson's study of urban politics echoes the depiction of subordinated working- and lower-class groups in the city, but identifies a somewhat different mechanism of exclusion (1981). The residential basis of local politics, coupled with residential segregation in US cities, downplays the importance of production-related issues such as workplace relations and distribution of the fruits of production. Workers are isolated from the dominant classes in homogeneous neighbourhoods, and are socialised into an ethnically based politics of distribution at the neighbourhood level. Conflict is limited to the scale of the neighbourhood, where groups fight for influence and control of local resources. Palliative actions by city elites mute more serious challenges to the distribution of power and resources.

Recent work focusing on the impact of economic structures and processes on cities theorises local economic autonomy as a necessary first step toward more egalitarian outcomes for the poor, and for their political empowerment. Although Katznelson implied that neighbourhood control merely diverted the attention of the working classes and racial minorities from broader inequalities, recent work examines local and neighbourhood institutions as mechanisms for effectuating broader change. Scholars argue that altering a locality's relations to capital is a precondition for political equality. The context of economic globalisation, capital mobility and the diffusion of neo-liberal policies does not mean that cities or workers are powerless in the face of international capital flows, beholden to multinational corporations acting in a global marketplace, and destined to ride the waves of global economic shifts, for good or bad. Instead, city leaders and residents can establish collectively owned institutions that bind capital to their cities, and distribute power widely. As the control of capital brings a measure of economic stability to places and their citizens, and as working and low-income people experience and exercise power within these new institutions, this ethos and these experiences will bleed into the political system, reinvigorating local democracy.

DeFilippis (2004) and Williamson et al. (2002) articulate this theoretical approach, and study examples of transformative arrangements for organising capital in cities. Many scholars assume that such strategies have limited prospects for enactment, especially in the US context. By drawing attention to actual cases, these researchers seek to normalise them, to show them in action even in the context of a hostile political economy. Williamson et al. (2002) present an array of 'community-centered, place-stabilizing policies', originating at the international, national, state and local levels, that they argue would invigorate community democracy and produce a more egalitarian distribution of resources and opportunities.

DeFilippis focuses on the collective ownership of work, housing and money: he examines cases of worker cooperatives, mutual housing associations, cooperative housing, land trusts, community-based financial institutions and credit unions. He finds that these alternative arrangements, which root capital to place and to a particular group of people, do improve the lives of collective owners.

Whether benefits spill over to help disadvantaged people more generally in a place is less clear, as is whether the presence of one kind of collective in a locality spurs the creation of others. Also, such cooperative institutions may not be sustained. DeFilippis argues for careful assessments of such projects' strengths and weaknesses; over-promising to 'solve' poverty risks generating a backlash that can erode support for partially successful programmes. Efforts to transform economic arrangements will be long-range and incremental, with inevitable setbacks. Both sets of authors set out a compelling, plausible logic about the link between economics and politics. DeFilippis suggests, however, that the shift from collective ownership of capital to more inclusive local democracies will not happen automatically (2004: 148). Rather, political leadership and/or a political movement are required. Shifts in the ownership of capital may set the stage for shifts in political arrangements if political leadership is exercised in that direction.

Social exclusion: a problem-centred approach

During the 1990s, the concept of social exclusion came to dominate urban policy and urban research in Europe. This approach to studying urban politics is inherently problem-centred. It advances a particular conceptualisation of 'the problem with cities' or perhaps 'the problem with some of the people' in cities. Although the concept of social exclusion is 'slippery and contested' (Geddes, 2000: 783), especially among academics, the European Union and national and local governments have used it to develop and to justify a range of reforms of social welfare policies and urban programmes relating to employment, education, housing and other elements of social provision (Atkinson, 2000).

The EU's URBAN programme, the French politique de la ville, the UK's New Deal for Communities and active citizenship programmes are only a few of the programmes aimed to reduce social exclusion, targeted at the urban and often at the neighbourhood level. The EU and its member states have funded research that examines conditions of social exclusion and evaluates policies. Many studies examine the relationship between neighbourhood conditions and individual indicators of social exclusion. In the UK, residence in a deprived area contributes to increases in some individual indicators of social exclusion (Buck, 2001). But neighbourhood resources may matter differentially to individuals. In a cross-national study spanning six European countries and 11 cities, and surveying a range of public programmes that aim to reduce exclusion, Murie and Musterd found that neighbourhood resources made the most difference for populations most marginalised by the economy or the welfare state (2004).

Particular anti-exclusion programmes include efforts to integrate policy delivery, to direct intensive services to particular targeted neighbourhoods, programmes focused on employment, or housing, and policies directed at particular groups of excluded people. The policy emphasis on social exclusion increasingly has shifted to focus on citizenship, with government officials and researchers articulating an ideal of inclusion and participation in policy creation and implementation (Davies, 2005; Brannan et al., 2006; Taylor, 2007).

Urban scholars have challenged many aspects of anti-exclusion policies and programmes. They critique the programmes' underlying causal theories about disadvantaged people in cities and their prospects for moving toward inclusion. For example, many scholars identify an implicit embrace of neoliberalism (e.g. Atkinson, 2000; Geddes, 2000; Davies, 2005; Taylor, 2007). That is, programmes tend to privatise and individualise the responsibility for social well-being by emphasising individual deficits that give rise to exclusion. While the notion of social exclusion can direct attention to social structural characteristics and distributional issues, the political rhetoric in some places emphasises individual factors and directs attention to equal opportunities rather than equal outcomes (Davies, 2005). Studies also question the degree to which local regeneration programmes and/or local social services can truly touch the national and international forces that produce exclusion, such as withdrawal of state welfare programmes, economic dislocations and restructuring. Some scholars note that policies focus on some dimensions of exclusion (class) and overlook others (e.g. gender and race). Finally, scholars critique local partnership efforts that often form the centrepiece of social inclusion programmes for shifting the burden of problem-solving to disadvantaged groups themselves, for failing to address limited capacity and power imbalances inherent in such arrangements, and for glossing over inevitable conflicts and questions of representativeness (Atkinson, 2000; Davies, 2005; Taylor, 2007).

Cross-cutting themes and points of difference

The major types of approaches to theorising the role of the poor in urban politics share a number of themes, and diverge in several additional ways.

Centrality of non-profits

A key theme of work about poor people in cities is the importance of non-profit and community-based organisations in representing the interests of the poor, in responding to their needs through policy development and delivery, and in acting to build more egalitarian and democratic cities.

From the perspective of regime theory, non-profits now are understood as critical members of a governing regime if it is to address the needs of the poor. The implication is that without an active non-profit sector, the regime is unlikely to respond to this population. As for research on community organising, studies present countless examples of non-profits delivering services, from aiding families to claim the Earned Income Tax Credit, to running job training programmes, aiding Hurricane Katrina victims, tutoring children, and more (Orr, 2007). Non-profits activate low-income people to participate in advocacy campaigns, play a role in shaping policy agendas, and develop innovative policy solutions of their own (Swarts, 2003). Organisations vary in their capacity and desire to build coalitions (e.g. Swarts, 2003 on PACT vs. MCU; Staudt and Stone, 2007 on IAF affiliates) and they confront various political and governmental contexts that affect their chances of success in achieving policy change, securing implementation and institutionalising reform.

Work emphasising the priority of economic arrangements envisions non-profits as key vehicles in rearranging capital relations. Williamson et al. describe numerous and varied types of third-sector institutions they refer to as place-based economic structures, including community land trusts, community development financial institutions, employee-owned businesses, and others. By rooting capital in place, such structures can bring economic stability to communities. But the existence of such structures does not guarantee long-term positive change. Community development corporations, once engaged in challenging uneven urban development and disinvestment, and fighting for community control, now often adopt entrepreneurial ways of doing business that mimic for-profit entities (DeFilippis, 2004). Scholars critique this turn to market logic, arguing instead for a return to community-based and collective logics that they believe have more potential to improve neighbourhoods and empower low-income people (Stoecker, 1994; DeFilippis, 2004). Studies document a growing antagonism between previously symbiotic community organising and community development.

Scholars examining anti-exclusion policies have extensively studied public–private community partnerships, offering insight and recommendations about the sorts of public investments required to give community partners a chance at real power. Reporting on a cross-national study of more than 80 local partnerships in 10 EU countries, Geddes finds that not all partnerships included community members in the first place, nor did all include key organisations (e.g. labour unions or local employer representatives) that could help disadvantaged people (2000). Participation in partnerships presents serious transaction costs for community organisations whose members may not be familiar with bureaucratic processes, and partners with technocratic orientations do not always value their experiential knowledge. Geddes argues that even when formal parity in representation occurs, actual power and resources remain imbalanced.

Non-profits and community-based organisations link directly to democratic practice in cities. Even when mobilisation fails to achieve its immediate goals, it can build organisational strength and political connections that may help the next time around, may inaugurate residents into a life of politics, as well as develop leaders. Organisational characteristics themselves can promote or constrain citizenship practice. DeFilippis found that few collectives operated in a truly member-led democratic manner; professional staff made most decisions (2004: 146). Organisations vary in the degree to which they represent diverse communities; especially if an organisation is supposed to represent the community in a wider partnership, finding ways to effectively represent inevitable diversity is an ongoing challenge (Taylor, 2007). Cooptation by government and other elites is a risk when community-based organisations participate in partnerships, but in some cases, these opportunities afford residents the chance to resist government power. Taylor notes that if community members have 'popular spaces' in which to independently develop their voice, they are better prepared to engage in the 'invited spaces' of local partnerships (2007). When community organising strategies truly start at the grassroots level, developing community campaigns from the ground-up, they can '[replenish] democracy in communities not generally associated with civic engagement' (Orr, 2007: 252).

Policy or process

Theoretical approaches vary according to whether they advocate particular policy changes or emphasise instead the processes of policy-making. Politics-centred approaches tend to focus on process. They identify which stakeholders take part in decision-making: are the poor or their advocates consulted, are they active participants in shaping policy? In addition, politics-centred work focuses on the durability of reforms. Thus, Stone et al.'s work on education and human capital networks establishes institutionalised or sustained reform as an important, if not the primary, standard by which to judge success. Stone's recent work on models of reform (with Orr and Worgs, 2006) further develops these ideas. The authors argue that interpersonal and inter-organisational networks can successfully institutionalise social policy reforms, and thus lock in attention to impoverished and disadvantaged populations in cities. Stepping back from the 1993 argument that mass mobilisation of low-income populations is necessary if cities are to address the needs of the poor, here Stone et al. illustrate that connections between staffed non-profit organisations, government and the private sector can produce sustained policy change that benefits the poor.

Theories that emphasise economic arrangements are more likely to recommend specific types of changes that theoretically will lead to political empowerment of the poor. Thus, DeFilippis advocates the creation and proliferation of collectively owned institutions, because they directly alter the inequality-generating forces of capital mobility. Williamson et al. offer a broader, though conceptually similar, range of solutions aimed to build economically stable places. They advocate building on and expanding existing place-focused national, state and local programmes that would temper the negative consequences for cities and their neighbourhoods of globalisation and free trade, economic restructuring and job loss, and sprawl.

Social exclusion approaches articulate an overarching goal of policy (to achieve social inclusion). The concept's focus on multiple and reinforcing dimensions of exclusion suggests that solutions must also be multidimensional, thus include attention to the labour market, education, housing, income, health, crime, civic participation, etc. Murie and Musterd catalogue a range of programmes in place to combat exclusion, but hesitate to posit any as universal 'best practices' or even best practices for particular types of neighbourhoods, because their comparative case study finds outcomes to be so deeply contextual. Outcomes are embedded in particular communities within neighbourhoods, within cities, regions and nations, all with particular configurations of policies and policy histories that affect an individual's experience at the neighbourhood level.

These findings are consistent with the impulse of many anti-exclusion programmes to rely on local partnerships that will develop and coordinate locality-specific solutions. But scholars express ambivalence about partnerships as panacea. On the one hand, they acknowledge the intuitive appeal of the logic that, as Geddes puts it, partnerships will increase capacity to address problems by generating knowledge, trust, policy coordination and innovation, and leveraging resources. Many studies have by now demonstrated the difficulties in translating the theoretical logic of partnerships into reality.

The role of ideas and discourse

Both economics- and politics-driven theories increasingly consider the importance of ideas and political discourse in shaping urban politics and prospects for the poor. Because particular ideas about problems, about how society works, and about groups of people, support specific policy solutions, authors often recognise that changing political discourse may be a first step toward changing policies. Regime theory and related politics-driven theories highlight the ways that ideas can mobilise and sustain coalitions. Stone et al. describe articulation of a compelling purpose as the first step toward building a reform coalition; subsequent tasks for reformers include operationalising the purpose, and consistently articulating to stakeholders how programmes advance it (2006). A public culture in the US, constituted of ideas and norms related to individualism, competition and consumerism, presents particular challenges to community organisers at present, according to Orr, because their task is to mobilise people around a common good, and to build a sense of collective community.

This situation – a mismatch between the dominant discourse and that of disadvantaged people or their advocates – is frequently described. Reform becomes more difficult not only because of these different ideas, but because institutions and structures embody the dominant ideas as well. For example, Katznelson argues that African-American activists in New York articulated a set of claims that challenged existing institutional arrangements by spanning and linking the politics of work and the politics of community. Excluded from both spheres, black leaders articulated this exclusion in a global way rather than in the segmented way that ethnic groups used. In this case, the institutional structure persisted through partial incorporation of blacks into the politics of community – creating neighbourhood institutions to contain conflict to the neighbourhood level, thereby rebuffing the larger discourse.

Critical to the projects of DeFilippis and Williamson et al. is the challenge to conventional discourse about capital mobility that animates economic development policies in cities and, they argue, leads to economic instability, especially for the poorest residents. By acting in accordance with ideas about competition for private investment in a global era, leaders actually bring the ideas to life (see also Hay, 1999 on New Labour discourse in Britain). Luring private investment with tax breaks and other incentives fails to root capital in cities, thus making corporate departure easier. Rethinking the meaning of local autonomy from the ability of a city to offer incentives to business to actually transforming the relationship between capital and place, and acting in accordance with this new definition, would bring about change on the ground, according to these authors.

Similarly, scholars examining anti-exclusion policies are sceptical about the discourse of social exclusion. Part of their work is to consider whether the concept and the programmes emerging from it, represent a politically palatable way of talking about poverty in a political and economic environment increasingly focused on scaling back government and maximising individual autonomy and responsibility. Thus they take an ambivalent stance. On the one hand, they document conditions of exclusion, and appreciate the concept's ability to describe something important about the experience of disadvantage. They also evaluate programmes intended to reduce exclusion. Yet they step back from the technical programme evaluations to critique the broader project itself and to place it in a historical context.

Limits of the local scale

Scholarship across theoretical approaches points to the local level as the site where regional, national and international forces hit the ground, thus where authorities grapple most directly with problems of poverty. Most urban scholars note that local actors are limited in what they can do on their own to make significant changes in the lives of the poor. In the literature on social exclusion, authors express scepticism that local partnerships can accomplish more than marginal improvements in the face of shrinking welfare states and restructured economies. Atkinson argues that local programmes need to be nested within national, regional and European policies in order to have an impact (2000).

Advocates for the poor in cities thus face a context continually shaped by external factors. Staudt and Stone's work on El Paso shows this vividly with an extreme example – in this border city, actors face challenges stemming from immigration policy, trade policy and drug policy set at the national levels in two countries, and at the international level. Local actors grapple with the adverse consequences of contradictory policies. In cities across North America and Europe, community organisers confront a fragmented local business sector as the economy restructures, and new issues raised by changes in the nature of employment. Efforts to organise federations of community organisations that can work at the national or even international levels represent a response in the United States to the constraints of the local scale (Orr, 2007).

Most scholars note the small victories or local-level changes that can make a difference in people's lives, though some warn of parochialism that can result when politics occurs at a very localised level. Still, scholars assert that the power of external forces does not render local action irrelevant, inconsequential or unnecessary – only acknowledging that its consequences may be limited or constrained without complementary and even stronger measures at higher levels. In different ways, most work across theoretical approaches implicitly or explicitly makes the case that democracy can, and even must, be rebuilt from the ground up.

Directions for research

Building theory about variation across policy areas

The concept of social exclusion reminds us that disadvantage occurs across many dimensions of experience. Yet the bulk of the research on urban politics and the poor focuses on urban development (economic development and housing). A growing body of work examines education. There is less work examining policy areas such as labour, health and environmental health, youth services, crime and public safety, and infrastructure, though decisions and political processes in these areas critically affect poor people's experiences and opportunities.

Even less work compares political processes and outcomes across policy sectors. Each policy arena involves different government actors and institutions, different private- and non-profit-sector players, different laws and policies, different problem definitions and animating theories, so sustained reform may be more likely in some policy areas. Some policy arenas may be more responsive than others to claims and participation from less powerful groups. That is, advocates may have more success in gaining a voice for the poor in certain sectors. Some issues are more amenable to distributive politics and the creation of selective incentives, some issues are handled in more public arenas, some issues involve more elected officials, some have a stronger base of knowledge about factors causing problems and effective solutions, some require longer time-horizons before change will be visible, some are simply more expensive to address. These are just some of the ways in which policy sectors vary, but they suggest that cross-sector research could shed light on the position of the poor in urban politics.

Theorising conflict

Given that theories of urban politics expect poor people to face difficulty gaining responsiveness, influence and power, it is surprising that the role of conflict is under-theorised. An important direction for theory development is to consider the role that conflict plays in securing a voice for disadvantaged groups, or inhibiting that voice. Work on governing regimes and partnerships, on civic renewal and inclusion evokes images of peaceful deliberation as the valued mode of interaction. Conflict is presented as a barrier to consensus-building, mutual understanding and social learning, and as a brake on reform. The ideal of stakeholders joined in common purpose is presented as the prerequisite for improving outcomes for the poor. Can't we all just get along? It would be worthwhile to explicitly revisit these assumptions. After all, conflict may indicate that powerless groups have achieved a modicum of voice, that they have mobilised enough to make their views known.

At a minimum, case studies could depict the work of brokering conflict in more detail. But there is a need for a wider range of models of interaction, such that consensus-building and collaboration stand alongside other modes through which voice and influence might be realised. Whereas Politics First work tends to take interest formation as an empirical question, work in the Economics First tradition tends to be sceptical that consensus around common goals is possible across groups positioned differently in the economy (DeFilippis, 2004). Taylor, citing Fung and Wright (2003), suggests that real community empowerment requires the construction of a countervailing power (2007). In this model of interaction, some groups exist in perpetual conflict with elites, while others work in partnership with them.

Which poor people?

Urban scholars commonly refer to the fragmentation of the private sector in contemporary cities, but there is less explicit theoretical attention to different groups of poor people. Theories could lay out expectations about which sub-groups will achieve voice and policy responsiveness, and which groups are likely to be more visible and valued members of the polity. Some sub-groups are subjects of study, if not of explicit theorising. Racial and ethnic groups within cities makes up a significant part of the urban politics literature, and these works certainly speak to the situation of poor people in cities, their demands and responses to them. There is increasing attention to immigrants – first and subsequent generations, documented and undocumented – who certainly constitute a portion of the impoverished populations in cities. The increasing body of work on education means that youth are considered in urban politics research, although the needs and experiences of youth in cities go beyond the schools. Research on welfare reform focuses on single mothers, and ex-offenders are increasingly the subject of studies.

Which groups do we as scholars render even less visible by our lack of attention? To what extent is the full range of poor people's experiences and positions included in urban politics research? Can patterns be identified, and is there a relationship to the popular image – deserving or undeserving – attached to particular sub-groups? For example, children are considered the deserving poor, whereas single men of working age may not be. Do scholars disseminate these images or challenge them? How do research funding streams affect which sub-groups receive attention?

Relatedly, more attention is warranted to how actors construct sub-groups of the poor and their neighbourhoods (for examples, see Allen and Cars, 2002; Camou, 2005), how community issues are defined, and the biases at work within this process (for example, the discussion of 'women's issues' in Staudt and Stone, 2007 and women's lack of participation in partnerships as noted by Geddes, 2000 and Taylor, 2007). In addition, research should demonstrate the differences in how sub-groups experience poverty and lack of power (e.g. Murie and Musterd, 2004). Fine-grained analysis of urban problems and policies alerts us that all poor people are not the same.

Constructivist, interpretive urban analysis

Analysis of poverty, inequality and politics in cities would benefit from the explicit development and application of constructivist and interpretive approaches. These theoretical and methodological approaches are well developed in the study of international relations and of public policy, and have proved especially useful in examining inequalities and power disparities in political life, but they are used infrequently to study urban politics (e.g. Yanow and Schwartz-Shea, 2006; Klotz and Lynch, 2007). Stated simply, a constructivist perspective sees individuals and groups as both shaping, and being shaped by, the world around them; structure and agency are mutually constitutive. People and collectivities interpret the world around them and act according to these interpretations, leading constructivists to assert that interpretations shape social reality. Institutions, standard practices and policies emerge from collective interpretations; identities and relationships (alliance, divisions, hierarchies) do as well.

Constructivist, interpretive work on urban politics and poverty would reflect critically on the larger system(s) in which local politics and policy-making processes occur, and on the dominant ideas that these systems and their institutions embody. Relatedly, such research would analyse the paradigms that guide action in cities – how they emerge, how they manifest themselves, who contests them and with what ideas and resources. In doing so, studies would map the major groupings of identities and interests in cities, linking these to the nested contexts within which they make sense, and considering whether, where, and how actors and/or groups might prompt change. The constructivist ontology is deeply contextual, making it compatible with a good deal of the Politics First work described above, but pointing to an expanded range of contexts interacting at the local scale.

Some of the Economics First and Problem-Centred scholarship cited here gestures toward constructivism as it interrogates dominant paradigms such as neoliberalism and social exclusion. These works pull such paradigms to the surface, up from the embeddedness of taken-for-granted or conventional wisdom, to consider their assumptions, and to trace how the discourse of local actors and of public policies manifest their concepts, causal arguments and values. Other examples of constructivist urban research include Taylor (2007) and Goode and O'Brien (2006), who each use Foucault's notion of governmentality to investigate how non-state actors come to assume and enforce the state's ideas about local partnerships in the UK, and economic development in Philadelphia – and more broadly, related norms and values about appropriate social behaviour in cities and methods of problem-solving. Klinenberg's (2002) social autopsy approach examines the collective production of urban disadvantage, vulnerability and death. His study of Chicago's 1995 heatwave situates urban politics within a complex context of multiple actors and institutions. Local officials symbolically construct the heatwave, offering interpretations of statistics that deflect responsibility and using language to undermine dissenters' claims. The impact of meaning-making and interpretation extends to policies and their legacies as Klinenberg traces the deadly results of 'reinventing government' to conceptualise citizens as consumers. Constructivist interpretive approaches are not without their limitations and challenges. But the same sort of lively debates that have marked the evolution of politics- and economics-centred approaches could be brought to bear on constructivist studies of the city. Such studies could begin to fill some of the gaps that I have identified as marking our research on poverty, inequality and social exclusion in cities.

Note

1 The author wishes to thank David Imbroscio and Jonathan Davies for their helpful comments and their patience; Susan Clarke and Laura Lomas for good ideas; and Kyle Farmbry, Gabriela Kutting and Tod Mijanovich for last-minute assistance.

References

Allen, Judith and Cars, Goran (2002) 'European urban policy and disadvantaged neighborhoods', *European Spatial Research and Policy*, 9 (1): 21–40.

Atkinson, Rob (2000) 'Combating social exclusion in Europe: the new urban policy challenge', *Urban Studies*, 37 (5–6): 1037–55.

Brannan, Tessa, John, Peter and Stoker, Gerry (2006) 'Active citizenship and effective public services and programmes: how can we know what really works?', *Urban Studies*, 43 (5–6): 993–1008.

Buck, Nick (2001) 'Identifying neighbourhood effects on social exclusion', *Urban Studies*, 38 (12): 2251–75.

Camou, Michelle (2005) 'Deservedness in poor neighborhoods: a morality struggle', in Anne L. Schneider and Helen M. Ingram, *Deserving and Entitled: Social Constructions and Public Policy*. Albany: SUNY Press. pp. 197–218.

Davies, Jonathan S. (2005) 'The social exclusion debate: strategies, controversies and dilemmas', *Policy Studies*, 26 (1): 3–27.

DeFilippis, James (2004) *Unmaking Goliath: Community Control in the Face of Global Capital*. New York: Routledge.

Dreier, Peter, Mollenkopf, John and Swanstrom, Todd (2001) *Place Matters: Metropolitics for the Twenty-first Century*. Lawrence: University Press of Kansas.

Fagotto, Elena and Fung, Archon (2006) 'Empowered participation in urban governance: the Minneapolis neighborhood revitalization program', *International Journal of Urban and Regional Research*, 30 (3): 638–55.

Ferman, Barbara (1996) *Challenging the Growth Machine: Neighborhood Politics in Chicago and Pittsburgh*. Lawrence: University Press of Kansas.

Fung, A. and Wright, E.O. (2003) *Deepening Democracy: Innovations in Empowered Participatory Governance*. London: Verso.

Geddes, Mike (2000) 'Tackling social exclusion in the European Union? The limits to the new orthodoxy of local partnership', *International Journal of Urban and Regional Research*, 24 (4): 782–800.

Goode, Judith and O'Brien, Robert T. (2006) 'Whose social capital? How economic development projects disrupt local social relations', in Richardson Dilworth (ed.), *Social Capital in the City: Community and Civic Life in Philadelphia*. Philadelphia: Temple University Press. pp. 159–176.

Harding, Alan (1995) 'Elite theory and growth machines', in David Judge, Gerry Stoker and Harold Wolman (eds), *Theories of Urban Politics*. London: Sage Publications. pp. 35–53.

Hay, Colin (1999) *The Political Economy of the New Labour: Labouring under False Pretences?* Manchester & New York: Manchester University Press, St. Martins Press.

Jargowsky, Paul A. (2003) 'Stunning progress, hidden problems: the dramatic decline of concentrated poverty in the 1990s', Washington, DC: Brookings Institution, Living Cities Census Series.

Judge, David (1995) 'Pluralism', in David Judge, Gerry Stoker and Harold Wolman (eds), *Theories of Urban Politics*. London: Sage Publications. pp. 13–34.

Katznelson, Ira (1981) *City Trenches: Urban Politics and the Patterning of Class in the United States*. New York: Pantheon Books.

Klinenberg, Eric (2002) *Heat wave: A Social Autopsy of Disaster in Chicago*. Chicago: University of Chicago Press.

Klotz, Audie and Lynch, Cecilia (2007) *Strategies for Research in Constructivist International Relations*. Armonk, NY and London, England: M.E. Sharpe.

Le Gales, Patrick (2002) *European Cities: Social Conflicts and Governance*. Oxford: Oxford University Press.

Logan, John R. and Molotch, Harvey L. (1987) *Urban Fortunes: The Political Economy of Place*. Berkeley: University of California Press.

Murie, Alan and Musterd, Sako (2004) 'Social exclusion and opportunity structures in European cities and neighborhoods', *Urban Studies*, 41 (8): 1441–59.

Orr, Marion (2007) 'Community organizing and the changing ecology of civic engagement', in Marion Orr (ed.), *Transforming the City: Community Organizing and the Challenge of Political Change*. Lawrence: University Press of Kansas. pp. 1–27.

Staudt, Kathleen and Stone, Clarence N. (2007) 'Division and fragmentation: the El Paso experience in global–local perspective', in Marion Orr (ed.), *Transforming the City: Community Organizing and the Challenge of Political Change*. Lawrence: University Press of Kansas. pp. 84–108.

Stoecker, Randy (1994) *Defending Community: The Struggle for Community Development in Cedar-Riverside*. Philadelphia: Temple University Press.

Stoker, Gerry (1995) 'Regime theory and urban politics', in D. Judge, G. Stoker and H.Wolman (eds), *Theories of Urban Politics*. London: Sage.

Stone, Clarence N. (1993) 'Urban regimes and the capacity to govern: a political economy approach', *Journal of Urban Affairs*, 15 (1): 1–28.

Stone, Clarence, Orr, Marion and Worgs, Donn (2006) 'The flight of the bumblebee: why reform is difficult but not impossible', *Perspectives on Politics*, 4 (3): 529–46.

Swarts, Heidi J. (2003) 'Setting the state's agenda: church-based community organizations in American urban politics', in Jack A. Goldstone (ed.), *States, Parties, and Social Movements*. Cambridge: Cambridge University Press. pp. 78–106.

Taylor, Marilyn (2007) 'Community participation in the real world: opportunities and pitfalls in new governance spaces', *Urban Studies*, 44 (2): 297–317.

UN-Habitat (2006) *The State of the World's Cities Report 2006/2007*. London: Earthscan.

United Nations Human Settlement Programme (2003) *The Challenge of Slums: Global Report on Human Settlements 2003*. London and Sterling, VA: Earthscan Publications Ltd.

Williamson, Thad, Imbroscio, David and Alperovitz, Gar (2002) *Making a Place for Community: Local Democracy in a Global Era*. New York: Routledge.

Yanow, Dvora and Schwartz-Shea, Peregrine (eds) (2006) *Interpretation and Method: Empirical Research Methods and the Interpretive Turn*. Armonk, NY and London, England: M.E. Sharpe.

12

RACE AND URBAN POLITICAL THEORY

J. Phillip Thompson

Many classic studies in urban politics discuss race, yet race has not been theoretically central to the field of urban politics. Robert Dahl's *Who Governs?* (1961) examined New Haven on the eve of race riots but did not foresee racial unrest. Floyd Hunter's *Community Power Structure* (1953) examined Atlanta during the midst of black civic protest against racial segregation, but the book considered race to be a false diversion from 'real' social and economic issues. Clarence Stone's studies of Atlanta examined black politics during the transition from white to black rule, yet his studies focused on political economy, organisational resources and elite coalitional arrangements. Despite the history of US slavery and racial apartheid, these studies implicitly took on board an ecological view of race relations that treated black racial integration as an evolutionary process comparable to earlier integration of European immigrants into 'the mainstream' of society.

The diminution of race in urban theory has come at considerable analytical cost. There is still no adequate answer in urban politics as to why there is not a labour party or a strong class politics, across race, in the US. The role of physical place and local culture in the formation of racialised social and political identities, explored in depth in relation to class in Ira Katznelson's *Marxism and the City*, has only recently been seized upon by scholars to explain current political dilemmas in US politics (Katznelson, 1993). All of this despite continued *de facto* racial segregation: more than three-quarters of white Americans live in suburbs, and a majority of blacks and Latinos live in cities. As Robert Beauregard writes:

> Of course, while the suburbs were physically open – spaces between houses, backyards open to view, the boundaries between lawns indistinct, the streets ungated – they were not socially open. The identity being formed was a white identity.
>
> ... A combination of geographical concentration and media stereotyping, not to mention the well-known anxiety that middle-class and white suburbanites have about minorities, has stamped the cities with the stigma of race. ... Race, poor people, and the cities were forged into a single symbol of American fear and ambivalence. (Beauregard, 2006: 143, 17)

Issues concerning black and Latino political agency are also not well understood in the discipline. This neglect in urban political studies contributes to an inability of urban theory to explain why minority political mobilisation remains low despite a plethora of social and economic problems minority communities, and it leaves wanting an examination of the racial role of cities: whether some cities play a designated racial role as repositories for historically non-white, semi-slave and excess labour.

This chapter will first discuss how race has been presented in urban political theory followed by a critique of urban theories and race. It will briefly contrast race politics in the US and Britain, and conclude with a call for a return to long-standing basic questions regarding race and democracy.

Race in urban political theory

One of the earliest studies of race in urban politics was James Q. Wilson's 1960 article, 'Two negro politicians: an interpretation' (Wilson, 1960). In his study of Harlem's Congressman Rev. Adam Clayton Powell and Chicago's Congressman William Dawson, Wilson maintained that churches such as Rev. Powell's Abyssinian Baptist were politically important in the black community 'only' where there was no African-American political organisation. Wilson contrasted Harlem to Chicago, where he described the urban political machine as strong, centralised, with extensive patronage in the African-American community, and thereby able to control elections without civic race leaders like Powell. Wilson's own data, however, revealed that blacks in New York received substantially more patronage than did African-Americans in Chicago. Wilson had difficulty explaining why the Tammany machine was not able to oust Powell in the late 1950s, a period of machine strength. Wilson never considered that Harlem's black 'machine' leader, J. Raymond Jones, could have harboured resentments against the white machine and out-manoeuvred it, as Jones did. Wilson greatly underestimated the mass appeal of Powell's outspoken black radicalism and he misjudged black political alienation already being prominently expressed in 1960 by the Nation of Islam (NOI), headquartered in Chicago, and by Malcolm X, assigned by the NOI to Harlem.

Robert Dahl's *Who Governs?*, published in 1961, maintained that no group dominated the city of New Haven, and that power was distributed across all sections of the city (Dahl, 1961). Dahl did not view lack of black political involvement in the city as a major act of racial exclusion, undermining the tenets of pluralism. Dahl's view was not shared by many in the black community; blacks rioted in New Haven soon after the book's publication. Many pluralists following Dahl also held that there is nothing particularly wrong with low levels of black political mobilisation. Black political non-participation was seen as part of a normal evolutionary process of ethnic elite incorporation and domination of ethnic group life. Pluralists simply assumed that race was not a fundamental social division in the US. Many anticipated (or more accurately, hoped) that the end of Jim Crow in the South would be the death knell for popular racism.

Writing in the wake of urban riots during the 1960s, urban political science could hardly avoid addressing intense racial conflicts. It was during this period that some of the most enduring work on race and cities was written. Richard Cloward and Frances Fox Piven argued that the black poor lack resources for sustained participation in politics and public policy:

> Much Negro leadership exists largely by the grace of white institutions: white political parties and government agencies, white unions and businesses and professions, even white civil-rights organisations. Everything in the environment of the Negro politician, civil servant or professional makes him attentive to white interests and perspectives. If black leadership were based in separatist institutions – particularly economic ones, such as black labor unions – it might be capable of some independence, but those separatist institutions do not now exist. (Cloward and Piven, 1974: 252)

They concluded that traditional mass-membership organisations, such as the NAACP, were not an effective model for organising the black poor because the poor had no resources to sustain such organisations. Leaders of mass organisations, they said, promote the false belief that the poor can alter politics and policy through regular political channels and they noted that external resources made available to the poor in the 1960s was a response to poor peoples' organisation rather than 'widespread black unrest' (Piven and Cloward, 1999: 336). Once leaders become 'enmeshed in a web of relationships with governmental officials and private groups', 'external resources become a substitute for a mass base', and as mass unrest subsides the external resources are withdrawn and the result is 'organisational collapse' (Piven and Cloward, 1999: 317, 331). To Piven and Cloward, disrupting the operation of mainstream economic and political institutions was the poor's only effective option to gain the attention of elected officials, and they viewed the post-1960s ascension of blacks into elected office and bureaucracies as tokenism intended to deplete the strength of black movements (Piven and Cloward, 1999: 255). Piven stated recently, with substantial justification, that, 'we were pessimistic, but the subsequent losses in all of the policy areas championed by these [1960s poor peoples'] movements shows that we were correct' (Piven, 2004). The thrust of Piven and Cloward's persistent argument – that the poor cannot be empowered within the present political–economic structure – remains highly influential in black political studies and deserves more attention in urban politics. Although effective black politics has not declined in all cities and at all times and call into question the generality of Cloward and Piven's theses, the dominant trend matches their analysis.

Ira Katznelson's *City Trenches*, published in 1981, drew several lines in the sand of urban theory that have yet to be fully incorporated into the field (Katznelson, 1981). Katznelson asserted that race is as deep or deeper a fissure in cities than class. He maintained that the cultural reproduction of racism has to be accounted for in institutions; that racism is not simply a cultural residue of a past era. Challenging a public management/pluralist perspective on cities (and the state), he characterised city administrations as having less to do with substantive problem-solving than with channelling and controlling discontent. What needed explanation in his view was not an absence of class conflict in cities but its limitation to the arena of the workplace while excluding 'community' (race) issues such as mass black unemployment. Katznelson noted that black protest had been channelled into party politics and community development, but he questioned whether the mediating institutions of 'party, union, church and voluntary associations' could contain blacks' marginalisation in the political economy.

In the 1980s, attention in the discipline turned away from the unresolved and vital issue of how institutions reproduce racial divisions in cities to focus on political economic studies (including public choice theories) de-linked from race, and also to a revived pluralism centred on black elite integration into urban political structures. Paul Peterson's *City Limits* (1981) asserted the primacy of unitary economic interests based on a particular ideology of economic self-interest over the primacy of political contestations. He wrote that:

> Like all social structures, cities have interests. ... The interests of cities are neither a summation of individual interests nor the pursuit of optimum size. Instead, policies and programmes can be said to be in the interest of cities whenever the policies maintain or enhance the economic position, social prestige, or political power of the city, taken as a whole. ... Any time that social interactions come to be structured into recurring patterns, the structure thus formed develops an interest in its own maintenance and enhancement. ... Land is the factor of production that cities control. Yet land is the factor to which cities are bound. ... To its land area the city must attract not only capital but productive labor. Yet local governments in the United States are very limited in their capacities to control the flow of these factors. ... Local governments are left with a number of devices for enticing capital into the area. They can minimize their tax on capital and on profits from capital investment. (Peterson, 1981)

Peterson did not consider race one of the primary 'social interactions that come to be structured into recurring patterns' or white residential segregation as having 'an interest in its own maintenance and enhancement'. He instead conceptualised racial inequality as a residue of economic decisions to minimise the cost of supporting the poor (among whom minorities are heavily concentrated). This remains the dominant view of race – that it is subservient to non-racially conceived economic interests – in urban politics.

Clarence Stone's *Regime Politics*, published in 1989, synthesised elite, pluralist and resource-mobilisation theories of urban politics (Stone, 1989). Stone traced the ascent of black mayors in Atlanta beginning in the early 1970s. The newly elected black mayor, Maynard Jackson, initially demanded that the city devote primary funding to providing jobs for unemployed blacks, to low-income neighbourhood development, and to increased business contracts for black firms. When white business balked at these demands and began to flee the city, Jackson (and later Mayor Andrew Young) reached an accommodation with the white business community and narrowed their demands to more contracts for black businesses and increased business investment in their cities. Stone found that the mayors did not have the staff resources to generate alternatives to development ideas proposed by private developers, so traditional patterns of city form and function were replicated (Stone, 1993). Thus, to minimise racial conflict and the risk of business flight to the suburbs, black mayors de-linked poor black communities from local policy-making and politics soon after they came into power.

Although Stone's description of black politics in Atlanta could apply to many, and perhaps most, cities with black mayors, it does not explain the trajectory of black politics in all cases. Chicago's Mayor Washington was an exception to the prevailing stance of black mayors: he did not accept cooptation by the business community, choosing instead to mobilise Chicago's poor black constituency. Washington, unlike most other black mayors, made little effort to conceal Chicago's deep racial antagonisms. He strived to develop alternative models of community building and economic development that might encourage low-income blacks to participate in the political process, working with community organisations and academic think-tanks to shape alternative economic development policies (Giloth, 1991). Stone's analysis is not a good fit with Chicago under Mayor Washington because Stone subordinates racial ideology, racial identity, or 'value consensus', as central to regime and public policy formation. Stone finds 'values' unwieldy and too diffuse to be a part of policy development:

> Problems big enough to contend for priority status on a city's governing agenda are unlikely to evoke value consensus as a basis for action. Hence regime analysis should look to coalition politics rather than shared values as the path to explanation. Any consensus is likely to be too general to explain a concrete course of action. (Stone, 2004: 11)

Stone's argument runs directly counter to the earlier argument by Katznelson that cultural reproduction must be explained through analysis of institutions, such as political parties and government. It also runs against the finding by Thompson that it is precisely during high stakes policy conflicts – such as increasing taxes on segments of the population, or policing policies – where struggles over dominant values and racial identity come to the fore (Thompson, 2006).

In recent years, the continued demographic isolation and poverty of minorities in central cities has gained attention and again led to a renewed discussion of race in urban politics. Analysts have noted that the 'civil rights' model of racial representation, for African-Americans at least, has reached its demographic limit and that 'civil rights' candidates seem to have lost the enthusiastic support of the black poor (Gilliam and Kaufman, 1998; Banks, 2000; Mollenkopf, 2003: 136). Low-political turnout in central cities, particularly among blacks and Latinos, is attributed to their continued poverty and weak political influence at the state and federal level. Low-income whites, now concentrated in suburbs, are likewise said to be overshadowed politically by their wealthy suburban white counterparts. In *Place Matters*, Peter Dreier, John Mollenkopf and Todd Swanstrom argue that the key to progressive Democratic control of Congress is both increasing minority political turnout in central cities and defeat of Republican strategies aimed at splitting off low-income white suburban from minority central city voters. They advise Democrats, 'whatever the obstacles, only when the party creates synergies between central-city and inner-suburban constituencies will it be able to build a durable electoral majority' (Dreier et al., 2001: 240). The core policy prescription of *Place Matters* is that metropolitan coalition builders make 'clear, effective substantive policy appeals to white, Catholic, blue-collar suburbanites, whose once strong familial attachment to progressive positions has weakened, by addressing their actual needs, which revolve around the reality that they are working harder but not gaining a higher standard of living or achieving a more family-friendly workplace' (Dreier et al., 2001: 246). They advise blacks and Latinos to, 'communicate with and mobilise emerging black and Hispanic suburban populations with nonracial appeals that speak to the same kinds of needs [as those of white suburbanites].' Here again, racial divisions are seen as secondary to non-racially conceived economic issues and non-racial 'class' identity. Their arguments beg the question of why such cross-racial coalitions have not emerged heretofore.

Race and the urban question: renewed

Three fundamental questions regarding race, none of them new, remain unresolved and largely ignored in urban politics. The first is an analysis of the social basis of society: whether white racism produces a fundamental divide, as deep or deeper than class, in social life and political behaviour. There is a substantial body of empirical evidence to suggest that it does (Bobo, 2000), but such evidence has not caused a fundamental rethinking of urban theories. The early pluralists were aware that social cohesion was a fundamental premise of pluralism. Dahl wrote in 1956 that, 'in the absence of certain social prerequisites, no constitutional arrangements can produce a non-tyrannical republic … the first and crucial variables to which political scientists must direct their attention are social and not constitutional' (Dahl, 1956: 83). The inclusive sense of community assumed by pluralists does not really exist: blacks and whites remain largely segregated in metropolitan regions, despite the achievements of civil rights reform in the 1960s. This is cause for serious reflection on the role of cities in relation to racial separation.

One of the most important topics is the conceptualisation of the state. It should not be assumed that democracy in the US is genuine for blacks given a strong majority rule system, widespread white racial prejudice, and a white voting majority in nearly all states and at the national level (constitutional powers are concentrated at both sites, but not in cities). The fact that a *majority* of black high school drop-outs (roughly half the total black male population) will serve prison sentences as young adults, for example, raises fundamental questions about whether the state is 'policing' or repressing. There has also been little to no attention given to the long-term effects of official government repression of black movement organisations in the 1960s and 1970s on contemporary black political discourse and movement activity – urban political studies rarely even consider state repression as an aspect of urban governance. These issues bear on the question, posed long ago by Piven and Cloward and

Katznelson, of whether coopting black activists into electoral politics and social welfare programmes could contain racial conflicts arising from blacks' subordinate economic and social position. Paul Peterson, writing over a decade ago, concluded that democratic institutions were not up to the task. He wrote that in order to avoid racial conflict that could upset the political order, pluralist politics requires keeping black radicals out of mainstream politics (Peterson, 1995).

The avoidance of questions of profound racial divisions in social life, of systematic economic marginalisation of poor blacks, and of state repression, clouds what should be a dynamic inquiry in urban politics into black political alienation. Studies of black opinion show continued strong racial identity among African-Americans, a deep distrust of whites and of government, and rising mass dissatisfaction with black political leadership. Seventy-one percent of African-Americans in 2000 believed that racial progress in the US would either not be achieved in their lifetime or would never be achieved (Dawson, 2001: 318). Beginning in the 1990s, surveys show that affluent African-Americans are as likely to be disillusioned and alienated with US institutions as lower-income blacks. A consequence has been significant black withdrawal from formal politics. Black political turnout in city elections involving black candidates, for example, has declined sharply since the 1970s (Gilliam and Kaufman, 1998). Organisations that might have once organised protest have disappeared. Cohen and Dawson state that, 'The state of nearly permanent economic depression in many black communities harmed their organisational base. Black organisations shrank and disappeared when their financial status worsened and their programmes were seen as less relevant to solving the problems of a devastated economy' (Cohen and Dawson, 1993).

Despite increased black alienation, much of what has been written about black urban politics in recent decades celebrates the election of black mayors and other black electoral victories in cities. The image is one of great racial progress against a backdrop of racial segregation or white-machine domination in the past. There tends to be an assumption that these elections symbolise progress of the black community as a whole. Yet urban black communities in the United States are in a state of economic and social turmoil. In the year 2000, 39 percent of black families had incomes putting them among the bottom 10 percent of the national distribution of income. The situation is dire for poor blacks: the top 20 percent of black families earn 48.6 percent of total black income, while the bottom fifth earns a mere 3.7 percent of total black income (Nemhard et al., 2005: 216). Blacks are far more likely to do jail time today than before black 'incorporation'. Since 1972, the US prison population has increased sixfold. Although blacks are only 12 percent of the national population, blacks are half of those in jail. Blacks were three times more likely to be in jail in the 1990s than in the 1970s. Nearly all of this increased risk is experienced by blacks with a high school education or less. As mentioned earlier, a black male drop-out, born in 1965–1969, had a nearly 60 percent chance of serving time in prison in the late 1990s (Pettit and Western, 2004: 161).

Many of the problems of blacks in cities were clearly shown in the aftermath of Hurricane Katrina in New Orleans. Thousands of residents did not own personal means of transport, did not have enough money to relocate, or were too sick to leave the city before the storm. Residents fleeing for higher ground across a bridge to the neighbouring white suburb of Gretna were met on the bridge by town police who shot over their heads and prevented their entry into Gretna. Rebuilding is proceeding at a snail's pace since the storm. Construction training centres are finding it difficult to train young black adult men entering job centres who frequently have a fourth-grade reading and maths level. Watching scenes of the flood on television, many white Americans expressed shock that the US still had such a serious race and poverty problem. Their shock is directly related to misleading images of progress prevalent in the media and urban academic discourse.

The analytic questions flowing from critical appraisals of race in cities are quite different from those usually found in urban political studies: how do blacks criticise the legitimacy of US institutions while not angering the vast majority of whites who believe in their fairness and impartiality (Hochschild, 1995; Bobo and Kluegel, 1997; Feagin, 2000; Kluegel and Bobo, 2001)? In today's climate of fear regarding terrorism, and increasing restrictions of civil liberties, how do black leaders avoid state repression for radical criticism of US institutions and policies? Given blacks' predominate political attitudes, radical when compared with those of most whites, how can black elected officials appeal to the black poor without fundamentally challenging the legitimacy of the social order and undermining their electoral appeal among whites? If black elected officials do choose to mobilise blacks, and to advocate for social justice on behalf of the black poor, how can they avoid giving license to misdirected black rage and promoting racial divisiveness and destructive social disorder?

Increased racial diversity and new structural inequalities

The racial landscape in the US is rapidly changing. The Latino population has recently surpassed the African-American population in size, due to high levels of immigration from Latin America, and it is growing at a more rapid rate. The Asian population is smaller than the African-American or the Latino population, but it too is growing rapidly and it is concentrated in some cities on the West and East coasts. The white population, by contrast, is growing slowly. By 2050, the US will be around 50 percent white, or perhaps majority non-white.

The terms 'black', 'Latino' and 'Asian' are inadequate for interpreting the complexity of racial identity in the US, and even worse is the false impression that race is a matter of the colour of one's skin: yellow, black or brown. Although native-born African-Americans are by far the largest 'black' ethnic group, there are increasing numbers of Caribbean, African and Latin American immigrants who also identify themselves as 'black'. 'Latino' likewise covers an extremely broad number of ethnic groups. Unlike the United States, which has a majority population of European descent designated 'white'. most Latin American and Caribbean countries have majority non-white populations (mestizos and mulattos), leading white elites in those countries to de-emphasise race in politics. During colonialism and after, again unlike the US, selected mulattos and mestizos in Latin America and the Caribbean gained honorary white status, and many participated in policing non-whites. In Brazil, Mexico, Bolivia and elsewhere, there are rising political movements among disadvantaged indigenous and black groups that are protesting racial discrimination. And, there is a backlash among those asserting that racial advocates in Latin America are importing a racial paradigm from the United States that does not fit Latin American history or culture (Nobles, 2005). The 'Asian-American' category has no fewer racial complexities (Tuan, 1999). Thus, thinking of race in the US as a simple 'Black–White' issue is misleading.

Aside from increasing numbers and diversity among blacks, Latinos and Asians, there are major differences in the structure of incorporation of immigrants into the US today versus the late nineteenth century (a comparable period of heavy immigration) that have profound implications for urban politics. European immigrants in the nineteenth and early twentieth century often had voting rights in state and local elections before obtaining citizenship (Hayduk, 2006). This is rarely the case today. Today, as before, most immigrants are migrating to cities. However, today they are migrating into a racialised metropolitan landscape, settling near African-Americans and native-born Latinos already segregated into cities and inner-ring suburbs. With large populations of immigrants ineligible to vote (nearly half of New York City's and 36 percent of Los Angeles County's population in 2000 were foreign born), central cities and inner-ring suburbs have far less voting power (per capita) than predominately white suburbs. Given black political withdrawal noted in the previous section, many cities are in a profoundly weakened political position in their competition with suburbs for state resources. High demands on public services for the mostly low-income immigrant population, coupled with the existing needs of impoverished inner-city residents, cause cities to need more assistance from state governments, not less. In the context of competition for scarce resources, it is not surprising to find economic competition and friction between native-born and immigrant minorities. On the other hand, they share many of the same problems of low-pay, unemployment, lack of access to health care, failing schools, high levels of crime, and in the case of Latinos and blacks, high rates of incarceration.

Among minority citizens eligible to vote, there have been signs both of intra-minority political cooperation and conflict in cities. Puerto Rican support was critical to the election of black mayors in Chicago and New York in the 1980s, and black and Chinese support was critical to the recent election of Antonio Villaraigosa, Los Angeles's first Latino mayor. Yet, blacks and Latinos split their votes in Villaraigosa's first run for mayor and also in recent mayoral elections in Houston. Demographic patterns suggest that political leadership in cities will increasingly depend on patterns of black, Latino and Asian cooperation. A key urban question is whether blacks, Latinos and Asians will frame their identities in opposition to each other, or whether they will form durable political coalitions (Hernandez, 2005). It is conceivable that the possibilities for non-white, low-income majorities or near-majorities in many cities and states, and the potential for major shifts in public policy, could serve as an attractant for both blacks and Latinos to increase their participation in electoral politics.

Race in Britain

There are many racial commonalities between the US and Britain. Both nations were actively involved in African slavery. Race was an important part of the identity of the working classes of both countries from their formation (Robinson, 1983). Both countries experienced large influxes of blacks into their cities following the Second World War, from the rural South in the US and from the West Indian colonies in Britain. The liberal-left in both countries have attempted, without great success, to supplant a politics of race with 'colour-blind' class politics (Katznelson, 1973). There are also socioeconomic similarities. Blacks in Britain are about three times more likely to be unemployed than are whites (Adams, 2006). Blacks also tend to be residentially segregated, although not nearly as much as blacks are in the US. Tensions between black youth and police agencies are high in both countries. Britain suffered urban race riots in the 1980s, appearing to replicate US patterns. Race is a widely perceived social problem in both countries. A 2002 BBC poll reported that more than half of the British public believes that Britain is a racist society (Cowling, 2002).

There are equally important racial differences between the two countries. Most obviously, there are demographic differences. Although the non-white population is growing rapidly in the UK, it is not nearly as large proportionately as is the US non-white population. Non-whites constituted 7.9 percent of the total UK population in 2001. Moreover, nearly half of non-whites in Britain are Asian, with most from India, followed by Pakistan and Bangladesh. Blacks constitute about 25 percent of the non-white population. Blacks are not the poorest, and arguably are not the most culturally ostracised, minority group in Britain. With the war in Iraq and recent terrorist attacks in London attributed to radical Muslims, Muslims (largely of Asian ancestry) have reported large numbers of racial incidents. Moreover, nearly 68 percent of Pakistani/Bangladeshi families are low-income in Britain, compared to 31 percent of Caribbean blacks and 49 percent of non-Caribbean blacks. Blacks are 14 times more likely to be stopped and searched by the police than white people, but Asians are six times more likely to be searched than white people and Asians also report sharp increases in recent years (Adams, 2006). As a result of close parallels in residential living circumstances and political interactions, and quite unlike the US, some Asian groups in Britain self-describe themselves as 'black' (Small, 1997: 370). Another important difference between the US and Britain is that government and public policy in Britain is more centralised. There are fewer minorities holding elected office in Britain and fewer opportunities for minority political patronage in comparison to the US (Katznelson, 1973). On the other hand, blacks in Britain are more fully incorporated into social welfare programmes in Britain than in the US (Lieberman, 2005).

Despite differences in political structure, history and demography, there are certain areas where cross-national comparison of race in cities may be of use in both countries. How do both countries reconcile class and race politics rooted in centuries of capitalism, slavery, segregation and colonialism? There is already a lively cross-continental debate about whether a US 'race-relations' paradigm, exported to Britain, reifies race and obscures class, or whether class-oriented scholars underestimate the cultural significance of race and the interaction of culture and political structure in both countries (Darder et al., 2004). How do both countries handle tensions arising from residentially segregated minority neighbourhoods characterised by high unemployment, relatively low educational attainment, social marginalisation, high crime, and high levels of distrust of the police and public authority? And, what accounts for relatively high levels of intra-minority cooperation in Britain as compared with the US? Are, David Goldberg suggests, 'Muslims the new niggers of [a] globalizing racial Americanization', threatening white civilisation on a global scale (Goldberg, 2005: 99)? If so, how will blacks and other non-whites react on both sides of the Atlantic?

Unfinished revolutions

Continued racial polarisation (both political and geographic) and increased numbers of disenfranchised foreign immigrants in cities pose sharp dilemmas for US cities. Without major reform of the political structure, it appears that minorities are trapped in cities with little political power to obtain the resources they need to advance economically and socially. With the normal political process reinforcing rather than diminishing racial polarisations, it is a good time to revisit the basic tenets of political society. Urban politics has not devoted much space to normative questions. But, locked opportunities in poor black and Latino urban neighbourhoods, huge influxes of undocumented Latinos into cities and declining standards of living amongst working class whites in suburbs raise fundamental questions about the meaning of US citizenship (why is it bereft of social supports?) and the persistence of political divisions among these groups – making them unable to change these conditions.

A citizen is a member of the political community of the nation. Yet, democratic citizenship does not begin with membership and rights, it begins with political imagination and empathy. The pluralist E.E. Schattschneider wrote that, '*democracy is first a state of mind*' that '*begins as an act of imagination about people*', meaning that people are '*equal in the one dimension that counts: each is a human being, infinitely precious because he is human*'. 'As a moral system', he said, 'democracy is an experiment in the creation of a community', and, '[to] put it very bluntly, democracy is about the *love* of people' (Schattschneider, [1960] 1975: xii–xiii). Throughout US history, racism constricted democratic imagination and empathy for non-whites, leading to limited notions of political community and citizenship. President Lyndon Johnson, speaking during the height of racial protest in 1965, encouraged whites in the US to imagine an inclusive citizenship that gives, '20 million Negroes the same chance as every other American to learn and grow, to work and share in society, to develop their abilities – physical, mental, and spiritual – and to purse their individual happiness', This vision was crushed by a politics of white resentment which framed attempts at improving conditions for minorities as encroachments on job security, school quality and neighbourhood stability for whites. This fits into a familiar pattern in the US of pitting minority advancement against 'white citizenship': the achievements of whites in securing rights and economic improvements. Low-income whites, beginning as indentured servants, gained citizenship rights in the US in part because elites sought their support in enforcing African slavery and conquest of Native Americans. Their citizenship was mainly negative, it provided poor whites with few opportunities for prosperity and only a measure of protection from the worst aspects of capitalism and government repression practised against non-whites – genocide, slavery and segregation. White citizenship bred an affinity between poor whites and white elites (in contrast to dark peoples), and accounts for much of white workers' historic conservatism in the US. When blacks finally did secure civil rights, most importantly in the 1960s, this threatened the meagre 'freedom' of whites as it was no longer certain that they would remain protected from the degradations heaped upon blacks historically (Olson, 2004). Moving beyond current racialised divisions between city and suburb requires, first of all, an ability to imagine and desire a different kind of society where minorities are cared for, and their advancement is not pitted against the needs of whites. Embedded in such a vision must be major alterations in the political economy and state. This is, in essence, a return to the unfinished civil rights revolution.

No less pressing is the issue of immigration. Historically, most African-American leaders were of the opinion that racial problems in the US were inseparable from racial struggles in the global South. As Walter White, longtime head of the NAACP, put it in 1945, African-American struggles were inseparable from 'problems of other colored peoples in the West Indies, South America, Africa, the Pacific and Asia'. White became a champion of human rights, warning Allied leaders in 1945 'to revolutionize their racial concepts and practices, to abolish imperialism and grant full equality to all of its people, or else prepare for World War III' (White, 1945: 154). Just as African-Americans, repressed and nearly starved in the rural South, were used to break strikes of militant northern white workers, repressed and nearly starved immigrants of colour from the global South today are used to weaken labour organisations in the US, and they compete with native-born minorities for poorly paid work in cities. This is the legacy of slavery and colonialism, and there is continued global inequality in the form of rapacious loans, unfair trade agreements, low pay for minerals, and political clientelism between the US and global South. Here again, there may be no way out of conflict between low-income citizens and immigrants, short of a new imagination of political community that transcends nation borders and supports policies promoting equitable trade and development between the global north and global South. This is the unfinished human rights revolution.

The state of urban theory regarding race

Urban theory has not made significant advances in understanding the role of race in cities over the last 30 years. Important insights developed in the 1970s have not been pursued. Treatment of the new influx of non-white immigrants into cities has been primarily descriptive, with little reflection in urban theory. Below, I summarise the perspective advanced in this chapter regarding African-Americans in cities. I seek to illustrate some new lines of analysis that could be applied to other groups in the US or in Britain.

How and *where* are tensions between capitalism and mass democracy reconciled? In the period of developing capitalism, the plantation economy and repressive regional government fuelled capitalist wealth accumulation while mass democracy was limited to the North – and primarily to whites even there. With the mechanisation of agriculture, blacks left the rural South and migrated into cities in search of industrial employment and also in search of democracy and a better life. Black demands put great pressure on business and government, provoked a crisis of urban governments in the late 1960s/early 1970s, and intensified a mass exodus of whites from cities. Industry responded by moving operations, whenever possible, to low-cost countries with weaker labour organisations and fewer democratic rights. Government responded by capping social welfare spending in urban areas and by initiating repressive criminal justice policies (such as the War on Drugs) in black neighbourhoods. Suburban whites turned inward, supporting policies aimed at reducing taxes funding inner cities and maximising their ability to fund their own neighbourhood schools and social welfare. De-funded, repressed and politically isolated and demobilised, black urban areas became *de facto* urban 'reservations' for unemployed and under-employed urban blacks, still adamantly demanding democracy and a better life. Without a docile black workforce, businesses providing services in metropolitan areas increasingly turned to immigrants (often illegal) willing to postpone – often as a matter of survival – demands for democratic rights and a better life.

By this account, the historical tension between mass democracy and capitalism must be addressed (again) in this new situation. Political crisis has been avoided only by repressive criminal justice policies, strong white majorities in state and national electorates, and urban black political demobilisation. This perspective suggests that some cities (or sections of cities) play a structural role in the larger political economy as 'urban reservations' (Detroit, Buffalo), just as other cities are centres of international finance and commerce (San Francisco, Manhattan). The issue of political stability looms large here, as tensions with African-Americans are not resolved, and large numbers of immigrants working at poverty wages and without voting rights may, if they follow the pattern of African-Americans, make their own demands for democracy and a better life in the near future.

There are a number of research questions that flow from this analysis. Should democracy be thought of territorially within states? Should cities, where immigration patterns and states' ex-felon voting prohibitions exclude large proportions of the population from voting, be considered democratic? Given repeal of laws allowing immigrant voting in many states long ago, increasing costs of political campaigns in large cities, the disappearance of political machines, weakening of unions, and dependence of minority civic associations on external funding, has democracy waned in cities in the US? How do indigenous and immigrant minorities interpret and respond to their circumstances? What kind of coalitional possibilities exist? Is spatial fragmentation, or containment of low-income minorities in segregated areas, key for political/economic stability? If so, how can this be reconciled with climate change/energy cost pressures for limiting sprawl and re-densifying cities?

Another large question is why has urban theory not advanced its understanding of race in over a generation? I suggest that it is because urban politics has emphasised political and economic procedures and processes to the exclusion of political (human) agency. 'People make history', constrained but not determined by circumstances. No modern economic system can function without government. No government can survive for long without 'the people'. The tension between degrading people in the economy and uplifting people in democratic discourse is a profound challenge to governance. It is in this realm that race has proved invaluable, and also that cities have proved invaluable. Race allows for degradation of minorities, without provoking a larger legitimacy crisis of democracy. Cities allow for the spatial concentration and containment of degraded minorities. Politicians and judges have found clever ways to manage this racial/spatial tension – by targeted enforcement of drug laws, by restricting forced school busing to integrate schools, and by turning a blind eye to exploitation of immigrants in urban areas.

It is important to remember that only human agents can manage the contradictions of capitalism and democracy, and they must constantly adjust to new circumstances. Perhaps by considering the larger problems of social and political stability, and by paying more attention to how local actors conceive and manage racial tensions, urban theorists can provide new insights into the role of race in cities. Race lives in the gap between capitalism and democracy.

References

Adams, Audrey (2006) *Race Audit of Social Policy Areas – A Snapshot of Black and Ethnic Minority Communities in the UK* [www.blink.org.uk]. The 1990 Trust, September.

Banks, Manley Elliot (2000) 'A changing electorate in a majority black city: the emergence of a neo-conservative black urban regime in contemporary Atlanta', *Journal of Urban Affairs*, 22 (3): 265–78.

Beauregard, Robert A. (2006) *When America Became Suburban*. Minneapolis: University of Minnesota Press.

Bobo, Lawrence (2000) 'Implications for planners of race, inequality, and a persistent "Color Line", in *The Profession of City Planning: Changes, Images and Challenges: 1950–2000*. New Brunswick: Rutgers University Press.

Bobo, Lawrence, and Kluegel, James R. (1997) 'Status, ideology, and dimensions of whites' racial beliefs and attitudes: progress and stagnation', in S.A. Tuch and J.K. Martin (eds), *Racial Attitudes in the 1990s: Continuity and Change*. Westport: Praeger.

Cloward, Richard A. and Piven, Frances Fox (1974) *The Politics of Turmoil*. New York: Pantheon Books.

Cohen, Cathy, and Dawson, Michael (1993) 'Neighbourhood poverty and African American politics', *American Political Science Review*, 87 (2): 286–302.

Cowling, David (2002) *What the Survey Reveals* at http://news.bbc.co.uk/hi/english/static/in_depth/uk/2002/race/what_the_survey_reveals.stm.

Dahl, Robert (1956) *A Preface to Democratic Theory*. Chicago: University of Chicago Press.

Dahl, Robert A. (1961) *Who Governs?: Democracy and Power in an American City*. New Haven: Yale University Press.

Darder, Antonia, Torres, Rodolfo D. and Miles, Robert (2004) 'Does "race" matter: transatlantic perspectives on racism after "race relations"', in A. Darder and R.D. Torres (eds), *After Race: Racism and Multiculturalism*. New York: New York University Press.

Dawson, Michael C. (2001) *Black Visions: Roots of Contemporary African-American Political Ideologies*. Chicago: University of Chicago Press.

Dreier, Peter, Mollenkopf, John and Swanstrom, Todd (2001) *Place Matters*. Lawrence: University of Kansas Press.

Feagin, Joe R. (2000) *Racist America: Roots, Current Realities, and Future Reparations*. New York: Routledge Press.

Gilliam, Franklin D. Jr. and Kaufman, Karen M. (1998) 'Is there an empowerment life cycle?', *Urban Affairs Review*, 33 (6): 741–66.

Giloth, Robert (1991) 'Making policy with communities: research and development in the Department of Economic Development', in P. Clavel and W. Wiewel (eds), *Harold Washington and the Neighbohoods: Progressive City Government in Chicago, 1983–1987*. New Brunswick: Rutgers University Press.

Goldberg, David Theo (2005) 'Racial Americanization', in K. Murji and J. Solomos (eds), *Racialization: Studies in Theory and Practice*. London: Oxford University Press.

Hayduk, Ron (2006) *Democracy for All: Restoring Immigrant Voting Rights in the US*. New York: Routledge Press.

Hernandez, Tanya (2005) *Is There Racism in Latin America and What Does That Mean for Race Relations in the United States?* at www.blackprof.com/archives/2006/05/is_there_racism_in_latin_ameri_1.html]. blackprof.com.

Hochschild, Jennifer L. (1995) *Facing Up to the American Dream: Race, Class, and the Soul of the Nation*. Princeton: Princeton University Press.

Hunter, Floyd (1953) *Community Power Structure: A Study of Decision Makes*. Chapel Hill: University of North Cardina Press.

Katznelson, Ira (1973) *Black Men, White Cities: Race, Politics and Migration in the United States 1900–30, and Britain, 1948–68*. Chicago: University of Chicago Press.

Katznelson, Ira (1981) *City Trenches: Urban Politics and the Patterning of Class in the United States*. Chicago: University of Chicago Press.

Katznelson, Ira (1993) *Marxism and the City*. Oxford: Clarendon Press.

Kluegel, James R. and Bobo, Lawrence D. (2001) 'Perceived group discrimination and policy attitudes: the sources and consequences of the race and gender gaps', in Alice O'Connor, Chris Tilly and Lawrence D. Bobo (eds), *Urban Inequality: Evidence from Four Cities*. New York: Russell Sage Foundation. pp. 163–213.

Lieberman, Robert C. (2005) *Shaping Race Policy: The United States in Comparative Perspective*. Princeton: Princeton University Press.

Mollenkopf, John (2003) 'New York: still the great anamoly', in R.P. Browning, D.R. Marshall and D.H. Tabb (eds), *Racial Politics in American Cities*. New York: Longman.

Nemhard, Jessica Gordon, Pitts, Steven C. and Mason, Patrick L. (2005) 'African American income inequality and corporate globalization', in J.W. Cecilia, A. Conrad, Patrick Mason and James Steward (eds), *African Americans in the U.S. Economy*. New York: Rowman & Littlefield Publishers, Inc.

Nobles, Melissa (2005) 'The myth of Latin American multiracialism', *Daedalus*, 134 (1): 82–6.

Olson, Joel (2004) *The Abolition of White Democracy*. Minneapolis: University of Minnesota Press.

Peterson, Paul E. (1981) *City Limits*. Chicago: University of Chicago Press.

Peterson, Paul E. (1995) 'A politically correct solution to racial classification', in P.E. Peterson (ed.), *Classifying by Race*. Princeton: Princeton University Press.

Pettit, Becky and Western, Bruce (2004) 'Mass imprisonment and the life course: race and class inequality in U.S. incarceration', *American Sociological Review*, 69 (2): 151–69.

Piven, Frances Fox (2004) 'Retrospective comments', *Perspectives on Politics*, 1 (4): 709.

Piven, Francis Fox and Cloward, Richard A. (1999) *Poor People's Movements*, 2nd edn. New York: Vintage Books.

Robinson, Cedric J. (1983) *Black Marxism: The Making of the Black Radical Tradition*. Chapel Hill: University of North Carolina Press.

Schattschneider, E.E. ([1960] 1975) *The Semisovereign People: A Realist's View of Democracy in America*. Hinsdale, IL: Dryden Press.

Small, Stephen (1997) 'Racism, black people, and the city in Britain', in C. Green (ed.), *Globalization and Survival in the Black Diaspora*. Albany: State University of New York Press.

Stone, Clarence N. (1989) *Regime Politics: Governing Atlanta, 1946–1988*. Lawrence: University of Kansas Press.

Stone, Clarence (1993) 'Urban regimes and the capacity to govern: a political economy approach', *Journal of Urban Affairs*, 15 (1): 1–28.

Stone, Clarence N. (2004) 'It's more than the economy after all: continuing the debate about urban regimes', *Journal of Urban Affairs*, 26 (1): 1–19.

Thompson, J. Phillip (2006) *Double Trouble: Black Mayors, Black Communities, and the Call for a Deep Democracy*. New York: Oxford University Press.

Tuan, Mia (1999) *Forever Foreigners or Honorary Whites? The Asian Ethnic Experience Today*. New Brunswick: Rutgers University Press.

White, Walter (1945) *A Rising Wind*. Garden City, NY: Doubleday, Doran.

Wilson, James Q. (1960) 'Two negro politicians: an interpretation', *MidWest Journal of Political Science*, 4 (4): 346–69.

13

GENDER AND SEXUALITY

Judith A. Garber

At the heart of all theories of gender and sex lies the observation that gender systems are the result of socially produced and maintained understandings about the many matters related to sex – about bodies, roles, identities and practices. This general observation has specific, profound relevance to urban politics. First, there are distinctively urban gender systems. Configurations of gender are noticeably urban in so far as they arise within the context of modern- and postmodern-era cities and metropolitan areas, which are characterised by highly specialised capitalist economies, intensified development and regulation of spaces, social and cultural permeability, diversified opportunities for political engagement, and integration into all channels of globalisation. Second, politics pervades urban gender systems. It rests in the role of gender systems in distributing power, rights and moral standing among city-dwellers; in the processes, both inside and outside of the local state, through which collective understandings about gender are generated; and in the interplay among opposing understandings about the propriety and mutability of any prevailing gender or sexual system.

Gender systems are richly complex and, hence, interpretable in endless ways. It is true that the male/female and heterosexual/homosexual distinctions are associated with highly recognisable aspects of patriarchy and heterosexual privilege – as Linda McDowell (1999: 21) reminds us, 'It is still habitual practice to assume that the former constructions are inferior to the latter'. However, this familiar model is also partly a caricature of gender systems. The complexity of gender gives the lie to any presentation of urban planning regimes as ratifying the power of generic men over generic women, or of globalised cities as sites of either pure sensual pleasures or pure corporate exploitation. Likewise, they bedevil blanket claims about the democratic potential that the public spaces of the city offer to sexual minorities, or about the barriers that those same spaces pose for women's citizenship. Hence, theorists must tackle difficult, persistent questions: How do gender and sex even interact with each other, let alone with race or ethnicity, class, citizenship status, (dis)ability, age and other 'urban' identities? Under what conditions can gender or sex be a positive force in the political sphere (and what 'counts' as politics)? How is gender mediated by space and time?

A remarkable fact about gender-based urban theories is the steep trajectory of their development. Feminist scholars and graduate students brought women – with varying degrees of attention to differences among women – into urban studies research in a noticeable way only in the 1970s. These studies explored the 'domestic' sphere of family, home, and neighbourhood, the public sphere(s) of economy and politics, and the public–private relationship (e.g., Lofland, 1975; Hayden and Wright, 1976; Cockburn, 1977; Mezey, 1978; Markusen, 1980; Saegert, 1980; Wekerle et al., 1980; Mackenzie and Rose, 1983; Gelb and Gittell, 1986).[1] Although Marxism (or socialism) and liberalism undergirded this research, radical (heterosexual and lesbian) feminist approaches to gender issues in cities were also represented among these early interventions (e.g., Burnett, 1973). At about the same time, a smaller body of work began to examine the formation and presence of communities of lesbians and gay men in big cities (e.g., Ettore, 1978; D'Emilio, 1981). By the 1990s, it was already taken for granted that cities are implicated in the systems of beliefs, norms and rules about gender and sexuality; furthermore, there had already been a major shift in theoretical weight towards gender and sexuality studies coloured by postmodernism (and post-structuralism and post-colonialism). What exists now is a substantial, multifaceted engagement with fundamental urban phenomena, concepts and research tools, including visions for the reconfiguration of citizenship, family, work, identity, space and other dimensions of urbanity.

This chapter is concerned with theories of urban politics whose *raison d'être* is the critique of gender systems that rest upon the dualistic, hierarchical constructs of male/female and heterosexual/homosexual. In approaching these theories about gender and sex, I first explain the use of 'systems' to conceptualise gender in cities, then highlight the interest in an inclusive, urban (and feminist or sexual) citizenship that follows from gender theorists' critiques of existing urban gender systems. Next, I focus on the relationship between feminist and queer theory, highlighting areas of convergence, crossover and divergence. I set out two aspects of the fundamental shift in our understanding of urban politics that has been produced most notably by postmodernists but that was instigated by early feminist and lesbian and gay work on cities. This shift encompasses, first, the disruption of the fiction of separate public and private spheres and, secondly, an expansive, interdisciplinary redefinition of politics that has opened a gap between queer and feminist approaches to cities and the predominant understanding of urban politics within political science. Throughout the chapter, I point to the dramatic shift in thinking about urban space – that is, in determining which spaces deserve attention, in uncovering the processes by which urban space is gendered and sexed, and in debating the conceptualisation of space as metaphorical or physical. These feminist and queer theories rarely claim to resolve the kinds of open-ended questions posed above. Rather, they provide empirically grounded as well as abstract models (Clarke et al., 1995: 206; Ahrentzen, 2003: 188) of the functioning (and dysfunctioning) of gender systems.

Urban gender systems

How best to characterise the organisation of gender is a subject of some controversy among urban theorists (Bondi and Davidson, 2003). Postmodern theory has shifted the terms of debate toward an increasingly widespread assumption of 'the impermanence of the very categories "woman" and "man"' (McDowell, 1999: 21). As a result, the conceptualisation of gender as stable structure has been eclipsed within urban theory by its presentation as a performance (or subversion) of discursively constructed gender norms (Butler, 1993). Finding 'a third way' (McDowell, 1999: 20) is difficult – McDowell and others use 'gender regime' (Appleton, 1995). Viewing gender as a *system* is helpful because it evokes movement but also a discernible form; systems have purposes but are dependent on various components that are not always functional, stable or predictable. Even within a gender system as pervasively, historically dominant as patriarchy, the essential 'female'/'male' dualism and hierarchy is understood differently across contexts. Hence, expectations about sex and gender might well shift between wartime and peacetime, a park at noon and midnight, a computer memory fabrication facility and an automobile assembly plant, or a province or state and its capital city. The 'same geographic point at the same time of day may have two or more different meanings', as in Robert Bailey's example of the meat market district of New York, where in the middle of the night, 'truckers and meat packers work side by side while younger gay men congregate in and around bars and sex clubs in the same section of urban space' (1999: 91). References to gender *systems* (in the plural) reflect the possibility of social understandings that do not assume a 'female'/'male' core of sexuality and may well actively abandon it. In most places and at most times, state rules and societal conventions privilege 'male'/'female' over various alternative arrangements of sexual identities and affinities, because 'masculinity and femininity [are] constructed in/by/for heterosexuality' (Brown and Knopp, 2003: 315). However, in both practice and theory, there are currently unclassifiable biological statuses and sexual (and related political) identities – for example, intersexuality and transgenderism – that make more sense than the familiar 'gay'/'lesbian' and 'male'/'female' binaries.

The sub-cultures and sub-spaces of cities do seem, historically, to support parallel, minority or oppositional gender systems at least as well as anywhere else. However, the general claims that are made about pluralism, tolerance and 'eroticism' as inherently urban (e.g., Young, 1990: 239; Deutsche, 1994: 195–253) reveal an impetus to universalise, along with a spatial determinism, that would usually receive a cool reception within contemporary approaches to gender and sex. Lawrence Knopp argues against the generalisation:

Anonymity, voyeurism, tactility, motion, etc. are all human experiences that can be, and arguably have been, sexualised and desexualised in a variety of places and fashions (and for a variety of reasons), throughout history. Thus they bear no *necessary* relationship to the city. The issue is ... how and why urban space has been sexualised in the particular ways that it has. (1995: 160, italics in original; also see Bell and Binnie, 2000: 83–91)

Within feminist and lesbian urban theory, there are longstanding debates about the gender privileges embedded in the idea of the city's openness. Much of this debate is concerned with the nineteenth-century Parisian literary figure of the *flâneur*, a male who aimlessly strolls the crowded streets as a voyeur of, but not a participant in, the city's diverse stimulations (see Kataoka, in this volume). Janet Wolff maintains that women have never been afforded this 'privilege of passing unnoticed in the city' (Wolff, 2006: 19) – in the past, they would have been read, at least by men, as prostitutes; in the present, women are rarely purposeless in public (2006: 21). In contrast, Elizabeth Wilson (2001) has posited the existence and liberatory possibilities of the (female) *flâneuse*, and Sally Munt (1995) has written about the *lesbian flâneur*, whose relationship to urban space is not governed by the opposite-sex dichotomy. Others have pointed out, more broadly, that the celebrated urban characteristics of anonymity, tolerance, variety, etc. are actually contingent on the intersection of many identities and systems of power. Urbanity clearly 'does not work to preserve the prerogatives of those people who enter urban public space having been pre-identified as posing a threat' because of skin colour, aboriginality, religion, age or gender (Garber, 2000b: 32). The identities of young minority and immigrant males in North America, Europe, and Australia and New Zealand are therefore, as Elspeth Probyn puts it (2003: 297), 'overdetermined' in certain spaces, and there are dangers in the reactions to them of police and other city-dwellers. Similarly, the liberatory potential and safety of city life are diminished for people with evident disabilities, not the least because they are the objects of curiosity but sometimes also of hostility (Chouinard and Grant, 1995: 140–1).

Citizenship

The previous discussion suggests that the ideal of the city as tolerant and heterogenous promises a universality of sexual and gender freedom that does not actually exist. Gender-based theorists therefore have an important role as critics of urban gender systems. Just as crucially, critique is often followed by imagining the conditions in which women and sexual minorities would have full 'urban citizenship' (or, relatedly, 'feminist citizenship' or 'sexual citizenship'). Here, citizenship signifies a relationship to the city that is far more encompassing, and more creatively political, than legal membership in a nation-state. Citizenship is frequently discussed in conjunction with Henri Lefebvre's 'right to the city' (1996), for both suggest the possibility of individuals exercising ownership of cities in ways that 'challenge the segregating and isolating ambitions of the state and private enterprise' (Deutsche, 1999: 199). Urban citizenship is premised on the basic belief that neither one's body nor identity should, on moral or democratic grounds, determine one's ability to inhabit, use, flourish in and act upon cities (and therefore requires that the *regular* liberal citizenship rights to voting, speech, state recognition, privacy, procedural fairness, non-discriminatory treatment, etc. be enjoyed city-wide, which they currently are not to varying extents in various countries). Precise definitions vary, but the following rights are commonly included as central elements of urban citizenship: economic, physical and environmental security; mobility and access to space; democratic political forums; and expression of personal and collective identities, including sexual expression. This denser understanding of citizenship speaks equally to the day-to-day conditions of city-dwellers' existence (food and housing, a healthy environment, protection from violence or other abuse, practicable means of travel, childcare, recreational spaces) and to a long-term, psychologically rooted capacity to develop one's identity and political voice, as well as to enjoy life (e.g., Andrew, 1992; Wekerle, 2004).

Gender-based theories have a heavy normative investment in recognising that systems of oppression are multiple and that they interact with each other. Thus, the integration of disabled people, immigrants, children, the elderly, the homeless, and religious minorities into the cities where they live (or want to live) cannot be separated from the 'primary' goal of removing gender and sexual hierarchies as determinants of urban citizenship. Feminist and queer urban citizenship are inconsistent with anything less than city-wide citizenship, because gender and sex are impossible to abstract from the entire set of characteristics that define any individual's lived experience. It follows that urban citizenship as articulated within feminist and queer frameworks *necessarily* looks to the types of spaces where people who are marginal to the formal channels of politics and power are likely to be, and to be acting. Michael Brown makes the point that '[i]f we open up citizenship to numerous social identities it has not been previously associated with, we must also open it up to a wider variety of material spaces across ... the city' (1997: 15). These are spaces that are typically considered to be private (bars, kitchens), public but non-political (art installations, street vendor stalls), only tangential to cities (border-crossings, penitentiaries), or not real space (graffiti, media coverage of urban issues). Citizenship may be measured by the kind and extent of citizenship granted within those spaces; it may be tied to the acts and expressions of citizenship – politics the occurring there. I will return below to the expansive understandings of politics and space that feminist and queer theories have introduced into the study of cities.

Feminist and queer theories of the city

Feminist theory and queer theory exist, simply put, because gender does. Specifically, their concerns are ultimately traceable to the social understanding that there is actually a male/female division that has some comprehensible relationship to the way power is distributed among groups. Objections could certainly be made to this typology of gender theories. The labels 'feminist' and 'queer' are clearly helpful as shorthand but are, admittedly, too broad to do full justice to the diversity of either category – for instance, the label 'queer' has the potential to create 'a dichotomy with heterosexuality as dominant and all other sexuality thrown together into one big oppositional construct' (Chouinard and Grant, 1995: 147). Probably the most obvious criticism of tying sexuality to gender is that the framework could easily subsume sexual identities and practices within a predominantly, historically feminist approach to gender studies. In contrast, I take feminist and queer theories as equivalently situated with respect to the study and critique of urban phenomena that stem from the convention of a male/female dualism, but the relationship between these theories is complex enough to require elaboration.

Gender-based theories of cities are, of course, comprised in part of a significant body of work by and about lesbians. Lesbian urban theorists have identified lacunae in the theoretical starting points of both gender studies and gay studies. Liz Bondi argues that feminists' insistence on treating gender as a social artefact rather than a biological fact has 'disembodied, de-sexed and de-eroticized' the city (1998: 180). The economic, racial, medical, sexual, and gender positions of bodies in urban space is, however, a growing area of emphasis in feminist as well as queer theory (Moss and Dyck, 2003). In political terms, an 'embodied' perspective on the city brings to the fore how the state acts directly upon bodies by determining acceptable places for sleeping, having or selling sex, breastfeeding, urinating and defecating, gathering in groups – or by not protecting people from crimes aimed at disfavoured kinds of bodies (e.g., Bailey, 1999: 249–79). In the political economy, male and female bodies – bodies that are always also marked by race, class, age and (dis)ability – are regulated at the local-scale sites of transnational-scale economic imperatives; the relationship between bodies, identities and work is particularly evident during structural shifts, such as during the period of post-industrialisation (see McDowell, 1999: 134–45). In homes, construction sites, farms, restaurants, sweatshops, and every sort of proper factory and office, bodies physically reflect the demands of different types of work assigned to different categories of workers. At the same time, workers' identities – as, for instance, sufficiently masculine, young, skilled or presentable – are affected by the type of work they (are expected or permitted to) do.

Lesbian theory, and especially empirically based theory, has paid especially close attention to the fact that women's identities intersect (as, say, woman *and* lesbian *and* Latino *and* able-bodied) and shift in prominence across locations (from the heterosexualised workplace to the lesbian social club to the mixed-ethnicity neighbourhood) and lifespan (see Valentine, 2007). This focus is in part a response to the fact that, until recently, the particularities of lesbian women's urban lives have been less studied than, and may be confused with, those of gay men and in part a desire to theorise intersectionality (Valentine, 1993; Cooper, 1994: 177; Chouinard and Grant, 1995: 146–8; Nast, 2002). Lying at the intersection of feminist and queer theory are distinctive political stances about coalition-building, representation and policy concerns regarding mothers and children, health, housing, violence and safety, and a wide scope of social justice issues. These critiques and new paths of inquiry suggest that a key issue is not whether feminist and queer theoretical stances are adequately distinguished from each other, but whether both have fields of vision expansive enough to permit a good look at who exists and what occurs in cities at the crossroads of gender and sex.

Queer and feminist theories are separate but inextricably linked, with an overlapping concern in the mutually constitutive relationship between the controlling male/female dichotomy and the politics, culture, economies, families, and built and natural environments of cities. There have always been, as Larry Knopp (2007) has pointed out, affinities between the study of gender and the study of sex and sexuality. In the early years of women's studies and gay and lesbian studies, many writers in and out of the academy held a shared perspective – essentialised – on identities ('man', 'white', 'immigrant'), and they placed similar emphases – liberal and Marxist – on legal and economic equality. By the turn of the millennium, it was postmodernism that had produced a degree of convergence among feminist and queer theorists coming from an array of disciplinary homes. This agreement revolves around the normative and analytical necessity to 'complicate' (2007: 49) fixed meanings ('economy', 'private', 'borders') inherited from modernism. It permits ongoing dialogue and debate between feminist and queer theorists over the definition and utility of urban concepts no less fundamental than 'politics' and 'space'. More empirically, gender-based theorists have forged paths, sometimes separate and sometimes joined, leading to core urban issues such as the safety, publicity, meaning, and politics of public spaces, but, again, complicated by difficult questions – for whom? when? with what tradeoffs?

In the end, however, insofar as queer theories 'foreground issues of sexuality and desire', whereas feminist theories 'foregroun[d] women's experiences and issues of gender' in society (2007: 48), they will frequently not be speaking from or about comparable urban experiences. This divergence can easily be spotted in the types of issues that receive sustained attention in the empirical research agendas about women and gays in cities. An interest in gay men's presence in and uses of urban public space for various combinations of social, political, and sexual reasons links successive generations of researchers. The overlap of sexuality with race, class and age means that not all gay men occupy space similarly, even in the same city or 'gay' neighbourhood or even during single events like pride parades or protests. Nonetheless, gay men's sexuality generally remains regulated through homophobic (legal and informal) controls on space (Valverde and Cirak, 2003), as well as through the actual contraction of public space in the service of consumption-based urban economic development (Bell and Binnie, 2000: 85–6; cf. Nast, 2002). For feminists, no single issue plays an analogously dominant role in research; however, to take one prominent example,[2] there are more than three decades of inquiry into the challenges and choices that women face in their regular travels within (and between) cities. Commuting is especially fraught for women because of their need to fulfil multiple job and family responsibilities, and in the context of their identities as members of (class, sexual, racial/ethnic) communities, the nature of female employment opportunities, marital status, child (or parent) care availability, state regulation of social programme recipients, housing discrimination, and lesser access to private cars (Hanson and Pratt, 1995; Miranne, 2000; also see Boo, 2003).

A vocabulary of urban politics and space

Feminist and queer theorists have contributed to the development of a sophisticated, persuasive language for use in conceptualising and discussing the most central aspects of urbanity, among which are politics and space. It is now totally unremarkable to talk about 'the politics of space' and 'the space(s) of politics', whether or not in reference to cities. These phrases have very recent origins, though, and are part of a largely post-modern vocabulary that construes 'politics' and 'space' in sweeping terms. The revisions are attributable to the epistemological goal of debunking essentialised, categorical, or otherwise limited meanings. As Doreen Massey puts it:

> [T]he mode of thinking that relies on irreconcilable dichotomies ... has in general recently come in for widespread criticism. All the strings of these kinds of opposition with which we are so accustomed to work (mind-body, nature-culture, reason-emotion, and so forth) have been argued to be ... a hindrance to either understanding or changing the world. Much of this critique has come from feminists' (1994: 255).

While Massey's observation is aimed at another dualism that pervades and genders urban studies, that of space/time,[3] it is the public/private distinction that is most immediately relevant to urban politics and most accessible to attack. *Some* version of separate public and private spheres exists at the core of liberal, Marxist, communitarian and radical democratic political thought, although all cities remain the product of liberalism and neoliberalism and, hence, of their dualisms.

Public, private and urban politics

By their very existence, every critical perspective on gender or sex poses a challenge to the basic terms of the public/private dualism. Postmodernism (and the related post-structural and post-colonial critiques of modernism) can claim the greatest responsibility for dampening the overt scholarly reliance on dualisms over the past 20 years. It was, by contrast, the *modernist* theorists of gender and sex – including, notably, urbanists interested in women's locality and their locatedness in various identities – who began questioning the legitimacy of the traditional public/private framework as either empirical fact, analytical framework or normative ideal. Indeed, the first political task feminist urban scholars accomplished was breaking the imaginary seal between the household and the city. Unmasking the fiction of separate spheres entailed identifying where (and which) women were already participating in urban politics and economies, even if these activities were not widely recognised as political or economic. It also required illuminating the political, social and economic processes through which the urban 'private' sphere is constructed, hence deprivatising gender and sex.

Beyond the insistence of feminists in the 1960s–70s that sexual and familial relationships are infused with power – the theoretical core of the mantra 'the personal is the political' – lie a wealth of more concrete and detailed observations about the interconnectedness of what previously were assumed to be separate spheres. The range of such observations has enlarged tremendously with the rise of post- and anti-modernist epistemologies, the proliferation of scholarship viewing urban politics and political economy through the lens of identity and subjectivity; and the actual trajectories of globalisation, urbanisation and oppression. Subject matter that was radical is now part of its own 'mainstream', yet there is no foreseeable limit to what we can learn about where urban politics is located, whether conceptually or materially, relative to publicity and privacy. Among the issues that have continually been revisited – with far more attentiveness over time to the intersectionality of gender with sexuality, and of gender and sexuality with other identities – are: the gender burdens of housing and neighbourhood design, and urban and metropolitan form (Whitzman, 2007); gaps in welfare state support for women, families and cities (Haylett, 2006); the contribution of women's domestic labour to capitalist reproduction and collective consumption (Katz, 2008); the dynamics, successes and failures of grassroots and social movement organising (Williams, 2005); the determinants and policy impacts of local electoral leadership (Flammang, 1997); the inclusion of equality concerns within local state structures (Bashevkin, 2006); and the nature and historical imprint of women's civic volunteerism (Spain, 2000).

In the next section, I discuss the redefinition of urban politics to include phenomena that are far from the common understanding of what constitutes politics. Here, though, I want to stress that dismantling the public–private duality also speaks to conventionally political topics, and does so in ways that have developed only because theories of gender and sex have been brought to bear on urban studies. The integration of the local state – a term first used by Cynthia Cockburn in her Marxist feminist analysis of governance in a London borough (1977) – into a broad collection of social forces (rather than government and capitalism only) is one example. Another is the related contention that the distinction between 'formal' and 'informal' political action directed toward the same goal is as untenable as the public/private binary (Brownhill and Halford, 1990). Municipal government structure can be seen to result from processes that have historically involved discourses of racism, patriarchy and heterosexual privilege (Dilworth and Trevenen, 2006). Political attitudes and behaviour are a manifestation of sexual, gender, racial and ethnic identities that exist in urban space, whether the spaces of neighbourhoods and streets or households and places of employment. At the same time, the actual and perceived receptiveness of local political institutions to minority groups' and women's claims conditions political attitudes and behaviours (Bailey, 1999; Staeheli, 2004; Sharp et al., 2005).

Redefining urban politics

Although urban studies is already an interdisciplinary endeavour, in the case of the gender and sexual politics of cities (and the urban politics of gender and sex), interdisciplinarity has special influence. Interventions from far beyond the usual suspects of political science, public administration and political economy – from art history, architecture, planning, geography, sociology, anthropology, history, literary studies, film studies, philosophy, psychology, psychoanalysis, ethnicity and area (e.g., Latino/a, Middle East, Native) studies, women's studies, gay and lesbian studies, development studies, and environmental studies – have pushed aggressively against the idea that urban politics is coterminous with that which occurs in what Ruth Fincher calls 'the famously "big-P" political sites of public space, the parliament, the city council, and the large unionized workplace' (2004: 49). Indeed, the project of theorising gender at any scale or level has gone hand-in-hand with numerous efforts, some quite conscious, to revise *the very definition of politics* that drives scholarly assumptions and norms, as well as research methods (Klodawsky, 2007).

These efforts have succeeded, at least in the sense that the dominant approaches taken by gender theories of urban phenomena are quite obviously 'concerned less with an official or privileged order of power in the city – the geography of political regimes or economic elites – than with more oppositional, informal or everyday spatial politics' (Tonkiss, 2005: 59). The tangible result of this shift lies in *what* is called 'politics' for the purpose of urban research and *who* is doing that research. Unquestionably, 'urban politics' topics have inspired rich treatments informed by feminist and gay and lesbian perspectives, as the previous section suggests. This literature exists only because gender theories have been brought to bear on urban studies generally. Urban politics is nevertheless mostly *not* viewed as resting within formal institutions and processes of cities, nor are political scientists responsible for more than a small fraction of the gendering and queering of the study of 'politics' in cities. Indeed, urbanists in other fields distance themselves from 'the traditional dualities bequeathed by mainstream political science' (Kofman and Peake, 1990: 315; c.f. Brown, 1999).[4]

Removing politics from the orbit of the state often – but not necessarily – goes hand-in-hand with wresting space from its material referents. In more resolute critiques of modernism, any division of urban space into the categories of 'physical' and 'abstract' – in essence, into space and 'space' – reinforces the other modernist, patriarchal dualisms and hierarchies related to aspects of reality, truth and significance. In this view, dualising space serves to deny its discursive, symbolic and subjective aspects; it short-circuits feminist and queer versions of political space(s) (Deutsche, 1999; Whitzman, 2007). To some degree, there is a universal acceptance within feminist and queer theory of the metaphorical 'spaces of' as being as equally real as the ground or built structures. However, the conceptualisation of space is a subject of some debate. In so far as gendered and sexed politics is increasingly being associated with particular places (see Hanson and Pratt, 1995; Watson, 2006), retaining an interest in the materiality of urban space may seem especially necessary even from some critical theoretical perspectives (Smith and Katz, 1993; Garber, 2000a).

In the wake of these important shifts, the study of politics in cities, as distinguished from an 'urban politics' oriented to the state (Clarke et al., 1995: 221–2), is motivated largely by the political content of activities and spaces that would likely previously have been overlooked as trivial, apolitical or not actually urban. There is increasing attention being paid to the (gendered, sexualised, racialised, and classed) uses of streets and plazas, parks, public toilets, playgrounds, museums, shops, houses, gardens, university campuses and community organisations (e.g., Watson, 2006). First, gender, sex, race and class systems are taken in and of themselves as constructed features of cities from which nobody, and no space, is exempt. Every body, identity and space is political, in short. Secondly, politics is ascribed to the activities that take place in those spaces. Because they are substantially less visible to the average political observer, there is special interest in activities that transgress or oppose accepted social and spatial rules – for middle-class, white Victorian

American women, by shopping downtown (Domosh, 1998); for gay Canadian men, by patronising policed bathhouses (Valverde and Cirak, 2003); for young Turkish Muslim women, by deciding when to wear or not wear the veil (Secor, 2002). Activities that occur in hidden political spaces may be recognised as transgressive in some ways and simultaneously complicit in processes that produce oppression, as with Emanuela Guano's (2006) study of underemployed, middle-class women in Genoa, Italy, who have moved their domestic role of caretaker of family antiques into the entrepreneurial sphere of antiques-selling. In so doing, they 'utilize their gendered skills ... to establish their own public and professional identities' (2006: 108) but 'become the enthusiastic foot soliders of Genoa's bourgeoning culture industry', (2006: 106) and thus of the city's integration into the global economy.

Postmodernist theorists have been a motive force in proliferating what counts as urban politics (and as space), but within postmodernism, there may be an urge to go farther than adding to the modernist conceptual repertoire. The quest to revise the definition of urban politics may take the form of a dismissal of the relevance to 'postmodern cities' of conventional, discipline-bound conceptions of politics, including communitarian, liberal, socialist and radical democratic models. Sophie Watson and Katherine Gibson (1995) reject the notion of political progress as male: 'What interests us is how heroic visions of modernist politics, that of mass mobilization and emancipation of the oppressed, have eclipsed ... the many possibilities of a post-modern politics' such as 'design[ing] and build[ing] postmodern spaces' (1995: 254–5). This version of postmodern urban politics is radically disaggregated and devolved in accordance with attention to the specificities of people's daily lives. In relegating 'simplistic notions of class alliances or urban social movements' (1995: 262) to the realm of 'wistful' (1995: 9) thinking, the position represented by Watson and Gibson leaves little room for politics as defined within political science, even if it is politics that takes place outside of the realm of the state.

Further options

A dualistic choice between public/private and modernist/postmodernist dichotomies would not be compelling, nor is it necessary – for Bondi and Davidson (2003: 326), 'feminist perspectives need to deploy both Enlightenment and post-Enlightenment ways of thinking'. Many feminist and queer theorists present options for defining and interpreting politics that are useful because they do not entail a predefinition or foreshortening of what 'counts', politically, in the city. I briefly describe two of these options (one an example of abstract theory and one an example of empirically grounded theory).

Political theorist Diana Coole (2000) characterises feminists as ambivalent about the public/private dichotomy of liberalism – able 'to perceive the *location* of any line dividing public from private as intrinsically unstable' but unprepared to approach the actual *existence* of the line as 'a general theoretical question' (2000: 342, emphasis added). For Coole, a number of transformations have so blurred the 'line' that it remains barely discernible. First, liberal thinkers long ago subdivided public/private into a state/economy/family/civil society categorisation that is not coterminous with the original binary. Secondly, feminism itself successfully destabilised the categories in ways that have made them theoretically and conceptually suspect. Thirdly, the processes of globalisation and technological change have rendered 'actual spaces' (2000: 349) unrecognisable within the old terms of discourse, as is evident from the compression of geographical scales. On the one hand, the complexity of space means that public/private no longer helps us understand oppression (even in seemingly simple cases that concern feminists, like domestic violence), or the world more generally. On the other hand, postmodernists' certainty in representing space in metaphorical and abstract terms is prematurely confident, given the changes still in progress. Coole's conclusion is that a post-dualism 'cartography' remains to be produced.

Geographer Michael Brown's (1997) study of AIDS activism in Vancouver's gay community begins with a trichotomy of state, family and civil society, where the (local) state is widely assumed to be, among the three spheres, the space of politics. While Brown's reexamination of the urban sites of citizenship practices implicates liberalism, he is responding directly to the post-structural, radical democratic political theory of Chantal Mouffe, which he characterises as 'steering between' liberalism and communitarianism (1997: 11). Brown demonstrates 'the confluences or overlap of these three spheres in actively promoting radical democratic citizenship' (1997: 28) among civil society and domestic-sphere actors, in the form of contributions to the gay community. In an effort to provide services and support to people with AIDS, family members, volunteers, paid employees in voluntary organisations, and bureaucrats necessarily moved among the three spheres. These interactions among service-providing government agencies, the voluntary sector and grassroots organisations, and the homes of men with AIDS cultivated politics outside of the state and, thus, provided opportunities for citizenship to non-state actors. For Brown as for Coole, then, simple dichotomies, which do not even test the limits of liberalism itself (Brown, 1999), cannot capture the contingency of the interactions of space, action, identity and power.

Conclusions

It is, to put it mildly, a challenge to encapsulate the influence of theories as sweeping and diverse as those discussed in this chapter. Feminist and queer interventions are especially sensitive to specificity of people, places and contexts. Thus, there is a growing literature on cities in the South, in the globalised mega-cities of East Asia and throughout Europe that I have not addressed, and missing along with that literature are some important intersectional approaches to urban gender and sex (see Nelson and Seager, 2005). Finally, the newness and rapid proliferation of gender- and sex-based theorising – and, crucially, its self-consciously critical stance – means that there are few canonical guideposts for those making their way through these approaches to urban politics.

One area of concern is the yawning communication gap between these theories and the conventional study of politics (or the study of conventional politics), which rests largely in apparently incompatible political vocabularies. But these new and old vocabularies actually share a key concept – *power*. The study of power is the traditional, core business of political science, and this concern with power is as true in the area of urban politics as in the study of national elections or international affairs. The expansive, interdisciplinary definition of urban politics discussed above is also largely that of power – that is, prevailing arrangements of power and oppression within social systems such as gender and race constitute power, and so do acts and other displays of resistance against those arrangements. Ruth Fincher describes urban processes with 'particular significance ... to gender or sexuality in place or space' as '*political because* they have these uneven outcomes' (2004: 62, emphasis added). Whether planners and other local decision-makers intend to institutionalise gender and sexual hierarchies when they limit the number of unrelated people occupying single-family dwellings, or skateboarders are conscious of their empowerment when they appropriate public sidewalks meant for shoppers, or patrons of revitalised arts districts would understand that they are participating in a commodification process that marginalises previous users of those spaces, they are seen as political actors. Among gender and sexuality theorists, there is widespread use of the formulation 'the politics of' – of location, of meaning, of built space. This is a coded language of power, which can usually be read as 'the awareness of the power relations implicated in' – in the organisation of urban life and forms.

For feminist and queer theories to 'speak urban politics' to urbanists who are modernists – to scholars who study 'big-P' politics like regional economic development policy or 'heroic' politics like demonstrations against repressive immigration regimes – it may be necessary to bring the language of power (and empowerment) more to the foreground. Power is not the only or necessarily the best way to talk about deepening and extending urban citizenship; a transformative politics aimed at 'unequal outcomes' must also involve proliferating opportunities for collective self-governance and action, whether locally or at multiple scales. Nevertheless, the comprehensibility and transportability of the language of power is a potential bridge between theories of gender and sex and the accepted approaches to urban politics.

Ultimately, the gendered and sexed study of more conventional urban political institutions, processes and behaviours will continue to be the tiny exception to the mammoth rule if scholars of urban politics treat identities besides class, and to a lesser extent race and ethnicity, as ancillary to the field. It is possible to take seriously gender and sex *and also* politics that occurs within and with reference to the local state, including in the context of such central theoretical frameworks as urban regime theory (e.g., Bailey, 1999; Brown, 1999). But this requires an understanding of patriarchy and heterosexual privilege as key components of globalisation, and as intersecting with other hierarchies of power and oppression but not being reducible to them. The growth over multiple decades of feminist and queer approaches to cities suggests that they are engaged in an important conversation that must not be limited to feminist and queer students of urban politics.

Notes

1 There is simply too much important literature to mention here. However, in addition to the works cited in the text, the state of urban gender and, although to a lesser extent, sexuality theory into the early 1990s can be seen in the 1978 'Women and the City' issue of *International Journal of Urban and Regional Research*, the 1980 'Women in the American City' issue of *Signs*, the 1984 'Women and the Environment' issue of *Antipode*, and the 1990 *Political Geography Quarterly* special issue on gender. For more recent snapshots of the state of the art, see Clarke et al.'s (1995) essay in the previous edition of this volume, McDowell's (1999) chapter-end bibliographies, Ahrentzen's (2003) review article, and the collection edited by Nelson and Seager (2005). Lest I appear to be relegating to history the pathbreaking urban scholars of gender and sexuality, it should be stressed that the graduate students of the 1970s (and before) are ongoing contributors to the theoretical developments I am discussing.

2 Another is women's fear in cities. See Whitzman (2007) for an insightful discussion of the treatment of fear as it relates to public and private spaces and to immigrant and other groups of women.

3 A number of the essays in Massey's brilliant 1994 collection, *Space, Place, and Gender*, reveal the masculinist assumptions within very prominent treatments of locality and globalisation by Marxist, postmodernist and radical democratic male thinkers in the late 1980s. In these theories, taken collectively, the time/space (or time/place) dichotomy harbours numerous others, including: travel/home, abstract/embodied, theoretical/atheoretical, political/apolitical, process/thing, progress/stasis, radical/defensive and masculine/feminine. The point, not surprisingly, is that the first half of each dichotomy is privileged, and that the dichotomies are false. Rosalyn Deutsche sharply criticises a similar body of urban political economy literature in her discussion of 'certain neo-Marxist geographers' who are 'trying to maintain a traditional division between what they call "material" or "concrete" space, on the one hand, and "metaphorical" or "discursive" space on the other' (1999: 177–8).

4 This incongruity undoubtedly lies as much in the marginality of urban politics within (North American) political science as it does in the still rather modest influence of gender on the discipline. Kofman and Peake (1990: 315) observe that even feminist political theory was 'generally not ... greatly concerned with the spatial dimensions of political affairs'. While this is less true than when they were writing, geographers are ostentatiously responsible for the lion's share of feminist and queer urban theory.

References

Ahrentzen, S. (2003) 'The space between the studs: feminism and architecture', *Signs*, 29 (1): 179–206.

Andrew, C. (1992)) 'The feminist city', in H. Lustiger-Thaler (ed.), *Political Arrangements: Power and the City*. Montreal: Black Rose Books. pp. 109–22.

Appleton, L. (1995) 'The gender regimes of American cities', in J.A. Garber and R.S. Turner (eds), *Gender in Urban Research*. Newbury Park, CA: Sage Publications. pp. 44–59.

Bailey, R. W. (1999) *Gay Politics, Urban Politics: Identity and Economics in the Urban Setting*. New York: Columbia University Press.

Bashevkin, S. (2006) *Tales of Two Cities: Women and Municipal Restructuring in London and Toronto*. Vancouver: University of British Columbia Press.

Bell, D. and Binnie, J. (2000) *The Sexual Citizen: Queer Politics and Beyond*. Cambridge: Polity Press.

Bondi, L. (1998) 'Sexing the city', in R. Fincher and J.M. Jacobs (eds), *Cities of Difference*. New York: Guilford Press. pp. 177–200.

Bondi, L. and Davidson, J. (2003) 'Troubling the place of gender', in K. Anderson, M. Domosh, S. Pile and N. Thrift (eds), *Handbook of Cultural Geography*. London: Sage Publications. pp. 325–43.

Boo, K. (2003) 'The marriage cure: is wedlock really a way out of poverty?', *The New Yorker, 79* (18 & 25 August): 105–20.

Brown, M.P. (1997) *Re/Placing Citizenship: AIDS Activism and Radical Democracy*. New York: Guilford Press.

Brown, M. (1999) 'Reconceptualizing public and private in urban regime theory: governance in AIDS politics', *International Journal of Urban and Regional Research*, 23 (1): 70–87.

Brown, M. and Knopp, L. (2003) 'Queer cultural geographies – we're here! We're queer! We're over there, too!', in K. Anderson, M. Domosh, S. Pile and N. Thrift (eds), *Handbook of Cultural Geography*. London: Sage Publications. pp. 313–24.

Brownhill, S. and Halford, S. (1990) 'Understanding women's political involvement in local politics: how useful is a formal/informal dichotomy?', *Political Geography Quarterly*, 9: 396–414.

Burnett, P. (1973) 'Social change, the status of women and models of city form and development', *Antipode*, 5: 57–61.

Butler, J. (1993) *Bodies That Matter: On the Discursive Limits of 'Sex'*. London: Routledge.

Chouinard, V. and Grant, A. (1995) 'On being not even anywhere near "The Project": ways of putting ourselves in the picture', *Antipode*, 27 (2): 137–66.

Clarke, S.E., Staeheli, L.S. and Brunell, L. (1995) 'Women redefining local politics', in D. Judge, G. Stoker and H. Wolman (eds), *Theories of Urban Politics*. London: Sage Publications. pp. 205–27.

Cockburn, C. (1977) *The Local State: Management of Cities and People*. London: Pluto Press.

Coole, D. (2000) 'Cartographic convulsions: public and private reconsidered', *Political Theory*, 28 (3): 337–54.

Cooper, D. (1994) *Sexing the City: Lesbian and Gay Politics Within the Activist State*. London: Rivers Oram Press.

D'Emilio, J. (1981) 'Gay politics, gay community: San Francisco's experience', *Socialist Review*, 11: 77–104.

Deutsche, R. (1994) *Evictions: Art and Spatial Politics*. Cambridge, MA: MIT Press.

Deutsche, R. (1999) 'Reasonable urbanism', in J. Copjec and M. Sorkin (eds), *Giving Ground: The Politics of Propinquity*. London: Verso. pp. 175–206.

Dilworth, R. and Trevenen, K. (2006) 'When cities get married: constructing urban space through gender, sexuality, and municipal consolidation', *Urban Affairs Review*, 40 (2): 183–209.

Domosh, M. (1998) 'Those "gorgeous incongruities": polite politics and public space on the streets of nineteenth-century New York City', *Annals of the Associations of American Geographers*, 88 (2): 209–26.

Ettore, E.M. (1978) 'Women, urban social movements and the lesbian ghetto', *International Journal of Urban and Regional Research*, 2 (3): 499–520.

Fincher, R. (2004) 'From dualisms to multiplicities: gendered political practices', in L.A. Staeheli, E. Kofman and L.J. Peake (eds), *Mapping Women, Making Politics: Feminist Perspectives on Political Geography*. New York: Routledge. pp. 49–69.

Flammang, J. (1997) *Women's Political Voice: How Women Are Transforming the Practice and Study of Politics*. Philadelphia: Temple University Press.

Garber, J.A. (2000a) 'The city as a heroic public sphere', in E.F. Isin (ed.), *Democracy, Citizenship, and the Global City*. London: Routledge. pp. 257–74.

Garber, J.A. (2000b) 'Not named or identified': politics and the search for anonymity in the city', in K.B. Miranne and A.H. Young (eds), *Gendering the City: Women, Boundaries, and Visions of Urban Life*. Lanham, MD: Rowman and Littlefield. pp. 19–39.

Gelb, J. and Gittell, M. (1986) 'Seeking equality: the role of activist women in cities', in J.K. Boles (ed.), *The Egalitarian City: Issues of Rights, Distribution, Access, and Power*. New York: Praeger. pp. 93–109.

Guano, E. (2006) 'Fair ladies: the place of women antique dealers in a post-industrial Italian city', *Gender, Place and Culture*, 12 (2): 105–22.

Hanson, S. and Pratt, G. (1995) *Gender, Work, and Space*. London: Routledge.

Hayden, D. and Wright, G. (1976) 'Review essay: architecture and urban planning', *Signs*, 1 (4): 923–33.

Haylett, C. (2006) 'Working-class subjects in the cosmopolitan city', in J. Binnie, J. Holloway, S. Millington and C. Young (eds), *Cosmopolitan Urbanism*. London: Routledge. pp. 187–203.

Katz, C. (2008) 'Bad elements: Katrina and the scoured landscape of social reproduction', *Gender, Place and Culture*, 15 (1): 15–29.

Klodawsky, F. (2007) '"Choosing" participatory research: partnerships in space-time', *Environment and Planning A*, 39: 2845–60.

Knopp, L. (1995) 'Sexuality and urban space: a framework for analysis', in D. Bell and G. Valentine (eds), *Mapping Desire: Geographies of Sexualities*. London: Routledge. pp. 149–61.

Knopp, L. (2007) 'On the relationship between queer and feminist geographies', *The Professional Geographer*, 59 (1): 47–55.

Kofman, E. and Peake, L. (1990) 'Into the 1990s: a gendered agenda for political geography', *Political Geography*, 9 (4): 313–36.

Lefrevbre, H. (1996) 'The right to the city', in E. Kofman and E. Lebar (eds and trans.), *Writings on Cities*. Oxford: Blackwell. pp. 147–59.

Lofland, L. (1975) 'The thereness of women: a selective review of urban sociology', in M. Millman and R.M. Kanter (eds), *Another Voice: Feminist Perspectives on Social Life and Social Science*. New York: Doubleday Anchor. pp. 144–70.

MacKenzie, S. and Rose, D. (1983) 'Industrial change, the domestic economy and home life', in J. Anderson, S. Duncan and R. Hudson (eds), *Redundant Spaces and Industrial Decline in Cities and Regions*. London: Academic Press. pp. 81–99.

Markusen, A.R. (1980) 'City spatial structure, women's household work, and national urban policy', *Signs*, 5 (3): S22–44.

Massey, D. (1994) *Space, Place, and Gender*. Minneapolis: University of Minnesota Press.

McDowell, L. (1999) *Gender, Identity and Place*. Minneapolis: University of Minnesota Press.

Mezey, S.G. (1978) 'Support for women's rights policy', *American Politics Research*, 6 (4): 485–97.

Miranne, K.B. (2000) 'Women "embounded": intersections of welfare reform and public housing policy', in K.B. Miranne and A.H. Young (eds), *Gendering the City: Women, Boundaries, and Visions of Urban Life*. Lanham, MD: Rowman and Littlefield. pp. 119–35.

Moss, P. and Dyck, I. (2003) 'Embodying social geography', in K. Anderson, M. Domosh, S. Pile and N. Thrift (eds), *Handbook of Cultural Geography*. London: Sage Publications. pp. 58–73.

Munt, S. (1995) 'The lesbian *flâneur*', in D. Bell and G. Valentine (eds), *Mapping Desire: Geographies of Sexualities*. London: Routledge. pp. 114–25.

Nast, H.J. (2002) 'Queer patriarchies, queer racisms, international', *Antipode*, 34 (5): 874–909.

Nelson, L. and Seager, J. (eds) (2005) *A Companion to Feminist Geography*. London: Blackwell.

Probyn, E. (2003) 'The spatial imperative of subjectivity', in K. Anderson, M. Domosh, S. Pile and N. Thrift (eds), *Handbook of Cultural Geography*. London: Sage Publications. pp. 290–9.

Saegert, S. (1980) 'Masculine cities and feminine suburbs: polarized ideas, contradictory realities', *Signs*, 5 (3): S96–111.

Secor, A. (2002) 'The veil and urban space in Istanbul: women's dress, mobility and Islamic knowledge', *Gender, Place and Culture*, 9 (1): 5–22.

Sharp, E.B., Clarke, S. and Sarbaugh-Thompson, M. (2005) 'Gays, rights, and local morality politics', in E.B. Sharp, *Morality Politics in American Cities*. Lawrence, KS: University Press of Kansas. pp. 129–61.

Smith, N. and Katz, C. (1993) 'Grounding metaphor: towards a spatialized politics', in M. Keith and S. Pile (eds), *Place and the Politics of Identity*. London: Routledge. pp. 67–83.

Spain, D. (2000) *How Women Saved the City*. Minneapolis: University of Minnesota Press.

Staeheli, L.A. (2004) 'Mobilizing women, mobilizing gender: is it mobilizing difference?', *Gender, Place and Culture*, 11 (3): 347–72.

Tonkiss, F. (2005) *Space, the City and Social Theory: Social Relations and Urban Forms*. Cambridge: Polity Press.

Valentine, G. (1993) '(Hetero)sexing space: lesbian perceptions and experiences of everyday spaces', *Environment and Planning D: Society and Space*, 11: 395–413.

Valentine, G. (2007) 'Theorizing and researching intersectionality: a challenge for feminist geography', *The Professional Geographer*, 59 (1): 10–21.

Valverde, M. and Cirak, M. (2003) 'Governing bodies, creating gay spaces: policing and security issues in "gay" downtown Toronto', *British Journal of Criminology*, 43: 102–21.

Watson, S. (2006) *City Publics: The (Dis)enchantments of Urban Encounters*. London: Routledge.

Watson, S. and Gibson, K. (1995) 'Postmodern politics and planning: a postscript', in S. Watson and K. Gibson (eds), *Postmodern Cities and Spaces*. Oxford: Blackwell. pp. 254–64.

Wekerle, G.R. (2004) 'Framing feminist claims for urban citizenship', in L.A. Staeheli, E. Kofman and L.J. Peake (eds), *Mapping Women, Making Politics: Feminist Perspectives on Political Geography*. New York: Routledge. pp. 245–59.

Wekerle, G.R., Paterson, R. and Morley, D. (eds) (1980) *New Space for Women*. Boulder, CO: Westview Press.

Whitzman, C. (2007) 'Stuck at the front door: gender, fear of crime and the challenge of creating safer spaces', *Environment and Planning A*, 39: 2715–32.

Williams, R.Y. (2005) *The Politics of Public Housing: Black Women's Struggles against Urban Inequality*. New York: Oxford University Press.

Wilson, E. (2001) *The Contradictions of Culture: Cities, Culture, Women*. London: Sage.

Wolff, J. (2006) 'Gender and the haunting of cities (or, the retirement of the *flâneur*)', in A. D'Souza and T. McDonough (eds), *The Invisible Flâneuse? Gender, Public Space, and Visual Culture in Nineteenth-Century Paris*. Manchester: Manchester University Press. pp. 18–31.

Young, I.M. (1990) *Justice and the Politics of Difference*. Princeton: Princeton University Press.

14

SOCIAL CAPITAL

Helen Sullivan

The idea of social capital has become ubiquitous within the social sciences and amongst policy-makers at all levels. Its penetration of academic and public policy circles has been swift and comprehensive, although accompanied by intense debates on all aspects of the concept including its definition, theoretical coherence, empirical development, measurement, and utility in theory and practice (Portes, 1998; DeFilippis, 2001; Mayer, 2003; Lowndes, 2004). Social capital can be defined as a resource that is generated via regularised interactions between actors who have developed relationships with each other based upon shared values, and who can use this resource for the attainment of individual or collective benefits that would not otherwise have been (easily) obtainable. Social capital draws attention to the role of networks, shared values and norms of reciprocity lubricated through trust, in generating and maintaining social order. It valorises the contribution of relationships in analyses of governance, staking a claim alongside structural and behavioural approaches.

This chapter focuses on what social capital can contribute to our understanding of urban politics. This is important not least because while social capital as currently understood is neither an exclusively 'urban' nor 'political' concept, its supporters make a variety of claims for it that have particular resonance in an urban political arena. These claims include linking social capital with the promotion of good governance, improved policy outcomes and the development of stronger communities (Putnam, 2000; Halpern, 2005). For cities faced with the combined challenges of declining public trust in the institutions of governance, rising public expectations about public service quality, and increasing levels of poverty and inequality that undermine social cohesion, these claims have strong appeal. However, the adoption of social capital as a key policy instrument in urban governance raises some important questions for policy-makers and scholars. These concern the roles of the local state and civil society organisations in contributing to or constraining social capital, the interaction of social capital with 'race'/ethnicity, gender and class, and the influence of wider contextual factors on its development.

Prior to exploring these questions, the chapter provides an overview of the conceptual development of social capital, describing and discussing the contribution of key thinkers and their relevance to urban politics.

Definitions and developments

Contemporary accounts of social capital tend to be associated with a core group of scholars from different social science disciplines, including sociology, economics and, latterly, political science. Predominant amongst contemporary contributors are Europeans such as Bourdieu, as well as several US scholars, particularly Coleman and Putnam but also including others such as Becker and Loury (see Portes, 1998 for a review).

Bourdieu's perspective on social capital was influenced by but also a reaction to Marxist sociology. He acknowledged economic capital as the most important form of capital, but argued that the maintenance of the hierarchical class relationships that prevailed within society depended upon the interaction and combination of economic with social and cultural capital. Bourdieu defined social capital as 'the aggregate of the actual or potential resources which are linked to possession of a durable network of more or less institutionalized relationships of mutual acquaintance or recognition' (1985: 248). The particular value of social capital lay in the access to individual benefits (not collective), that participation in these 'durable networks' facilitated. These benefits could be direct access to economic resources or access to other forms of capital that ultimately conferred economic benefits, e.g. contacts with notable individuals or affiliations to powerful institutions. Such networks did not arise spontaneously but were in Bourdieu's terms, a form of 'accumulated labour'; the product of deliberate investment effort on the part of individuals who might benefit from the transformation of human relationships into stable social group relationships marked by obligations. The relationship between investment in social relationships and the benefits that would accrue was neither direct nor entirely predictable; some degree of trust in the ultimate reciprocity of the relationship was necessary.

For Fine (2001), Bourdieu's analysis of social capital is important because it incorporates an understanding of the contribution of class, economics and the constitutive role of politics in differentiating between levels of social capital, core factors in the study of urban politics. Field (2003) concurs that Bourdieu's focus on the way in which social capital is used by elites to maintain their privileged position is important, but argues that it is limited by his relatively 'static' view of social relations – Bourdieu does not consider the possibility that individuals from other social classes might use social capital to change their position in the social structure. However, Field does emphasise the importance of Bourdieu's theoretical contribution to our understanding of social capital, in particular the ways in which he described the interaction of different kinds of capital and the role of 'accumulation'.

If Bourdieu provided the catalyst for developing analyses of social capital in Europe, then Coleman is considered to have fulfilled the same function amongst sociologists in the US. Coleman drew on rational choice theory to shape his analysis of social order and his approach to social capital. On this basis, all social interaction is understood as a form of exchange. Coleman's development of social capital can be seen as an attempt to link economics and sociology, and to present social capital as a means of explaining why people cooperate within a social system that is driven by self-interest and where immediate gratification may be derived from competition.

For Coleman, social capital was important because it was 'productive' – it enabled the attainment of ends that could not otherwise have been achieved, and it also made a particular contribution to the human capital of individuals, i.e. their individual capacity to act outside of social networks. Coleman considered social capital a public good, created as a by-product of individuals' pursuit of self-interest. Consequently, it could be deployed to help solve collective action problems as it was created by and afforded benefits to both those that were necessary to its creation but also all who were part of a structure (Coleman, 1988: s116). Field (2003) is unconvinced by Coleman's explanation of why rational actors should invest in social capital instead of pursuing self-interest. He argues that by identifying social capital as a by-product of the pursuit of self-interest, and therefore a public good to be used in addressing collective action problems, Coleman bypasses rather than resolves this question.

Coleman defined social capital as 'a variety of entities with two elements in common: they all consist of some aspect of social structures, and they facilitate certain actions of actors whether persons or corporate actors within the structure' (Coleman, 1988: s98). A sufficient level of trust between individuals was essential to facilitate the release of social capital, and social capital in turn helped to generate future trust. Coleman identified the primary source for the generation of social capital as the family. Other 'constructed' forms of social organisation were less effective in generating social capital, though Coleman believed that some, such as the church, were more effective than others. In the context of contemporary urban politics, this points to the targeting of resources in support of families to help protect this source of social capital.

While Bourdieu and Coleman conceived of social capital as inherent in relationships between individuals in social networks, the work of political scientist Robert Putnam was to take social capital into new (and controversial) territory, via his claim that social capital might also be the property of cities and nations. Drawing on an empirical study of Italian regional government, Putnam claimed that 'good governance' in the north was associated with mutuality between institutions of government and civil society, while under-performance of governments in the south was characterised by the mutual suspicion operating between government and civil society.

A crucial ingredient in the Italian case was the existence of a healthy 'civic life', characterised by high levels of associational activity (participation in sports clubs, choral societies, etc.) which had direct benefits for members (in terms of enjoyment) but also had broader consequences, generating a stock of social capital that could be drawn on to achieve wider public purposes.

First, networks of civic engagement foster sturdy norms of generalized reciprocity … Networks of civic engagement also facilitate coordination and communication and amplify information about the trustworthiness of other individuals. ... Finally, networks of civic engagement embody past success at collaboration, which can serve as a cultural template for future collaboration. (Putnam, 1993: 35–42)

In *Bowling Alone* (2000), Putnam applied his analysis to American civic life. Drawing on a range of data (political participation, volunteering, formal association membership and participation in informal networks), as well as attitudinal and societal data, Putnam concluded that social capital in America was in significant decline and that this was adversely affecting societal well-being. Improvements in well-being should therefore, according to his analysis, be based upon initiatives to foster greater social capital, in part through support for civic life.

Putnam refined his definition of social capital in *Bowling Alone*, describing as 'connections among individuals – social networks and the norms of reciprocity and trustworthiness that arise from them' (2000: 19), which can affect the productivity of both individuals and groups. He also specified two distinct kinds of social capital: bonding social capital which he described as acting as a kind of 'sociological super-glue' in terms of 'mobilising group solidarity'; and bridging social capital which he saw as a form of 'sociological WD-40' lubricating the development of broader identities and reciprocal relationships (2000: 22–3).

These dimensions of social capital have been further refined by Michael Woolcock who added a third – linking social capital which enables the development of vertical as well as horizontal relationships. His definition which has been widely adopted is as follows:

- bonding social capital, which denotes ties between like people in similar situations, such as immediate family, close friends and neighbours
- bridging social capital, which encompasses more distant ties of like persons, such as loose friendships and workmates and
- linking social capital, which reaches out to unlike people in dissimilar situations, such as those who are entirely outside the community, thus enabling members to leverage a far wider range of resources than are available within the community. (2001: 13–14)

Putnam's work and his dramatic claims for social capital have generated huge interest and critique amongst academics and policy-makers. As with Bourdieu and Coleman, Putnam has been criticised for downplaying (at least in his early work) the negative impacts of social capital compared to the benefits (Misztal, 2000). Some contest his thesis about the decline of social capital in America and how this might be reversed (DeFilippis, 2001; Szreter, 2002), while others dispute its universality arguing that context is a significant contributor to the development of social capital (Hall, 1999; Rothstein, 2001). Political scientists have taken issue with him for not paying enough attention to politics and institutions in his elaboration of the workings of social capital. Before turning to these issues, we reflect on some of the theories that underpin conceptions of social capital for the insights they provide into the relevance of social capital for the study of urban politics.

Social capital, theory and urban politics

Field (2003) focuses on the contribution made to social capital formulations by social theorists' analyses of human relationships. He highlights the work of de Tocqueville in delineating the way in which voluntary associations in America bound individuals together, provided education for citizenship and underpinned democracy in contrast to the traditional and hierarchical relationships that prevailed in European societies, and he detects de Tocqueville's influence in Putnam's enthusiasm for volunteering and associationalism. Misztal (2000) cites Durkheim's analysis of how purposive relationships between individuals developed in the move from feudal to industrial societies and sees in Putnam's work references to Durkheimian ideas of group solidarity, expressed in associations beyond kinship through looser and/or weaker ties, as well as references to rational choice theory, the latter a key influence over Coleman. Field (2003) highlights Marx's formulation of a 'class for itself' (providing the basis for the emergence of new forms of social solidarity amongst class members) as informing Bourdieu's ideas about social capital.

This focus on the quality of human relationships and the ways in which they contribute to socialisation, social ordering and solidarity in communities is relevant to the study of urban politics as it speaks to policy and popular concerns about the decline of 'community' and sociability and the corresponding increase in social atomisation and anxiety in cities that are increasingly economically and socially divided. The link between associationalism and the construction of 'good citizens' is of particular importance here, as is the suggestion that social and economic instability can stimulate the emergence of new human relationships and connections.

Cunningham (2002) highlights the conceptions of democracy that shape the development of social capital. He situates social capital in the context of participatory democracy as described by Rousseau but also linked to the more recent developments in associationalism proposed by Hirst (1994) among others. There are links here too with de Tocqueville, with regard to the potential of social capital to improve the effectiveness of government through the development of stronger trust relations that facilitate coordinated action. For Cunningham, this is 'fully in the tradition of participationism, according to which cooperative citizen involvement in joint activities nurture just those values conducive to the accumulation of social capital and hence, on the thesis of Putnam and Coleman, to effective undertaking of human projects' (2002: 135).

Linking social capital with participatory democracy and suggesting that the quality of governance and outcomes will improve as a result addresses another matter of core concern to urban politics; declining democratic participation and trust in governments to deliver what communities want. It also prompts consideration of other features of participatory democracy, such as strategies for decentralised decision-making and the participation of citizens as 'co-producers' in governance.

Roberts (2004) challenges the idea of social capital as a neutral concept with positive or negative consequences contingent upon context. He understands social capital as a manifestation of the further evolution of capitalism, part of 'a "socialised" and "humanitarian" ideology associated with neo-liberalism ... [that] is still reliant upon a coming together of ordinary people in their communities to solve common problems' (2004: 489).

Walters (2002) links neo-liberalism with governmentality and argues that the use of the term social capital, with its links to other more tangible forms of capital, reflects an attempt to render associationalism and civic orientation both calculable and therefore governable. Mayer (2003) develops this point, arguing that by casting civic resources as economic resources, the World Bank has been able to use social capital as an instrument through which nation states can improve social conditions for economic performance. This supports a discourse of social capital that neutralises the macro changes wrought by globalisation and makes welfare crises inevitable, impacting on all equally.

Communities, neighbourhoods, women and workers as well as the unemployed – all must adapt to these forces, must flexibilize, learn, empower themselves and put pressure on urban administrators, in short: develop their social capital. Then urban poverty – which tacitly became constructed as the product of ineffective local governance and underdeveloped social capital – can be alleviated. (Mayer, 2003: 125)

These contributions draw attention to the role of the state, casting it as an agent of neo-liberalism in helping to create the conditions for capitalism to flourish, through the provision of social support to help communities help themselves. They raise questions about the role of the local state in urban politics and the extent to which local governance institutions have the capacity (and the willingness) to adopt and effect alternative strategies in the prevailing political economy.

Context and social capital

Drawing on analyses of social capital trends in democracies (including the UK, Sweden, Australia, Japan, France, Spain, Germany), Putnam (2002) concludes that what he detected in the US is now becoming apparent in these other territories, though there are contextual differences. Important exceptions to this thesis include Japan and the Scandinavian countries, where the contextual differences are so profound as to have generated very different outcomes (from each other as well as in comparison to America).

Putnam (2002) detects the following common features: declining electoral turnout and declining trade union membership (except Scandinavia); declining engagement in political parties; and declining church attendance. Putnam refutes arguments that suggest that these declining forms of social capital are being replaced by others that are more appropriate to the times. Instead, he argues that these new forms of association are weaker and have more limited scope for generating societal solidarity among communities in neighbourhoods, cities, states and beyond. 'The older forms that are fading combined individual fun with collective purpose, and they were multi-stranded, as in Catholic unions or party sports leagues. The new forms of social participation are narrower, less bridging, and less focused on collective or public-regarding purpose' (2002: 412), for example issue oriented, grassroots networks that exist for only as long as the issue is pertinent.

Rothstein's (2001) analysis of social capital in Sweden provides important evidence of the way contextual factors shape the design and significance of social capital as well as supplying an interesting alternative to Putnam's thesis of social capital in decline. He argues that the character of social democracy in Sweden – its universalist approach to welfare provision and the way in which government programmes have been institutionalised – has supported the generation of social capital. Della Porta's (2000) study of contemporary Italian government (at all levels) reveals how trust in government, government performance and social capital can develop into 'virtuous' or 'vicious' cycles. In a 'vicious' cycle, corruption, poor government performance and public mistrust combine with 'bad' social capital – networks that lubricate corrupt decision-making and enable citizens to get things done in maladministration – to ensure that decisions get made and services supplied. Although the causal relationships are not easily untangled, della Porta argues that each component 'feeds' the others, so 'bad' social capital

> is needed to produce the reciprocal trust that is all the more indispensable for conducting deals in the shadows, where no formal laws, police, or judges are available to uphold agreements. Political corruption, in turn, reproduces this 'bad' social capital, rewarding those who belong to the 'right' networks and follow the 'right' norms. (2000: 205)

Bull and Jones (2006) show how local and national contexts interact affecting the impact of social capital in practice. Through a comparative study of Bristol and Naples, they reveal how the kind of social capital that can flourish is contingent upon 'the past political history of each city and the nature of local social networks' (2006: 782). Of particular significance was the extent to which autonomous authentic civil society organisations were established in each city and the connections they had made with governance processes. At the same time, this local interaction was mediated by the power relations in operation between different tiers of government.

Putnam's (1993) work also provides some insights into the importance of local context for shaping social capital. He shows how social capital is differentiated by neighbourhood and community effects. 'Where you live and whom you know – the social capital you can draw on – helps to define who you are and thus to determine your fate' (1993: 40). Linked to this are the ways in which inequalities in social class and racial discrimination can adversely affect social capital. Putnam illustrates that minority communities have their own vehicles for the generation of bonding social capital, such as the role of black churches, though others conclude that these vehicles may be less effective at generating bridging social capital (Orr, 1999).

These findings suggest that urban policy-makers need to be sensitive to the particular factors that might inhibit the development of social capital and be equipped to provide support to particular communities where necessary, though they will be constrained by broader contextual influences such as intergovernmental relations and macro economic trends.

The role of the state

The social capital formulations presented by Bourdieu, Coleman and Putnam are largely silent on the contribution of the state to the development of social capital. Putnam's work has been the subject of most criticism, in part because it is his formulation of social capital that takes it into the political arena and because of his 'society centred' analysis which conceives of social capital as operating in a 'one way relationship' in which strong civil society impacts positively on politics (Szreter, 2002). In response, political scientists have focused their attention on the contribution of the state to the development of social capital (in its bonding, bridging and/or linking forms), and its potential for enhancing political participation.

Advocates of a more developed analysis of the role of the state argue that governments in particular have considerable influence over the constitutional environment within which politics and civil society are conducted. Foley and Edwards (1996: 47) draw attention to the way in which institutions 'govern who plays, the rules of the game, and acceptable outcomes', while Szreter (2002) reflects on the importance of values in underpinning emergent institutions, arguing that the kind of social capital that develops in any given context is linked to the 'moral, cultural and ideological discourses of a society' (2002: 595) which includes a particular perspective on the appropriate role of the state.

Local government and related agents of local governance are of particular significance as they shape local priorities, deliver a range of key services and respond to matters of local concern raised by citizens. Although the respective influence of national and local government will vary across countries, for example the extent to which local government implements national policies, in general, elected local government has a more intimate and dynamic relationship with citizens than national government. Kearns considers the shape and nature of a city's political opportunity structure as of huge significance for the distribution of social capital, 'for such a structure provides incentives, expectations and openings for people to undertake collective action within the political system' (2003: 45). Lowndes and Wilson (2001) develop this point, arguing that there are:

> four, interacting dimensions of institutional design within local governance that shape the creation and mobilization of social capital: relationships with the voluntary sector; opportunities for public participation; the responsiveness of decision-making; and arrangements for democratic leadership and social inclusion. (2001: 633)

The experience of the UK Government under New Labour provides a helpful illustration of state attempts to make use of social capital to achieve urban revitalisation. A key issue for New Labour on taking office in 1997 was how to address the persistent poverty and inequality that existed in parts of its major cities and urban areas. One strategy, rolled out across England from 2000, focused on taking action within urban neighbourhoods.

The National Strategy for Neighbourhood Renewal (SEU, 2000), aimed to tackle disadvantage within deprived neighbourhoods and reduce the gap between them and the rest of the country. Its aims of reviving economies and communities, ensuring decent services improved leadership and joint working were to be achieved through special targeted funding initiatives such as the New Deal for Communities and the Neighbourhood Renewal Fund, but also through initiatives to 'join up' service delivery through the introduction of neighbourhood management. Underpinning this policy programme was an emphasis on community revival through self-help, based upon the 'vital resources of social capital' (SEU, 2000: 25). The importance of social capital and self-help to neighbourhood renewal are evident from New Labour's conception of 'well-functioning communities', summarised by Kearns (2003) as:

- local management of services and partnership approach by service providers
- commitment to resident participation
- a broad social mix
- agreed set of rules among residents that are consistently applied
- places and facilities where people can interact, such as shops and community venues
- ethos of volunteering (broaden social networks and improve job prospects as a result). (2003: 45)

The New Deal for Communities (NDC) programme was central to the strategy for neighbourhood renewal. It operated in deprived urban neighbourhoods of up to 4000 households and had four objectives: tackling worklessness, improving health, tackling crime and raising educational achievement. It was funded by central government but was delivered through a locally based multi-sector partnership in which local communities were to play a major part. The first phase of the programme was given over to capacity building within local communities so that local leaders emerged able to sit on the partnership board, and others developed sufficient confidence and skills to enable them to participate in other aspects of the programme. Local government was expected to both support the development of the neighbourhood partnerships in whatever way necessary and to participate in the programme as a key partner along with other relevant service providers.

In the NDC programme, the development of social capital was implicitly linked to the success of the initiative. Its development was sought in a number of ways. Bonding and bridging social capital were to be developed through the creation of opportunities for association amongst community members such as social events, workshops on local needs, and through the provision of information exchange opportunities such as neighbourhood radio broadcasts. Resources for this were provided as part of the NDC budget. Linking social capital was to be developed between community members and local government elected councillors and officials, as well as officials from other local delivery bodies through the development of personal relationships amongst members of the local partnership board overseeing the programme. Local governance institutions had a responsibility to both support the development of these local partnership arrangements but also to ensure that their organisations were responsive to the decisions taken by the partnership. The long-term goal was to parallel the revitalisation of these urban neighbourhoods with the reinvigoration of democracy, drawing on the capacity created through these processes.

Subsequent New Labour programmes have continued this emphasis on social capital and self-help. For example, the Civil Renewal Agenda initiated in 2003 aimed to create 'strong, empowered and active communities, in which people increasingly do things for themselves and the state acts to facilitate, support and enable citizens to lead self-determined and fulfilled lives' (Blunkett, 2003: 43). At the centre of civil renewal are 'active citizens', individuals who recognise the importance of self-discipline and family life, and who are prepared to take on the obligations of citizenship, through individual and collective action (Barnes et al., 2007).

Running through each of these policy programmes is a conception of responsible, functioning, self-sufficient and entrepreneurial neighbourhoods underpinned by high levels of social capital, which can be fostered by state intervention. There is little acknowledgement of, or connection with, the impact of macro-level factors on national economic performance, employment trends and income levels. However, what is evident from New Labour's experience is the importance of the local state in helping to realise the goals of these ambitious programmes. This finding is supported by Saegert and Winkel's (1998) study of housing reprivatisation in New York concluded that:

> while social capital, even among very poor tenant populations, can add value to government investment in housing ... all reprivatization programmes involved substantial public investment in both capital and operating expenses ... [and] the persistence of these gains may be threatened over time if such subsidies disappear (1998: 48).

The emphasis on a changing, more enabling, role for local government and its relationship to social capital is picked up by Akkerman et al. (2004) in their study of local state/civil society relations in the Netherlands. The Netherlands' model of the 'interactive state' in which popular engagement in local decision-making is encouraged (but not required) is highlighted as one example of this new role. However, they argue that an 'interactive state' may be unhelpful in terms of generating bonding social capital. This must be done by individual groups with common and shared identities, who can also contribute to democracy via the pressure they exercise in pursuit of their rights. Where the 'interactive state' can help is in overcoming the exclusivity and homogeneity associated with these closely bonded groups through acting to create overlapping networks which may generate bridging social capital. This may only link the 'elites' but it can nonetheless help to integrate otherwise isolated groups.

A similar point is made by Smith et al. (2004) in their study of the interactions between local government and voluntary sector bodies in two British cities, though here they are focusing on the way in which social capital may be generated across sectors rather than within them. Szreter (2002) also addresses this issue, arguing that the state can play a role in facilitating the development of 'linking' social capital which supports the emergence of institutionalised relationships among unequal agents.

Katzenstein (2000) takes a contrary view to supporters of state-sponsored social capital. He argues that the absence of a strong welfare state and inclusionary politics in America has resulted in it 'leading the way' in developments in social capital. He cites evidence to suggest that citizens are themselves changing the sources of civil society support that they invest in and also changing the way they approach politics.

For Katzenstein, the new social movements offer important alternatives for citizen participation and association that compensate for the decline in attachment to national parliaments and political parties. Consequently, to better understand the possibilities for social capital, we need to pay more attention to the past and potential future role of civil society organisations. This is considered in the next section.

Civil society and social capital

For Akkerman et al. (2004), the 'interactive state' and the cross-sector collaboration integral to it can be understood as one way of responding to the demands of an increasingly complex and fragmented governance environment. Collaboration between actors for public purpose is now largely accepted among policy-makers and third sector or civil society organisations are invariably included as key stakeholders in collaborative governance, particularly at the urban scale (Sullivan and Skelcher, 2002). This, in combination with the dominant social capital discourse, has had an important impact on the constitution and capability of civil society actors.

Writers have pointed to the way in which the term civil society has been interpreted for the purposes of prescribing social capital. For example, both Mouritsen (2003) and Mayer (2003) show how social capital advocates have emphasised the engagement of community associations but not political institutions, employer organisations or trade unions. This emphasis is important because it excludes those bodies more likely to have an oppositional political agenda and the resources to pursue it.

The negation of conflict as a key feature of state/civil society relations is another aspect of some social capital formulations that critics have drawn attention to. Foweraker and Landman (1997) argue that making links between social capital and democracy perpetuates the notion that consensus and trust (activated by associational activity) generate democracy whereas history suggests that the creation of democracy requires struggle (see Rabrenovic, this volume). DeFilippis (2001) argues that the social capital agenda has fundamentally redefined civil society bodies – 'voluntary associations, therefore, are not confrontational encounters based on vested interests, but rather features of social life, through which participants come together to pursue shared objectives' (2001: 787). This reconstitution of civil society both homogenises it and reinvents it for a new purpose. In so doing, it denies the role of civil society in sponsoring 'counter publics' (Barnes et al., 2007), instead attaching to it a new role in managing communities in accordance with an ideology that addresses poverty through workfare or training, rather than protest. 'Urban social movements are thus transformed from potential social movement actors demanding recognition of their social rights into "social capitalists", whose "belonging" is conditional on their mobilising the only resources they have as a form of capital' (Mayer, 2003: 125).

Research into civil society organisations provides evidence of the tensions identified above, but also of the ways in which some civil society bodies have developed alternative strategies which include a positive assessment of the potential of social capital. For example, Gittell et al.'s (2000) examination of the work of women-led, neighbourhood-based, community development organisations (CDOs) in America highlighted the pressures on those organisations in the 1980s and 1990s to move away from a comprehensive approach to neighbourhood support (meeting the needs of women, children and families) towards physical development (housing) and economic regeneration through business support. The resistance of these organisations often led to funding cuts but they remained committed to comprehensive programmes of support as a key response to 'the failure of the economic and political systems to meet their communities' most basic needs' (2000: 145).

Gittell et al. (2000) found that in these women-led CDOs, social capital was acknowledged as a key ingredient in making social change, and the generation of social capital was linked to a holistic approach to community development, coupled with a commitment to participation and local democracy. They found that 'women-led CDOs are building the norms, trust, and networks that are essential to social capital, and they are also engaged in civic action for social change' (2000: 124). The organisations were engaged in generating bonding, bridging and linking social capital, for example:

> Multiple layers of networks were created, such as those of community residents with each other, ties between community residents and CDO staff members, and relationships between CDO directors and community residents or directors of other organisations. CDO activities also brought individuals and the organisations themselves into official networks, such as coalitions, or cases in which members represented the CDO at public events or met with public officials. (2000: 124–5)

Pharr (2000) also provides a rather different perspective on the interaction between civil society organisations and social capital. Drawing on evidence from Japan, she suggests that the emergence of new social movements there can act to disrupt the prevailing 'clientilism' between social networks and government. Here the emergence of new civil society bodies may have the effect that Katzenstein (2000) claimed for them (above), developing a new kind of social capital not aimed at generating confidence in government.

These findings reinforce the importance of context in supporting our understanding of the contribution of social capital. They also point to the need for dynamic analytical frames that can take account of the past, present and potential futures for social capital. In this vein, Bang (2005) argues for the need to find ways to understand new kinds of citizen participation in politics that do not fit within traditional prescriptions of 'strong government' and 'thick communities' but instead rely on 'being ordinarily engaged in the construction of networks and locales for the political governance of the social' (2005: 172).

Power, diversity and inequality

An understanding of how social capital is informed by matters of power, diversity and inequality is essential if the concept is to have any utility in urban politics.

Amongst those who advocate the potential of social capital to lead to improved community well-being, reviews of recent trends in social capital make disturbing reading. For example, Putnam (2002) draws attention to the impact of inequality and declining community cohesion in his review of cross-national studies of social capital, concluding that '[t]he apparent increase in class bias in social capital may be related to growth in income inequality noted in many advanced countries, as well as by growing ethnic fragmentation. Concern about inequalities, especially growing inequalities, in the social capital domain is perhaps the most important common thread' (2002: 416).

Some contributors argue that inequality and exclusion are inherent in social capital. For example, Bourdieu (1986) refers to the 'closed' nature of social capital when defined as a property of individuals. People who realise their capital through their networks do so precisely because others are excluded. Social capital is therefore as likely as other forms of capital to reproduce socioeconomic inequalities. DeFilippis (2001) makes this point starkly, arguing that 'for social capital to make sense as a concept in a market economy, then networks, formal or informal, must operate in the competitive realm of market relations. And while the individuals in such a network might share common interests that allow them to act as a network, these networks, because of the competitive nature of capitalism, cannot be extended to everyone in society' (2001: 793).

Szreter's (2002) response to this is to advocate a greater role for the state in supporting the developing of 'linking social capital' to help enable poor communities to access the resources to 'get on' rather than merely 'get by'. DeFilippis (2001) by contrast argues for greater power and control to be devolved to communities themselves, to enable them to have access to sufficient physical and monetary capital to really make an impact on their social and economic circumstances.

An early and important contribution to understanding the interaction of social capital with inequality is that of Loury's (1977, 1981) work made an early and important contribution to our understanding of the interaction of social capital with inequality. He drew attention to the ways in which social capital can be impacted on, positively *and* negatively, by factors such as race and class. His assessment of the perpetuation of racial inequality in incomes concluded that legal prohibitions on racial discrimination and the development of positive equality policies would, by themselves, be insufficient for addressing the condition of poor black communities in America. This was because such communities were disadvantaged by other potent factors including the transmission of poverty from one generation to another, and the relative paucity of connections those communities had into the labour market, in particular their absence from networks that would facilitate access to employment opportunities and greater material resources. Szreter (2002) reinforces this point, arguing that poor people may only be able to access 'bonded' social capital, which consequently may hold them prisoner rather than help them break out of their circumstances.

Orr's (1999) research into the role played by social capital in school reform in Baltimore provides ample illustration of this. In a city experiencing poverty, racial division and financial constraints, education was identified as a key means of securing well-being in later life. Orr found that social capital was important in generating and maintaining community support for school reform but was also limited in important ways. Education reform relied upon a broad coalition of diverse interests taking collective action. While black churches and the civil rights movement were powerful forces for creating social capital and thence collective capacity among black leaders and within black communities, they were not sufficient for extending that leadership to a broader coalition, i.e. drawing in the white elites in control of political and economic resources (moving from bonding to bridging social capital). Local mayors were however important in generating that bridging social capital reinforcing the potential of local state institutions.

Other research suggests that local state interventions can in fact further exacerbate inequalities, in terms of class, race/ethnicity or gender. The popular focus on neighbourhood interventions in urban areas is one example. Levi (1996) points to the way in which simply supporting the development of social capital in neighbourhoods can result in them reproducing their own circumstances.

> By themselves dense networks support localism, which is often extremely resistant to change ... Neighbourhoods (and certain other networks of civic engagement) are a source of trust and a source of distrust. They promote trust of those you know and distrust of those you do not, those not in the neighbourhood or outside the networks. (1996: 51)

Briggs' (1998) research into housing policy in New York found that extended social networks were more important than neighbourhood effects in supporting individual well-being.

The experience of three northern towns in England illustrates the negative consequences of urban policy that is perceived to take insufficient account of inequalities and discrimination within diverse communities. Tensions between whites and Asians, predominantly Pakistani and Bangladeshi communities, resulted in riots in 2001. An official review into the causes of the unrest focused attention on a lack of 'community cohesion'. It explored how community cohesion could be built deploying a framework that included social capital as one of five pillars of community cohesion. Social capital was considered important for the following reasons:

- Social capital allows people to resolve collective problems more easily.
- Businesses and social transactions work better and are less costly if people trust one another and repeatedly interact with one another.
- Social capital widens people's awareness of the way in which their fates are linked to each other.
- Networks serve as conduits for flows of information that facilitate the achievement of common goals. (Home Office, 2001, cited in Kearns, 2003: 48)

The findings of the review included a requirement that local areas develop 'cohesion plans' which included the promotion of cross-cultural contact between black and minority ethnic and white communities to foster understanding and break down barriers. Some critics of the report argued that the recommendations relied too heavily on assumptions about the power of a unitary sense of place and also denied the legitimacy of conflict and an 'agonistic politics', in the emphasis on the possibility and desirability of cross-community consensus (Amin, 2002).

Forrest and Kearns (2001) express concern at the singular way in which social capital prescriptions are implemented without attention to other policy levers that might be needed. They argue that while the components of social capital may be important in facilitating connections and cooperation between residents in neighbourhoods, social capital is insufficient of itself. Rather, it needs to be accompanied by other factors such as resources and opportunities if it is to realise the potential that policy-makers claim for it. Without these other elements, social capital may in fact have a limited impact, enabling individuals and communities to 'cope' but not enabling them to 'overcome' (Forrest and Kearns, 2001: 2141).

The work of Lowndes (2004), Gittell et al. (2000), and Barnes et al. (2007) emphasises to the importance of a gendered understanding of social capital. Lowndes (2004) argues that social capital formulations have tended to be developed in a gender-biased way, for example, focusing on male dominated activities in considering the empirical sources of social capital. This serves to reproduce the 'public/private split', rendering women's activity as irrelevant in improving our understanding of the practice of citizenship. Lowndes reviews a range of sources and concludes that men and women display similar levels of social capital but have distinctive 'social capital profiles', with women's social capital more strongly embedded in neighbourhood-specific networks of informal sociability.

The importance of the neighbourhood to women is emphasised in research by Gittell et al. (2000) into women-led CDOs in America. They highlighted the importance of leadership style and institutional design in creating the right conditions for the generation of social capital amongst community members. They concluded that:

In terms of leadership, we found that women are deeply committed, community-based leaders who foster community participation and use a collaborative approach to create social change. The participatory structure of most of the CDOs in our study and the way the organisations built participation into their programmes created a democratic space where community residents could both form ties with each other and develop as individuals while collectively working for the betterment of the whole community. (2000: 125)

Barnes et al. (2007) drew similar conclusions about the importance of institutional design and a participatory culture to the generation of social capital Their research into public participation initiatives in two English cities found the culture and practices at a 'women's centre' to be 'inclusive and participative ... a real attempt to overcome power imbalances between full time staff and volunteers. The result was a strong sense of attachment and involvement: "It's the first place I've been where I feel on an equal with paid workers"' (2007: 149). The centre made use of strategies such as the use of personal narration (storytelling) as a way of:

affirming membership and connecting individuals to each other. There were deliberate attempts to make connections across lines of difference amongst women and interviews with women involved suggested this had a transformative impact – not simply on women's opinions, but a deeper transformation of their sense of self. (2007: 143)

In the case of the 'women's centre', the social capital generated had been used to very powerful effect, both in terms of the personal and professional 'successes' of the women who had been members of the centre, and in terms of the place the women's centre occupied in the local governance arena. Other research, such as that by Lowndes (2004), suggests that this may not always be the case. Instead, 'women earn social capital that is then spent by men', for example in the pursuit of political careers (2004: 55).

Future directions in urban social capital research

While the idea of social capital may have become all pervasive in some sections of academia and policy-making, there remain important questions about its potential contribution to our understanding of urban politics.

First is the need for further theory refinement, specifically in terms of situating social capital within a context in which the dynamics of power relations and the potential limits of social capital are more evident. These developments need to be informed by emerging understandings about changes in citizen participation and the role of the state and civil society – be wary of easy appeals to overarching explanations that describe either 'win–win' or 'lose–lose' outcomes. In the same way that the possibilities of 'social capitalism' and 'participative democracy' need to be tempered by an understanding of the dynamics of neo-liberal capitalism, so too do the limits of neo-liberalism need to be acknowledged. As Clarke (2004) helpfully points out, neo-liberalism is not a single dominant ideology but a strategy that has to operate within particular contexts within which resistance and reaction will occur. This points to the value of further and closer examination of the way in which social capital develops and operates in very different urban contexts.

Secondly, if social capital does have a role to play in fostering democratic renewal, then further investigation is needed into what kinds of social capital can generate political capital and in what circumstances. This requires both methodological refinement (in the way that Lowndes describes above) so that our consideration of what constitutes 'social capital' is not limited by 'norms' of investigation, and analytical flexibility so that our conceptual frames are relevant for present and future formulations of social capital.

Finally, we need rigorous examination of empirical evidence to increase our understanding of social capital's contribution to individual, community, neighbourhood and/or national well-being. Some recent contributions provide critical coverage of what is available (see Halpern, 2005, for example). However, these need to be complemented by a meta-analysis of the impacts of the wide range of policy programmes (in the public and third sector) that have sought to sponsor social capital as a means to achieve improved social outcomes over the last decade.

References

Akkerman, T., Hajer, M. and Grin, J. (2004) 'The interactive state: democratization from above?', *Political Studies*, (1): 82–95.

Amin, A. (2002) 'Ethnicity and the multicultural city: living with diversity', *Environment and Planning A*, 34 (6): 959–80.

Bang, H. (2005) 'Among everyday makers and expert citizens', in J. Newman (ed.), *Remaking Governance*. Bristol; Policy Press. pp. 159–78.

Barnes, M., Newman, J. and Sullivan, H. (2007) *Power, Participation and Political Renewal*. Bristol: Policy Press.

Blunkett, D. (2003) 'Civil renewal, a new agenda', Edith Kahn Memorial Lecture, 11 June.

Bourdieu P. (1985) 'The forms of capital', in J.G. Richardson (ed.), *Handbook of Theory and Research for the Sociology of Education*. New York: Greenwood. pp. 241–58.

Briggs, X. de Souza (1998) 'Brown kids in white suburbs: housing mobility and the many faces of social capital', *Housing Policy Debate*, 9 (1): 177–221.

Bull, A.C. and Jones, B. (2006) 'Governance and social capital in urban regeneration: a comparison between Bristol and Naples', *Urban Studies*, 43 (4): 767–86.

Clarke, J. (2004) 'Dissolving the public realm? The logics and limits of neo-liberalism', *Journal of Social Policy*, 33 (1): 27–48.

Coleman, J.S. (1988) 'Social capital in the creation of human capital', *American Journal of Sociology*, 94: S95–121.

Cunningham, F. (2002) *Theories of Democracy*. London: Routledge.

DeFilippis, J. (2001) 'The myth of social capital in community development', *Housing Policy Debate*, 12 (4): 781–806.

Della Porta, D. (2000) 'Social capital, beliefs in government and political corruption', in S.J. Pharr and R.D. Putnam (eds), *Disaffected Democracies. What's Troubling the Trilateral Countries?* Princeton: Princeton University Press. pp. 202–30.

Field, J. (2003) *Social Capital*. London: Routledge.

Fine, B. (2001) *Social Capital Versus Social Theory: Political Economy and Social Science at the Turn of the Millennium*. London: Routledge.

Foley, M. and Edwards, B. (1999) 'Is it time to disinvest in social capital?', *Journal of Public Policy*, 19 (2): 141–73.

Forrest, R. and Kearns, A. (2001) 'Social cohesion, social capital and the neighbourhood', *Urban Studies*, 38 (12): 2125–43.

Foweraker, J. and Landman, T. (1997) *Citizenship Rights and Social Movements: A Comparative and Statistical Analysis*. Oxford: Oxford University Press.

Gittell, N., Ortega-Bustamante, I. and Steffy, T. (2000) 'Social capital and social change, women's community activism', *Urban Affairs Review*, 36 (2): 123–47.

Hall, P. (1999) 'Social capital in Britain', *British Journal of Political Science*, 29 (3): 417–61.

Halpern, D. (2005) *Social Capital*. Cambridge: Polity.

Hirst, P. (1994) *Associative Democracy. New Forms of Economic and Social Governance*. Cambridge: Polity Press.

Katzenstein, P.J. (2000) 'Confidence, trust, international relations, and lessons from smaller democracies', in S.J. Pharr and R.D. Putnam (eds), *Disaffected Democracies. What's Troubling the Trilateral Countries?* Princeton: Princeton University Press. pp. 121–48.

Kearns, A. (2003) 'Social capital, regeneration and urban policy', in R. Imrie and M. Raco (eds), *Urban Renaissance? New Labour, Community and Urban Policy*. Bristol: Policy Press. pp. 37–60.

Levi, M. (1996) 'Social and unsocial capital: a review essay of Robert Putnam's *Making Democracy Work*', *Politics and Society*, 24: 45–55.

Loury, G.C. (1977) 'A dynamic theory of racial income differences', in P.A. Wallace, A.M. La Mond (eds), *Women, Minorities, and Employment Discrimination*. Lexington, MA: Heath. pp. 153–86.

Loury, G.C. (1981) 'Intergenerational transfers and the distribution of earnings', *Econometrica*, 49: 843–67.

Lowndes, V. (2004) 'Getting on or getting by? Women, social capital and political participation', *British Journal of Politics and International Relations*, 6 (1): 45–64.

Lowndes, V. and Wilson, D. (2001) 'Social capital and local governance: exploring the institutional design variable', *Political Studies*, 49: 629–47.

Mayer, M. (2003) 'The onward sweep of social capital: causes and consequences for understanding cities, communities and urban movements', *International Journal of Urban and Regional Research*, 27: 110–32.

Misztal, B.A. (2000) *Informality: Social Theory and Contemporary Practice*. London: Routledge.

Mouritsen, P. (2003) 'What's the civil in civil society? Robert Putnam, Italy and the Republican tradition', *Political Studies*, 51 (4): 650–68.

Orr, M. (1999) *Black Social Capital. The Politics of School Reform in Baltimore 1986–1998*. Lawrence: University Press of Kansas.

Pharr, S.J. (2000) 'Officials' misconduct and public distrust: Japan and the trilateral democracies', in S.J. Pharr and R.D. Putnam (eds), *Disaffected Democracies. What's Troubling the Trilateral Countries?* Princeton: Princeton University Press. pp. 173–201.

Portes, A. (1998) 'Social capital: its origins and applications in modern sociology', *Annual Review of Sociology*, 24: 1–34.

Putnam, R.D. (1993) 'The prosperous community: social capital and public life', *American Prospect*, 13: 35–42.

Putnam, R.D. (2000) *Bowling Alone: The Collapse and Revival of American Community*. New York: Simon and Schuster.

Putnam, R.D. (2002) 'Conclusion', in R.D. Putnam (ed.), *Democracies in Flux. The Evolution of Social Capital in Contemporary Society*. New York: OUP. pp. 393–416.

Roberts, J.M. (2004) 'What's social about social capital?', *British Journal of Politics and International Relations*, 6 (4): 471–93.

Rothstein, B. (2001) 'Social capital in the social democratic welfare state', *Politics and Society*, 29 (2): 207–41.

Saegert, S. and Winkel, G. (1998) 'Social capital and the revitalization of New York City's distressed inner-city housing', *Housing Policy Debate*, 9 (1): 17–60.

SEU (2000) 'National strategy for neighbourhood renewal', consultation paper. London: SEU.

Smith, G., Stoker, G. and Maloney, W. (2004) 'Building social capital in city politics: scope and limitations at the inter-organisational level', *Political Studies*, 52 (3): 508–30.

Sullivan, H. and Skelcher, C. (2002) *Working Across Boundaries*. Basingstoke: Palgrave.

Szreter, S. (2002) 'The state of social capital: bringing back in power, politics and history', *Theory and Society*, 31 (5): 573–621.

Walters, W. (2002) 'Social capital and political sociology: re-imagining politics?', *Sociology*, 36 (2): 377–97.

Woolcock, M. (2001) 'The place of social capital in understanding social and economic outcomes', *Isuma, Canadian Journal of Policy Research*, 2 (1): 1–17.

15

URBAN SOCIAL MOVEMENTS

Gordana Rabrenovic

Over the last several decades, many cities around the world have become the locale for national and international protests. Anti-Iraqi war demonstrations in Berlin, gatherings of mothers and grandmothers at the Plaza de Mayo in Buenos Aires, student demonstrations in Beijing, and anti-globalisation demonstrations in Seattle were all locally staged protests that addressed much larger national and international issues. These demonstrations attracted attention, in part, because they involved a large number of people and took place in world capitals where many national and international political and economic institutions are located.

What all these protests have in common is their concern for social and economic justice and for participatory democracy. They often target political and economic leaders on local, national and international levels. Finally, although protesters are increasingly concerned with global issues, they are also concerned with how they play out at the local level in terms of neighbourhood quality of life, access to jobs, economic opportunities, health status and the ability to participate in political debate and decision-making.

The world in which we live is becoming more global and urban. In 1950, only 29.8 percent of the world's population lived in cities. Today 47.2 percent of the world's population lives in urban areas, and by 2030, approximately 60 percent of the world's population is projected to live in urban areas (United Nations, 2002). As a result, urban issues can be expected to continue to dominate the agenda of social movement organisations. This chapter examines how urban social movements are formed, the political and social contexts within which they emerge, how movement issues are framed, and the impact of globalisation on local organising. I will offer some examples of urban social movements both locally and globally, and conclude by discussing future directions and challenges facing urban social movements.

Understanding urban social movements

The term urban social movement first appeared in the 1970s in the work of Manuel Castells. His primary focus was on issues of power and conflict in the city (Castells, 1983). He examined various types of issues, including collective consumption and labour issues in the city, the development of cultural identities and demands for an increased role for citizens in decision-making regarding the division and use of urban space (see Geddes, this volume). For Castells, urban social movements were the rarest and perhaps most important examples of collective action: those conflicts that create fundamental changes in power relations at the urban and societal levels. He saw the potential for such change in the emergence of cross-class alliances among residents of urban communities who were organising in the 1970s and 1980s around the shared interests of improving collective consumption in the cities, creating and maintaining the cultural identity of their cities and promoting political self-management.

Over time, the concept of urban social movements was broadened to include other, less radical, examples of popular organising and direct political participation, such as grassroots citizen initiatives, ethnic self-help organisations, community-based developments and service delivery programmes, as well as locally focused political advocacy. These initiatives, programmes and organisations have emerged in response to a changing economic and political landscape (Fisher and Kling, 1993). Shifting boundaries between public and private space, the transfer of wealth from the public to private sphere, increasing social inequalities in cities, and the privatisation of government functions and public spaces have created new issues for the urban social movements. Finally, as the influence of globalisation trends became more apparent, researchers began to broaden their view to include international and regional actors as part of the social movement landscape.

Urban social movements were also part of the development of a new wave of activism known as 'new social movements' that grew in the 1970s and 1980s, in part as a reaction to a decline in class-based movements and ideologies. The post-industrial economy decreased the influence of traditional working class organisations and diminished the possibilities for economic redistribution based on class struggle (Pichardo, 1997). Although the fight for economic justice continues to be an important urban issue, its formulation, strategies and actors have changed. A myriad of movements such as the environmental movement, women's and gay liberation, the anti-nuclear peace movement, and various cultural movements flourished – attracting a variety of activists (Boggs, 1986). Their concerns dealt with quality of life issues, recognition of their lifestyle choices and a push for more direct citizen participation in decision-making. Also known as 'identity politics' and under the slogan 'the personal is political', these new social movements questioned the notion of what was considered political by politicising previously invisible issues, and led to the development of new collective identities that became a driving force for mobilisation.

Scholars of urban social movements focus on several important empirical and theoretical questions: what are the effects or outcomes of mobilisation? How do urban movements interact with state authorities? How does such interaction influence a movement's choice of strategies and tactics? What type of resources do movements need in order to be successful? Are protests or moderate strategies more likely to lead to policy change? And, finally, how does the political context in which movements develop contribute to the success or failure of a particular mobilising strategy? In answering these questions, researchers draw on several different theoretical approaches, including most prominently resource mobilisation theory political opportunity structure theory and framing theory.

Resources for mobilisation: forming and sustaining urban movement organisations

Resource mobilisation theory (RM) developed as a response to and a critique of theories that explained crowds and rioting as irrational behaviour (Le Bon, 1960) and focused on shared grievances and generalised beliefs as impetus for social mobilisation (Turner and Killian, 1972). RM was also sympathetic to civil rights movements and new social movements. Instead of grievances, RM emphasises the importance of mobilising a variety of resources to support movements, such as money, human time and effort, establishment of social ties and networks with other groups, along with the choice of tactics used by political officials to control or coopt movements (McCarthy and Zald, 1977: 1213). Although some early work of resource mobilisation theorists was influenced by rational choice theory and Olson's (1965) utilitarian logic, its later development turned toward explaining how people organise and use resources to address their shared goals. Thus, RM moved the analysis of social movements from individual actors and psychological factors to collective mobilisation, and organisational and structural explanations.

Edwards and McCarthy (2004: 125–8) distinguish between four different types of resources: moral resources which are seen as gaining legitimacy and solidarity for movements and their organisations from external actors; cultural resources, such as cultural competences and collective identities of social movement participants; social–organisational resources, such as existing infrastructure, social networks and organisations that movements create or appropriate; and human resources, such as the experience, expertise and skills of movement participants. Theorists recognise that resources are unequally distributed in society and that some movements are in a better position to mobilise them than others.

Once movement organisations become established, they must mobilise resources to accomplish their goals and secure their own survival and viability. Typically, movement organisations engage in the following activities: they formalise their organisational structures, recruit members and recognised leaders, identify a wide variety of resources and develop communication networks to reach both movement members and potential allies. They also define organisational goals, select issues to address and articulate organisational strategies and tactics that will retain the loyalty of their constituency. Social movement groups that succeed in influencing the political process and/or changing public policy tend to be more bureaucratised and centralised (Gamson, 1990), which may, however, limit their ability to effectively work for change.

In the field of community studies, access to resources is a key factor in distinguishing community development versus community organising approaches to urban change, development and/or services (Stoecker, 2002). Community organisations embrace a community development approach in order to address directly the production and delivery of social, economic and housing services to community residents (Gittell and Vidal, 1998). In order to secure resources for these services, they collaborate with existing political and economic power structures. In addition to resources from federal, state and local government, community development organisations (of which Community Development Corporations are the most common form) also seek resources from foundations and corporate grants, as well as from fees for their services. The greatest challenges these organisations typically face are how to maintain local autonomy by ensuring that local residents have control over economic resources, how to maintain citizen involvement in decision-making and how to maintain focus on community needs.

In contrast to the service and partnership orientation of community development, community organising focuses on creating organisations to work for social justice and social change.[1] According to this approach, community is a resource and a potential power base for organising. Thus, community organising is focused on obtaining, maintaining or restructuring power in the community for the community. Community organisations who embrace this approach have a more adversarial relationship with the existing political power structure. Because of that, they have a harder time obtaining financial resources from government and/or other establishment institutions to address local needs.

Connected to the question of organisational resources is the choice of organisational strategies. Specifically, does the use of protest and/or disruptive tactics increase a movement's chances of influencing political decision-making? Based on his analysis of 53 social movement organisations, Gamson argues that it does (Gamson, 1990). His findings support Piven and Cloward's (1977) argument that in order to achieve social change, groups have to use a confrontational or protest strategy. Piven and Cloward's research was based on an analysis of 'poor people's movements' that developed in the American cities during the 1960s and 1970s (see Thompson, this volume). Supporters of this argument insist that the ability to mobilise and to protest is the only resource available to the poor and they use it in place of financial resources to achieve political objectives.

A good example of such grassroots mobilisation is the nationwide anti-poll-tax movement developed in opposition to local tax changes in Great Britain piloted in Scotland from April 1989 and introduced in England and Wales in April 1990. The Conservative government of Prime Minister Margaret Thatcher developed a plan to replace a local property tax known as domestic rates with a 'community charge' – an individual-based flat-rate tax that applied uniformly to all adult residents.[2] This tax became widely known as the 'Poll Tax'. Ordinary people saw the proposed change as grossly unfair and under the leadership of the All Britain Anti Poll Tax Federation organised a widespread effort to undermine the new tax system. In response to organising efforts, local residents made enforcement of the new tax system nearly impossible by refusing to pay the poll tax, organising mass demonstrations against the tax, petitioning the local court system for tax relief, and the physical defense of property against bailiffs seeking to recover the tax on behalf of local authorities by sequestering and selling personal goods. According to some accounts, 17.5 million people refused to pay the poll tax (Burns, 1992: 176).[3] The most visible side of what became known as 'poll tax rebellion' was the protest of over 200,000 people at Trafalgar Square in March 1990. Even though the protest was planned as a peaceful demonstration, it turned into a riot when police, not expecting such a large number of people, overreacted and used force to disperse protesters. Many protesters were injured and arrested. However, this 'poll tax riot' also brought global visibility to the issue of poll tax. The anti-poll-tax movement was a key contributory factor, together with Conservative Party splits over integration with Europe, in the downfall of Prime Minister Margaret Thatcher. The poll tax was replaced by the Council Tax, which combined elements of the personal and property tax systems (Butler et al., 1994).

Most recently, support for use of disruptive strategies was on display in protests that erupted in many world cities around the issues of economic and cultural globalisation. The organisations that have participated in those protests used a strategy of transnational coalition building and the internet to coordinate international protest campaigns. The sheer number of people that participated in these events attracted media attention and made the movement's goals more visible to the general population. Another important characteristic of the anti-globalisation movement is its ability to bring together protesters from many points on the political spectrum. For example, the slogan 'Teamsters and turtles, together at last' used in anti-globalisation protest in Seattle exemplified the common ground between labour and the environmental movement.

The political opportunity structure and social movements

To study the interrelation between urban social movements and the political context in which they emerge, researchers use the political opportunity structure approach. They focus on the 'configurations of options, chances and risks originating outside the mobilising group' (Koopmans, 2004: 66). Some of these externalities are relatively stable and fixed, such as the characteristics of the existing political system and its institutions, or relatively volatile and unexpected, such as natural disasters, economic changes and/or shifts in political alignments. In addition, the political opportunity structure can provide both constraints and incentives to a social movement.

The political opportunity structure approach is especially well suited for comparative research. Using this approach, researchers compare social movements, their strategies and outcomes based on structural and cultural opportunities for political mobilisation. Structural opportunities are conceptualised as the degree of openness of the political system, such as levels of decentralisation and the functional separation of power. Cultural opportunities refer to prevailing norms, ideas and conflict resolution models accepted by the public in a particular society.

Within the urban context, some researchers use the concept of urban political regimes to examine opportunities for mobilisation as well as its outcomes (Stone, 1989; see Mossberger, this volume). Urban political regimes focus on the power arrangements (based on political, economic and social ties) among major stakeholders within a city and examine how such arrangements potentially influence the strategies and resources available to urban social movements. Policy-makers, government officials, members of the media, political parties and related movement organisations are potential allies or enemies to urban movements depending on pre-existing structural and political arrangements (Eisinger, 1973; Kriesi, 1996). Typically, political regimes based on progressive or social-reform coalitions are the most sympathetic or open to community-oriented activities and, as a result, urban movement organisations are more likely to flourish during their regimes. On the other hand, pro-growth coalitions are often seen as opponents to community interests, both generating the urban problems they have to face and restricting resources available to address them.

Depending on its political orientation, an urban regime may try to repress or integrate a social movement into the existing regime. Repression can lead to radicalisation of the movement participants, increase the media attention for their causes and even help them recruit more members. It also can lead to the movement's demise if movement goals are misinterpreted, their leaders arrested, or their strategies discredited. Integration of the movement, on the other hand, often leads to the institutionalisation of movement organisations and their goals. For example, in many cities, neighbourhood organisations became part of structural citizen participation by successfully challenging local political administrations and business alliances and by making residents' issues part of local political agendas (Rabrenovic, 1996).

Social movements and their leaders can also be coopted and/or adjust their goals and strategies to diminish the threat they represent to the legitimacy of a political regime. Movement leaders may become salaried employees of the city or movement organisations might be transformed into service providers. These outcomes are not necessarily bad for a movement if integration increases its ability to influence public policy and/or better address needs of a movement's constituency. But in order to do that, they have to resolve potential contradiction between their community organising and community development activities and strategies (Stoecker, 2003; Saegert, 2006).

As is the case for many different types of economic and social phenomena, an important issue is how do changes brought on by globalisation influence the political opportunity structure of urban social movements? Specifically, who are the movement's targets, allies and enemies in a particular locale, will depend to what degree globalisation processes have: (1) shifted power from local and national political entities to international and regional institutions, (2) increased the power of multinational corporations over local institutions, and (3) reduced the capacity of traditional state structures to control them.

Nevertheless, the most recent comparative research on urban movements shows that local activists continue to identify local or regional governments as the primary source of their problems and the focus of their protests continues to be local (Shepard and Hayduk, 2002). The budget deficit cutting measures forced upon many individual countries by the requirements of the Maastricht Treaty in Europe and the austerity policies of the International Monetary Fund forced on Latin American countries have often provoked mobilisation at the local level. In their analysis of social movement actions against the European Union in Europe, Imig and Tarrow found that between 1984 and 1997, domestic governments and domestic private actors were the targets in 74.1 percent of the protests (Tarrow, 2005: 93). Given that local activists identified local or regional governments as the primary source of their problems, it is not surprising that the focus of their protests was also local.

Framing the issues

Successful collective action also depends on how movement issues are framed. Mediating between the opportunity for mobilisation and concrete actions that get implemented are the subjective meanings that people attach to their situations (Goffman, 1974). The concept of framing is rooted in symbolic interactionist and social constructionist approaches and is based on three basic premises: people are seen as active assemblers of meaning; the creation of meaning through framing occurs in various forums; and political conflicts on particular issues are fought out as symbolic contests between contesting frames (Sasson, 1995). Framing, within the context of social movements, is different from everyday interpretive frames. Referred to as 'collective action frames', they are used by the members of the movements to produce and maintain the meaning of particular situations in order to mobilise the members of their constituency, transform bystanders into supporters, exact concession from targets of their mobilisation and demobilise their antagonists (Snow and Benford, 1988: 198).

Researchers have distinguished between diagnostic framing and prognostic framing. Diagnostic framing focuses attention on a particular issue. It helps shape how an issue is perceived, and identifies who or what is responsible for the problems underlying the issue. Diagnostic framing also identifies the targets or sources of the outcomes sought. For example, if urban residents and their organisations frame crime problems as a 'breakdown of community', they are likely to interpret neighbourhood crime as a consequence of a breakdown of the social order (Sasson, 1995). Broken windows, loud and uncivil youth, trash and junk in the streets, vandalism and graffiti and boarded up or abandoned buildings are seen as creating perceptions of fear that in turn induce residents to withdraw from social life. The sense of danger and the residents' withdrawal lead to a decrease in informal social control, which is conducive to crime. On the other hand, if they frame those conditions as a consequence of 'blocked opportunities', they stress structural factors such as unemployment, poverty and inadequate social services that are seen as causing neighbourhood decline that in turn causes crime.

Prognostic framing develops specific remedies or goals that social movement organisations want to accomplish and it defines the means and tactics for achieving these objectives. Within the framework of a 'breakdown of social order', prognostic framing may encourage residents to develop community-wide alliances to address both the social and physical deterioration of their communities. In the 1990s, many neighbourhoods across the United States responded to widespread increases in crime by developing neighbourhood-based crime prevention programmes that took advantage of community resources to increase informal social control, to develop a sense of community and/or to deter potential offenders with the ultimate goal of minimising victimisation in the community.

Prognostic framing using a 'blocked opportunity' framework, on the other hand, might stress the importance of addressing sources of unemployment, poverty and inadequate services. Residents and their organisations could be encouraged to work in partnership with business, government and labour organisations to improve the school system, provide structural activities for children and youth, create opportunities for new employment, build affordable housing, and/or get resources from state and federal government for various social and economic programmes.

The concept of master framing is another useful approach to understanding social movements, especially transnational movements (Snow and Benford, 1988; Tarrow, 1992). Master frames focus on ways in which diverse groups can integrate their objectives and goals, and are useful concepts for studying transnational mobilisation.

Within transnational mobilisation movements, two important master frames have emerged: one of globalisation and the other of global justice. For example, protesters who came to Seattle, Genoa, Quebec City and Prague were brought together under the globalisation frame that was used as a frame-bridging tool to connect opponents of free trade and neo-liberal policies with supporters of a cleaner environment and global democracy (Broad, 2002). Similarly, the concept of global justice has been used as a master frame to confront global organisations regarding their lack of electoral responsiveness and accountability in the public sphere. Global justice also stresses the need to incorporate values other than profit making into global economic institutions.

Once social movement organisations define their collective action frames, they often articulate them into their written documents such as brochures, fliers and placards. They also coordinate their own frame with the frames of other organisations and then use master frames to integrate different groups and organisations around common themes. Women, environmentalist and peace movement organisations have successfully used these techniques to participate in transnational movements.

As local and national organisations cooperate and participate more with transnational movements, they are increasingly likely to incorporate globalisation issues and themes to frame their own issues. In addition, as particular tactics and framing strategies are found to be successful across different locals, they are more likely to become institutionalised by the movement organisations and get repeatedly used in different places.

Illustrations and application

Urban social movements address issues that affect residents at the local level, including a lack of affordable housing, the physical deterioration of neighbourhoods and a need to secure local services. Immigration, ethnicity, race, class, gender and sexual orientation continue to contribute to the heterogeneity of cities and make the issues of identity and belonging important factors in our urban communities. What accounts for successful mobilisation around these issues? In order to answer this question, I will use several examples of urban social mobilisation and show how social movements form organisations, develop coalitions, frame their issues and take advantage of local and global political opportunities. The authors of these studies use a combination of resource mobilisation, political opportunity structure and framing analysis in order to explain mobilisation efforts as well as their outcomes.

Mobilising around homeless issues

One of the most persistent urban social problems is homelessness. It is caused by a variety of factors, including decreases in affordable housing, cuts in health and human services, and changing local economies that are losing jobs that pay sustainable wages. In order to respond to the needs of the homeless, many urban residents have mobilised and formed organisations to campaign for more resources and better treatment of the homeless. Although it is difficult to assess the success of such efforts, Cress and Snow (2000) conducted a study of 15 homeless social movement organisations in eight cities across the United States. They examined factors that contributed to successful mobilisation and found that the homeless social movements that had viable organisations were the ones that were able to take advantage of supportive political contexts and were active participants in developing diagnostic and prognostic issue frames. They also found that there are multiple strategies that can lead to positive outcomes. Depending on the local political opportunity structure, organisations used advocacy, coalition building, protests and media attention to push for their understanding of the problems and to secure benefits for their constituencies.

Cress and Snow (2000) found that successful homeless movements produced a variety of benefits for their constituents. In some instances, homeless social movements improved the living conditions of the homeless by securing their rights, such as protection from police harassment, obtaining welfare benefits and registering to vote. In addition, in some cities, successful movements helped ameliorate the conditions of the homeless by expending shelters, food programmes, job training programmes, sanitation facilities and permanent low-income housing. The types of programmes most often identified as a success were usually ones directly connected to a social movement's goals and organisational ideology.

The researchers also found indirect benefits to the homeless from various social movement initiatives. These outcomes were less directly connected to social movements' organisational goals, and had more to do with engaging homeless constituents in the political and government process, which sometimes led to life-changing experiences. In addition, movement activities were important, sometimes changing public perceptions of the issue and public opinion of the homeless population and its needs.

Battles over highway construction

Another important urban issue is the battle over land use and the protection of neighbourhood quality of life. Highway construction projects can have especially detrimental effects on urban neighbourhoods. Residents affected by highway construction often organise to stop or change the scope/size of these projects. The targets of their mobilisation are typically local and regional actors are involved in the project. The ability of residents to challenge highway projects often depends on how well they can reach individuals and organisations beyond their own neighbourhoods. In addition, the existence of formal citizen organisations and how issues are framed are contributing factors in securing successful outcomes. Manlio Cinalli's study (2003) of urban mobilisation around neighbourhood opposition to Westlink, a transportation project in Belfast, Northern Ireland, illustrates this point well. Cinalli studied two mobilisation campaigns. The first campaign took place in the 1970s; the second in the 1990s. 'Westlink' was the name of the Department for Regional Development's transportation plan to build several new roads in order to improve the flow of traffic to, from and within the city of Belfast.

During the first campaign, urban protesters came from polarised social groups. Protesters were linked to mostly religiously homogeneous organisations. To bring these groups together, the West Belfast Community Association and the Belfast Urban Study Group were set up. Although cooperation worked for a while, increased ethnic polarisation in the late 1970s and a greater preoccupation with local neighbourhood issues produced a break-up of the alliance. As a result, a failure to develop a united front weakened opposition to the Westlink plan.

The second campaign in 1996 was triggered by a plan to upgrade Westlink. This time, political conditions were different from those of the 1970s. Significantly improved political conditions in Northern Ireland allowed neighbourhood groups to overcome their sectarian differences and develop strong personal and interorganisational linkages, which facilitated the development of a common opposition movement. Better relationships also developed between neighbourhood and environmental organisations. Improved relations and the greater participation of a broader range of social movement groups enabled the movement to create a master frame focusing on concerns for social and environmental justice. They also elevated public support for their objectives through the use of local and national newspapers. These efforts enabled the activists to gain the support of established political leaders and formal institutions in the community, including universities. Finally, the movement succeeded in getting the Department for Regional Development to conduct a comprehensive review of the Westlink expansion project. Although the expansion plan was not stopped, the successful integration of different groups under a set of shared goals at least forced a reconsideration of the Westlink scheme.

Community response to hate against immigrants

Hate group provocations to immigrants is a growing problem in many communities. This type of problem can be especially difficult for smaller, less diverse American cities. Rabrenovic (2006) studied how one small American city, Lewiston, Maine, responded to an influx of immigrants from Somalia, and how this community challenged the provocations of an outside hate group.

Problems in cities like Lewiston often develop around the financial costs of incorporating immigrants into a community and around the cultural threat that immigrants represent to the local way of life. In addition, in these smaller communities, a lack of experience with ethnic/racial minorities, along with the fear provoking impact of 9/11, has given racial supremacists an opportunity to expand their membership base by promoting racial hatred and fear across these communities. This is what happened in Lewiston in 2001 when an influx of new immigrants and refugees from Somalia created tensions in the city and lead to the World Church of the Creator, a neo-Nazi hate organisation, to announce their intention to organise a rally to protest against Somalis' presence in Lewiston.

To address the threat posed by the World Church hate rally, city officials, community activists and religious leaders came together and created a community-based coalition under the name *Many and One Coalition*. Their strategy was to marginalise the hate mongers by organising a diversity rally at the same time but at a different location. They wanted to avoid violent confrontation with the members and supporters of the World Church so as not to publicise their message. Most importantly, the alternative rally was intended to show the coalition's support for Somalis and also help articulate their vision of Lewiston's future as a racially diverse and welcoming place.

Only about 30 people attended the World Church's rally, and few of these individuals were Lewiston residents. In contrast, more than 4000 people showed up for the Diversity Rally organised by the *Many and One Coalition*. The results of Lewiston's *Many and One* mobilisation demonstrated effective ways of organising against hate, avoiding violence and marginalising hate provocateurs by decreasing their ability to recruit new members. The emergence of an urban-based social-movement organisation created a space for the community to come together around more inclusive and supportive attitudes towards immigrants. Equally important, the ability of the coalition to frame their mobilisation around a future of the city as a more diverse community helped to avert violence.

The impact of globalisation on urban social movements

In order to understand contemporary urban social movements, it is important to examine the impact of globalisation on issues, resources and strategies. Globalisation processes and policies have often led directly to a worsening of local economic and/or political conditions such as damage to local economies and tax bases, increased unemployment, unequal distribution of local services and environmental degradation. The response to such problems has included both local and international mobilisation. Environmental justice organisations provide a good example of this type of coalition building in that they are increasingly connecting local concerns with issues at the national and global level. Although these types of organisation first developed in poor urban neighbourhoods, they grew over time to incorporate a variety of other social movement organisations that have their roots in civil rights, occupational health and safety, immigration rights, the concerns of indigenous communities for retaking and protecting their traditional lands, and environmental health (Faber and McCarthy, 2001).

Today, environmental justice movement organisations typically bring together concerns for environmental degradation, economic inequality, racism and the lack of opportunities for participatory democracy around the master frame of environmental justice that links racism, injustice and environmentalism (Taylor, 2000: 514). What unites these different organisations is the common goal of finding solutions to problems that encompass the issues of environmental abuse, racial oppression, poverty and political disempowerment. In order to do that, they pay attention to systematic causes of environmental injustice and elevate their struggle to both a national and international level.

Activists may also organise locally even when they identify the source of the problems as transnational. For example, Mexican-American women in El Paso reacted to deterioration of their local circumstances, which they attributed to the international NAFTA agreement, by staging actions against local and national actors. Their organisation, La Mujer Obrera, was formed to support women's concerns for decent and stable employment, housing, education, nutrition, health care, peace and political liberty by addressing the large political and economic forces shaping the political economy of their cities. The organisation's leaders used religious, political and cultural symbols as a basis for their mobilising efforts and as a way to link individual members to their organisation. Their goal was to obtain resources from both local and national leaders to address the plight of displaced workers even though the source of their problems was a transnational trade agreement (Navarro, 2002).

The second and increasingly common way to address local problems, caused at least in part by transnational forces, is through international mobilisation. Using this approach, social activists are increasingly forging transnational ties and articulating common transnational agendas to address issues such as immigration, social and environmental justice, and labour rights. Because these transnational movements are loosely organised associations, their members come from a variety of ideological and activist backgrounds, including groups opposed to globalisation, anti-capitalist groups, churches and social justice organisations. They use a broad spectrum of political activities such as protests, participation in political campaigns, petition campaigns and declarations. They also challenge prevailing political relationships and power structures, and attempt to educate the public about the malign effects of global capitalism. They coordinate international campaigns and share organising practices utilising new communication and transformational technologies. These relationships are often being facilitated by international non-profit and non-governmental organisations.

However, there are difficulties facing both local and international mobilisation around issues created by global forces. For example, how can they transform region-specific problems that may have transnational roots into global struggles? Or, how can they choose appropriate strategies to address them? In addition, even when strategies lead to success, their prolonged use can produce backlash. A good example of the backlash phenomenon can be found in the massive street demonstrations that have followed meetings of international organisations. Such protests are increasingly being met with harsher and more punitive police reactions, as the violence that erupted in Genoa have shown (Tarrow, 2005). Another example of backlash is the increasing tendency of national governments to exclude international activists from participating in protests by denying them visas. Finally, international organisations and institutions have begun to move their meeting sites to more remote locations such as Singapore and Dubai where there is less opportunity for mass street mobilisations (Smith, 2002).

In the future, an important potential obstacle to transnational social movements may be the profound disparities in the resources, information and legitimacy controlled by activists and organisations that come from places with different levels of economic, political and social development. Because activists from more developed places often have more experience, command a better knowledge of English as a language of cooperation, have easier ways of accessing communicational channels including the internet, and are more likely to participate in international conferences, they are thus more likely to control or exercise a disproportionate influence over issue framing and the choice of strategies in transnational movements. Given these disparities, a major consideration for transnational movements is how to better incorporate the knowledge and values of groups from different economic, political and geographic backgrounds.[4]

The future of urban social movement theory and research

Globalisation has intensified competition among nations and communities for economic resources, often pitting one location against another. In addition, because of flexible financial markets, companies can easily transfer their capital from one place to another; thus they are less likely to make concessions to local demands. These global processes will increasingly elevate globalisation issues on many urban social movement agendas. However, within social movement theory, there is not enough attention paid to the urban context of social movements. There is inadequate attention to the operationalisation of economic forces and how they affect cities and the political environment is often too broadly defined. For example, on some issues, some government agencies or officials can be allies of social movement organisations and other government agencies can be the opponents. As a result, we need more research on conditions under which movement organisations benefit from cooperation with government and, similarly, under which conditions opposition is the better strategy. Also, enhancing our understanding of the potential interactions between local, national and international forces is an important avenue for future research. For example, why do transnational social movements emerge in some cities and in others do not?

Another potentially valuable area for future research is how collective interests emerge among urban residents and how they influence collective action. Does the 'urban way of life' have anything to do with identity formation among residents?

What is the role of mass media in solidifying those identities? How does participation in urban social movements influence the lives of individuals?

Very few studies that examine social movement outcomes and/or successes have been conducted. This is perhaps not surprising because of the complexity of studying social movements. For example, it is difficult to assess the cultural and institutional changes that result from social movement activities because these are likely to emerge over fairly long periods and are also likely to be affected by additional factors than those associated with social movements' activities.

On the other hand, the diversity of movements and their strategies demonstrate that there are multiple ways to address problems and concerns at the local levels. However, we need more research on how movement participants make their choices. How do they become aware of opportunities for mobilisation? How do they resolve ideological differences that exist between their members? When is it appropriate to act locally and when do they need to use international pressure to get results at the local level?

Another complicating factor in studying urban social movements is that their impact may vary by type of community in which they are operating. State and national policies regulate economic and political life and can be influenced or changed by grassroots mobilisation. Thus, many studies use the case study approach that provides a rich analysis of particular mobilisation efforts, but makes it hard to develop more generalisable sets of propositions. For example, our understanding of the impact of social movements could be improved by more systematically collecting data over time and across space, in order to determine when and under which conditions movements are successful.

Finally, domination of structural approaches to explaining social movements downplayed the role of emotions, perceptions and individual choices. In order to fully understand and explain why and how people act, we need to better integrate this wide variety of perspectives.

Notes

1 The most famous community organiser in the United States was Saul Alinsky who mobilised Chicago neighbourhoods in the 1930s (Stoecker, 2002). Today organisations such as Association of Community Organisations for Reform Now (ACORN), Industrial Area Foundation (IAF) and National Organisers Alliance provide support to local groups and neighbourhoods.
2 Not everyone had to pay full rate. There were rebates of up to 80 percent for students and other individuals with limited income. However, the principle was that everyone had to pay something toward community tax.
3 In a speech to his supporters, Prime Minister John Major cited the figures of 17.5 million people who 'either had not paid or were in serious arrears – about half of those liable to pay' (Burns, 2002: 176).
4 National and transnational feminist networks have provided a good example of how a movement can facilitate the flow of ideas and activism from many places and avoid domination of one group of activists over the other (see Desai, 2002).

References

Boggs, Carl (1986) *Social Movements and Political Power: Emerging Forms of Radicalism in the West.* Philadelphia, PA: Temple University Press.

Broad, Robin (2002) 'Introduction: of magenta hair, nose rings, and naivete', in Robin Broad (ed.), *Global Backlash.* Lanham: Rowman & Littlefiled Publishers, Inc. pp. 1–10.

Burns, Danny (1992) *Poll Tax Rebellion.* Stirling, Scotland: AK Press, and London: Attack International.

Butler, David, Adonis, Andre and Travers, Tony (1994) *Failure in British Government: The Politics of the Poll Tax.* New York: Oxford University Press.

Castells, Manuel (1983) *The City and the Grassroots.* Berkeley and Los Angeles: University of California Press.

Cinalli, Manlio (2003) 'Socio-politically polarized contexts, urban mobilization and the environmental movement: a comparative study of two campaigns of protest in Northern Ireland', *International Journal of Urban and Regional Research*, 27 (1): 158–77.

Cress, Daniel M. and Snow, David A. (2000) 'The outcomes of homeless mobilization: the influence of organization, disruption, political mediation, and framing', *American Journal of Sociology*, 105 (4): 1063–104.

Desai, Manisha (2002) 'Women's transnational solidarity: women's agency, structural adjustment, and globalization', in Nancy A. Naples and Manisha Desai (eds), *Women's Activism and Globalization.* London: Routledge. pp. 83–98.

Edwards, Bob and McCarthy, John D. (2004) 'Resources and social movement mobilization', in David A. Snow, Sarah A. Soule and Hanspeter Kriesi (eds), *The Blackwell Companion to Social Movements.* pp. 116–52.

Eisinger, Peter K. (1973) 'The conditions of protest behavior in American cities', *American Political Science Review*, 67: 11–28.

Faber, Daniel and McCarthy, Deborah (2001) 'The evolving structure of the environmental justice movement in the United States: new models for democratic decision-making', *Social Justice Research*, 14 (4): 405–21.

Fisher, Robert and Kling, Joseph (1993) 'Introduction: the continued vitality of community mobilization', in Robert Fisher and Joseph Kling (eds), *Mobilizing the Community*, Urban Affairs Annual Reviews series, 41. Newbury Park, CA: Sage. pp. xi–xxiii.

Gamson, William A. (1990) *The Strategy of Social Protest*, 2nd edn. Belmont, CA: Wadsworth.

Gittell, Ross and Vidal, Avis (1998) *Community Organizing: Building Social Capital as a Developmental Strategy.* Thousand Oaks: Sage.

Goffman, Erving (1974) *Frame Analysis.* New York: Harper & Row.

Kriesi, Hanspeter (1996) 'The organizational structure of new social movements in a political context', in Doug McAdam, John D. McCarthy and Mayer N. Zald (eds), *Comparative Perspectives on Social Movements: Political Opportunities, Mobilizing Structure, and Cultural Framings.* Cambridge: Cambridge University Press.

Koopmans, Ruud (2004) 'Protest in time and space: the evolution of waves of contention', in David A. Snow, Sarah A. Soule and Hanspeter Kriesi (eds), *The Blackwell Companion to Social Movements.* Oxford: Blackwell Publishing. pp. 19–46.

Le Bon, Gustave (1960) *The Crowd: A Study of the Popular Mind.* New York: Viking Press.

McCarthy, John D. and Zald, Mayer N. (1977) 'Resource mobilization and social movements: a partial theory', *American Journal of Sociology*, 82 (6): 1212–41.

Navarro, Sharon Ann (2002) 'Las mujeres invisibles/the invisible women', in Nancy A. Naples and Manisha Desai (eds), *Women's Activism and Globalization.* London: Routledge. pp. 83–98.

Olson, Mancur (1965) *The Logic of Collective Action.* Cambridge: Harvard University Press.

Pichardo, Nelson A. (1997) 'New social movements: a critical review', *Annual Review of Sociology*, 23: 411–30.

Piven, Frances Fox, and Cloward, Richard A. (1977) *Poor People's Movements: Why They Succeed, How They Fail.* New York: Vintage.

Rabrenovic, Gordana (1996) *Community Builders.* Philadelphia: Temple University Press.

Rabrenovic, Gordana (forthcoming) 'When hates comes to town: community response to violence against immigrants', *American–Behavioral Scientist*, 51 (2): 349–6.

Saegert, Susan (2006) 'Building civic capacity in urban neighborhoods: an empirically grounded anatomy', *Journal of Urban Affairs*, 28 (3): 275–94.

Sasson, Theodore (1995) *Crime Talk*. New York: Aldine de Gruyter.

Shepard, Benjamin and Hayduk, Ronald (2002) *From Act Up to the WTO: Urban Protest and Community Building in the Era of Globalization*. London: Verso.

Smith, Jackie (2002) 'Globalizing resistance: the battle of Seattle and the future of social movements', in Jackie Smith and Hank Johnston (eds), *Globalization and Resistance*. Lanham: Rowman & Littlefiled Publishers, Inc. pp. 207–27.

Snow, David A. and Benford, Robert D. (1988) 'Ideology, frame resonance, and participant mobilization', *International Social Movement Research*, 1: 811–33.

Stoecker, Randy (2002) 'Community development and community organizing: apples and oranges? chicken and egg?', in Benjamin Shepard and Ronald Hayduk (eds), *From Act Up to the WTO: Urban Protest and Community Building in the Era of Globalization*. London: Verso. pp: 378–88.

Stoecker, Randy (2003) 'Understanding the development-organizing dialectic', *Journal of Urban Affairs*, 25 (4): 493–512.

Stone, Clarence N. (1989) *Regime Politics*. Lawrence: University Press of Kansas.

Tarrow, Sidney (1992) 'Mentalities, political cultures, and collective action frames: constructing meanings through action', in Aldon D. Morris and Carol M. Mueller (eds), *Frontiers in Social Movement Theory*. New Haven: Yale University Press. pp. 174–202.

Tarrow, Sidney (2005) *The New Transnational Activism*. Cambridge: Cambridge University Press.

Taylor, Dorceta (2000) 'The rise of the environmental justice paradigm', *American Behavioral Scientist*, 43 (4): 508–80.

Turner, Ralph H. and Killian, Lewis M. (1972) *Collective Behavior*, 2nd edn. Englewood Clifs, NJ: Prentice-Hall.

United Nations (2002) *World Urbanization Prospects: The 2001 Revision*. UN: Department of Economic and Social Affairs, Population Division.

Part V

CHALLENGES

16

WHO IS GOVERNED? LOCAL CITIZENS AND THE POLITICAL ORDER OF CITIES

Clarence N. Stone

Confidence in representative government appears widely on the wane, and local democracy seems particularly lacking in vibrancy. The claim that local representatives are close to the people rings somewhat hollow. Instead of uniting people in civic work, office holders typically preside over a high level of apathy and in the worst cases, their actions give rise to active distrust. Further, as put by one pair of authors: 'If a basic aim of institutional design is to nurture a sense of shared fate among citizens, local political institutions are failing badly' (Macedo and Karpowitz, 2006: 59). Fresh thinking about the study of urban politics is thus very much in order, and a new urban scholarship might well be built around the idea of refashioning local democracy. In this chapter, my aim is to suggest ways of thinking about urban politics in light of democratic ideals. I recommend a nine-step effort.

Step one: seeing democracy as an inclusive process

Self-government rests on the principle that those who are governed have a role in governing. An ancient Greek version was that all would rule and be ruled in turn. Everyone would have a hand in governing, but in such a way as to have reason to accommodate the concerns of others. No one would get her or his way all of the time, but all would be part of a system in which their concerns were assured consideration. No group would be consigned to the position of a permanent minority, and conciliation would be extended to all (Crick, 2000). Thus, we draw from Greek wisdom an understanding of democracy as an inclusive process.

Today voting, combined with the right of dissent, is widely seen as fundamental to achieving the incorporation of all. Paying heed to Patrick Dunleavy's caution about excessive emphasis on such input processes (1980), I argue here, however, that we need a broader understanding of political inclusion, one that involves the total fabric of the polity, that is, the way in which state, civil society and market weave together. This is an unconventional understanding, but one that provides a way of addressing the fact that many localities contain populations that are disconnected from the mainstream of governance, and find themselves in a position of unending marginality. The presence of such a 'permanent minority' falls short on a basic requirement of democracy.

Step two: understanding elections as an inadequate expression of democracy

Our understanding of representative government thus is somewhat shallow. If elections are open and contested and citizens enjoy an opportunity to vote, then we tend to assume that democratic representation is at work. But, let us bear in mind the limits of electoral accountability as a form of representation. Although voting is the most conspicuous form of citizen participation in politics, elections are in reality a highly limited form of political expression. For multiple reasons that need not be elaborated here, elections provide inadequate ground on which to rest democratic representation. Voting itself involves what might be termed a 'blunt' choice, imperfectly matched to the complexity of the alternatives that may be at stake (Verba, 1967). The framework within which voter choices are made sometimes lacks a coherent and relevant issue content. Turnout is often low and class-skewed. And, of fundamental importance, elected officials are only part of what makes up a governing arrangement.

Step three: recognising that protest movements are not endpoints in political change

One response to shortcomings in official channels of representation is to mount a social movement. Indeed, much of the politics of the latter half of the twentieth century was dominated by such phenomena as the civil rights movement in the US and movements for independence in countries whose citizens suffered under the political debility of colonial status. Important as these liberation episodes were, a movement is only a prelude to the main event. When one political order is destabilised (and destabilisation is perhaps the major strategy of social movements), the central issue becomes one of the terms of a new political settlement. The resources and strategies used in destabilising an old order might be quite different from those required in constructing a new and durable political settlement. How, then, does a change become institutionalised? As a new order takes shape, we need to ask how far-reaching the change is. In the US, the follow-through to the civil rights movement shows us that many things remained unaltered, and new relationships took shape as buffers against racial integration. White flight, for example, was a powerful new force giving rise to consequences greatly at odds with the goal of ending racial segregation (Kruse, 2005).

We have long understood that 'protest is not enough' in bringing about lasting change (Browning et al., 1984). Protests are subject to various short-term counterattacks, and can be outlasted by those in power (Lipsky, 1970). Targets of movement mobilisation often have a significant arsenal of defences, and they may even relocate and redirect investments. Thus, over time, the US labour-union movement found itself weakened by the relocation of business operations away from the older urban centres, where unions had their greatest successes, to areas of the country that were less union-friendly (Mollenkopf, 1983). Now, overseas investment and outsourcing have taken an additional toll.

For protest movements, then, an oppositional strategy of putting pressure on established centres of governing power is insufficient. Negotiated settlements may prove to be ephemeral. Lasting change is a matter of establishing durable relationships of a kind that are a part of the system of governance. Incorporation rather than simply 'pressure on' is the key, but incorporation into what?

Leverage within local government is by no means an insignificant factor (Button, 1989), but much is outside the reach of city hall, not only in the US with its incomplete powers of home rule and limited capacity to raise revenue (Elkin, 1987; Frug, 1999; and Barron, 2003), but also in much of Europe (Stoker, 2003). Investment activity, informal networks of access to employment, control over patterns of migration, and much more are beyond the scope of local authority. Because official actions are themselves only part of the process of governing, we need to look more widely. Unless members of a movement can incorporate themselves productively into the web of relations between governmental and non-governmental actors, they have limited capacity to define the terms on which political change is institutionalised. To understand what it means to be productively incorporated, we need now to turn our attention to policy and the form that policy takes in the real world of governing and being governed.

Step four: rethinking what policy is

We have long understood that policy is not what is formally enacted. Policy is what is implemented, but even that insight does not take us far enough. Policy implementation is itself not something with a disembodied form separate from the people affected (Honig, 2006). Policy is how official initiatives and programmes actually mesh with the behaviour of citizens as they respond from the varied positions they occupy in the total order of things. It flows from complex interactions within the polity. *Policy therefore is not a unidirectional force applied to a uniform body of people* (McLaughlin, 2006). It is instead a complex set of interactions with which citizens may be aligned in various ways.

Consider the experience with evacuation in New Orleans as Hurricane Katrina swept through the area. In the face of imminent flooding, the mayor gave an official order to evacuate. Initially, an unstated assumption was that residents would simply exit the city and locate temporary housing outside the flood zone. Many residents did so, but many others, lacking automobiles and credit cards, were unable to do so. For the latter, there was no coordinated plan of evacuation. Other than opening the Superdome as an emergency (but ill-equipped and poorly managed) facility, officials at all levels did little except launch belated rescue efforts. In short, official action served some but not others. In the manner initiated, emergency evacuation assumed that residents had a capacity, on their own, to leave the city and find shelter else-where. As became evident during a badly executed implementation effort, the initial policy plan was seriously flawed. The evacuation aim was not aligned with the inabil-ity of a sizeable segment of the population to respond in the anticipated way.

Formal policy is often announced in a universal form. Everyone is to evacuate, or all students are to meet high academic standards. Some policy pronouncements are largely symbolic. They embody good intentions, but change little about how the world operates. Some may be understood as symbolic from the beginning. Others may represent wishful thinking and lapse quickly into an empty gesture. Many others will undergo significant change and adjustment as they move from enactment to execu-tion. Policy is shaped by the way various people are perceived and treated by others, by their own inclinations, and especially by the resources and capacities they enjoy.

As in the case of the Katrina evacuation, it often happens that declared policy is made with little understanding for how it will be carried through as citizen responses come into play. *De facto* policy is therefore what governmental and non-governmental actors produce through their joint action. Coordination may be tacit rather than explicit, and it may be weak and friction-laden. But joint action, not government action alone, determines policy reality.

Step five: re-examining policy-making

If policy is *de facto* what results from the interplay between the behaviour of citizens (documented and not) and the actions of governmental actors, then we need to re-think the policy process. Patrick Dunleavy took urban political science to task for being 'overwhelmingly input-oriented' (1980: 13). Elections, followed by legislative enactments, he argued, are not the main dynamic of politics. Because government is not an independent force acting upon a passive society and economy, policy-making involves much more than activity in which initiatives move from advocacy to poten-tial enactment and, if enacted, onto implementation (cf. Sabatier, 1999).

Significantly, however, even those who call for a balanced or polity-centred approach tend to put the spotlight on actors within the governmental sphere. In her influential work, aimed at reversing society-centred analyses, Theda Skocpol argues: 'Both appointed and elected officials have ideas and organizational career interests of their own, and they devise and work for policies that will further those ideas and interest, or at least not harm them ...' (1992: 42). Put another way: 'Because states are authoritative and resourceful organizations – collectors of revenue, centers of cultural authority, and hoarders of means of coercion – they are sites of autonomous action, not reducible to the demands or preferences of social groups' (Skocpol, 1985: 42).

In countering social determinism, Skocpol tends to describe the policy process as autonomous, with social input, but largely directed by professional politicians and administrators. Yet, at other times, she talks about a 'need to analyze states in relation to socioeconomic and sociocultural contexts' (1985: 20). However, framing the matter around the conceptual distinction between state and society captures only a partial reality. There are ways in which state and society mesh so thoroughly that the notion of one influencing the other implies a degree of separation that ill fits how the process works.

It fell to Robert Putnam's work on social capital in Italy (1993) and subsequently in the US (2000) to put civil society in the spotlight and move scholars toward a more balanced polity-centred approach (see, for example, Saegert et al., 2001). While state actions shape civil society, civil society also profoundly penetrates policy-making. Consider the case of AIDS prevention. Studies of Christchurch, New Zealand (Brown, 1999) and Zurich, Switzerland (Neueschwander et al., 2004) underscore the enormous importance of civil society. In Christchurch, for example, prevention policy is achieved through a tight-knit *community*, consisting of volunteers, health and social work professionals, and other activists on the issue. Without a strong sense of community, AIDS prevention runs the risk of what Michael Brown terms 'clientilization and poor service delivery' (1999: 80). In his view, effective AIDS prevention depends on bonds that extend beyond officially defined responsibilities, and grow from 'a sense of caring and unity' that enhances communication, information sharing and intensity of effort beyond what a formal relationship is able to evoke. As one AIDS worker put it: 'There's no contractual obligation to perform some of the work we do ...' (quoted in Brown, 1999: 80).

In matters as intimate and sensitive as those involved in the spread of AIDS, it is particularly important that professionals and target groups have a basis on which personal trust can be built. In Switzerland, gay organisations and social work professionals were the early responders to the crisis: 'As self-help organisations or professionals with a long experience in working with the different target groups, they were extremely well rooted in the various milieus (prostitution, homosexual community, drug users, etc) that are normally quite difficult to penetrate – especially for state actors' (Neuenschwander et al., 2004: 7). Hence as AIDS prevention unfolded in Switzerland, public authorities found it essential to collaborate with pertinent self-help organisations 'in order to gain access to the relevant target groups' (2004: 8). As Brown observes, 'AIDS politics do not just work on policy mandates alone. They work effectively because [key players] are part of the communities in which they serve' (1999: 80).

AIDS prevention is, of course, an atypical policy in many regards. Still, even in less intimate matters such as neighbourhood revitalisation, effectiveness depends on a meshing of efforts from government agencies (often at multiple levels), neighbourhood groups and various financial and technical-assistance intermediaries (Von Hoffman, 2003). Still, market forces have to be reckoned with. Some alignments are weak. Neighbourhood revitalisation sometimes fails to take hold or occurs at only a modest level. Or, in the case of ending racial segregation in America's highly decentralised school system, legal doctrine failed to align with operational reality and in fact contributed to a drastically reconfigured metropolitan pattern along with significant rethinking about public education (Kruse, 2005).

———— **Step six: rejecting functional necessity as an overriding cause** ————

Given the complexity of the policy process, we face the question of what drives policy actions. One possibility is that individuals are largely pawns moved by larger systemic forces. There is no question but that structural forces, such as economic competition between localities, are an important factor (Peterson, 1981), but caution is in order. Because intermediate links constitute a significant force, functional necessity has become a largely discredited form of argument (Hay, 1995; Hall and Taylor, 1996; Jacobs and Skocpol, 2005). Alvin Gouldner long ago spotlighted political agency within a corporate setting. Foreshadowing James March (1962), Gouldner argued that powerful individuals within a corporate structure 'do not respond directly to all of the tensions of the organization as a whole; they respond with greater readiness to those organizational tensions which threaten their own status' (1954: 240–1). This means that what is functional or efficient for an organisation does not *control* the behaviour of individuals within that setting. Concerns that impinge directly on actors may carry more weight than some broadly defined version of the interest of the whole. School reform may be deemed important for the well-being of the city, but the teachers union may have a different set of focal concerns.

In his work on social history, Arthur Stinchcombe observes that human agency stems from understandings that are immediate and contingent, but not randomly subjective. He argues that while structural factors help shape the cognitions of people, many factors come into play. Stinchcombe notes that a 'general difficulty with "functional" arguments that explain social behaviour as attempts to solve "system problems" of one sort or another is that people quite often solve the wrong problem, or give the wrong solution to the right problem' (1978: 110; see also Rothstein, 1992). Hence, useful as abstract theories that highlight functional 'necessities' may be in identifying general patterns of history, they are not sufficient. There is an intermediate level of events where the contingent nature of development reveals important variations and alternative paths of development (Thelen and Steinmo, 1992: 28; Weir, 1992).

Human agency figures importantly in how structures are adapted to form governing arrangements and thus how governing arrangements favour some courses of action and disfavour others. Yet agency, which is often seen through a lens of elite behaviour, has to be understood within a structured context. The nature of the intersection between agency and structure is one of the most difficult puzzles to solve.[1] On the one hand, 'because humans shape the constraints in which they interact through choice and design', it is important to look at 'moments of institutional change' (Thelen and Steinmo, 1992: 27). On the other hand, 'human agency occurs and acquires meaning only in relation to already preconstituted and deeply structured settings' (Hay, 1995: 200). Unanticipated outcomes play a large role, and some of these have to do with the ways in which those in socioeconomically subordinate positions adjust to the flow of broad changes around them. Thus, we need to appreciate that civic and political relations are at least as much a product of unintended and piecemeal adjustment as of interventions driven by elite aims and ambitions. There is reason therefore to think broadly about the nature of local political orders, how they take shape and the implanted ways in which the formation of new arrangements are constrained.

Step seven: looking beyond elite clashes and coalitions

In an assessment of the concept of an urban regime in this first edition of this volume, Gerry Stoker called for greater attention to the 'wider relationship between government and its citizens' (1995: 60). Concentrating on elites and their interests can, among other things, underplay the role of race, class and gender in politics (cf. Wilson, 1985).[2] What, then, does a local political order look like from the bottom up? What place do ordinary citizens, especially those of lower socioeconomic status (SES), occupy in the political order? We cannot assume that citizens are simply passive recipients of the actions of distant policy-makers, hence not an integral part of the policy process itself. Consider what happens if we shift from asking how various policies affect citizens to a slightly more refined question of how people at the grassroots engage with a range of initiatives and programmes (Handler, 1996). Are citizens deemed to be part of the process? What does it mean if their engagement is marked by alienation and resentment? Is there recognition that the varied actions and reactions of citizens help make policies what they actually are?

Although it is important to consider how elites build support for an agenda and attempt to engineer changes, we should concurrently consider how these changes affect the lives of ordinary people *and how they adjust*. In short, what influences how ordinary citizens of varying means align with sundry policies and programmes? One tenet of classic pluralism holds that citizens facing limited life chances have a special incentive to act to expand their opportunities (Dahl, 1961: 293–6). Yet clearly there are many situations in which no such action is observable, and we cannot attribute such passivity to satisfaction with things as they are.

It seems especially urgent then to understand why misaligned policy configurations, with their hampered capacity for problem-solving, have a tendency to perpetuate themselves. Urban school reform faces that challenge, as do other areas of policy, such as crime control in inner-city areas. Partly, it is a matter that problems are interrelated. Efforts to expand opportunity through workforce development, for example, run up against the harsh reality that segments of the population are disconnected from the world of mainstream employment in a manner that is hard to overcome without taking on such broad issues as low-wage work and multigenerational poverty (Stone and Worgs, 2004). There is a tendency toward triage responses in which small numbers of the least disconnected are assisted while larger numbers in worse straits are neglected. Bold declarations that 'all children can learn' run afoul of the reality that, for some students, actual conditions perpetuate low expectations and resources are allocated accordingly (Oakes and Rogers, 2006).

Although at this stage the concept of a political order remains underdeveloped, it can expand our analytical horizons beyond elite-level clashes and coalition-building efforts. It gives us an opportunity to consider how race, class and other social identities align with systemic inequalities and how these inequalities are perpetuated. The concept of a political order thus enables us to put aside the myth of distinct spheres of government and society (Orren and Skowronek, 2004: 80). It gives us a useful lens for looking at politics, focusing not on who governs, but instead on how governing occurs.

Because political order fits comfortably with the notion of a polity-centred approach (Orren and Skowronek, 2004), the term avoids giving primacy to socioeconomic processes, but without any implication that the state is detached from its moorings in civil society and economy. Since change is not readily achieved by pulling a single lever, mobilising for change is likely to be beyond the capacity of those who are lightly resourced. The notion of a political order thus brings into consideration the multiple strands that weave together politics with society's system of stratification. Stereotypes, past experiences and fears of 'the other' help form a fabric of relationships that are too important to disregard, though they are not always readily observable as distinct events or strategic manoeuvres.

A local political order occupies a stratified terrain, and that terrain poses a test for how inclusive a political order is. And from limited degrees of inclusiveness there are significant policy consequences. For example, social housing planned and developed through a male-dominated order may be sterile and therefore quite different from the kind of housing that might have been built through an order in which women had greater voice (Strömberg, 1996).

That localities exist in an intergovernmental context means that there may be levers of change beyond the reach of those in key institutional positions locally, and it is well to remember that those levers of change may not be in the service of local democracy and may instead operate on behalf of a much different agenda. Still, as conditions alter, new ideas come into play, resources shift and change is possible – sometimes by accretion and sometimes by dramatic shift. Ideas, however, do not operate independent of resources, material and otherwise (Sewell, 1992), some of which may flow through intergovernmental channels (Savitch and Kantor, 2002).

—— Step eight: heeding technocratic ascendance as well as globalisation ——

The study of urban politics has long struggled with the challenge that mobile capital poses for local democracy (Imbroscio, 1999), and several chapters in this collection call attention to the enormous importance of the global economy. The mobility of capital is a leading concern of local officials everywhere and their desire to attract investment confers on business what Charles Lindblom terms a 'privileged position'

(1977). Yet, when Patrick Dunleavy called for urban political science to move beyond preoccupation with input processes and take greater account of the context within which local politics takes shape, he had in mind an even broader picture of modernity and its consequences (1980). As a student of British housing policy, Dunleavy knew how the growth of the welfare state had created an intergovernmental edifice within which local decisions were made.

After the erosion of an earlier way of life created needs that private markets were ill-suited to meet, housing became a significant collective good, planned and operated through the public sector. As social housing came under the sponsorship of the national welfare state, that move greatly expanded the role of professional planners and other social-policy experts, with their own particular networks. A case study of the London Borough of Southwark shows how the growth of the welfare state weakened the local labour movement and altered the policy process (Goss, 1988). With decision-making becoming more technocratic, it also became less oriented to local concerns, and the populace felt disconnected from the process. Of the post Second World War years, one author talks of 'a defeat for localist values' and 'a growing tendency to sacrifice civic engagement on the altar of centrally determined efficiency' (Marquand, 2004: 69).

The welfare state assumed a smaller role in the US, but policy experts nevertheless came to occupy an important position. In his study of New Haven, Robert Dahl captures this trend when he talks about the growing importance of planners, technicians and professional administrators. As he put it: 'The new men in local politics may very well prove to be the bureaucrats and experts – and politicians who know how to use them' (1961: 62). Recent historical studies of New Haven (Rae, 2003) and Boston (O'Connor, 1993) – both places where city hall, not the business sector, was the prime initiator of redevelopment – highlight a striking parallel with Southwark. Though elected officials held centre stage in both places, urban redevelopment imposed hardships on those with lower incomes and status, caused significant social disruption, and in the process generated resentments. New Haven's redevelopment agency was sufficiently disconnected from the populace to be known as 'the Kremlin' (Rae, 2003: 318).

What to make of these experiences, now part of an earlier urban history? Redevelopment is not an isolated experience. Across a wide range of services, professionalisation and bureaucratisation have opened a deep divide between non-affluent citizens and government that we continue to struggle to bridge (Handler, 1996; Schorr, 1997; Fung, 2004). Southwark, Boston and New Haven are places in which a sizeable segment of the population found itself on the margins of an emergent order, without an effective voice in how policy might be adjusted. By prediction from classic pluralism, a largely working-class electorate would be expected to bring about responsiveness to their situation. Events, however, took a different course. Seen through the lens of shifting political orders, the lower ranks in socioeconomic standing lost ground. The new political force was a professional and technocratic element, with its own agenda and connections but only weakly linked to the non-affluent citizenry. A point to be explained is thus why this tie is so slack. Neither local elected officials nor administrative professionals displayed a hostile stance toward the lower classes. To the contrary, efforts were made to be responsive to their needs. For their part, supralocal actors provided support for what they often regarded as aims of social equity. Still, good intentions or not, their initiatives often damaged ties to the less affluent.

A central puzzle is thus why emerging political orders have weakened rather than enhanced the position of lower socioeconomic groups. One possibility is post-industrial capitalism with its diminished place for unskilled workers. No doubt, global capitalism is a contributor, but the politically diminished position of the lower classes preceded deindustrialisation. Hence, advanced capitalism cannot be the whole story. Similarly, the rise of conservative, anti-poor governments in the US and the UK is a likely contributor, but the political debility of the lower socioeconomic ranks was evident prior to the Thatcher and Reagan eras in the two countries. Racism is yet another possibility and a strong candidate for a supporting role, but middle-class minorities have found wider opportunities available, even as their non-affluent counterparts faced continuing, if not worsening, marginalisation.[3]

Perhaps we need to consider something beyond 'the usual suspects'. An advantage of viewing experience through the lens of local political orders is that it enables us to ask how the process of governing relates to the lives of ordinary citizens and what voice they have as policy is put into practice. We see that, for example, both New Haven and Southwark have undergone a transition from a neighbourhood-based form of politics in which citizens were connected in highly personal ways with the political and civic life of their communities to a kind of politics in which professionalisation played a central role, but failed to find effective links to citizens as they underwent damaging forms of social and economic change. David Marquand points to a shift in ethos among professionals from being contributors to a 'broader civic community' to that of being possessors 'of technical skills, technical knowledge and technical qualifications', beyond the ability of the lay public to understand and assess (2004: 75). In this process, constructive alignment did not take hold and inclusion faltered.

While professionalism is a necessary element in the overall governance of modern communities, professionalisation itself leaves us uncertain about how to put together a political order that is inclusive and effective. From Southwark, we can see that a national welfare system oriented toward social equity can still be inadequate for delivering inclusion. From New Haven, we also know that an executive-centred approach for governing can be far off the mark. Both experiences fall well short of inclusiveness, and the policies as put into practice failed to align constructively with the lives of substantial segments of the population. Powerful forces from the global economy and from the expanded role of expertise have converged in such a way as to leave policy misalignments in which lower SES populations are increasingly marginalised. Managerialism seems to have eclipsed representation.

Step nine: reconsidering the pluralist model

It is time to rethink the pluralist model, with its notion of governing as guided centrally by an input process and as characterised by openness. Talk of a shift from government to governance may imply that governing once operated in a chain-of-accountability manner. Yet governing *never* operated in this way. Policy and policy-making fit such a model poorly, elections are (and have been) a highly inadequate link between citizens and their governors, and powerful forces have long been at work outside the conventional input process. Classic pluralism comes nowhere near capturing the reality of local politics.

In Dahl's account of the evolution from an oligarchy, ruled by a cohesive elite, to a pluralist democracy, political development consists essentially of role differentiation. Wealth separates from social standing, and then electoral popularity separates from both. Seeing that as the master process historically, Dahl believed that the addition of policy expertise further dispersed power. He further assumed that the authority attached to holding elected office can override competing claims. From the fate of the once-dominant patricians, Dahl concluded that any big power move by Social and Economic Notables would be checked: 'competitive politics would lead in the end to the triumph of numbers over Notability' (1961: 84).

Who Governs? conflates electoral competition with elite competition. The historical process it examines centres on control of elected office, hence Dahl treats the differentiation of wealth and social standing from electoral popularity as the definitive step. Functional specialisation, however, sets in motion a different dynamic. After all, functionally differentiated elites do not compete for the same position. Differentiation produces interdependence, thereby providing a basis on which elites can cooperate rather than compete when they work out congruent aims. Under these conditions, economic and political elites are no longer countervailing forces, but potential allies able to act in alignment with enough combined resources to pre-empt much of a city's agenda-setting capacity. Thus, they in turn become attractive partners for policy experts because an elite coalition stands out as allies who make programmes of action feasible. Thus, the urban regime argument is that domination is more complex than 'power over' (Stone, 1989: 226–31). 'Power to' can work in such a way as to leave segments of the community outside the circle of effective governing. This is the misalignment that surfaced in Southwark, Boston and New Haven. Economic and political elites found common ground at the very time that policy and programme professionals were disconnecting from the lower classes.

Role differentiation created no foundation for competing for the support of the lower SES population. Indeed, given the action agendas of various experts, including social-policy specialists, the lower strata of society found themselves often regarded as obstacles rather than as attractive allies (Stone, 1980). Addressing the resulting disconnections and misalignment thus becomes a challenge in the revitalisation of local democracy.

Put the matter in deeper context. Pluralism rests on an assumption that what is true formally – that the major institutions of society enjoy a high degree of legal autonomy and a considerable amount of operating autonomy – determines what is true informally. The reality, however, is that a web of interdependence provides a basis on which efforts and resources can be combined to pursue some aims, often at the expense of alternative efforts. In other words, the formal autonomy of various elements of the social order is only the surface of a more complex ordering of society. Because the legal element of the overall order is limited in its reach, much is settled by informal understandings and extra-legal arrangements. The *de jure* equality attached to citizenship notwithstanding, the *de facto* reality of socioeconomic inequality impinges on these extra-legal arrangements and related understandings. The core of the political order is therefore not about elections and the exercise of formal authority, but about relationships that both reflect and give shape to the varied and, as it often turns out, uneven capacities to identify and address problems.

Conclusion

Campaigns and elections are only the tip of the political iceberg. Beneath the water line of overt political activity, citizens interact with official agents of the state and with one another in numerous ways. The conception of policy offered in this chapter encompasses the idea of co-construction, the idea that policy is what is yielded by governmental and citizen actions combined.

When we try to take into account the multitude of factors that shape the education experience of children or the level of public safety in a neighbourhood, we get a look at the political order that is different from one narrowly focused on who holds office. Some citizens enjoy a network of relationships that give them a strong sense that they have a place in society. At the other extreme are citizens whose relationships provide little collective capacity to respond to challenges, and they see themselves as outside the mainstream of society. They may be citizens in name, but they have little reason to believe that their concerns will be addressed in an effective manner. Furthermore, their view of reciprocity and conciliation is confined to a few friends and family members, who may also regard themselves as largely powerless outsiders. What does it mean, for example, that New Haven's poverty commission held hearings, and 'virtually no one came forward'? (Fox, 1988: 127).

A broad understanding of politics directs our attention to how various sectors of society are connected and the extent to which each sector views itself as in a position to receive consideration from others as they encounter challenges. A democratic order is one in which all sectors see themselves as possessing recourse to respond to problems that arise. Such problems come in many particular forms: a natural disaster, a weakness or decline in the level of public safety, diminished access to gainful employment, an inadequate system of transportation, extraordinary circumstances requiring a safety net, environmental degradation, to name a few.

Much overt political activity is about what agencies of government should and should not do, but below the surface in a political order lies a set of sometimes contested but always important arrangements through which state, civil society and market intersect. Public policy is therefore not about what, in some disembodied way, government agencies do or don't do. It is about these intersections and their consequences. It follows, then, that we should not reduce citizenship to membership in an apolitical audience, which reacts periodically to a drama on a remote stage. Democracy is not just about the accountability of elected officials for the decisions they make and the programmes they oversee.

Of necessity, democracy is about how market, government and civil society intersect and interact. If, as seems probable, the continuing expansion of market relations weakens civil society and undercuts the sense that a web of interdependence binds a people together at some fundamental level, then the prospects for democracy are waning. And there is need to find ways to reverse the trend. But first we have to understand the trend and its political implications. Looking at the larger order through a local lens makes the matter concrete in a way that highlights state/civil society/market connections. The central political question is about how citizens align with various interwoven elements of the polity in matters ranging from childcare to emergency evacuations.

Why have emerging political orders weakened rather than strengthened the position of the lower strata in today's world? By simply asking who governs, we run the risk of limiting inquiry to a search for some elite group that actively suppresses a more inclusive politics. To ask who is governed and how points to a broader inquiry. What would a different and more democratic configuration of state, market and civil society look like, and how might we get there?

Although the outcome of a continuing tension between persisting inequality and democracy depends on a full range of activities from local to global, much can be gained by a view from below. For that reason, it is important to ask how local citizens fit into the picture. How are they governed? What steps can be taken to enable them to occupy their rightful role as constructive contributors to governing?

In modern political life, a low position in the system of social stratification often carries with it multiple political handicaps. As the Katrina experience illustrates, lower SES populations lack the market capacity officials sometimes assume to be in place. In addition, the lower classes are widely perceived as social and economic liabilities, and thus are often unattractive as coalition partners. Although the record is far from uniform, many service-providing professionals relate ineffectively to lower strata populations, who, out of accumulated experiences with negative stereotypes, ill treatment and unkept promises, often harbour a high level of alienation and distrust toward the larger society and those acting in official capacities. The result is sometimes called the 'two world' phenomenon (Stone and Worgs, 2004; cf. Mollenkopf and Castells, 1991).

Urban political study faces a dilemma. Describing the problem in itself yields no solution. Indeed, the more thoroughly the problem is delineated, the less susceptible it seems to corrective action. The analytical challenge is to break the vice of structural determinism. That cannot be done by simply laying out a programme of action. The task is to confront the full reality of structural forces, acknowledge their potent character and detect leverage points that may be mutually reinforcing.

Part of this challenge is critical and ideational – to identify weaknesses in current arrangements and show why change is in order. The tension between capital accumulation and reproduction of the labour force is one version of this effort. It, however, tends to devolve into a dead-end discussion about redistribution and the equity–efficiency trade-off. A more apt angle might be to look at the issue as a matter of social investment. Here the trade-off is short-run benefit versus long-term return. Both profit-taking and election cycles tend to work against long-term consideration of what may serve society well. One question, then, is how to introduce into policy deliberations a time frame that is less tied to immediate return.

A major factor to be confronted is the pervasive influence of the market, not just in locational decisions about investment, but also in altering the character of civil society. In housing and transportation particularly, there is an increasing tilt toward private consumption and away from reliance on public provision (Goss, 1988; Kearns, 1992). While one-time common forms of mutual assistance have declined (Rae, 2003), those with less income are often unable to use the private market effectively. Consequently, non-affluent citizens find themselves increasingly in policy company with the poor in hurricane-stricken New Orleans – that is, when they are unable to use private means to meet their needs, they find little in the public sector with which to link constructively. A cultural tilt away from recognising conditions of interdependence and toward what one author calls 'personalized realities' is in evidence (Bennett, 1998). Exploration of alternative mechanisms and what makes them feasible stands as an appealing research target. The workings of community development corporations are an example (Peterman, 2000; Von Hoffman, 2003).

Along with market biases, another structural challenge stems from the growing complexity of contemporary life. Complexity raises the hurdle of reconciling democracy with 'techno-bureaucratic administration' (Fung and Wright, 2003: 3). In dealing with society's lower ranks, most professionals see themselves as the embodiment of essential expertise. Moreover, 'reinvented government', despite its customer orientation (Osborne and Plastrik, 1997), has pushed the master source of expertise to a point remote from the direct provision of public services. As put by Marquand: 'Trust ... was displaced from professionals directly engaged in service delivery to more remote professionals engaged in scrutinizing other professionals' (2004: 111). The British experience with the 'audit explosion' parallels the education reform process in the US.

Today, the relevant expertise is increasingly a managerial and entrepreneurial one about orchestrating market and outcome-evaluation processes so as to bring about sought-after performance standards. The process has become more, not less, technocratic, and the guardians of expertise are far removed from the lives of people in the lower ranks of society. Thus, one problem is the emergence of a new class of policy Mandarins little connected to lower SES populations and without much of a record of success in devising effective schemes for addressing social exclusion. Line agencies have lost considerable political ground, and the voluntary and for-profit sectors have gained political footing but without so far showing large breakthroughs in solving social problems.

As new and complicated schemes of service provision are devised, a relevant question is who is guarding the guardians – not who is evaluating single programmes, but who is subjecting the grand schemes, the 'big pushes' to scrutiny? Who is analysing critically the bases of political support that undergird these schemes, locally and beyond? Are there alternative coalitions and new forms of professional training that can bring policy practice into closer and more constructive connection with the marginalised populations in today's society? The AIDS prevention experience points in a useful direction. Professionals understood that they could not solve the problem alone, and they realised that they needed to enlist the active cooperation of the target population. Most professions, however, have not moved very far in that direction. They have little grasp of how the complex weaving of state, civil society and market define the situation in which some citizens operate.

Although the outcome of a continuing tension between inequality and democracy depends on a full range of activities from local to global, much can be gained by a view from below. For that reason, it is important to ask how local citizens fit into the picture. How are they governed? What steps can be taken to enable them to occupy their rightful role as constructive contributors to governing?

At the heart of our quest for inclusiveness is a realisation that local democracy is far from being a mere luxury we can indulge in only after technical effectiveness is satisfied. Seen through a polity lens, technical effectiveness includes constructive ways of melding the roles of citizens and professionals. It means holding in check the tendency of market relations to downplay interdependence and long-term consequences. It means constructing a civil society in which those with fewer worldly advantages are not isolated and rendered marginal. Discovering how to move toward such a world is the research task confronting the field of urban politics. It is a challenging task, but one that is filled with potential excitement and fulfilment because much is at stake.

Notes

1 The literature on this matter is vast. I find especially useful Stinchcombe (1978), Abrams (1982), Tilly (1984), Sewell (1992), Hay (1995) and the edited volume by Steinmo et al. (1992).
2 It might be noted that those politically associated with the more privileged segments of society tend to dismiss the importance of these categories as 'political correctness' while stressing 'personal responsibility' as if it somehow transcends such labelling.
3 This is not to suggest that race is unimportant in the experiences and opportunities for middle-class African-Americans, but it is the case that a lower-class position carries with it disadvantages that cut across racial lines – see Lareau, 2003; and Kusserow, 2004.

References

Abrams, Philip (1982) *Historical Sociology*. Ithaca, NY: Cornell University Press.
Barron, David J. (2003) 'Reclaiming home rule', *Harvard Law Review*, 116 (8): 2255–386.
Bennett, W. Lance (1998) 'The uncivic culture: communication, identity, and the rise of lifestyle politics', *PS: Political Science and Politics*, 31 (4): 740–61.
Brown, Michael (1999) 'Reconceptualizing public and private in urban regime theory', *International Journal of Urban and Regional Research*, 23 (March): 70–87.

Browning, Rufus P., Marshall, Dale R. and Tabb, David H. (1984) *Protest Is Not Enough*. Berkeley: University of California Press.

Button, James W. (1989) *Blacks and Social Change*. Princeton, NJ: Princeton University Press.

Crick, Bernard (2000) *In Defence of Politics*, 5th edn. London: Continuum.

Dahl, Robert A. (1961) *Who Governs?* New Haven, CT: Yale University Press.

Dunleavy, Patrick (1980) *Urban Political Analysis*. London: Macmillan Press.

Elkin, Stephen L. (1987) *City and Regime in the American Republic*. Chicago: University of Chicago Press.

Fox, Kenneth (1988) 'Who can govern? Dahl's *Who Governs?* revisited', in Ian Shapiro and Grant Reeher (eds), *Power, Inequality, and Democratic Politics*. Boulder, CO: Westview Press. pp. 123–31.

Frug, Gerald E. (1999) *City Making*. Princeton, NJ: Princeton University Press.

Fung, Archon (2004) *Empowered Participation: Reinventing Urban Democracy*. Princeton, NJ: Princeton University Press.

Fung, Archon and Wright, Erik Olin (2003) 'Thinking about empowered participatory governance', in Archon Fung and Erik Olin Wright (eds), *Deepening Democracy*. New York: Verso.

Goss, Sue (1988) *Local Labour and Local Government*. Edinburgh: Edinburgh University Press.

Gouldner, Alvin W. (1954) *Patterns of Industrial Bureaucracy*. New York: Free Press.

Hall, Peter A. and Taylor, Rosemary C.R. (1996) 'Political science and the three institutionalisms', *Political Studies*, 44: 936–57.

Handler, Joel F. (1996) *Down from Bureaucracy*. Princeton: Princeton University. Press.

Hay, Colin (1995) 'Structure and agency', in David Marsh and Gerry Stoker (eds), *Theory and Methods in Political Science* Basingstoke: Macmillan.

Honig, Meredith I. (2006) 'Introduction: complexity and policy implementation', in Meredith Honig (ed.), *Confronting Complexity*. Albany: SUNY Press. pp. 1–23.

Imbroscio, David L. (1999) 'Structure, agency and democratic theory', *Polity*, 32 (1): 45–66.

Jacobs, Lawrence R. and Skocpol, Theda (2005) 'Studying inequality and American democracy', in Lawrence R. Jacobs and Theda Skocpol (eds), *Inequality and American Democracy*. New York: Russell Sage Foundation. pp. 214–36.

Kearns, Adrian J. (1992) 'Active citizenship and urban governance', *Transactions of the Institute of British Geographers*, 17 (1): 20–34.

Kruse, Kevin M. (2005) *White Flight*. Princeton, NJ: Princeton University Press.

Kusserow, Adrie (2004) *American Individualisms*. New York: Palgrave Macmillan.

Lareau, Annette (2003) *Unequal Childhoods*. Berkeley: University of California Press.

Lindblom, Charles E. (1977) *Politics and Markets*. New York: Basic Books.

Lipsky, Michael (1970) *Protest in City Politics*. Chicago: Rand McNally.

Macedo, Stephen and Karpowitz, Christopher (2006) 'The local roots of American inequality', *PS: Political Science and Politics*, 39 (1, January): 59–64.

March, James G. (1962) 'The business firm as a political coalition', *Journal of Politics*, 24 (November): 662–78.

Marquand, David (2004) *Decline of the Public*. Cambridge: Polity Press.

McLaughlin, Milbrey W. (2006) 'Implementation research in education', in Meredith I. Honig, *Confronting Complexity*. Albany: SUNY Press. pp. 209–28.

Mollenkopf, John (1983) *The Contested City*. Princeton, NJ: Princeton University Press.

Mollenkopf, John and Manuel Castells (eds) (1991) *Dual City: Restructuring New York*. New York: Russell Sage Foundation.

Neuenschwander, Peter, Kübler, Daniel and Frey, K. (2004) 'From loose networks to exceptionalist alliances: power relations between the state and NGOs in Swiss HIV/AIDS prevention'. Paper prepared for the European Consortium of Political Research, Joint Sessions of Workshops, Uppsala, Sweden, 13–18 April.

Oakes, Jeannie and Rogers, John (2006) *Learning Power: Organizing for Education and Justice*. New York: Teachers College Press.

O'Connor, Thomas H. (1993) *Building a New Boston*. Boston: Northeastern University Press.

Orren, Karen and Skowronek, Stephen (2004) *The Search for American Political Development*. New York: Cambridge University Press.

Osborne, David and Plastrik, Peter (1997) *Banishing Bureaucracy Complexity*. New York: Plume.

Peterman, William (2000) *Neighborhood Planning and Community-Based Development*. Thousand Oaks, CA: Sage.

Peterson, Paul E. (1981) *City Limits*. Chicago: University of Chicago Press.

Putnam, Robert D. (with Robert Leonardi and Rafaella Nanetti) (1993) *Making Democracy Work*. Princeton, NJ: Princeton University Press.

Putnam, Robert D. (2000) *Bowling Alone*. New York: Simon & Schuster.

Rae, Douglas W. (2003) *City: Urbanism and its End*. New Haven: Yale University Press.

Rothstein, Bo (1992) 'Labor-market institutions and working-class strength', in Sven Steinmo, Kathleen Telen and Frank Longstreth (eds), *Structuring Politics*. New York: Cambridge University Press.

Sabatier, Paul A. (1999) 'The need for better theories', in Paul A. Sabatier (ed.), *Theories of the Policy Process*. Boulder, CO: Westview Press.

Saegert, Susan, Thompson, J. Phillip and Warren, Mark (eds) (2001) *Social Capital and Poor Communities*. New York: Russell Sage Foundation.

Savitch, H.V. and Kantor, Paul (2002) *Cities in the International Marketplace*. Princeton, NJ: Princeton University Press.

Schorr, Lisbeth (1997) *Common Purpose: Strengthening Families and Neighborhoods to Rebuild America*. New York: Doubleday.

Sewell, William H. (1992) 'A theory of structure', *American Journal of Sociology*, 98 (1): 1–29.

Skocpol, Theda (1985) 'Bringing the state back in: strategies of analysis in current research', in Peter B. Evans, Dietrich Rueschemeyer and Theda Skocpol (eds), *Bringing the State Back In*. New York: Cambridge University Press. pp. 3–37.

Skocpol, Theda (1992) *Protecting Soldiers and Mothers*. Cambridge, MA: Harvard University Press.

Steinmo, Sven, Thelen, Kathleen and Longstreth, Frank (eds) (1992) *Structuring Politics*. New York: Cambridge University Press.

Stinchcombe, Arthur L. (1978) *Theoretical Methods in Social History*. New York: Academic Press.

Stoker, Gerry (1995) 'Regime theory and urban politics', in David Judge, Gerry Stoker and Harold Wolman (eds), *Theories of Urban Politics*. London: Sage. pp. 54–71.

Stoker, Gerry (2003) *Transforming Local Governance*. New York: Palgrave Macmillan.

Stone, Clarence N. (1980) 'Systemic power in community decision making', *American Political Science Review*, 74 (4): 978–90.

Stone, Clarence N. (1989) *Regime Politics*. Lawrence: University Press of Kansas.

Stone, Clarence and Worgs, Donn (2004) 'Poverty and the workforce challenge', in Robert P. Giloth (ed.), *Workforce Development Politics*. Philadelphia: Temple University Press. pp. 249–80.

Strömberg, Thord (1996) 'The politicization of the housing market', in Klaus Misgeld, Karl Molin and Klas Åmark (eds), *Creating Social Democracy*. Pennsylvania: Pennsylvania State University Press. pp. 237–69.

Thelen, Kathleen and Steinmo, Sven (1992) 'Historical institutionalism in comparative politics', in Sven Steinmo, Kathleen Thelen and Frank Longstreth (eds), *Structuring Politics*. New York: Cambridge University Press.

Tilly, Charles (1984) *Big Structures Large Processes Huge Comparisons*. New York: Russell Sage Foundation.

Verba, Sidney (1967) 'Democratic participation', *Annals of the American Academy of Political and Social Science*, 373 (September): 53–78.

Von Hoffman, Alexander (2003) *House by House, Block by Block*. New York: Oxford University Press.

Weir, Margaret (1992) 'Ideas and the politics of bounded innovation', in Sven Steinmo, Kathleen Telen and Frank Longstreth (eds), *Structuring Politics*. New York: Cambridge University Press.

Wilson, Ernest III (1985) 'Why political scientists don't study black politics, but historians and sociologists do', *PS: Political Science and Politics*, 18 (Summer): 600–7.

INDEX

accelerator model 119
accountability
  Europe 133–4
  governance 140, 148
accumulation process
  Marxist perspectives 57–8
  neo-liberalism 66
activism 244–5
Africa, globalisation 153, 156, 160–1
African-Americans
  activism 181
  poverty 194–5
  urban migration 200
  see also black minorities
agency
  political leadership 126, 128
  poverty 163–4
AIDS
  activism 215
  prevention 261, 271
Althusser, Louis 56–7, 75
amalgamation strategies 117
America *see* United States
anti-exclusion programmes 177–8, 180, 181–2
Asia, globalisation 153, 156, 160
Asian-Americans 195, 196
  see also black minorities
Atkinson, Rob 182
Atlanta, U.S. 29–31, 42–4, 49
  black politics 191
  community power 29–31
  racial segregation 188
  urban regime analysis 42–4, 49
authority migration 9, 139, 148
autonomy, economic 176

Balbo, Marcello 156
Baltimore, U.S. 233–4
Batley, Richard 156–7
Bayat, Asef 164
behaviourism 92, 95
Belfast, Northern Ireland 248
Benjamin, Walter 77–8, 81
Benton-Short, Lisa 154
'biological' leadership 130
Bish, Robert 110
black minorities 11
  British 197
  civil rights 199
  cooperation 196
  exclusion 181
  mayors 191–2, 194, 196
  metropolitan government school 110
  politics 188, 189, 190, 194
  poverty 190, 194–5

black minorities *cont.*
  protest 191
  see also African-Americans
Blair, Tony 94
Bolivia 67–8, 157
Bond, P. 67
Bondi, Liz 209
bonding social capital 154, 224, 229, 234
Bordieu, P. 222, 233
Borraz, - 133–4
bottom-up influences 96, 100
Bowling Alone (Putnam) 224
Brazil 157–8
Brenner, N. 65–6, 107, 115, 119
bricolage, institutional 102
bridging social capital 154, 224, 227, 229, 234
Bristol, England 46, 227
Britain
  ethnic minorities 197
  race 197–8
brokers, leaders as 128
Brown, Michael 49, 208, 215, 261
bureaucracy 19, 137–52
business
  governance 149
  power types 33–5
  urban regime analysis 40–2, 47

Caldeira, Teresa 158
Calvino, Italo 84
Canada 116–117, 154, 215
Cape Town, South Africa 157
capital
  community power 32
  mobility 181
  ownership 176, 177
  see also social capital
capitalism
  anti-globalisation activities 250
  democracy 200
  Marxist perspectives 55, 57
  neo-liberalism 65–6
  post-structuralism 75, 79
  spatial analysis 59
carceral cities 80
case study approach 252
Castells, Manuel 56–7, 59, 68, 74–5, 164, 239
CDOs *see* community development
  organisations
CDPs *see* community development projects
Chakrabarty, Dipesh 160
chance, post-structuralism 83–4
change
  bureaucracy theories 138–43
  effects 13

change *cont.*
  new institutionalism 95, 96–8, 101–3
  urban regime analysis 43–4
Chicago
  black politics 192
  heat wave study 185
Chicago School 28–9
Christchurch, New Zealand 261
cities
  administration 34–5
  classifications 158–61
  definitions 17–18
  democracy 200
  inequality 172–3
  political order 257–73
  poverty 172–3
  racial politics 190, 201
citizens 5, 10–12, 169–254
  policy-making 263
citizenship 198, 207–8
city–county consolidation 107, 110, 114, 119
city-region concept 115, 119, 155, 159
civic activities 223–4
civic capacity concept 50–1
civic domain, rules-in-use 99
Civil Renewal Agenda 230
civil rights 199
  model 192
  movement 11, 258
  resource mobilisation theory 241
civil society 269
  markets 270
  policy-making 261
  social capital 231–2
class identities 193
class politics
  Marxist perspectives 57–8, 61, 68–9
  public choice school 111–12
classical theory, Marxism 56–8
Cloward, Richard 190
CNH *see* Collingwood Neighbourhood House
co-production framework 142
coalition theory 33, 35–7, 42–3
Cockburn, Cynthia 212
Cole, Alistair 21
Coleman, J. S. 222–3
collaboration, urban regimes 40–1, 49–50
collective action 251
  Atlanta, Georgia 43
  frames 245–6
collective consumption 57
collective form, political leadership 129–30
collective rules 100
collectives 177, 179, 180
Collingwood Neighbourhood House
    (CNH) 78–9
command power 36
committee-leader systems 129–30
communication skills 142
communism 63
community cohesion 234
community development organisations (CDOs)
    174, 178–9, 232, 241–2
community development projects (CDPs) 63
community power 5, 6, 27–39, 183
  analysis 37–8
  debate 27–33, 91
commuting 210

comparative research
  community power 37
  conceptual sketching 142–3
  future directions 164–5
  globalisation 160, 164–5
  numerosity 22
  political leadership 131
  urban regime analysis 7, 45, 46–8, 51
  see also cross-national research; research
competitiveness 116
complex environments 95–6
conceptual sketching 142–3
concessionary regimes 43
conditions of possibility 78–9
conflict theories 183
conflicting interests 145–6
consensus 145
Conservative Party 64
consolidation
  metropolitan government school 107, 110
  new regionalism 114, 119
constitutions of local authorities 100
constructivism, poverty analysis 184–5
consumption 57
context
  city classifications 160
  political leadership 127–8, 129, 132–3
Coole, Diana 214–15
cooperation 223
corruption 227
cosmopolitanism 78
council-manager form 129–30
councillors' positions 131
county–city consolidation 107, 110, 114, 119
creativity
  ethics 80
  leadership 125, 133
crime
  globalisation 153–8
  prevention programmes 245
crisis management
  power relationship 81
  regulation theory 62
critical perspectives
  comparative research 165
  Marxism 58–63
  post-structuralism 7–8, 73–85
  'posty' urban political theory 7–8, 73–4, 81–5
cross-national research 5
  change effects 13
  community power 6, 37–8
  urban regime analysis 40, 45–8
  see also comparative research;
      research
Cuban communities 154
culture
  political leadership 127, 132
  post-structuralism 82–3
  resources 241
Cusack, T. 130

Dahl, Robert 18, 30, 31–2, 188, 189, 193, 265, 267
Davies, Jonathan 1–14, 45, 146, 148
Davis, Mike 59–60, 66–7, 69, 162
Dear, M. 60–1
decentralisation
  developing countries 155
  new regionalism 112

decision-making processes 17
  community power 29–32, 34–5
  mayoral systems 131
DeFilippis, James 176–7, 180
Deleuze, Gilles 73–4, 83–4
deliberative democracy 147–8
Della Porta, D. 227
democracy 12–13
  capitalism 200
  citizenship 198
  developing countries 155
  governance theory 139–41, 146–7
  local 257–73
  neo-liberalism 67
  post-structuralism 79
  social capital 225, 231, 236
  urban regime analysis 42
demography 153–8
Denmark, nature politics 145–6
descriptive–inductive methods 92
determinism
  economic 115
  social causation 133
developing countries
  comparative research 165
  fragmentation patterns 155–8
development
  politics 34
  regimes 44
'developmentalism' 161
devolution 117–18
diagnostic frames 245
'difference'
  local authorities 98–9
  Marxist perspectives 68
  post-structuralism 83–4
DiGaetano, Alan 47–8
disabled people 207
disciplinary approach, post-structuralism 82
'disciplinary clusters' 160–1
discursive institutionalism 93, 97
disenfranchisement 200
dispossession 66
distance-minimisation 29
diversity 154, 234
divisible conflicts 146
domination, power types 36–7
downtown development 79
Dunleavy, Patrick 265
Durkheim, Émile 225

economics
  autonomy 176
  community power 29, 33–7
  determinism 115
  governance 138, 149
  'posty' urban political theory 73
  reterritorialisation 115–17
  theories 175–7, 180, 183
  urban regime analysis 40–1, 49, 50–1
education policy 50
efficiency
  governance theory 139–41
  metropolitan government school 106, 110
  public choice school 112
El Paso, U.S.
  national policies 182
  social movements 250
elections 258, 267, 268

elites 263, 264, 267
  theory 18, 29–30, 32–3
  see also neo-elite theory
Elkin, Stephen 42, 44, 48–9
embeddedness
  local governance 96
  rules 95, 100–1
empiricism
  theories 1–2
  vs theoretical premises 98
empowerment
  governance theory 147
  of the poor 180, 183
enabling state concept 143
England
  local–national relationship 19
  new left 63–4
  political leadership 125, 130–1, 133–5
  public-private partnerships 46
  see also Britain; London
entrepreneurs
  institutions 101, 103
  regimes 43–4
environment
  Marxist perspectives 69
  social movements 249–50
equity
  metropolitan government school 106
  public choice school 111
  see also inequality
Escobar, Arturo 161
ethico-politics 80
ethics 74, 79–80
ethnic minorities see minorities
Europe
  globalisation 160–1
  nature politics 145–6
  political leadership 125–6, 133–4
  poverty 172
  urban regime analysis 46
  Urban Research Association 4
European Union 96, 244–5
everyday life 56, 77–9, 81
evolutionary perspectives 58–63
exchange-values, community power 35–6
exclusion see social exclusion

Fainstein, Susan and Norman 41–2, 43–4
families, social capital 223
female identities 210, 214
feminism
  Marxism 61
  theories 205, 207, 215–16
  urban space 208–15
Ferman, Barbara 174–5
Fincher, Ruth 212
flâneur/flâneuse 77–8, 207
followers, political leadership 130
Fordism 62
  see also post-Fordism
Foucault, Michel 79–80
fragmentation
  international patterns 155–8
  metropolitan government school 107, 120
  public choice school 111–12
  socioeconomics 157–8
frames
  social movements 245–6, 251
  theory 12

France, urban regime analysis 46
Friedmann, John 158–9
functional necessities 262–3
functional specialisation 267
functionalism 58

Garber, Judith A. 11, 204–20
gay community
   citizenship 215
   urban space use 210
Geddes, Mike 7, 18, 55–72
gender 11, 204–20
   Marxist perspectives 61, 68–9
   social capital 235
   systems 204, 205, 206–7
genealogies (Foucault) 79–80
Genoa, Italy 214
geography 28–9
Germany
   political leadership 130
   urban regime analysis 46
Gibson, Timothy 79
GLA see Greater London Authority
GLC see Greater London Council
global city concept 76, 82–3, 116, 158–61
global justice 246
globalisation 10, 153–68, 216
   master frames 246
   neo-liberalism 65
   progressive theories 73
   protest strategies 243
   social movements 12, 239, 244, 249–51
   urban space 215
Goldsmith, Mike 96
Goodwin, M. 62
governance 3, 5, 8–10, 89–168
   bureaucracy 137–52
   change effects 13
   citizens 10
   complex environments 95–6
   definitions 142–3
   globalisation 153–68
   government distinction 138
   human agency 262–3
   local 228, 229, 259
   new institutionalism 91–105
   pluralism 267
   political leadership 125–36
   regionalism 106–24
   social capital 231
   theory 9–10, 137, 139–50
   urban regime analysis 40, 47–8, 51
government
   business collaborations 41
   governance distinction 138
   new regionalism 112
Graham, Stephen 156
Greasley, Stephen 9, 125–36
Greater London Authority (GLA) 117–18, 125, 131
Greater London Council (GLC)
   63–4, 113, 117
Greater Toronto Area (GTA) 116–17
growth coalition/machine thesis
   33, 35–7, 42–3
growth machines 175
GTA see Greater Toronto Area

Harding, Alan 6–7, 27–39, 46
Harlem, New York city 189

Hart, Keith 163
Harvey, David 56, 57–8, 60–1, 65–6, 68, 156
hate groups 248–9
Hay, C. 100
heat wave study (Chicago) 185
hierarchies
   conflicting interests 146
   governance dependency 148
high-poverty neighbourhoods 172
highway construction protests 247–8
Hispanic communities 154, 195, 196, 198
historical institutionalism 93
history, community power 27–39
homelessness social movements 247
homicide rates, Brazil 158
housing policy 265
human agency see agency
human rights movement 11
humanism 56–8
Hunter, Floyd 29–30, 31, 35, 188
Hurricane Katrina 194–5, 259–60
hyperspace 82–3

identity politics 210, 214, 240
Imbroscio, David 1–14, 48, 114
IMF see International Monetary Fund
immigrants 184
   community response to hate against 248–9
   political rights 200–1
immigration
   flows 154–5
   US cities 196
in-divisible conflicts 146
incarceration 194
incentives 43, 44–5, 47, 49
inclusion
   governance theory 141–2, 147
   urban poor 174
income data 173, 194
individualism 29, 35, 37
individuals
   leadership 125, 127–9, 132–3, 134
   new institutionalism 94, 102
   New Public Management 140
inductive methods 92
industrial–urban distinction 77
inequality 171–87
   cities 172–3
   political economy 149
   political order 264
   racial 191
   social capital 233–4
   see also equity
'informal sector' 163–4
infrastructure fragmentation 156–7
institutional bricolage 102
institutionalism 8, 91–105
   change 13, 95, 96–8
   governance theory 148–50
   political leadership 127, 129–33, 134
   power 95, 98, 101
instrumental power 33, 34
integration, social movements 244
interactive state 230, 231
interest-mapping 150
'interests'
   city administrations 35
   conflict 145–6
   networks 149–50

international fragmentation 155–8
international migration 154–5
International Monetary Fund (IMF) 66, 68, 162
international organisations 161–4
interpretive approaches, poverty 184–5
Invisible Cities (Calvino) 84
Italian Communist Party (PCI) 63
Italy, social capital 223, 227

Jackson, Maynard 191–2
Japan, social capital 232
Jessop, B. 62, 65, 150
John, P. 2–3, 5–6, 17–23, 133–4
joined-up government 143–4
Jones, B. 130
Jones, J. Raymond 189
Jones, Victor 107

Kataoka, Serena 7–8, 73–87
Katrina, Hurricane 194–5, 259–60
Katzenstein, P. J. 230–1
Katznelson, Ira 188, 190–1
Kjaer, Anne Mette 9–10, 13, 137–52
Klinenburg, Eric 185
Knopp, Lawrence 206
Krasner, S.D. 2

Labour Party 63–4
    see also New Labour
labour restructuring 64
land titling programmes 163
language, post-structuralism 79–80
Lanzara, G. 102
Lasswell, Harold 12
Latin America
    globalisation 156, 157, 160
    neo-liberalism 67–8
Latinos 195, 196, 198
    see also black minorities
layman rule 129
Leach, S. 126–8, 133
leadership 9, 125–36
    context 127–8
    costs 129
    new institutionalism 99–101
    styles 126, 131
Leeds, England 46
Lefebvre, Henri 56–7, 74–84, 207
left politics 63–4, 67–8, 69
Leftwich, A. 3
legislative rules 100
legitimacy
    governance theory 141
    political leadership 133–4
Leland, Suzanne 119
lesbian theories 207, 209–10
Lewiston, Maine, U.S. 248–9
Lindblom, Charles 33–4
linking social capital 224, 230, 233
LIS *see* London Industrial Strategy
living costs 173
Livingstone, Ken 131–2
local activism 244–5
local authorities
    change 101
    community power 32–3
    culture 127
    governance 91
    leadership 99–100

local authorities *cont.*
    organisations 94
    participation differences 98–9
    quangos 146–7
local democracy 257–73
local governance 91
    embeddedness 96
    institutional matrix 94–5, 101
    local government distinction 95
local government 259
    fragmentation 111, 120
    local governance distinction 95
    social capital 228, 229, 230
    values 19–20
Local Government Act 2000 99, 130
local growth machines 175
local partnerships 178, 179, 180, 229
    governmentality 185
    limitations 182
local politics
    definition 17
    leadership 127, 132–4
    propinquity 21–2
local public economies perspective 120
local regime 41–2
local scale 182
local state 212, 215
    governance 140
    social capital 230
localisation
    neo-liberalism 65–6
    new regionalism 113
    politics 161–4
Logan, John R. 35, 37–8
London 159
    new regionalism 117–18
    political leadership
        125, 131–2, 134
London Industrial Strategy (LIS) 64
Los Angeles 196
Lousville, U.S. 113–14
Lowndes, V. 8, 91–105, 127, 133
Lyons, W.E. 112

McDowell, Linda 204
Magnusson, Warren 82–3
maintenance regimes 44
male/female division 208, 209
Many and One Coalition 249
marginalisation 171
    poverty 10–11
    working-class 266
markets
    civil society 270
    mechanisms 148
Marquand, David 266
Marvin, Simon 156
Marxism 5, 7, 55–72
    community power 35
    post-structuralism 74, 83
    regime theory comparison 2
    social capital 225
    urban poverty 175
    see also neo-Marxism
MAS *see* Movimiento al Socialismo
Massey, D. 61, 211
master frames 246
master planning 161
Maxey, Chester 107

mayoral systems 9, 125–33, 134
   see also black minorities
MDGs *see* Millennium Development Goals
megacities 66, 153
meta-perspectives 68–9
metaphorical treatment of the urban 83
metropolitan government school 8–9, 106,
   107–11, 113–14, 116, 119–20
Mexican-Americans 250
Miami, U.S. 154
migration, international 154–5
Millennium Development Goals (MDGs) 162–3
'mimetism' 133
minorities 11
   metropolitan government school 110
   polarisation 198
   political turnout 192–3
   poverty 192
Mitchell, Don 79
mobilisation
   international 250
   resources 12, 44
   social movements 241–3, 246–9
modernism
   gender 211
   Marxist critique 61
   see also postmodernism
Molotch, Harvey L. 35, 37–8
moral resources 241
Morgan, D. 131, 133
Morgan, K. 144
Mossberger, Karen 6–7, 40–54
Mouritzen, P. 129–30
Movimiento al Socialismo (MAS) 67–8
Mullin, M. 131
multi-level governance 96
multidimensional solutions to social exclusion 180
murder rates, Brazil 158
Muslims, British 197

Naples, Italy 227
national contexts *see* cross-national research
National Strategy for Neighbourhood Renewal 228–9
nature politics 13, 145–6, 150
neighbourhood agendas 174–5
neo-elite theory 30–1
   see also elites
neo-liberalism 62, 64–8, 69, 226, 236
   ethico-politics 80
   globalisation 156
neo-Marxism 69
   community power 31, 33
   see also Marxism
neo-pluralism 33–5, 36–7
   see also pluralism
neo-Weberian theory 31
Netherlands, social capital 230
networks
   governance 9–10, 13, 143–50
   social capital 222, 223, 233, 234
Neuwirth, Robert 162
New Deal for Communities 229
'new governance' 138–9
   see also governance
New Haven, U.S. 265, 266, 268
   community study 30, 31–2
new institutionalism 8, 91–105
   case studies 98–102
   core premises 92–3

New Labour 143–4, 228, 230
new left 63–4, 69
new localism 113
New Orleans 194–5, 259–60
New Public Management (NPM) 137–41
new regionalism 9, 106–7, 108–9, 112–18, 119–21
new social movements 240, 241
New York city 65, 127–8, 132, 159
   black politics 189
   social capital 230
   urban space use 206
'newtonian' leadership 130
non-profit sector 178–9
non-Western globalisation 153–68
normative perspectives
   institutionalism 92–3, 97, 103
   regionalism 120
North America
   globalisation 161
   see also Canada; United States
North, the
   comparative research 164
   see also South, the
NPM *see* New Public Management
numerosity 6, 21, 22

Oakerson, Ronald 112–13
OECD *see* Organisation for Economic
   Co-operation and Development
O'Neal, Tip 21
operational rules, local authorities 100
Organisation for Economic Co-operation and
   Development (OECD) 116
organisations
   change 97
   international 161–4
   rules 94
   set-ups 143
organised crime 153–8
Ostrom, Elinor 97, 110, 142
Ostrom, Vincent 110

Painter, J. 62
Paris 159
   riots (1968) 79
Parks, Roger 112–13
participation
   accountability mechanisms 133–4
   governance 141–2, 145, 147
   local differences 98–9
   reform strategies 135
   urban regime analysis 49
party politics
   leadership 132, 134–5
   rules-in-use 99
path dependency
   institutions 97, 101
   research 20–1
patriarchy 204, 206
PCI *see* Italian Communist Party
performance pay 141
Perlman, Janice 164
Peters, G. 93, 102, 138
Peterson, Paul 34–5, 38, 41, 191
Pickvance, C. 58–9
Pierre, J. 48, 95, 137
Pittsburgh, U.S. 175
Piven, Frances Fox 190
place-shaping decisions 32

planning 75, 77
pluralism 18, 20
    model 266–8
    poverty 173–4
    theory 29–32, 37
    see also neo-pluralism
police stop-and-searches 197
policy
    choices
        education 50
        variation 43–5
    economic constraints 41
    enabling state concept 143
    implementation 259–60
    poverty 163
policy-making 149, 260–2, 267
political economy
    governance 138, 149
    regime analysis 33–7, 49, 51
political leadership see leadership
political opportunity structure approach 12, 243–5
political order 257–73
political spaces 214, 216
politics
    community empowerment 28–30, 183
    definitions 3–4
    development 34
    globalisation 10, 153–8, 160–5
    inclusiveness 257
    national 17, 19
    parties 99, 132, 134–5
    poverty 173–5, 180, 181
    theories 173–5, 180, 181, 183
poll tax protests (U.K.) 242–3
polycentrism
    new regionalism 112
    see also public choice school
poor people
    empowerment 180, 183
    protest strategies 242
    social capital 233
    sub-groups 184
    see also poverty
Portes, Alexandro 154
'positions', rule creation 95
positivism 29
post-Fordism 62, 64
post-structuralism 7–8, 73–85
    see also structuralism
postmodernism 5, 7
    gender 206, 210, 211
    Marxist perspectives 57, 59–61, 68
    urban space 214
'posty' urban political theory 7–8, 73–87
poverty 171–87
    change effects 13
    cities 172–3
    concentration 172
    globalisation 162–4
    marginalisation 10–11
    measurement 172, 173
    rates 172
    theories 173–8
    see also poor people
Powell, Adam Clayton 189
power 5–8, 25–87
    change effects 13
    cities 18, 155

power cont.
    citizens 10
    community power 5, 6, 27–39, 91
    crisis management 81
    deflation model 119
    governance 139–42, 149
    institutions 95, 98, 101
    Marxist perspectives 55–72
    politics 216
    'posty' urban political theory 73–87
    propinquity 21
    urban regime analysis 40–54
practice–theory relationship 1–14
pragmatic approach 93, 97
prison population 194
private sector
    globalisation 156
    multi-level governance 96
    New Public Management 138
    see also public-private partnerships
probabilistic approaches, social causation 133
problem-centred approaches, social
        exclusion 177–8
professionalism, political leadership 129
prognostic frames 245–6
progressive regimes 43, 44–5
progressive theories 73
property strategy 64
propinquity 2, 3, 6, 21
protest movements 258–9
public choice school 106, 108–12, 114, 120
public choice theory 140
public management
    assumptions 139–42
    reform strategies 137–8
    rules-in-use 99
public safety, regime analysis 50
public service delivery
    bureaucracy 148
    globalisation 156–7
    rules-in-use 99
public-private partnerships 46, 113, 144, 156–7, 179
public/private dualism 211–12, 214–15
Putnam, Robert 12, 154, 223–4, 226–7, 228, 233

quangos 146–7
queer theories 205, 215–16
    urban space 208–15

Rabrenovic, Gordana 12, 239–54
race 11
    in Britain 197–8
    community relations 197–8
    diversity 195–6
    hatred 249
    identity 194
    inequality 191
    Marxist perspectives 61, 68–9
    minorities see minorities
    polarisation 198
    politics 188–203
    riots 197
    segregation 188, 193, 196
    spatial tension 201
racism 189, 190, 193, 197, 198
    Collingwood Neighbourhood House 78–9
radical perspectives 74, 76–7, 80–2
rational choice theory 92–3, 97, 103

reciprocity 144, 146
redistributive policy 41
reform strategies
    leadership 125–6, 133, 134–5
    new institutionalism 97–8, 103
    new regionalism 119–20
    public management 137–8
regime analysis *see* urban regime analysis
regionalism 8–9, 106–24
    European Union 96
    research 118–19
    see also city-region concept
regulation theory 62
representative democracy 147
repression of social movements 244
reputational analysis 29–30
rescaling approach
    new regionalism 9
    regionalism 107–9, 115–20
research 17–23
    social exclusion 182–5
    see also comparative research; cross-national
        research
researchers' reputations 21
residential segregation 197
resource distribution 176
resource mobilisation (RM) 12, 44, 241–3
reterritorialisation approach
    new regionalism 9
    regionalism 107–9, 115–21
'rights to the city' 56, 75, 79–81
Riis, Jacob 171
RM *see* resource mobilisation
road building protests 247–8
Roberts, J. M. 225–6
Robinson, Jennifer 160
Rose, Nikolas 80
Ruble, Blair 154
rules, governance 94–5, 97, 98–9, 100–3
rules-in-form 97
rules-in-use 97, 99, 100–3
rural life, urbanisation 3
Rusk, David 114

safety, public 50
Sandercock, Leonie 77–8
Sao Paulo, Brazil 157–8
SAPs (structural adjustment programmes) 162
Sartori, Giovanni 142
Sassen, Saskia 116, 159
Saunders, Peter 91–2
Savitch, Hank 8–9, 106–24
Schattsnieder, E. E. 198
Schmidt, Vivien 93
schools, social capital 233–4
Seattle, U.S. 79
segregation, residential 197
selective incentives 43, 44–5, 47, 49
self-government 257
self-help 229
self-interest 223
SES (socioeconomic status) 98–9
sexuality 204–20
Sidney, Mara 10–11, 171–87
Siegel, Fred 111
Sites, W. 132
Skocpol, Theda 260–1
slums 66–7, 162–3

Smith, Laïla 157
Smith, Michael Peter 154–5
Smith, Neil 59
social autopsy approach 185
social capital 11–12, 221–38
    civil society 231–2
    definitions 221–4
    democracy 225, 231, 236
    international migration 154
    new institutionalism 96, 98–9
    state role 228–31
    theories 225–6
social causation 133
social exclusion 171–87
    measurement 173
    problem-centred approach 177–8
social housing policy 265
social investment 270
social movements 12, 239–54
    globalisation 239, 244, 249–51
    Marxist perspectives 57
    mobilisation 241–3, 246–9
    outcomes 252
    political context 243–5
    protest 258–9
social production model 42, 45, 51
socialism 64
socioeconomic fragmentation 157–8
socioeconomic status (SES) 98–9
Soja, Ed 59–61
Somali immigrants 248–9
South Africa 67, 157
South, the
    city classifications 158–61
    comparative research 164
    international organisations 161–4
    neo-liberalism 66–8
    see also North, the
South Wales Regional Development 144
Southwark, London Borough 265, 266
spatial analysis 18
    capitalism 59
    community power 28–9
squatters 162
stability of institutions 96
state
    governance 140–2
    Marxist perspectives 55, 57
    repression 193
'state capture' 149
Stepick, Alex 154
Stinchcombe, Arthur 262
Stoker, Gerry 9, 18, 47, 125–36, 148
Stone, Clarence 2, 5–7, 12–13, 36, 42, 44–5, 49, 51,
    125, 128–9, 132, 174, 180, 188, 191–2, 257–73
Storper, M. 60
Stren, Richard 10, 153–68
structural adjustment programmes (SAPs) 162
structural power 33–4
structuralism 56–8, 74–6
    see also post-structuralism
Studenski, Paul 107
sub-cultures 206
sub-groups, urban poverty 184
sub-national level politics 17
suburbs
    metropolitan government school 110–11
    new regionalism 113, 115

Sullivan, Helen 11–12, 221–38
sustainability 69
Svara, J. 129–30
Sweden, social capital 227
Sweeting, D. 131, 134
'Swiss cowbell theory' 20
Switzerland, AIDS prevention 261
Swyngedouw, Erik 157
systematic power 36

technocrats 139
Thatcher government 64
Theodore, N. 65–6
theoretical premises vs empirical
    observation 98
theory–practice relationship 1–14
third-sector institutions 178–9
Thompson, J. Phillip 11, 188–203
Thornley, A. 118
Thurmaier, Kurt 119
Tiebout, Charles 111
Tocqueville, Alexis de 225
tokenism 190
Tokyo 159
Tomaney, J. 118
top-down influences 96, 100
Toronto, Canada 116–17
transgressive behaviour 213–14
transnational social movements
    250, 251
transparency
    deliberative democracy 148
    quangos 147
trust 223, 231
    governance theory 144, 146, 150

UAA (Urban Affairs Association) 4
UN-HABITAT 161–2, 172
United Nations
    Human Settlements Programme 172
    Millennium Development
        Goals 162–3
    UN-HABITAT 161–2, 172
United States
    city–county consolidation
        107, 110, 114
    community power 27, 32–8
    downtown development 79
    immigration 196
    international migration 154–5
    political leadership 127–9, 131–2
    prison population 194
    public–private partnerships 113
    regional challenges 118–19
    social capital 224
    Urban Governance Theory 137
    urban regime analysis 40–2, 43–7
    see also individual cities
Urban Affairs Association (UAA) 4
urban geography 28–9
Urban Governance Theory 137
urban planning 75, 77

urban politics
    definition 18
    race 188–203
    redefinitions 212–14
urban poverty see poverty
urban regime analysis 2–3, 5–6, 40–54, 174, 181
    community power 33, 36
    future directions 50–1
    governance 149
    non-profit sector 178
    revision 48–50
urban social movements see social movements
urban space
    categories 213
    feminism 208–15
    postmodernism 214
    queer theories 208–15
urbanisation 3, 239
U.S. see United States
use-values, community power 35–6

values
    local government 19–20
    new institutionalism 95, 97–8
Vancouver, Canada 215
variation, policy choices 43–5
veto-player model 130
Villaraigosa, Antonio 196
visionary leadership 125, 133
Vogel, Ronald 8–9, 106–24
voluntary associations 145, 225, 231

Washington, Mayor 192
water systems 157
Watson, S. 131, 133
Weber, Max 138
welfare state 265, 266
Welsh Office 144–5, 150
Westlink project 248
'white citizenship' 198–9
white racism 193
White, Walter 199
Williams, Raymond 58
Wilson, James Q. 189
win–win situations 142–3, 145
Wincott, D. 100
Wirth, Louis 82, 83
Wolff, Goetz 158–9
women
    identities 210, 214
    political order 264
    social capital 235–6
Wood, Robert 107
Woolcock, Michael 224
working-class
    perceptions 269
    political order 265–6
World Bank 66, 67, 161–2
World Church of the Creator 249
world cities 158–61
World Urbanization Prospects (WUP) 153
WUP see World Urbanization Prospects

CPSIA information can be obtained
at www.ICGtesting.com
Printed in the USA
FSOW02n2139020116
15213FS